PUBLIC RELATIONS

A GUIDE TO STRATEGIC COMMUNICATION

PUBLIC RELATIONS

A GUIDE TO STRATEGIC COMMUNICATION

Young Joon Lim

University of Texas - Rio Grande Valley

cognella
SAN DIEGO

Bassim Hamadeh, CEO and Publisher
Carrie Montoya, Manager, Revisions and Author Care
Kaela Martin, Project Editor
Christian Berk, Production Editor
Jess Estrella, Senior Graphic Designer
Alexa Lucido, Licensing Manager
Natalie Piccotti, Director of Marketing
Kassie Graves, Vice President of Editorial
Jamie Giganti, Director of Academic Publishing

cognella® | ACADEMIC PUBLISHING
3970 Sorrento Valley Blvd., Ste. 500, San Diego, CA 92121

Brief Contents

Contents

CHAPTER 3

Fundamental Elements of Public Relations Profession   35

CHAPTER 4

Careers in Public Relations for College Students   53

CHAPTER 5

Communication Models and Messages for Public Relations   72

CHAPTER 6

Scholarly Research in the Field of Public Relations   88

CHAPTER 10

Corporate Relations   153

CHAPTER 11

Employee Communication   171

CHAPTER 18

Global Public Relations   292

Introduction to Public Relations for the Twenty-First Century

Things change fast in the digital age. New technologies introduce state-of-the-art products and services to us every day, including smartphones and mobile apps, electric and self-driving vehicles, and even personalized cancer vaccines. The advent of digitization and automation encourages people to adapt their current lifestyle to the quickly evolving online and off-line worlds. As a result, they get busier managing human connection on a personal and professional level. Since the ways of connecting humans and gathering information are diversified, we, as social animals, become increasingly aware of the importance of building and maintaining decent human relations in both online and off-line environments. A relationship can be built at work, home, school, any public or private events, and online with the most important element: communication. We communicate with others to build a positive relationship that helps us find better social opportunities and feel more supported, fulfilled, and connected. Building a positive relationship with other people or other social entities needs strategies, and this is where public relations plays a key role in creating a successful relationship.

Public relations, also simply known as PR, appears everywhere in social life. People don't often recognize how deeply public relations is involved in human relations. Humans are social beings, and they interact with family members, friends, coworkers, business partners, and even strangers to maintain their daily routines. Even though they don't think much about saying "hello," "good morning," and "thank you" to other individuals throughout the day, the bottom line is that people are educated to be nice to one another. In other words, we hope to live in a peaceful environment, and public relations serves as the backbone of interactive social harmony. Public relations begins with the social mantra of "be nice to others," which applies to individual relationships and even international relations.

Public Relations is?

Public relations is a complex of many practical applications to the real world, embracing every aspect of human activity. From a business perspective, it can be understood as a tactic to build good relationships with clients. Clients pay public relations professionals to make their businesses look great to the public and target audiences. In a similar way, public relations staff in an organization is assigned to deal with customers, consumers, and the target audience with any available communication tools to portray their organization in a positive light. The tactical landscape of public relations, however, is not limited to such a business function. This is why a public relations expert says very few people can explain what people in public relations really do.[1]

Everybody wants to be loved rather than hated. Individuals in society talk, fight, cooperate, negotiate, eat together, and hate or love each other. Building positive human relationships is one of the best ways to achieve a successful life, and public relations revolves around human interaction. Public relations serves as the driving force in promoting peace, encouraging humanitarian aid, promoting public virtue, and entertaining the human mind. New communication technologies, tools, and techniques are the essential elements for public relations to perform its functions with the aim of creating effective relationships.

The public is exposed to nonstop messages ranging from 24/7 traditional media, such as television, radio, and newspapers, to social media on the Internet. Public relations professionals are savvy about using communication tools to disseminate messages—more specifically customized messages—in hopes of informing, educating, entertaining, and persuading the target audience. To understand the notion of public relations and its relevant terms, we need to know what public relations is, who uses it in society, why it contains a promising future, and how it is adopted and conducted in the United States and the world.

1   "Five Things Everyone Should Know About Public Relations," *Forbes*. https://www.forbes.com/sites/robertwynne/2016/01/21/five-things-everyone-should-know-about-public-relations/#5e45ib122a2c

Public Relations and Definitions

Whenever confusing or unfamiliar terms and concepts are introduced to society, new definitions are created and introduced to the public by innovators who are mostly scholars, officials, inventors, entrepreneurs, and leaders of industries. Many different definitions of public relations have gone through the same process of being produced by multiple pioneers.

Edward Bernays, one of the two founding fathers of public relations (see Chapter 2), defined public relations in 1923 as

> information given to the public, persuasion directed at the public to modify attitudes and actions, and efforts to integrate attitudes and actions of an institution with its publics and of publics with those of that institution.[2]

More recently, public relations professionals and organizations have introduced further sophisticated definitions of public relations, as shown in Table 1.1.

Public Relations Society of America (PRSA) incorporated various definitions of public relations and introduces the most popular definition:

> Public relations is a strategic communication process that builds mutually beneficial relationships between organizations and their publics (2012).

One thing for sure is that there is no all-embracing definition of public relations because the profession of public relations is still growing and evolving. More importantly, public relations does not belong to the purview of natural science, which only defines 2 x 2 = 4, with no room for doubt; rather, public relations is associated with social science, opening up to any challenging possibility in eternal truth. By integrating all the definitions presented earlier, from Bernays to PRSA, this book proposes another definition of public relations: "A distinctive discipline and practice of managing stellar reputations and creating positive images for clients or organizations with the use of two-way communication strategies."

TABLE 1.1   Definitions of Public Relations by Public Relations Professionals and Organizations

Merriam-Webster Dictionary	Public relations is the activity or job of providing information about a particular person or organization to the public so that people will regard that person or organization in a favorable way.
The World Assembly of Public Relations	Public relations is the art and social science of analyzing trends, predicting their consequences, counseling organization leaders, and implementing planned programs of action that will serve both the organization's and the public's interest.
Chartered Institute of Public Relations	Public relations is the discipline that looks after reputation, with the aim of earning understanding and support and influencing opinion and behavior. It is the planned and sustained effort to establish and maintain goodwill and mutual understanding between an organization and its publics.
Middle East Public Relations Association	Public relations is the discipline that looks after reputation with the aim of earning understanding and support and influencing opinion and behavior.

---

2   Edward Bernays, *Crystallizing Public Opinion,* p. 55 (New York: Liveright, 1961).

Who uses Public Relations, and Why?

Public relations is the "it" item to own for individuals and organizations. Without the use of public relations, no organizations or public figures can operate their businesses or handle public issues. Public relations is a necessity for corporations, governments, educational institutions, hospitals, nongovernmental organizations, sports teams, religious institutes, celebrities, politicians, international organizations, and media outlets. In particular, it is impossible to find organizations that operate without the department of public relations or communication. The following are examples of five representative entities that show the widespread practice of public relations.

Five Representative Entities of Public Relations Practice

THE UNITED STATES OF AMERICA (GOVERNMENT)

The US government has 15 executive departments that represent the primary units of the executive branch of the federal government, such as the Department of State and Department of Defense. These departments have their own public affairs bureaus (the government prefers using the term *public affairs* instead of *public relations*; see Chapter 14). Such bureaus aim to inform domestic and foreign publics of the US government's policies and missions. For example, the Department of Veterans Affairs implements its public relations operations through the Office of Public and Intergovernmental Affairs, which focuses on "creative and innovative ways to connect with vets, the media, and other stakeholders."[3] In a similar vein, the Bureau of Public Affairs of the State Department "engages domestic and international media to communicate timely and accurate information with the goal of furthering US foreign policy and national security interests as well as broadening understanding of American values."[4] In a nutshell, the US government adopts public relations operational tactics to inform and connect with domestic and foreign publics.

WALMART (CORPORATION)

As the largest corporation (by revenue) in the world, according to the 2019 Fortune Global 500 list, Walmart has been a main target of the media and public criticism regarding its business operations. Walmart has confronted serious issues of poor employee relations, mishandled customer service, and an infamous reputation of not contributing to the community. Walmart needs to defend itself or fight against such relations issues raised by the media and the public. For example, in June 2014, *New York Times* op-ed writer Timothy Egan accused the company of a lack of contribution to American society. The company's vice president of Communications and Corporate Affairs fired back the next day on the Walmart corporate blog, pointing out that Walmart is the largest taxpayer in the United States, had hired more than 42,000 veterans in the first half of 2014, paid a full-time average associate wage of $12.91 (which was higher than market average), and had promoted 170,000 employees in 2013.[5] Corporations like Walmart adopt public relations defense mechanisms to correct inaccuracies like those they found in the article. In so doing, Walmart expects that the public and customers of the corporation are

---

3   "Office of Public and Intergovernmental Affairs," US Department of Veterans Affairs, http://www.va.gov/opa/.

4   "Bureau of Global Public Affairs," US Department of State, http://www.state.gov/r/pa/index.htm.

5   "Wal-Mart's Scathing Response To A New York Times Columnist Who Eviscerated The Company" Business Insider, https://www.businessinsider.com/walmarts-response-to-the-new-york-times-2014-6

better informed about the corporation's social contribution to the country and its employees in hopes of addressing the bad images and further building and managing a good reputation to stay on top of the Fortune 500. Public relations is an excellent management tool for corporations seeking to reform poor reputations and images under one condition: the more people (more particularly, target audience) are informed of their corporate good deeds, the higher the profits they could earn.

THE UNITED NATIONS (INTERNATIONAL ORGANIZATION)

The world's largest international organization operates its Strategic Communications Division under the Department of Global Communications. The organization's public relations practice aims at raising awareness of global conflict and international problems, such as war, poverty, human rights violations, and terrorism. The United Nations (UN) needs financial and diplomatic support from both the United States and other member nations. Governments of member nations carefully monitor their domestic public opinion on the UN to decide whether they will contribute to the organization. The United States, the single-largest contributor to the UN's regular budget, is the most prominent example. The US government has been sensitive to its domestic public opinion on the UN, particularly about how strongly the US public sees the UN as a vehicle for spreading American values around the world. If public opinion is positive, the government gains momentum for continuing to support the organization. Therefore, UN officers at the Strategic Communication Division focus their strategies on reaching out to the United States and global target audiences to inform them of the UN's humanitarian work in the areas of "climate change, health (HIV/AIDS, malaria, pandemic influenza), gender-equality issues and ending violence against women, and environmental issues (forests, water, biodiversity, oceans, desertification)."[6] The success of the strategies depends on how effectively the UN appeals to the target audience, highlighting the fact that the UN is the single-most unique international humanitarian organization that helps people in desperate situations on behalf of the UN's 193 member states as of 2020. The Department of Global Communications stated its mission: "To reach millions of people with trusted, objective information and an inclusive message that enables the public, civil society, private sector and Member States to engage in the work of the United Nations."[7]

CHARLIE SHEEN (PUBLIC FIGURE)

Charlie Sheen was the highest-paid actor in the TV industry in 2010, receiving $1.8 million per episode for his work on the popular CBS sitcom *Two and a Half Men*. However, Sheen, who may be enjoying his fame and fortune too much, entered rehab in January 2011, and the production of the show went on hiatus at the same time. During 2010, Sheen was in and out of jail, rehab, and tabloid news coverage. His public relations representative, Stan Rosenfield, defended Sheen in the media, saying that Sheen was "having severe abdominal pains" even after Sheen had been hospitalized because of drinking and a 36-hour, cocaine-fueled party with porn stars in his Beverly Hills home.[8] CBS and its holding company, Warner Brothers Television, released a joint public relations' statement: "We are profoundly concerned for his health and well-being, and support his decision [of entering rebab]." Surprisingly, in February, Sheen

6   "Strategic Communications," United Nations, https://www.un.org/en/sections/departments/department-global-communications/strategic-communications/index.html.

7   "Department of Global Communication," United Nations, https://www.un.org/en/sections/departments/department-global-communications/index.html

8   Luchina Fisher, "Charlie Sheen's Longtime Publicist Stan Rosefield Resigns," ABC News, January 28, 2011, http://abcnews.go.com/Entertainment/charlie-sheens-longtime-publicist-stan-rosenfield-resigns/story?id=12785991.

appeared on a call-in radio program and called Chuck Lorre, the producer of *Two and a Half Men*, a clown and a stupid little man. He also added a comment on Alcoholics Anonymous, portraying it as a "bootleg cult" with a five-percent success rate.[9] Sheen also demanded a raise to $3 million per episode to come back and shoot the sitcom. A few days later, a spokesman for Warner Brothers Television announced, "After careful consideration, Warner Brothers Television has terminated Charlie Sheen's services on *Two and a Half Men*, effective immediately, and no decision has been made about the future" of the show. Sheen's longtime PR representative, Rosenfield, announced his resignation, saying "I'm unable to work effectively as his publicist and have respectfully resigned."[10] The *Los Angeles Times* reported Rosenfield was the troubled actor's "consistent voice."[11] Troubled stars like Sheen seek public relations professionals who can manage and maintain their public and media images in a crisis. In 2015, Sheen revealed his HIV-positive diagnosis, and he said in a 2019 interview that he would want a possible reboot of *Two and a Half Men*.[12]

AMERICAN ASSOCIATION OF RETIRED PERSONS (ASSOCIATION)

Better known as AARP, which is a US-based interest group, the American Association of Retired Persons aims to empower people to choose how they live as they age. AARP provides specialized products and services for its over 38 million elderly members. "With a high projected increase due to the aging of baby boomers and an intensive minority membership drive," AARP decided to consolidate all communication strategies into the practice of public relations, which placed the *AARP Magazine*, *AARP Bulletin*, AARP.org website, AARP YouTube Channel content, and AARP events under the control of the AARP media relations team in collaboration with public relations firms in 2014.[13] AARP's public relations team focuses on informing the lives of people aged 50-plus of any updates or changes in legislative, regulatory and legal advocacy. The team launched the Life Reimagined campaign, which encouraged "a first-of-its-kind series of online and offline experiences" that guided US seniors through life transitions by "helping them discover new possibilities and connect with a community of people pursuing similar passions and goals."[14] In conjunction with the twenty-first century's buzzwords for baby boomers, such as "reinvent," "reimagine," "encore, " and anything that suggests a second chance or a new chapter, AARP's public relations campaign produced the rebranding of AARP in which joining AARP is to "become the go-to address for feeling good about aging."[15] AARP conveyed the successful message of reinvention for after-retiring life

---

9   James Hibberd, "Charlie Sheen Slams 'Two and a Half Men' Creator in Multiple Rants, *Entertainment Weekly*, http://www.ew.com/article/2011/02/24/charlie-sheen-slams-men.

10   Fisher, "Charlie Sheen's Longtime Publicist."

11   Christie D'Zurilla, "Charlie Sheen's Publicist Quits: Stan Rosenfield 'Respectfully' Resigns," *LA Times*, http://latimesblogs.latimes.com/gossip/2011/02/charlie-sheen-publicist-quits-stan-rosenfield-resigns.html.

12   Jessica Napoli, "Charlie Sheen Recalls 2011 Spiral, Talks Sobriety Journey, and More Revealing Moment from New Interview," Fox News, April 11, 2019, https://www.foxnews.com/entertainment/charlie-sheen-2011-spiral-sobriety-journey.

13   Richard D. Pace, "AARP Seeking Public Relations Firm—RFP Everything PR," Everything PR, December 19, 2014, https://everything-pr.com/aarp-public-relations/.

14   AARP, AARP Launches Life Reimagined to Offer Ways for Discovering New Possibilities and Navigating "What Next," Market Watch, May 28, 2013, https://www.marketwatch.com/press-release/aarp-launches-life-reimagined-to-offer-ways-for-discovering-new-possibilities-and-navigating-whats-next-2013-05-28-11183190.

15   Sharon Jayson, "AARP to Coach Aging Boomers 'Reimagining' Their Lives, *USA Today*, May 28, 2013, https://www.usatoday.com/story/news/nation/2013/05/28/aarp-boomers-jobs-coaching/2358551/

to the boomers. In early 2019, the AARP media relations team issued a press release noting that AARP was named one of the world's most ethical companies in 2019 that drove positive change in the business community and societies around the world.[16]

Why is Public Relations Promising as an Academic Course?

Studying public relations in college is fun, entertaining, and real. "Real" means that public relations explores the social activities of humans and acknowledges the importance of communicative human behavior. In the era of globalization, practices of free trade, capitalism, and democracy among seven billion people on earth have become a prime standard for global citizenship. Global corporations, international organizations, and global citizens embrace new communication technologies to communicate with their customers, business partners, and target audiences. Public relations positions itself at the center of the communicative activities.

The academic study of public relations focuses on nurturing future up-and-coming public relations practitioners who understand the media, use new communication technology, and are able to facilitate human communication skills to inform, persuade, influence, and entertain target audiences on behalf of organizations or clients. Public relations empowers college students who want to prepare for their future in a broad range of industries to build in-depth knowledge of all aspects of communication, including persuasion, media effects, social media strategies, and verbal and nonverbal communication. The following information discusses why public relations offers a bright future for college students:

- The US Bureau of Labor Statistics predicts employment of public relations specialists is projected to grow 9 percent from 2016 to 2026, about as fast as the average for all occupations. Employment growth will be driven by the need for organizations to maintain their public images. Candidates can expect strong competition for jobs at advertising and public relations firms with large media exposure. The public relations field has expanded to such a degree that these specialists now outnumber journalists by nearly five to one.[17]

- *Forbes* magazine placed public relations specialists as number nine on the list of "Most Promising Careers for Aspiring Entrepreneurs," indicating that they have the skills of communication, along with social and thought processing skills.[18]

- Advertising and public relations directors were the seventh highest-paid employees in the United Kingdom, according to the UK Office for National Statistics.

---

16 AARP, "AARP Named One of 2019 World's Most Ethical Companies by Ethisphere," PR Wire, February 26, 2019, https://www.prnewswire.com/news-releases/aarp-named-one-of-2019-worlds-most-ethical-companies-by-ethisphere-300802301.html.

17 "Public Relations Specialists," US Bureau of Labor Statistics, https://www.bls.gov/ooh/media-and-communication/public-relations-specialists.htm

18 "No. 9 Public Relations Specialists," *Forbes*, https://www.forbes.com/pictures/lml45lgdf/no-9-public-relations-specialists/#5ca9fed224b2.

- The business news channel, CNBC, ranked public relations as the fifth least stressful college major with a strong likelihood of finding well-paid, high-quality jobs upon graduation.[19]

Public relations practitioners pay attention to what is going on in society and the world. They stay current with the media and monitor social issues to educate themselves. They follow stories of politics, sports, Hollywood, culture, economy, and business, in addition to policy decisions and public opinion on special issues. Their habits of keeping up with society—even with the Kardashians—and of understanding social issues could stem from college courses, such as public relations, journalism, and communication.

How is Public Relations Processed?

The practice of public relations usually follows some standardized steps to anticipate and solve problems. There are four widely known models, each of which explains the steps with acronyms.

ROPE: Research, Objectives, Planning, and Evaluation

- *Research.* Public relations practitioners identify the situation organizations or clients confront. They aim to figure out what the issues and opportunities of the situation are.
- *Objectives.* With the understanding of the situation, public relations practitioners set goals to create strategies for public relations operations.
- *Planning.* Public relations practitioners strategize budget, time, and other resources to implement public relations campaigns to influence the target audience.
- *Evaluation.* Public relations practitioners analyze if their public relations strategies and campaigns were successful at influencing the audience.

RACE: Research, Action, Communication, and Evaluation

- Research
- *Action.* Public relations practitioners use what they have found in their research to determine the best course of action for the interest of clients or organizations.
- *Communication.* Public relations practitioners craft messages toward the target audience and distribute them through available communication channels.
- Evaluation

---

19   Abigail Hess, "The 10 Least Stressful College Majors Can Lead to Some of the Highest-Paying Jobs," CNBC, April 21, 2017, https://www.cnbc.com/2017/04/21/the-least-stressful-majors-can-lead-to-some-of-the-highest-paying-jobs.html.

GRACE: Goal, Research, Action, Communication, and Evaluation

- *Goal setting.* Public relations practitioners learn about the organization's or client's mission statement.
- Research
- *Assessment.* This step is similar to the planning step from the ROPE model.
- Communication
- Evaluation

RPIE: Research, Planning, Implementation, and Evaluation

This model is published on PRSA's website, explaining that the RPIE process (Figure 1.1) "transforms public relations measurement from output-based to outcomes-focused."[20]

- Research
- Planning
- *Implementation.* After the planning step, public relations practitioners conduct public relations. campaigns to influence a target audience as planned.
- Evaluation

Probably anybody can create new acronyms for the steps of public relations as a management function, but nobody should ignore the keywords of research, planning, communication, and evaluation. When public relations practitioners are assigned to promote the interest of organizations or clients, they first acknowledge the main issues of the situation in the environment through the process of research. Then they plan strategies and allocate resources to reach out to the target audience through communication channels. Finally, they analyze the outcomes of public relations practice. According to PRSA, public relations practitioners should act "as a counselor to management and as a mediator, helping to translate private aims into reasonable, publicly acceptable policy and action."[21]

The RPIE Acronym

Research: Identify the situations

Planning: Strategize budget, time and other resources

Implementation: Conduct public relations a campaign

Evaluation: Analyze if such public relations campaigns were successful

FIGURE 1.1 The RPIE process.

20   PRSA. https://apps.prsa.org/Learning/Calendar/display/5520/The_Four_Step_Process#.XoO2XIhKiUk
21   PRSA, https://prsay.prsa.org/2009/03/11/a-madd-look-at-public-relations/

Who are the Essential Publics of Public Relations?

Organizations and individuals use public relations to communicate with others in particularly customized settings. Another way of understanding public relations is to reverse the words: relations public or relations with the public regarding the essential publics of public relations. Creating and maintaining good relationships with essential publics is the key concept for the practice of public relations. The essential publics are referred to as those that closely interact with public relations practitioners.

1. *Media people/journalists.* Public relations aims to seek publicity in hopes of mass distribution of messages and information. Journalists have the power to reach out to the public, while public relations serves as a good news source for their media stories.

2. *Employees.* Public relations builds a communication bridge between management and labor inside organizations.

3. *Investors.* In order for an organization to launch or expand business, public relations aims to assure investors about the operational strengths of the organization.

4. *Politicians.* As those who are running for office vie for voters' attention and support, public relations spreads persuasive messages and creates positive images.

5. *Marketers.* Selling a product or service of the organization is not easy in a competitive environment. Public relations creates positive images and reputations for the product or service.

6. *Fundraisers.* Raising funds, even for a good cause, is one of the hardest tasks, but public relations makes it easier by creating a humanitarian position in contributors' minds.

7. *Officials/officers.* Preserving high public support is an ideal practice of federal and local governments. Public relations streamlines official information flow into the public.

These seven publics employ public relations to achieve their goals and make their jobs easier.

What are the Functions of Public Relations?

PRSA identifies the disciplines of public relations as follows:[22]

- Brand journalism/content creation
- Corporate communications
- Crisis communications
- Events
- Executive communications
- Internal communications

---

22   "About Public Relations," PRSA, https://www.prsa.org/all-about-pr/.

- Marketing communications
- Media relations
- Multimedia
- Reputation management
- Social media
- Speechwriting

What are the Stereotypes or Misperceptions about Public Relations?

As noted, public relations is excellent at both boosting an organization's business operation and understanding human relationships in society. Is this always true? As people say, there are always two sides to every story, and public relations surely bears the burden of a negative reputation, largely because of unflattering anecdotes throughout history. Ron Smith, a professor at Buffalo State (State University of New York System), characterized the negative anecdotes as fallacies about public relations:[23]

- Public relations is secretive and insidious.
- Public relations is just a form of propaganda.
- Public relations equates to lying, hype, and exaggeration.
- Public relations is only about spin, making bad guys look good.
- Public relations tries to keep the public ignorant about what's really happening.
- Public relations is the guy with the shovel following the elephants in a circus parade.
- Public relations works only for powerful groups with deep pockets: corporations, governments, lobbyists, and others who work against the best interests of average people.

The fallacies demonstrate the most negative stereotypes of public relations since its birth. They also reflect the negative view of the media and journalists. Communication strategist Molly Borchers argued that many journalists seem to have a profound aversion to public relations practitioners.[24] As a result, reporters painted public relations practitioners as spin doctors, flakes, manipulators, propagandists, or plain liars. However, this troubled relationship is changing. Public relations practitioners "no longer have to endure the indignity of getting dissed by a stressed-out reporter" because journalists' influence on the public becomes less powerful as the public migrates to social and digital media for their news and information.[25] Obviously,

---

23   Ron Smith. *Public Relations: The Basics, p. 6* (London: Routledge, 2014)

24   Molly Borchers, "Public Relations Has a PR Problem," Huffington Post, October 7, 2014, http://www.huffingtonpost.com/molly-borchers/public-relations-has-a-pr_b_5942660.html.

25   Peter Himler, "The Journalist and the PR Pro: A Broken Marriage?," *Forbes*, March 14, 2013, http://www.forbes.com/sites/peterhimler/2013/03/14/the-journalist-the-pr-pro-a-broken-marriage/.

the relationship between public relations practitioners and journalists is unfriendly, falling somewhere between mutual dependence and mutual distrust. To understand public relations in comparison with other similar occupations, it is important to learn about similar but different fields of practice, such as journalism, marketing, and advertising. This learning should give rise to an integrated understanding of public relations.

How Does Public Relations Differ from Other Similar Fields of Practice?

Advertising, marketing, and journalism have fundamentally intertwined relationships. They often share the same market values and outcomes while simultaneously building border walls against each other to mark their authentic territories.

Advertising versus Public Relations

These two industries are commonly considered nonidentical twins, similar but different in certain respects. The biggest difference lies in the method of payment for publicity. It is said that advertising pays for space, while public relations prays for space. Advertising specialists buy space in newspapers and broadcast time on television to place advertisements or commercials with messages created by organizations and individuals. In contrast, public relations practitioners produce messages to be chosen by media people or journalists who can publish and convey such messages to the public. Hence, advertising is categorized as paid media, whereas public relations is regarded as earned media.

With paid media, there is a financial expenditure by the organization: paying the media to promote its product or service with influential messages. Social media platforms such as YouTube, Twitter, Instagram, and Facebook also offer advertising space. With earned media, unlike advertising, public relations searches for the possibility of free publicity. If the media reported information or messages for the organization with no additional charge, the goal of earned media would be achieved.

Advertising exclusively focuses on consumers who purchase goods and services in comparison with public relations, which embraces a broader range of audiences, including employees, shareholders, and the public. Consumers are informed of what goods and services are available in the marketplace through straightforward messages in advertising. They carefully and smartly choose which ones they are going to purchase. Public relations, on the other hand, hopes that many people—including consumers, clients, and the public—are exposed to the messages reported by the media. For example, when a new electronic device is introduced to the marketplace, public relations practitioners for the device's manufacturer try to work with the media, hoping that the information about the device is reported nationally and internationally through as many media outlets as possible. If the device is shown in media coverage, the manufacturer gains greater credibility among potential consumers than it does through advertising since audiences are inclined to believe media sources better than direct advertising ones. A study by Nielsen, an information and measurement company, reported that public relations is almost 90 percent more effective than advertising when it comes to the role of content in the consumer decision-making process.[26]

---

26   Robert Wynne, "The Real Difference Between PR and Advertising," *Forbes*, July 8, 2014, http://www.forbes.com/sites/robertwynne/2014/07/08/the-real-difference-between-pr-and-advertising-credibility/.

TABLE 1.2   Advertising versus Public Relations

Advertising	Public Relations
Paid media	Earned media
The power of controlling content and messages	The reliance on the media for message distribution
Vertical decision-making process	Horizontal decision-making process
Direct exposure to consumers	Indirect exposure to audiences
Selling goods and services	Building relationships

Advertising has the power to control content and messages; advertisers decide what messages, graphics, photos, videos, songs, and people go into the advertisement. They may use animated characters, such as Queen Elsa from the movie *Frozen* with the song "Let It Go" or celebrities like Jennifer Aniston, who touts the advantages of Aveeno with the slogan "Get Skin Happy."

One weakness of advertising is huge cost. Public relations is just the opposite—it costs almost no money. However, public relations cannot guarantee that the media will cover the messages and content as the practitioner originally intended. For example, the media could evaluate the electronic device as a stale product and give it negative coverage. This means public relations practitioners need to convince journalists to report positive stories about their products or services.

Advertising usually goes through a stubborn decision-making process—one that is almost always top-down. For example, an advertising agency creates an ad for its client by embracing the view of the agency's senior management and the client's requests for "what a consumer or business-to-business buyer should think."[27] By contrast, public relations practitioners tend to be open to all conversations around them and embrace what people hope and want in a storytelling fashion. In short, advertising is one-way communication with consumers while public relations is more interactive with a wide range of audiences (Table 1.2).

Marketing versus Public Relations

Marketing and public relations used to be considered two different industries: the former is part of business, and the latter is part of communication. However, recently, they have become more integrated in the marketplace.

The American Marketing Association defines marketing as "the activity, set of institutions, and processes for creating, communicating, delivering, and exchanging offerings that have value for customers, clients, partners, and society at large." Like public relations, marketing includes the process of communicating with people in society, but marketing focuses most of its energy and time on selling products to increase revenue for the organization with the aim of increasing product demand. Public relations is more concerned with comprehensive images and the reputation of the organization.

MARKETING: PROCEDURES AND CORE COMPONENTS

Marketing focuses on increasing the customer's demand for products and services. In other words, marketing is connected to the process of producing and selling a particular item. Thus, marketers are

---

27   Wynne, "The Real Difference."

involved in the life of the product at each stage from the beginning to the end by following the procedures listed next:

- Research what services and products customers want and need.
- Identify target customers.
- Design the new product's appearance and name.
- Determine a means of distinguishing the product from competitors.
- Advise on the development of the new product.
- Explore distribution channels and stores.
- Fix prices.
- Find ways to inform customers about the product.
- Promote the product with events.
- Monitor customer response.
- Reorganize marketing strategies and operations.

The procedures originate from marketing's four core components—better known as the four Ps (Figure 1.2)—introduced in 1960 by Professor Edmund McCarthy as follows:

1. **Product.** The scope of a product can reach from a tangible good to an intangible service that meets the expectations of customers.

2. **Price.** Once a concrete promise of the product leads to an established time line, marketers need to get into the process of pricing decisions. To set a final price for a product, they take a comprehensive approach by considering such elements as profit margins, the costs of promotion and supply, the branding budget, and the extra costs in time and energy.

3. **Place.** It's always location, location, location. Marketing is about putting the right product, at the right price, in the right place at the right time. Finding the right place (or where the product should be sold) leads to convenience for customers who want to get to the product. Marketers consider customer demographics (gender, age, education, and income level) and geographic regions to find the optimal place.

4. **Promotion.** As soon as marketers have a product, a price, and a place, they sell it—or, from a marketing viewpoint, they promote it. Advertising and organizing events are the backbones of promotion that inform customers of the product. Personal selling and sponsorship can be categorized as tactics of promotion.

In addition to the four Ps, marketing and communication professionals try to add one more P to the list: some say it should be profit; others say it could be public relations; the rest say it should be people. Although all seem compelling, it is important to know that public relations is able to cooperate with marketing to achieve organizational goals.

Marketing is used to sell products for organizational profits, while public relations is designed to build and maintain positive image and reputation for the organization.

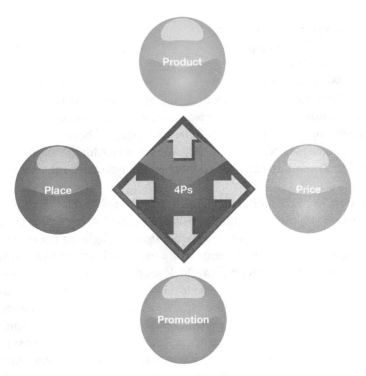

FIGURE 1.2 The four ps: Marketing's four components.

Journalism versus Public Relations

It can be a bit confusing to distinguish these two fields because the concept of journalism in a general fashion includes the practices of public relations and advertising, along with radio, TV, newspaper, magazine, and online reporting. The term "journalism" is even being used interchangeably with mass communication, which embraces advertising, public relations, news reporting, and any kind of media-related communication aimed at distributing information to a wide range of people.

An effective method of separating the characteristics of journalism from those of public relations is to study the job descriptions of journalists and public relations practitioners. Both professions have common activities: story writing and information distributing. They both produce stories, but their purposes are different. Journalists create stories to provide news and information to the public, whereas public relations practitioners produce stories that advocate their organizations or clients.

Imagine, for example, that Mayor Jason Bush of the city of Wonderland has asked the city council to approve a raise in the city's property tax; this means that homeowners in the city have to pay 1 percent more next year. It is a big issue in the city, and everybody is talking about the increase. Homeowners, of course, are mad at the mayor and the council members. To alleviate their anger, the city's public relations practitioner, Kellie Clinton, has sent a press release to the local TV stations and newspapers. The main points of the press release are that the city needs the additional revenue to provide more supplies to public elementary schools and acquire more police vehicles to enhance public safety. The tax revenues would only be used for the greater good—for security and children. In the press release, Ms. Clinton quoted the police chief and one of the school principals saying, "We both felt grateful to the city officials and people in the city. We promise that all city residents will be safer, and our children will receive a better education." The press release is intended to attract public support, even from homeowners, for the tax increase. In particular, it represents behavioral justification for the mayor and council members by showing support from the two most highly invested interest groups: school administrators and police officers.

On the other hand, *Wonderland Times* reporter Anna Trump covers the story by interviewing the mayor and homeowners, and both sides of the story will be highlighted in her article. The mayor explained the inevitable necessity for the increase. Angry homeowners, by contrast, said they would not support the increase because the management system of the city had collapsed because of the corrupt mayor and council members. The homeowners added that they would not vote for the mayor and council members in the next election. Ms. Trump's article also includes her findings of disorganized money expenditures by the city.

This imaginary story shows the different characteristics of public relations and journalism. Public relations practitioners are supposed to highlight positive aspects of anything done by their organization and its people, like the city and the mayor. They avoid shedding light on negative responses and outcomes; rather, they focus on making their clients look good, or at least not bad. Journalists do not care much about making organizations or individuals look good or bad. They are supposed to report both sides of the story and let readers and viewers decide. However, this does not mean that journalists are always objective and unbiased people. They are capable of slanting an article or a report. For example, Ms. Trump may place more quotes from angry homeowners and their family members attacking the city in her article, or she could hide the findings of suspicious city expenditures to support the mayor. In short, journalists have more power when it comes to the creation of informative messages.

Public relations practitioners, however, have better channels of information distribution. Whereas journalists usually reach audiences through one main medium, such as television, radio, and newspapers, public relations practitioners are able to simultaneously use many media channels—including social media, television, radio, online outlets, and newspapers—to reach the target audience.

Journalists' job descriptions often say that they are responsible for gathering and producing information as a media product that informs and educates the public. The descriptions also say that journalists are not supposed to influence public opinion in any single intended direction. By contrast, as an advocate, public relations practitioners' responsibility is to inform, educate, and influence the target audience on behalf of organizations, clients, or specific causes.

How Will Public Relations Evolve?

Public relations evolves in parallel with the development of new ideas, issues, and technologies. New definitions of public relations are continually being introduced. The practice of public relations is increasingly welcomed and adopted by more people and industries. Public relations courses are chosen by more college students, and strategies for public relations are being developed by more communication specialists.

Robert Wynne, president of Wynne Communications, pointed out that the media business is changing and so is public relations: fewer audiences are reading newspapers and magazines, while more are consuming their news online.[28] Wynne suggested that if traditional public relations is a megaphone aimed at a specific segment of journalists, then the new public relations of advocacy is a team of electric

28   Robert Wynne, "The Future of Public Relations—Three Forks in the Road," *Forbes*, December 9, 2014, http://www.forbes.com/sites/robertwynne/2014/12/09/the-future-of-public-relations-three-forks-in-the-road/2/.

guitars, drummers, and singers blasting the same message 24/7, using a row of speakers taller than the Empire State Building.[29]

It is increasingly obvious that public relations has to move quickly to adapt itself to the new communication environment. "The PR landscape has evolved to the point where the most effective practitioners are the ones who see themselves as facilitators of content and know how to adjust their communication efforts on a situational basis," says Matt Rizzetta, CEO of North 6th Agency, a public relations firm. "The media landscape is more expansive than ever before, with so many layers and nuances. The ones who can see clearly through all of the clutter and adjust their outreach strategies are the ones who will continue to reap the benefits."[27]

In the process of adaptation in public relations and other similar fields of communication, communication experts have come to realize that each field separately would not be able to achieve the organization's goals in the globalized digital age. There will come a time when the future heads toward a full integration of all the communication disciplines. This realization urges communication professionals to incorporate the fields of public relations, advertising, marketing, and journalism into an organized and cooperative entity of synchronized communication.

New terms such as integrated communication, convergent communication, integrated marketing communication, and communication in synchronization are gaining popularity in the developing field of strategic communication, which takes a comprehensive approach to public relations. Driven by the fast pace of technological improvements, strategic communicators expect the industrial evolution toward synchronized communication to move quickly. Collaboration between public relations, advertising, marketing, and journalism is not an option but a requirement for accomplishing the goals and missions of any organization in the digital age.

FIGURE CREDITS

---

29   Wynne, "The Future of Public Relations."

CHAPTER SUMMARY AND REVIEW

1. Define public relations.

2. Identify the five entities using the practice of public relations.

3. Conceptualize the processes of public relations.

4. Explain the differences between public relations and advertising and marketing and journalism.

5. Describe the evolving conceptual trend of public relations.

PUBLIC RELATIONS IN PRACTICE

FURTHER READING

PR Week's Awards For **Best PR Campaign**

Winner: Gerber and Edible
Campaign Name: Every Baby is a Gerber Baby

Using a social-by-design media strategy, the baby food brand engaged traditional outlets to announce the news, securing live and behind-the-scenes segments on *Today* and hosting a media tour with parenting and consumer lifestyle media.

Read more at
https://www.prweek.com/article/1579436/prweek-us-awards-2019-winners

Historical Evolution of Public Relations in the United States and the World

P ublic relations is evolving as a management function, professional practice, and field of scholarly study. In other words, it was not built overnight. The term *public relations* became recognizable to the public after the mid-1900s. Tracing the roots of public relations back to its origin is a good starting point for an understanding of the deeper historical background of public relations.

Ancient Roots of Public Relations

Today's civilizations owe a great debt to the ancient empires and cities of Egypt, Greece, and Rome. People from those times invented and advanced many techniques, concepts, and devices for human communication. When Egyptian pharaohs held absolute power in the golden age of peace and prosperity, they began to focus their attention on leaving a legacy. As a result, investing in symbolic statues and tombs became a means of impressing the public and eliciting their support. The pharaohs built massive funerary monuments (including the famous pyramids), which were designed to serve as the symbol of power. The wishes of the pharaohs to maintain their authority through eternity in a stable central empire were epitomized by such architecture, although the huge expense of pyramid building eventually led to the demise of the kingdom.

Another heritage of the Egyptian pharaohs is the Rosetta Stone (Figure 2.1), a text inscribed in 196 BC by a group of priests to praise the achievements of the king of Egypt, Ptolemy V. The priests used the stone as a publicity device to inform the public of the pharaohs' greatness so that they would give their support and trust to the king. The stone, almost four-feet long and two-and-a-half-feet wide, was found by one of Napoleon's soldiers in 1798, and it has been displayed at the British Museum in London since 1802.

While the pharaohs were not directly involved in honoring their own achievements, the Roman General Julius Caesar spearheaded the creation of his own legacy. Caesar, who deliberately took every opportunity to remind Romans that he was descended from the goddess Venus, used coins that told stories of his war victories abroad as a prime communication channel to justify his absolute power. His victory stories were further spread nationwide with the catchy phrase, "I came; I saw; I conquered." Caesar was the first Roman to put his portrait on Roman coins during his lifetime, spreading the symbolic message of his political and economic power to the public.

His efforts did not stop there. Caesar furthered the dissemination of his stories to the public via the publication of *Acta Diurna* (daily acts or daily records of doing). When he became consul, the highest elected political office of the Roman Republic, he ordered that the *Acta Diurna* be put in a public place where all interested citizens could follow the actions of his administration. Handwritten copies of this early publication were posted in public places in Rome. Later, it included court news and private notices, such as celebrations of births, marriages, or funeral announcements. Caesar maximized the impact of symbolic images and public information as a political leader. In short, he was adept at using creative, sophisticated image techniques through communication tools such as coins and public postings.

Much of the early history of public relations is associated with the growth and maintenance of Christianity at the height of Roman influence. As Christian churches were formed and teachings were established, believers sent the messages of Jesus through eloquent letters and speeches. For example, in 1095, Pope Urban II made a very persuasive speech to convince Christians to go to war against Muslims in an effort to reclaim the Holy Land. As a result, the Crusades, a series of religious war campaigns, were created. Armies of Christians from Europe responded to the pope's plea with the slogan "Deus vult!" or "God wills it!" Military elites and ordinary European citizens joined the Crusade forces, wearing crosses as a symbol of the church.

In the thirteenth century, philosopher-priest Thomas Aquinas studied the persuasive nature of religious communication, which became the bedrock for late medieval Catholic philosophy, theology, and science. Devoting himself to a life of traveling, writing, teaching, public speaking, and preaching, Aquinas wrote books and commentaries that were distributed to libraries across Europe. He understood that educating students and informing the public about religion and philosophy could be achieved through written materials.

In a similar way, in 1517, Martin Luther used writing as a means of public persuasion. When Pope Leo X announced a new round of indulgences to raise money for Catholic church construction, Luther expressed his anger at the pope by posting a sheet of paper containing 95 theses on the chapel door of the University of Erfurt. Although Luther did not imagine at the time that they would ignite the Protestant Reformation, the world-famous Ninety-Five Theses gained public support for criticizing the indulgences for corrupting people's faith. Luther gained public support for a reform movement against the church and the pope. The most significant vehicle for disseminating the movement's messages was the emerging technology of the printing press, which was used to spread copies of the Ninety-Five Theses throughout Europe in less than two months. Luther was officially excommunicated from the Roman Catholic Church after refusing to withdraw his public declaration that the Bible did not give the pope the exclusive right to interpret scripture. With his excommunication, he gained many more followers and received support from German princes.

FIGURE 2.1 The rosetta stone.

Propaganda and Public Relations

In response to Luther's growing popularity, the church, threatened by the emergence of the Protestant Reformation, used persuasive communication techniques, such as speeches, letters, books, and lectures to propagate its traditional authentic values. In 1622, Pope Gregory XV established the Sacred Congregation for Propagating the Faith (Congregatio de Propaganda Fide). It was a commission of cardinals who were obligated to spread the faith and regulate church affairs in non-Christian—more particularly non-Catholic—lands. The term *propaganda* was officially introduced with this commission. The religious mission of the Catholic Church populated the work of propaganda. The pope wanted the cardinals to orchestrate foreign missions and train priests to spread the Catholic faith through the activities of propaganda. Thus propaganda, at the time, was referred to as the deliberate, systematic attempt to achieve religious expansion to non-Catholic lands.

The meaning and definition of propaganda, however, changed radically after World War I. In the postwar years, communism and fascism manufactured the core principles of propaganda in a new fashion. Fascists and communists strategized to use propaganda to extend their power beyond their national borders, seeking to influence foreign audiences with their own tailored information and ideological teachings. In propagating these appeals, they used then-rising communication technologies, such as radio and newspapers, as quick and efficient tools of manipulative information distribution in international relations. In other words, communication tools were used for propagandistic purposes. The term *propaganda* began to acquire a negative connotation during this period of chaotic world politics.

Adolf Hitler, Benito Mussolini, and Hideki Tojo were iconic figures in the conversion of the meaning of propaganda from religious to political communication. Hitler, in his book *Mein Kampf*, wrote, "Propaganda tries to force a doctrine on the whole people. ... Propaganda works on the general public from the standpoint of an idea and makes them ripe for the victory of this idea." Hitler used propaganda expertly to spread the ideals of Nazism. He ordered his propaganda staff to make sure that "the Nazi message was successfully communicated through art, music, theater, films, books, radio, educational materials, and the press."[1] Hitler considered films valuable, using them in a pioneering way to spread the ideas of anti-Semitism and the superiority of German military power. For example, in 1935, the now-infamous movie *The Triumph of the Will* by Leni Riefenstahl depicted the glorifying aspects of Hitler and the National Socialist Movement; in contrast, in the 1940s, *The Eternal Jew* portrayed Jews as uncivilized and parasitic people consumed by sex and money. Hitler used propaganda quite effectively to garner German public support for his regime, which murdered millions of people. Nazi propaganda (Figure 2.2) served as a manipulative and persuasive communication apparatus for Hitler to mobilize German civilians and soldiers in his desire for power.

Some scholars and critics of public relations see Hitler's use of propaganda as the direct origin of public relations. They point out that there is no genuine difference between public relations and propaganda because public relations is associated with using misleading facts and glorifying the only positive side of messages to influence public opinion, and so is propaganda. In addition, the methods and activities of public relations are employed to create a favorable relationship with the public on behalf of a powerful group of people or organizations. Therefore, they argue that public relations is rooted in propaganda. Nazi propaganda with its egoistic and political motivations for abusing communication technology and channels still influences modern attempts to eliminate negative images of public relations.

FIGURE 2.2 Nazi propaganda.

---

1 "Nazi Propaganda," Holocaust Encyclopedia, http://www.ushmm.org/wlc/en/article.php?ModuleId=10005202.

Public Relations in Early US History

Samuel Adams and the Boston Tea Party

Samuel Adams and his group of American patriots probably did not intend to create a massive wave of publicity when they, masquerading as Indians, threw 342 chests of imported tea into the Boston Harbor to protest the repressive taxation in 1773. They staged the event, now known as the Boston Tea Party, to symbolize colonial defiance. It shed light on Samuel Adams's mastery of swaying public opinion; *PR Week* characterized the event as "arguably the greatest and best-known publicity stunt of all time, and certainly one that changed the course of history."[2] "Publicity stunt" refers to an event that is staged to attract public attention thanks to media coverage. In the same vein, an event that is staged and orchestrated to be recognized by the public and reported in the media is called a pseudo-event. Adams is considered the architect of the publicity stunt and is remembered as either a master of propaganda who provoked mob violence or an iconic orchestrator of motivation for independence before the outbreak of the Revolutionary War.

Thomas Paine

Thomas Paine, known as the godfather of the American nation, inspired the rebels in 1776 to declare independence from Britain with his persuasive writing. His pamphlet, "Common Sense," pointed out that many of the officeholder-oriented British rules were utterly senseless, lacking all sound ideas of America. The pamphlet sold 150,000 copies in 1776 and motivated the revolutionary movement. As the Revolutionary War began, Paine wrote in an essay to soldiers, "These are the times that try men's souls. The summer soldier and the sunshine patriot may, in this crisis, shrink from the service of his country." His messages encouraged the soldiers and inspired patriots to keep fighting for independence. He was a strategic communicator who mobilized forces toward the goal of independence.

Benjamin Franklin

Benjamin Franklin was one of the Founding Fathers who helped draft the Declaration of Independence and the Constitution of the United States. He is known as revolutionary America's best writer, inventor, and diplomat. From a public relations perspective, he was a community organizer. For example, his work led to the creations of a hospital, a university, a militia, a post office, a lending library, a fire brigade, and a home delivery system. Walter Isaacson, a Franklin biographer and former chairman of CNN, calls Franklin "the country's first unabashed public relations expert" who knew how useful a good reputation was.[3] Indeed, he was a publisher who understood well how to use the printing press to promote social causes in the court of public opinion. While serving as president of the Pennsylvania Society for Promoting the Abolition of Slavery, Franklin published several essays that called on Congress to abolish slavery and end the slave trade. His legacies come down through history, along with his image on the $100 bill.

---

2   Melanie Shortman and Jonah Bloom, "The Greatest Companies Ever," *PRWeek*, July 15, 2002, http://www.prweek.com/article/1234145/greatest-campaigns-ever-200-year-old-publicity-stuntthat-changed-course-history-product-recall-becomethe-model-crisis-comms-melanie-shortman-jonah.

3   American Library Association, http://www.ala.org/tools/programming/franklin/29entrepreneurben

The Arrival of Modern Public Relations

P.T. Barnum

P.T. Barnum, known as the "Greatest Showman on Earth" (Figure 2.3), opened the first stage of modern public relations with a focus on publicity in the 1800s, although some public relations practitioners see him as merely a flamboyant show business guy. Barnum operated a museum, circus, and other exhibitions. For more than 40 years, his career prospered as the press chased his sensational stories filled with gimmicks and hyperbole. In 1835, he fed journalists a story about a slave named Joice Heth, who claimed to be 161 years old and a former nurse for George Washington. Barnum placed her in shows and made a lot of money. The press neither refrained from reporting her appearances nor cared about checking whether the former nurse was a sham or not.

Owing to the trend of sensational journalism, Barnum found another lucrative opportunity with a four-year-old boy who was two feet tall and weighed 15 pounds. He trained the boy to sing and dance, then put him in a military uniform and touted him as "General Tom Thumb." The press covered the story, and people came to the exhibit to see the boy. It was a big hit that led to a traveling tour of Europe. The exhibit even attracted the attention of England's Queen Victoria.

Barnum became famous for showcasing the strange and unusual, and his strategy of attracting newspapers kept evolving. Swedish opera singer Jenny Lind was Barnum's next project for promotion and publicity. After he made a contract with Lind (whom Americans and Canadians had never heard of) for $1,000 per performance for 150 shows in the United States and Canada, Barnum launched a publicity campaign to inform the American public about her, nicknaming her the "Swedish Nightingale." He promoted her romantic, innocent image for six months before Lind finally arrived at New York Harbor, where thousands of people were waiting to hail her as she got off the steamship.

Barnum decided to retire from his show business career after the tour with Lind. He wrote his autobiography and served two terms in the Connecticut legislature and one term as mayor of Bridgeport, Connecticut. Then he returned to show business by launching Barnum & Bailey's Greatest Show on Earth. When he bought an enormous elephant from the London Royal Zoological Society to import to the United States for another exhibit, there was a public outcry of protest from all over England. Children and their mothers became hysterical over the English national pet. American newspapers did not miss the sensational story, and the English craze offered a lot of free publicity to Barnum. The deep public interest in both countries dominated the front pages of the press.

Barnum dubbed the elephant (whose name was Jumbo) the "Towering Monarch of His Mighty Race, Whose Like the World Will Never See Again." Jumbo arrived in New York in 1882 to a large welcome from thousands of people. The name "Jumbo" was popularized and became a part of the language.

The shrewd businessman believed in the power of promotion and publicity. After suffering a stroke in 1890, Barnum asked journalists to run his obituary early so he could read whether people thought of him as the greatest showman on Earth. Several weeks before his death in April 1891, the *New York Sun* published his obituary with the front-page headline, "Great and Only Barnum—He Wanted to Read His Obituary—Here It Is." The *New York Times*, after his death, ran his obituary:

> No man knew better than he the value of printer's ink. He made it part of his business to be talked about. The more attention he got in that way the better he liked it. Phineas Taylor Barnum was a good father, a faithful husband, a true friend, and an honest public servant. He was a shrewd manager, and in his business made money when he could. From the smallest of beginnings, he won notoriety, if not fame, on

two continents. His life was filled with the most striking examples of what may be accomplished by that peculiar quality known as Yankee push. His name will long be remembered in his native land.[4]

FIGURE 2.3 P.T. Barnum: The greatest showman earth.

Whether Barnum is remembered as a wicked, deceitful showman or savvy businessman who knew how to promote his exhibits for free, nothing is clearer than that he made the first historical step in public relations practice. He was an innovator in creating a wave of free publicity and promotion. In a public relations sense, he introduced the age of press agentry. As a press agent, he used the skills of making a person or thing look desirable or likable to the media in order to create public interest. The period of Barnum's success was the age of hype, in which newspaper reporters were seeking a stream of sensational and exaggerated news stories. Even though today's public relations practitioners rarely use Barnum's extreme tactics, they cannot ignore the fact that their occupational priority is to attract media attention. The practice of press agentry in the age of social media has been more populated with self-practicing press agents, such as Kim Kardashian, Dwayne Johnson, Justin Bieber, Donald Trump, Selena Gomez, and Kylie Jenner. Barnum deserves a big round of applause as a publicity promoter for the entertainment industry in the 1800s.

Robber Barons and Muckraking

During the Progressive Era from 1890 to 1920, the United States of America went through rapid social and economic changes with reforms in government and business. Big business was thriving, due in part to nationwide railroad lines and communication technology. Local business entrepreneurs expanded their fortunes nationwide. William Vanderbilt (railroads), J. P. Morgan (finance), William A. Clack (mining), John D. Rockefeller (oil), and Andrew Carnegie (steel) formed the invincible group of the wealthy and powerful. Such businessmen were socially disgraced as "robber barons," referred to as exploitative and greedy magnates who amassed their wealth at the cost of the struggle of low-wage workers and exploitation of national resources. The public and media saw them as being uncaring about the rest of society. The robber barons controlled and monopolized important industries. As a result, consumers had to pay more for goods and services. New immigrants worked for them in horrible conditions for little wages. The country was dealing with vice, crime, and corruption as the robber barons and politicians partnered up for their own benefit.

Journalists confronted the corrupt status quo. They exposed dirty businesses and corruption in government. Their investigative stories shocked the public, and public opinion was built up against the robber barons, and there was a call for progressive reform. Journalists focused their work on exposing social ills and corporate/political corruption. They kept digging up the dark mess of social problems to call on the country to address chronic urban poverty, unsafe working conditions, and child labor. President Theodore Roosevelt acknowledged the journalists as the men with muck rakes who were indispensable to the well-being of society. The journalists who wrote investigative articles were called "muckrakers," and their job was depicted as "muckraking," which exposed wrongdoing.

---

4   "The Learning Network," *New York Times*, http://www.nytimes.com/learning/general/onthisday/bday/0705.html.

Muckrakers reported exposés on the exploitation of children and women, crimes of capitalists, food adulteration, fraudulent claims for patents, and any other deceitful business practices. Hundreds of muckraking stories were published. Such exposés affected social sentiment about politics, economy, and culture. The public was deeply appalled by the disgusting practices of businessmen and politicians. As a result, the effect of muckraking on the soul of the country was epic.

The robber barons seriously began to recognize the public outcry for righteousness. They felt that ignorance about public hostility and negative publicity would not solve the issues they confronted. They learned that publicity was directly linked to the formation of public opinion, to which the government was most sensitive. In response to the wave of angry public sentiment, the government enforced tight regulations on what the robber barons could and could not do. It was time for the robber barons to realize that publicity could be used as a source against business threats; if they could not operate their business in secrecy because of muckraking journalism, then they would use publicity for their own purposes. Big businesses turned to public relations to cultivate public favor in hopes of shaking off public hostility. The public relations industry as a communication system was born.

Ivy Lee: Public Relations Comes with Honesty

Ivy Ledbetter Lee graduated from Princeton University and then worked as a *Wall Street Journal* reporter and presidential campaign staffer until he partnered with former Buffalo newspaperman George F. Parker. They opened a consulting firm, Parker and Lee, in 1905. At the firm, Lee was hired to represent Pennsylvania railroad tycoon George F. Baer to handle the 1906 Atlantic City train accident that claimed 53 lives. Lee advised the Pennsylvania railroad to distribute information about the accident to journalists before any rumors were heard and reported on. Lee also held on-site briefings about the accident with journalists who were invited to the scene. In addition, he handed out fact sheets and made railroad experts and executives available for interviews. That fact sheet is considered the first press release. The journalists praised Lee's professional move to help them both report the accident and address concerns regarding public transportation safety.

Lee was convinced that business had to tell stories honestly, accurately, and openly to build healthy public opinion. He believed that the public needed to be informed by business, which was responsible for presenting its side in an honest fashion. Since then, Lee produced press releases for any occasion he was working on. When he sent press releases to journalists, he included a copy of his "Declaration of Principles" statement, later recognized as essential principles for the public relations profession. The declaration reads in part,

> This is not a secret press bureau. All our work is done in the open. We aim to supply news. This is not an advertising agency. If you think any of our matter ought properly to go to your business office, do not use it. Our matter is accurate. Further details on any subject treated will be supplied promptly, and any editor will be assisted most carefully in verifying directly any statement of fact. In brief, our plan is frankly, and openly, on behalf of business concerns and public institutions, to supply the press and public of the United States prompt and accurate information concerning subjects which it is of value and interest to the public to know about.

In contrast to many hyperbole-spouting press agents of that era, Lee believed in openness with the media to build credibility between businessmen and journalists. He preached to businessmen that companies should send factual information to the press if they wanted to earn public confidence.

Because of his honest moves and trustworthy practices with journalists, Lee's services were sought by major corporations. The Rockefeller family was one of them. In the early 1900s, the public perceived

FIGURE 2.4 Ivy Lee.

John D. Rockefeller as a harsh, arrogant, and uncaring robber baron who had achieved his wealth by exploiting powerless people. The so-called Ludlow Massacre in 1904 worsened the family's image. On April 20, 1914, members of the Colorado National Guard killed 6 coal-mine workers, 2 women, and 11 children in Ludlow, Colorado, where 8,000 Colorado mine workers had been on strike since the summer of 1913, asking for better working conditions. The killings sparked ten days of widespread rioting in the coalfields, and more than 60 people were killed. The workers were employed by the Rockefeller-owned Colorado Fuel & Iron Company. People in Colorado went to New York asking for a meeting with Rockefeller Jr., who rejected the demand. Rockefeller Jr. hired Lee when the problem became a national issue. Lee visited the coalfields to talk to mine workers, politicians, and the guard members. After his visit, Lee advised Rockefeller Jr. to visit the Colorado minefields. His visit attracted a host of journalists to travel with him, and Rockefeller Jr. was photographed comforting the workers.

Lee gave more advice to Rockefeller to alter the long-held poor public perception of him. Lee understood the strategies of how to humanize the robber barons. Rather than making excuses for what he had done in the past, Rockefeller was advised to implement new business policies and practices, such as raising employee wages, improving working conditions, and making charitable contributions. Rockefeller was filmed giving away dimes to children. After his death, he was remembered more for the dimes he passed out than the massacre. Lee's goal was to achieve a better public image of Rockefeller. Today, the Rockefeller family's public image showcases the members as incredibly generous philanthropists instead of notorious robber barons.

Later in life, Lee attempted to represent the Soviet Union to improve trade relations with the United States, and he worked for the IG Farben firm, later taken over by the Nazis, to promote the international sales of its chemical products. He was accused of having a connection with communists and Nazis, but the accusation was never proven. Lee is remembered today as one of the two modern public relations fathers who separated press agentry from modern public relations. The other father is Edward Bernays.

Edward Bernays: Public Relations is Psychological Persuasion

Edward L. Bernays (Figure 2.5), the nephew of Sigmund Freud, was born in Vienna and grew up in New York. Bernays regarded himself as a professional opinion producer who could persuade people. Bernays viewed public relations as a part of social science studies, claiming that the public relations industry should focus on designing public persuasion campaigns based on psychology and its social application. He called this scientific application of persuasion the "engineering of consent."

Bernays brought up a provocative argument about propaganda and public relations. He argued that social manipulation by public relations practitioners would be justified by creating authoritative leaders who could assert elusive social control.

> If we understand the mechanism and motives of the group mind, is it not possible to control and regiment the masses according to our will without their knowing about it? The recent practice of propaganda has proved that it is possible, at least up to a certain point and within certain limits.[5]

5   "Edward Bernays," Fandom, http://pr.wikia.com/wiki/Edward_Bernays.

Bernays believed that public relations shifted its practice from the journalistic values of honest information distribution to psychological persuasion in reaching individuals. For him to succeed in public relations, advocacy and persuasion focused on his process of representing clients.

Applying advocacy and persuasion to the public sphere, Bernays believed that he could cause the public to dream about buying mass-produced goods in their subconscious minds. In essence, he organized campaigns aimed at shifting public perception from one of wanting products to one of needing products. Bernays wanted to establish a consumer-based culture, which continues to affect the world today; he created a culture of desire. Bernays opened his own firm in New York in 1919, serving a large number of major clients. He built a trading bridge between the goods and services of corporations and the buying desires of consumers. He created the following six historical campaigns:

FIGURE 2.5 Edward Bernays.

1. In 1915, Sergei Diaghilev, founder of the Ballets Russes, hired Bernays to convince the American public that ballet was fun to watch. Bernays, who knew Americans were not interested in ballet, tried to find the best way of distributing the core message of ballet as fun art; he wrote a ballet guide to target famous cultural magazines. He also sent photos of the ballet dancers to weekly newspapers while persuading American fashion designers to launch collections in the style of the ballet costume. Departing from Bernays' tactics, magazines and newspapers began to characterize ballet as a form of elegant art. Upon the arrival of Diaghilev's ballet artists at the New York docks, Bernays took pictures of the crowd of fans. He sent the pictures to the media, and tickets were sold long before the opening of the ballet tour.

2. In 1923, Bernays was hired to promote Ivory soap for Procter & Gamble. In his market research process, he discovered that people preferred a white unscented soap. At the time, Ivory was the only product on the market with those qualities. He sent his research findings to journalists who later reported that a plain, white, unscented soap was America's favorite. Bernays launched events, including a soap yacht race in Central Park and municipal building washes. He promoted the National Soap Sculpture Competition in which children carved sculptures out of Ivory soap at elementary schools. The country became familiar with using Ivory soap.

3. In 1924, Bernays worked for the president. While President Calvin Coolidge was running for reelection, he needed to alleviate his image as a cold, silent iceberg. Bernays orchestrated the campaign to portray Coolidge as an "Ordinary Joe" with a big smile. Bernays recommended that the president have a meet-and-greet event over pancakes at the White House. For publicity, Bernays said there was no doubt that actors and actresses carried a strong connotation of humanness, warmth, extroversion, and friendship. He invited celebrities to the pancake breakfast with the president. With the event, Bernays expected heavy media coverage of the president's warmth and human sympathy. The press reaction to the event was front-page news throughout the country. The headline in the *New York Times* read, "President Almost Laughs."

4. In 1925, the Beech-Nut Packing Company, a producer of pork products and nostalgic Beech-Nut bubble gum, hired Bernays to increase bacon sales. Instead of sending a simple message to eat bacon, he chose the method of third-party endorsement to prove scientifically that Americans would

benefit more from a heavy breakfast than a light one. Bernays asked his internal doctor if a heavier breakfast might be more beneficial for the American public, and his doctor confirmed that it would. The doctor sent letters to 5,000 fellow doctors nationwide, supporting his confirmation. Most doctors endorsed the importance of a heavier breakfast, and the media reported it. Bacon and eggs were presented as the best choices for breakfast, and the company's profits soared. Bernays used trusted authority figures for the birth of the American-style breakfast.

5. In March 1929, he organized a "Freedom for Women" campaign, which inspired women to smoke cigarettes as a symbol of liberation and power. Bernays hired a group of models to march on Fifth Avenue in New York City and signaled them to light Lucky Strike cigarettes in front of journalists and photographers who had been informed about the event. Bernays framed the event as "Torches of Freedom" (Figure 2.6). The next day, the *New York Times* had front-page headlines: "Group of Girls Puff at Cigarettes as a Gesture of Freedom." The American Tobacco Company praised his work.

FIGURE 2.6 Women and their "torches of freedom".

6. In October 1929, Bernays was involved in promoting Light's Golden Jubilee to celebrate the 50th anniversary of Thomas Edison's invention of the electric light bulb. The celebration lasted for six months across several major cities. The US Post Office issued a commemorative stamp. President Herbert Hoover, Thomas A. Edison, Henry Ford, Marie Curie, and many more dignitaries participated in the celebration. Bernays said that the participation of such important figures gave new meaning and status to public relations. Bernays was later hired by General Electric.

Bernays used the psychological principle that people are stimulated by subconscious desires. He synthesized the physical and mental elements of human behavior into motivating people. How to stimulate fresh desires, persuade reluctant desires, and wake up dormant desires was Bernays's focus while developing public relations. His public relations campaigns were legendary, like the "Torches of Freedom" campaign, which persuaded women to smoke in public to fight for gender rights (Figure 2.6). However, he regretted creating the campaign after research in the 1950s showed that smoking was linked to lung cancer. In the early 1960s, Bernays became a public opponent of smoking and took part in antismoking campaigns. Not only was Bernays a perceptive public relations practitioner, but he was also a prolific writer on public relations. He wrote four books: *Crystallizing Public Opinion* (1923), *Propaganda* (1928), *The Engineering of Consent* (1955), and *Biography of an Idea: Memoirs of a Public Relations Counsel* (1965).

Ivy Lee and Edward Bernays laid the foundation for modern public relations. They both acknowledged how public relations would evolve and what public relations practitioners should do in the rapidly changing 1900s. Ivy Lee's standards of practicing public relations toward the public and media with the principles of honesty and accuracy gave rise to the development of current public relations ethics. Edward Bernays's psychological approach to the practice of public relations broadened the application of public relations to the human mind and behavior, in which modern public relations offers counseling and consulting services. Lee and Bernays educated public relations practitioners and developed the values of public relations. Both deserve to be called the fathers of modern public relations.

Arthur W. Page: Corporate Public Relations

The American Telephone and Telegraph Company (AT&T), founded in 1885, was the most dominant telecommunication giant in the early 1900s. When the company was facing public hostility because of its market monopolization, AT&T's president, Theodore N. Vail, realized that companies should consider building positive reputations with the public and their customers. In fact, most press coverage of the company was negative. Vail was the first business leader who used the term *public relations* when he included it in the 1907 AT&T annual report; to him, public relations meant the whole scope of relations between the corporation and the public. He said, "If we don't tell the truth about ourselves, someone else will."

Vail's belief in public relations passed down through the culture of AT&T, and it was brought to realization with Arthur W. Page, who was hired as AT&T's first vice president of public relations in 1927. As a former journalist and member of the board of directors at Chase Manhattan Bank, Page understood the balanced functions of publicity and management. Page demanded, when taking the position, that he not be excluded from making management decisions and policies. He wanted to get involved in the corporate decision-making process to include public relations values for business performance. Page also stressed that strong maintenance of AT&T's reputation would be connected to proper corporate performance approved by the public. Page believed that the public had to be informed of what AT&T was doing and what its policies were. For AT&T's public relations programs, Page announced the five principles of corporate public relations, which have been considered the first corporate communications-management guidelines. The principles are as follows:

1. To ensure management thoughtfully analyzes its overall relation to the public,

2. To create a system for informing all employees about the company's general policies and practices,

3. To create a system giving contact employees (those having direct dealings with the public) the knowledge needed to be reasonable and polite to the public,

4. To create a system drawing employee and public questions and criticisms back up through the organization to management, and

5. To ensure frankness in telling the public about the company's actions.

Even after Page retired in 1947, his legacy of corporate public relations has been remembered through the Arthur W. Page Society, an organization founded by AT&T executives in 1983 to promote the management policy role of chief public relations officer. The organization's members include senior public relations and corporate communications executives from Fortune 500 companies. The members, based on Page's five principles, developed the following twenty-first-century corporate communication principles: (1) tell the truth, (2) prove it with action, (3) listen to the customer, (4) manage for tomorrow, (5) conduct public relations as if the whole company depends on it, (6) realize a company's true character is expressed by its people, and (7) remain calm, patient, and good-humored.[6]

The Oscar Mayer Wienermobile: Corporate Public Relations Campaign

While public relations pioneers established profound principles and practiced exemplary campaigns, corporations took advantage of such development to promote their products and services. In 1936, the Oscar Mayer Company came up with the idea of promoting its ham and sausage products through a symbolic icon: the Wienermobile. The hot-dog-on-a-bun-shaped mobile roamed America's highways and back roads. Drivers of Wienermobiles handed out toy whistles shaped like mini replicas of the Wienermobile to crowds on streets, and the media paid attention to the moving fake sausage. Drivers

---

6   The Arthur W. Page Society. https://page.org/site/the-page-principles

of Wienermobiles, who were known as hotdoggers, have been characterized as a group of media ambassadors. The company's public relations practitioners alerted local media about the impending arrival of the mobile, arranged public photo time, and set up media interviews. The hotdoggers, mostly public relations/communication college graduates, are responsible for attracting national attention with the help of media coverage. They give tours of the mobile and create memories for consumers of all ages with promotional events. In 2019, CNN described the public relations duty of hotdoggers: handing out wiener whistles and coupons, chatting with people, taking photos, attending events, doing media interviews, and otherwise promoting the company.[7]

The Wienermobile (Figure 2.7) as a brand symbol of Oscar Mayer is a driving force behind the brand's public relations strategies. Oscar Mayer continues to generate media coverage in every city where the mobile arrives. Despite the criticism of hot dogs as unhealthy food, the company focuses on stirring nostalgic memories: "Hot dogs are a fun, feel-good American food that brings families together at picnics and barbecues."[8] The mobile helps the company capitalize on its family-friendly brand image, although it does not carry actual hot dogs to sell. The Wienermobile was off the streets during World War II because of gas rationing, but the company has built several new Wienermobiles since the war. As of 2019, there are six active Wienermobiles traveling across the country. PRSA called the Oscar Mayer Wienermobile one of the most enduring marketing symbols in public relations.[9]

De Beers: The Tagline

Founded in 1888 by British businessman Cecil Rhodes, De Beers was a cartel of 12 companies spread across the globe, which owned 85 percent of the diamond market and had a notorious reputation for price-fixing and exercising a global monopoly over the diamond industry in the 1930s. While De Beers stockpiled diamonds to control price, then-chairman Sir Ernest Oppenheimer had to find markets to boost diamond sales during the global economic depression. He saw the United States as the powerhouse for supporting the diamond industry in the late 1930s and hired the Philadelphia ad agency N.W. Ayer to launch a marketing campaign. The agency researched the US diamond market and found that Americans viewed diamonds as a commodity for super-rich people and less practical than cars and home appliances.

The agency strategized to create a psychological demand for diamonds in consumers' minds by pushing the idea that diamonds are forever. It linked diamonds with psychological human activity—love and marriage. The main strategy was to associate diamonds with romance, so they created a new tradition of the diamond engagement ring. In short, the agency focused on creating the social trend of getting a diamond engagement ring as a

FIGURE 2.7 Current wienermobiles are the largest ever—27 feet long and 11 feet high.

7   Marnie Hunter, "Wienermobile: Drive a Hot Dog, See the Country," CNN, February 22, 2019. https://www.cnn.com/travel/article/wienermobile-oscar-mayer/index.html.

8   "News," UT Austin Advertising and Public Relations, http://advertising.utexas.edu/news/hot-dog-pr-alumna-says-driving-weinermobile-fun-time-serious-business.

9   CNN. https://www.cnn.com/travel/article/oscar-mayer-wienermobile-airbnb-trnd/index.html

prelude to marriage. Public opinion on diamonds was reformulated from a luxury to a romantic necessity by the agency, which, culturally and socially, convinced Americans that a diamond ring would complete the romantic journey.

To spread the message of diamonds with eternal and emotional value, the agency used newspapers, radio, and magazines, including direct advertisements. The agency's campaign led to newspapers to publish stories of Hollywood celebrities wearing diamond rings and necklaces, radio programs to announce diamond trends, and magazines to print instructions on how to buy a diamond. The instructions advised people to ask about color, clarity, and cutting, for these determine a diamond's quality and contribute to its beauty and value.[10] As a result of the campaign, De Beers enjoyed a 55 percent increase in diamond sales in the United States between 1938 and 1941. With the noticeable gain, De Beers and the agency began to further their marketing strategy in the 1940s.

Starting in the 1940s, De Beers and the agency decided to focus on positioning the engagement diamond tradition in young couples' minds. They invented a new message of a man buying a diamond ring for his soon-to-be wife. The more they were exposed to the message, the more likely the public came to see it as fact.

The famous slogan "A Diamond Is Forever," with its emphasis on both eternity and sentiment, became a huge hit in 1948. The simple audacity of these four iconic words has placed diamonds as by far the most precious gemstone of choice worldwide. The slogan cemented the marriage culture among Americans. In 1951, "eight out of ten American brides got a diamond," and girls would not feel engaged unless they had a diamond engagement ring.[11] The campaigns for De Beers succeeded in establishing the new social culture of diamonds, symbolically defined as the ultimate romantic gift of love from men to women, as well as an essential part of loving relationships.

Public Relations after World War II

The economic boom after World War II led to the prosperity of public relations. Corporations created public relations departments, and PRSA was founded in 1948. In the 1960s, social reform served as a key impetus for public relations activity and development. Political upheavals such as Vietnam War protests, the civil and women rights movements, and the environmentalist movement needed communication strategies. Public relations practitioners embraced new concepts of practical principles for societal changes and confrontations. If the 1950s were an age of what we should *say* to the public in public relations, then the turbulent 1960s would be an age of what we should *do* in public relations. They advanced the practice of public relations to focus on consumer rights rather than corporate reputations.

The consumer movement, as part of the rapid social changes in the 1960s, aimed to protect the average American against dysfunctional products, unfair pricing and, poor working conditions. An effort to raise awareness for consumer protection arose through an organized social movement, which created a wave of advocacy for the rights of consumers. The rights were infringed upon by misleading information, faulty

---

10   Lindsay Kolowich, "The Engagement Ring Story: How De Beers Created a Multi-Billion Dollar industry From the Ground Up," Hubspot, June 13, 2014, http://blog.hubspot.com/marketing/diamond-de-beers-marketing-campaign.

11   J. Courtney Sullivan, "Why a Diamond Is Forever Has Lasted so Long," *Washington Post*, February 7, 2014, http://www.washingtonpost.com/opinions/why-a-diamond-is-forever-has-lasted-so-long/2014/02/07/f6adf3f4-8eae-11e3-84e1-27626c5ef5fb_story.html.

products, and deceitful practices of corporations. The consumer movement pushed for increased rights and legal protection when corporations had something to do with any harmful business practices. When John F. Kennedy was a presidential candidate, he made a promise to support consumers. When Kennedy became president, the concept of professional regulations serving the public interest was articulated in his 1960 speech to Congress. The Consumer Bill of Rights is summarized as follows:[12]

- *The right to safety.* To be protected against the marketing of products and services that are hazardous to health or to life.

- *The right to be informed.* To be protected against fraudulent, deceitful, or grossly misleading information, advertising, labeling, or other practices and to be given the facts needed to make informed choices.

- *The right to choose.* To have available a variety of products and services at competitive prices.

- *The right to be heard.* To be assured that consumer interests will receive full and sympathetic consideration in making government policy, both through the laws passed by legislatures and regulations passed by administrative bodies.

- *The right to education.* To have access to programs and information that help consumers make better marketplace decisions.

Along with consumer rights, the "customer is king" trend spread throughout society in the 1970s. The practice of public relations was democratically inspired to oppose business interests. As consumer and civil interest groups blossomed (with little money and staff), social activists in close alliance with public relations practitioners were likely to use performing arts. For example, advocates of anti-deforestation staged a tree-hugging event by inviting the media to the mountains. Social concerns against big corporations prompted corporate communicators to focus new corporate communication strategies on community relations. Community relations required sustainable, constant communication with the people who constitute the environment in which corporations operate from which they draw resources. They needed to foster mutual understanding, trust, and support.

In the 1980s, public relations practitioners experienced strong demand for management functions from corporations, federal and local governments, and nonprofit organizations. Hence, the practice of public relations embraced the organizational concept of management by objectives (MBO), a process of defining goals within an organization to achieve its objectives between employees and employers. The MBO process consists of five steps: (1) review organizational objectives, (2) set worker objectives, (3) monitor progress, (4) evaluate performance, and (5) give reward. Based on the management approach to public relations, practitioners were asked if they would assist in addressing controversial issues between labor and management. As a result, employee relations were identified as a new public relations area of practice.

The 1990s and early 2000s were the eras of comprehensive communication strategies, in accordance with the lavish developments in the Internet, social media, global economy, and personal communication devices. In this environment, public relations practitioners are required to handle a multiplicity of assignments, including crisis management, investor relations, and cultural relations. Public relations in the twenty-first century has transformed into a versatile practice for organizations and individuals

---

12   "Consumer Bill of Rights," Massachusetts Office of Consumer Affairs, http://www.mass.gov/ocabr/government/oca-agencies/dpl-lp/consumer-fact-sheets/consumer-bill-of-rights.html.

all around the world. When Ivy Lee and Edward Bernays implemented the practice of public relations, their major target audience was journalists, most of whom worked for newspapers and magazines. The main communication technologies they depended on were telephone and "snail mail." Working for foreign clients was not easy because of the infant state of the air transportation system until the mid-1900s. After World War II public relations practitioners understood the power of television and radio as communication tools for corporations and other organizations to distribute messages and cultivate mutual relationships with their target audiences. As of today, visual graphics such as photos and videos on social media platforms have a strong effect on public relations campaigns.

Future of Public Relations

The Internet became popular in the late 1990s, and it served as another powerful communication tool for public relations practitioners to use in terms of sending press releases, building online public relations centers for organizations, organizing online campaigns, and connecting with more online media outlets. They are capable of getting their jobs done quickly and efficiently in the online world but the overwhelming flood of information and tense competition for attention requires more time and effort to accomplish positive outcomes.

The early 2000s saw enormous changes in the practice of public relations. Thanks to new personal communication devices, such as smartphones and tablet PCs, social media has become an essential communication channel for individual and organizational interactions. The practice of public relations has to become agile, broad, and sensitive. In the social media world, a small issue can grow into a national crisis, and a tiny feud can place an organization or an individual into a chaotic situation. Public relations practitioners tend to monitor social and organizational issues 24/7 in order to handle any danger while trying to spearhead communication strategies for their organizations and clients. It is a new trend in the practice of public relations, and it is backbreaking but rewarding.

CHAPTER SUMMARY AND REVIEW

1. Study the early development of communication for the powerful.
2. Identify why big US corporations were criticized in the early 1900s.
3. Identify the major figures of public relations and describe their legacies.
4. Discuss which public relations campaigns were impressive.
5. Describe the development of modern public relations.

PUBLIC RELATIONS IN PRACTICE

FURTHER READING

PR Week's Awards For **Best PR Data Insight**

Winner: Nestlé/Lean Cuisine and Weber Shandwick
Campaign Name: The it all Social Experiment

Lean Cuisine wanted to help women redefine what having it all means to them in this creative social experiment. To take on the unattainable idea of having it all, the company invited a group of women to take a survey about what they want out of life, such as if they want a family and what they want to achieve professionally.

Read more at
https://www.prweek.com/article/1579436/prweek-us-awards-2019-winners

3

Fundamental Elements of Public Relations Profession

he Bureau of Labor Statistics, a unit of the United States Department of Labor, explains that public relations practitioners create and maintain "a favorable public image for the organization they represent," aiming to shape positive public perception and gain remarkable notice for the organization. In doing so, public relations practitioners specialize in creating and maintaining a stellar reputation for the organization. With this explanation, a question arises: Is that it?

The Occupational Scope of Public Relations

The practice of public relations embraces the use of communication tools like a press release to build a good image for an organization. However, with the expansion of capitalism, globalization, democracy and technological innovations in the twenty-first century, job descriptions for public relations practitioners are increasingly dynamic and versatile. Issuing a press release to create and maintain mutual media relations is one of the core functions of public relations; other functions range from campaign management, employee training, investor relations, event organization, online/social media administration and damage control in communication. These descriptions plainly represent what public relations practitioners live for, every day and everywhere. They know how important it is to keep up with rapid social changes, which bring more job responsibilities. They acknowledge how overwhelming it is to stay current with all the new and evolving social phenomena in the business world.

It is widely believed among public relations practitioners and college scholars that creating and maintaining "a favorable image for the organization" is the ultimate goal of public relations. If so, it is necessary to acknowledge the extent to which the organization is referred. BusinessDictionary.com defines an organization as "a social unite of people that is structured and managed to meet a need or to pursue collective goals."[1] Based on that definition, an organization can be a company, corporation, firm,

---

1 "Organization," BusinessDictionary.com, http://www.businessdictionary.com/definition/organization.html.

FIGURE 3.1 A favorable image can be created by public figures like steve jobs.

institution, agency, government, association, group, club, administration, or consortium. Such organizations are major employers of public relations practitioners.

Individuals such as celebrities and politicians should also be included in the category of major employers. Although individuals do not belong to the scope of an organization, they hire public relations practitioners for personal image management. Celebrities and politicians are major clients who seek advice and strategy to deal with the media and the public. Hence public relations is considered an industry of image management for any organization and any individual.

Everybody Does Public Relations in Practice

Does "any organization and any individual" mean that anybody can practice public relations? The answer to the question is, "Why not?" As long as people communicate and interact with other people in private and public places, they are already involved in the practice of personal public relations. Most of them tend to be nice; they hope to make more friends; they need to cooperate; they wish to help (or be helped); they want to be loved. In short, they behave themselves in order to impress other people and to be (consciously or subconsciously) perceived as nice people. They were and are in the process of building good relationships and images with other people in a social setting. It is the practice of self-public relations whether they recognized the act or not. Humans in society are all self-practiced public relations beings.

Anybody can conduct public relations in his or her daily routine. Public relations does not require an official exam, a degree, or a license (like attorneys and dentists) to work in the profession. Then why does society acknowledge the professional occupation of public relations? More specifically, why do organizations and individuals need public relations practitioners? Professor Ron Smith has answers to these questions:

> Public relations is a profession rooted in research, ethics, strategic planning, and evaluation, as well as effective written, spoken, and visual communication. It is based on a course of study. So it's more appropriate to say that anybody who has acquired the skills and adopted the ethical standards can do the work of public relations.[2]

Public relations practitioners are a special group of people who have been trained for communication enhancement with a target audience and for problem solving in tough situations. Being armed with communication skills is the first step toward becoming a public relations practitioner who also views the general public as a target audience.

---

2   Ron Smith, *Public Relations: The Basics*, p.7 (London: Routledge, 2014),

The First Step to Becoming a Public Relations Practitioner

Communication skills are essential for future public relations practitioners. The most recommended and effective way of obtaining such skills is to take college courses. Taking classes in general communication, advertising, marketing, news reporting, and public relations is a common way of developing communication skills. In other words, a college education is a must to work as a public relations practitioner or strategic communicator in the future. Becoming a college student is the first step toward becoming a public relations practitioner.

For college students, general communication classes refer to basic English writing, news reporting, and public speaking courses. These courses are designed to help students increase their written and spoken communication skills. Writing and speaking should be the practical principles of communication skills, and, fortunately, all colleges nationwide offer such courses. A basic English writing course is required for college freshmen to learn how to read, think, and write. They are also encouraged to take a public speaking course to learn how to control the common fear of speaking in front of people while effectively delivering intended messages to audiences. Based on their experience, college sophomores are allowed to choose more specialized writing courses, such as news or business writing, if they decide to pursue communication-related majors: public relations, advertising, online journalism, broadcast media, mass communication, and so on.

In order for students who study in the communication field to achieve good writing skills, there are two instruments they are obliged to master. One is how to write a formal email and the other is how to write an article in Associated Press style.

Email

When college life begins, students usually receive an official email address ending with .edu. Colleges expect students to use their academic email accounts as an official means of communication between the student and the college faculty. The student is responsible for sending and receiving all information regarding school affairs via the assigned email account. Not responding to a question or request from the student's private email account, such as Gmail, has become a universal practice for professors and instructors. They often ask students to resend their messages via school email accounts. Using a college email account establishes an academic means of communication on campus.

With the advent of smartphone communication and its pervasive use, college students commonly prefer to text or leave a message on social media platforms. They do not care much about the influence of email communication. Email, however, is a powerful communication tool from a public relations perspective. When students have questions and concerns about their academic performance, especially about coursework, they usually send messages to their instructors via email. Further, instructors ask their students to send them an email if they need a meeting outside of normal office hours. In this respect, the way in which students communicate and present themselves when writing to instructors is extremely important. It creates a good or bad image of the student in the instructor's mind. More importantly, the student should see email as "a professional form of communication" that affects instructors' decisions on how they view the student and how much time and energy they want to invest in that student.

For college students, it is a mistake to be careless about how email communication reflects their attitudes and manners. If students want to build a good image for academic success, then email is definitely one of the strategic tools they should use impressively. It can represent "how courteous and well educated they are" in the academic practice of public relations.

A news reporter wrote, "Many students don't see the need to show even a modicum of respect for those in positions of authority, particularly in emails. ... Students fail to observe the existence of professional boundaries completely."[3] For college students not to fail at email communication with instructors in academic public relations, there is an army of suggestions from many academic organizations. The following are several "dos and don'ts" to keep in mind.

Crucial Email Dos

- *Make the Subject Line Informative.* The subject line should succinctly identify what the student is writing about.

- *Use the Instructor's Proper Title.* A good rule of thumb is to keep communication formal, so address an instructor as Dr. (if they have a PhD) or professor. Otherwise, use Mr. or Ms. with his or her last name.

- *Begin with a Greeting.* Writing "Dear Dr. Smith" or "Hello, Dr. Smith" is better than "Dr. Smith." "Hi" is way better than "Hey."

- *Use a Colon (:) or Comma (,) after the Greeting.* This is one of the email formats. For example, "Dear Dr. Smith," or "Dear Dr. Smith:" completes the greeting section.

- *Be Considerate of the Instructor.* It is important to convey clear and concise messages with proper paragraph breaks. Blank lines between each paragraph are highly recommended. Instructors prefer to read one paragraph with two sentences rather than five.

- *End Appropriately.* End an email with words or phrases like "Sincerely," "Kind Regards," or "Best Regards."

- *Add Contact Information.* Name, email address, phone number, or major will be added if necessary.

Crucial Email Don'ts

- **Don't email** the instructor complaining about grades. If you have an issue with grades, visit the instructor during office hours and talk.

- **Don't email** the instructor to ask for materials that are already posted on a course management system, such as Blackboard—much of the information about a class is usually posted in the online syllabus.

---

3   Denise D. Knight and Noralyn Masselink, "i don't mean too bother u but" student email and a call for netiquette," E-learning Magazine, May 2008. http://elearnmag.acm.org/featured.cfm?aid=1379051.

- **Don't email** the instructor and send the same email to other people. The email should be a private communication between the instructor and the student, not anyone else.

- **Don't email** disrespectful content. Rude and offensive messages will not be tolerated by any instructor.

- **Don't expect** an immediate response to your email. Rather than checking emails every hour, the instructor probably checks emails once a day. Wait at least one day for a reply.

A courteous, professional email enables the student to be recognized as a promising future public relations practitioner. The student should keep in mind that instructors are also humans with feelings, just like students, and they hope to exchange emails with students in a manner that is respectful and courteous.

The following two emails were sent to Dr. Smith, and they are nearly original.

From: Michelle JXXXXX — mf348762@XXXXX.edu
Subject: Exam

Hey.

I did not take the exam because I had to go to work. Can I take it? I want to take it maybe next week. Thank you.

Michelle JXXXXX

From: Becky LXXXXX — bl749305@XXXXX.edu
Subject: A chance for missing the exam

Dear Dr. Smith:

Hello. My name is Becky LXXXXX, and I am in your Introduction to Strategic Communication class.

I am rather embarrassed to ask this, but I am writing to ask you if there's a way I can have a chance to take the exam.

I missed the exam because I had to go to work to cover my manager's shift at XXXXX gas station on Main Street.
It has never happened before, but it did this time. It is true, and my manager is willing to explain the situation to you via email or phone conversation.

(Continued)

Could you let me know if I could take it? If not, I understand, but thank you for your time.

I am so sorry about this inconvenience, sir.

Have a nice day.

Sincerely,

Becky LXXXXX
Strategic Communication Junior
bl749305@XXXXX.edu

Regardless of the two students' chances for a make-up exam opportunity, Dr. Smith would view Becky as a courteous student, as opposed to Michelle, whom Dr. Smith would likely pity for her lack of basic communication manners.

Email in Business

The way Becky writes an email can give her a better chance of finding a future job as a public relations practitioner. Kelsey Casselbury, a communication expert, points out that email is widely used as a form of business communication, and, overall, it is a highly effective communication tool.[4] Casselbury explains the gist of writing effective business emails:

> The subject line should accurately represent the content of the email. Use proper punctuation and capitalization, and use bold, italics, and white space to make important information stand out from the rest of the content. Use a salutation to begin the email, and only send to individuals that readily need or request to receive information from your business. Business emails should be brief, positive, and professional.[5]

Be sure to write a business email with a greeting, such as "Hello, Director Smith:" or "Dear Ms. Smith:" If the student does not know the name of the receiver, the greeting can be "To whom it may concern:" or "Dear Sir or Madam:" but it would be more impressive to find out the name of the person who will be reading the email rather than using the salutation "To whom it may concern." Also, note that "Dear someone:" goes without a comma, while "Hello, Someone:" requires a comma. It is one of the email rules.

Email Rules for Applying for Jobs or Internships

College students often use email to apply for jobs or internships, although many online job sites offer automatic uploads of resumes and cover letters. According to the "Email Statistics Report of 2015–2019,"

---

4   Kelsey Casselbury, "The Use of Email in Business Communication" Chron. March 12, 2019, https://smallbusiness.chron.com/use-email-business-communication-118.html

5   Kelsey Casselbury, "The Use of Email in Business Communication" Chron. March 12, 2019 https://smallbusiness.chron.com/use-email-business-communication-118.html

over 124 billion business emails were sent and received every day, and about 50 percent of emails were read on mobile phones.[6] As a result, human resources professionals and recruiters spend just six seconds reviewing a resume or less time scanning a job seeker's email. When emailing a job or internship application, students should know that the subject line is everything. Filling in the subject line with a strong message is the best way to entice a recruiter to open the email. A vague subject line, such as "Resume for John Smith's Application," is destined to be beaten by another one that reads, "Entry-Level Communication Specialist Position # 1111 for John Smith."

The editor of Job-Hunt.org, Susan Joyce, has provided additional valuable advice for college job seekers who use email.[7]

- In the very first paragraph, explain who you are and why you are contacting them. Recruiters do not have much time to read the entire e-mail.

- Think and write like a good sales/PR person: instead of using many "I" sentences, use "My experiences of ... " and "My ability to ... " Try to use positive and active words.

- Use short paragraphs.

- Send from a "good" e-mail address: a school-issued e-mail will suffice.

- Include a business "signature" section at the bottom: This includes your name, e-mail address, website address, and phone number.

- Find someone else to proofread it. Before hitting the send button, a student should ask an expert from the campus career center to revise his or her e-mail.

In sum, the proper use of email represents what and who the student is. Even though fast and convenient texting and messaging via smartphone have become popular means of communication, effective and official email practice for college students is still alive. In fact, email is not only the first point of contact for college students looking for a job or internship, but it also functions as a main communication tool for professional interaction between students and instructors on campus.

Students majoring in communication-related fields should know about the benefits of using email in a strategic way to build good relationships with instructors and create a strong, positive image in the recruiter's mind.

Associated Press Style in Public Relations

The Associated Press (AP) is the largest news service in the world. It has published guidelines on how to write and report news stories since 1953. Reporters, editors, and strategic communicators in the media industry use the *AP Stylebook* as a guide for grammar, punctuation, and practices of news reporting. The book, updated annually, is referred to as the "journalist's bible," and the *AP Stylebook* website claims it is

---

6   The Radicati Group Inc., "Email Statistics Report 2015–2019," March 2015, https://www.radicati.com/wp/wp-content/uploads/2015/02/Email-Statistics-Report-2015-2019-Executive-Summary.pdf.

7   Susan P. Joyce, "Get That interview With a Great Email Message," Huffington Post, May 19, 2014, http://www.huffingtonpost.com/susan-p-joyce/get-that-interview-with-a_b_4996669.html.

widely used "as a writing and editing reference in newsrooms, classrooms, and corporate offices world-wide."[8] In other words, college students who want to become journalists should get familiar with the news writing rules guided by the book; however, it isn't readily apparent why corporate offices also use AP style. Even more curiously, why is AP style used by public relations students?

Why Do Public Relations Practitioners Use the *Ap* Stylebook?

Journalists and public relations practitioners have different boundaries regarding job practices, and the *AP Stylebook* is the journalist's bible. But why do public relations practitioners need to know how to write stories about their organizations and clients based on AP style? A good explanation is that one of their typical tasks is to write a press release that informs news outlets of the organization. The press release is expected to grab a journalist's attention, and the journalist will make a decision if the release has an opportunity to be reproduced or reported in the media. If it is, the public relations practitioner has made a big score for the organization.

News content in mass media, such as television, newspapers, magazines, and radio is produced by a wide variety of journalists, and they agree on consistent guidelines for news reporting in the AP style. It offers the fundamental principles of news reporting: consistency, clarity, accuracy, and brevity. Therefore, if a press release is read by a journalist who finds it poorly written and ignorant of the AP style, the release will end up in the journalist's trash can. One newspaper editor confessed, "We receive hundreds of press releases through fax, mail, and e-mail every week. But regardless of its newsworthiness, we don't publish a release with AP errors because we have no time to fix it."

Luke O'Neill, editor of Business Wire, points out that public relations, investor relations, marketing, and communication professionals should stay abreast of the AP style and its annual changes so that they can "relate to the media on their level, write cleaner press releases, increase message adoption, and simply sound cool."[9] The truth behind this writing style is connected with the feeling that journalists appreciate people who respect the media's language; public relations practitioners follow the style to build trustworthy relationships with journalists. As a result, a press release might have a better chance for publication. Again, public relations practitioners pray—not pay—for free space and airtime.

Becoming a good public relations practitioner equals mastering AP style. As colleges offer news writing or media reporting classes that educate students about AP style, it is also important to know that students in these classes consider the style most handy and practical for their future careers. An employer who plans to hire a college graduate for an entry-level position is likely to believe that a college degree guarantees that the job applicant is armed with a good mastery of writing skills. Hence, the applicant can contribute to the bottom line from the first day of work. The employer never appreciates some rookie employee's incompetence in writing, simply because their company would not waste time and money on retraining in basic writing skills (e.g., inverted pyramid, subject-verb agreement, verb tenses, relative pronouns, appositives, etc.). Organizations and media outlets are looking for employees who know what communication is and how to communicate with audiences. The mastery of writing skills is not an option but a necessity, and students in communication-related fields are expected to

---

8   AP Stylebook, "AP Stylebook 2014 Adds Religion Chapter with Over 200 Terms," May 28, 2014, http://www.ap.org/Content/Press-Release/2014/AP-Stylebook-2014-adds-religion-chapter-with-over-200-terms.

9   Luke O'Neill, Eight AP Style Mistakes Frequently Found in Today's Press Releases, https://thecentogroup.wordpress.com/category/press-releases/

understand and use AP style to become promising public relations practitioners or strategic communicators. In fact, many public relations/strategic communication firms and organizations ask job applicants to take a writing test (including an AP style quiz and a press release example) as part of the interview process.

Consider the advice of two public relations leaders who emphasize the importance of writing skills.

1. Dawn Miller, CEO of Miller PR, said, "Writing tests are a very important part of the interview process for us. Typically, we ask the applicant to prepare a press release, a pitch, a bio, or a company boilerplate, depending on the candidate and the skills required for the position we're looking to fill."[10]

2. Amy Bermar, president of Corporate Ink, a Boston-based agency specializing in technology clients, said, "We use writing tests for every single hire—at every level. We began this more than fifteen years ago, after the unhappy discovery that someone 'senior enough' to know how to write actually didn't write very well at all."[11]

FIGURE 3.2 AP logo.

Writing Mistakes to Avoid

The key to job security for future public relations practitioners is mastering writing that follows AP style. Table 3.1 lists the ten most frequent mistakes in college-level writing.

TABLE 3.1   Ten Most Frequent Mistakes in College-Level Writing

Dangling Modifiers. No word or phrase to describe	* After watching the great new movie, the book based on it is sure to be entertaining. — Who watched the great new movie? It is not the book; that can't watch the movie. A subject must be added so that the modifier has something to describe, change, or limit. In the sentence, the subject should be a person. ** After watching the great new movie, I thought the book based on it was sure to be entertaining.
Run-On Sentences. Two or more main clauses that are run together without proper punctuation	* I didn't know which course I wanted to take I was too embarrassed to decide. — Two independent clauses joined together without connecting words or punctuation to separate the clauses cause a grammar error. A period or a coordinating conjunction can prevent the error. ** I didn't know which course I wanted to take, and I was too embarrassed to decide.
Faulty comparison. Comparison to two unlike people or things	* The civil protests in 2016 were more numerous than 2015. — This sentence compares protests to 2015. ** The civil demonstrations in 2016 were more numerous than the protests in 2015.

10   PR News, "Rock the Job Interview: 5 Tips for Nailing Your PR Writing Test," October 30, 2019, https://www.prnewsonline.com/job-interview-5-tips-pr-writing-test/

11   Ibid.

Objective Pronouns. The objective pronouns are her, him, it, me, them, us, and you

* The fight began this morning between Matt and she.
— The pronoun is used as an object, so it should be in the objective case.
** The fight began this morning between Matt and her.

Prepositions in Subject-Verb Agreement. The relationship between other words in a sentence

* The tray of cocktail glasses have fallen on Mr. Smith's left foot.
— The subject of this sentence is the tray, not the glasses.
** The tray of cocktail glasses has fallen on Mr. Smith's left foot.

Compound Subjects. Two or more subjects for a verb

* The teacher, the secretary, or the student are going to school.
— Singular subjects are joined by or take a singular verb.
** The teacher, the secretary, or the student is going to school.

Colons. Introduction to particular information

* On his presidential campaign trip, Mr. Smith will stop by the following cities, San Antonio, Los Angeles, Seattle, Columbus, and Miami.
— A colon is used to enumerate a list.
** On his presidential campaign trip, Mr. Smith will stop by the following cities: San Antonio, Los Angeles, Seattle, Columbus, and Miami.

Sentence Fragments. A group of words that is not a sentence

* For engaging in pro bono work gives you practical experience and a chance to see how wonderful the legal field is.
— Removing the preposition removes the error, as there is no subject.
** Engaging in pro bono work gives you practical experience and a chance to see how wonderful the legal field is.

Gerunds. A verbal that ends in "-ing" and functions as a noun

* Singing is merely the art of keeping a large group of people from sleep.
— Singing is a gerund as a subject, and the gerunds "keeping" and "sleep" are objects of prepositions. "Sleep" should be in parallel.
** Singing is merely the art of keeping a large group of people from sleeping.

Progressive Tense. An illustration of an action in time

* Before Ms. Smith entered the conference room, she was hiding from her ex-boyfriend.
— The past progressive should be used to illustrate a past continuous action.
** Before Ms. Smith entered the conference room, she had been hiding from her ex-boyfriend.

The 11 Most Important Ap Style Rules

AP style is complex but efficient since it is designed to save time and space for the media. Mastering the art of AP-style writing is critical to public relations/strategic communication students because writing is what public relations practitioners do every day. In addition, writing in journalists' language establishes mutual credibility between the two professions; press releases written in AP style show respect to the editors and journalists, politely prompting them to consider choosing the news sent by the public relations practitioner. A press release that follows AP style means the journalist can use more of the news release, which makes it more likely that the media will publish the story.

Box 3.1 shows the 11 most important AP style rules for students majoring in public relations, advertising, print/online/television journalism, and strategic communications to practice.

Manners, Etiquette, and Protocol: It's All about Relationships

The practice of public relations in professional settings is based on human relationships, and human relationships are built from universally accepted beliefs in humane principles of harmony, virtue, love, consideration, kindness, courtesy, and compassion. Keeping these principles in mind, public relations practitioners are doing their job while traveling around the world, attending meetings, organizing events, constructing strategies, consulting with clients, and advocating the interest of organizations. One more principle that is embraced in the practice of public relations is loyalty. Public relations practitioners work to support their client, boss, and organization, not all the people in the world.

To support their clientele, public relations practitioners interact with a wide range of people in diverse industries and countries. Interacting effectively with people on behalf of clients or organizations requires establishing a decent human relationship first. When people meet each other in a business environment, they feel (consciously or subconsciously) pressured to impress each other. Etiquette expert Jacqueline Whitmore emphasized the importance of proper etiquette:

BOX 3.1: FUNDAMENTAL RULES OF AP STYLE

1. Numerals: one through nine are spelled out, while 10 and above are generally written as numerals. Spell out casual expressions. For ages, always use figures. If the age is used as an adjective or as a substitute for a noun, then it should be hyphenated.

   a. A 5-year-old boy walked home. The boy is 5 years old.
   b. The woman, 26, has a daughter 2 days old.
   c. The man is in his 50s.
   d. They had a fleet of 11 station wagons and two buses.
   e. They had four four-room houses, 10 three-room houses, and 12 10-room houses.
   f. Thanks a million.
   g. A thousand times no!

2. Names: always use a person's first and last name the first time. Only use last names on second reference. Never place Mr., Mrs., Miss or Ms. before their last names, except when they are part of a direct quotation.

   a. Sam Smith had a huge night at the Grammy Awards on Sunday, winning four awards. Smith thanked his friends.
   b. Hillary Clinton visited her hometown on Monday. Clinton is going to visit her husband's hometown on Wednesday.
   c. Apple CEO Tim Cook had a meeting with Google CEO Larry Page in San Diego. Cook said, "Mr. Page will make a new search engine soon."

3. Composition Titles: use quotation marks around the titles of books, songs, television shows, computer games, poems, lectures, speeches, and works of art, while capitalizing all the principal words. Do not put quotation marks around software titles such as Microsoft Word or WordPerfect. Do not use quotations around the names of magazines, newspapers, or the Bible.

   a. Author J.K. Rowling is not going to publish her new book, "The Rise and Fall of the Second Kingdom in Hogwarts."
   b. Tom Hanks appeared on "ABC Nightline News."

(Continued)

c. The New York Times reported that the classic "Gone with the Wind" would be remade.

d. Dvorak's "New World Symphony" will be played in the city hall.

e. People enjoyed the free version of "FarmVille" on Christmas.

4. Addresses: use the abbreviations "Ave.," "Blvd.," and "St." only with a numbered address. Spell these words out when used without a number. If a street name is a number, spell out First through Ninth and use figures for 10th and higher.

   a. Susan Smith lives at 4321 Main St.

   b. Her house is at 1234 Chicago Drive.

   c. The new building manager lives at North Fifth Avenue.

   d. The White House is located at 1600 Pennsylvania Ave.

5. Dates and Months: when a month is used with a specific date, abbreviate only the following months: Jan., Feb., Aug., Sept., Oct., Nov., and Dec. Do not use st, nd, rd, or th with dates. Use the letter *s*, but not an apostrophe after the figures when expressing decades or centuries. Do not abbreviate days of the week.

   a. President Donald Trump was born in June.

   b. President Barack Obama was born on Aug. 4.

   c. The event will be held on May 15.

   d. The 1400s was a big century.

   e. The car accident was reported on Monday night.

6. Times and time element: use figures except for noon and midnight. Use a period and a colon. Avoid redundancies like 10 a.m. this morning. Use days of the week, not today, tomorrow, or yesterday.

   a. John Smith is scheduled to have a meeting at 4:00 p.m.

   b. John Smith is going to see his doctor at noon.

   c. John Smith stopped by his son's school at 8:00 Tuesday morning.

   d. She will return Wednesday.

   e. The campaign took 50 hours, 23 minutes, 14 seconds to end.

7. Punctuations: do not use a comma before the last item. Periods and commas always go inside quotation marks. Use commas in numbers of 1,000 or more but not for year and Zip codes. A hyphen joins two or more words working as an adjective.

   a. She loves books, movies, newspapers and television.

   b. She has a lot of job experiences, such as a lawyer, judge, CIA agent, professor and professional driver.

   c. "We should fix this problem together," the CEO said. "I will do my best."

   d. He lives in Zip code 98765.

   e. When Tom Johnson got a full-time job, he went to see his father, who has a know-it-all attitude.

   f. He is anti-war.

8. Titles: capitalize formal titles when they are used immediately before a person's name, but lowercase titles if they are informal. Lowercase and spell out titles when they are not used with an individual's name. Abbreviate titles such as Gov., Rep., and Sen.

    a. Democrats knew President Obama had hoped to get the bill passed. The president will issue a statement Thursday.
    b. The vice president, Joe Biden, released a toughly worded statement.
    c. People in China welcomed movie star Jennifer Lopez.
    d. Gov. Mark Dayton said Wednesday he is seeking a meeting with Minnesota state employees.
    e. "I don't think there's any ill intent in this," Sen. Dianne Feinstein, Democrat of California, said Sunday.
    f. Mike Smith, journalism major, won the scholarship.

9. State names: states names should not be abbreviated when standing alone in the text, but when the name of a city and state are used together, the name of the state should be abbreviated, except for the states with four and five letters and outside the main territory of the United States (Alaska, Hawaii, Idaho, Iowa, Maine, Ohio, Texas and Utah).

    a. Susan Smith plans to travel from Tennessee to Massachusetts.
    b. Susan Smith plans to travel from Jackson, Tenn. to Logan, Mass.
    c. The couple had met in Akron, Ohio and moved to San Jose, Calif.
    d. The hurricane began in New York and moved north toward Maine.
    e. World travelers named Juneau, Alaska the best place for honeymoons.

10. Collective nouns: nouns that denote a unit take singular verbs and pronouns. Team, council, board, senate, group, class, committee, club, crowd, faculty, family, jury, orchestra, herd, and staff are all collective nouns, while players, New York Yankees, LA Lakers and Colts are all simply plural.

    a. The committee plans to meet at 10:00 p.m.
    b. The Packers do not participate in the draft league.
    c. The Utah Jazz are battling for third place.
    d. The communication team participated in its company's annual meeting.

11. Technology terms: a guide for spelling and capitalization rules for technology.

    a. Internet—always the big "I"
    b. email—no hyphen but a hyphen for e-book and e-reader
    c. smartphone and cellphone—one word
    d. website and web page—one word and two words
    e. iPad, iPhone, iPod—the small "i"
    f. tweet and retweet—lowercase
    g. Google and Googling and Googled—the big "G"
    h. Laptop and videoconference—one word
    i. Facebook and YouTube and Twitter and LinkedIn

Just as you evaluate potential business partners, employees, and personal acquaintances on your encounter with them, others will judge you and your business by how you conduct yourself.[12]

So how do people make good impressions on other people in the business world? Public relations practitioners are professionals—they know what they should do, and a failure to build good human relationships with people from the very beginning can make their jobs both difficult and miserable. For example, as we discussed earlier, a good relationship with a journalist promises a better chance of getting a press release published in the media. Simply put, public relations is all about human relations.

Good human relationships are built on the ways people act. The term *act* here can be better understood in the context of societal norms, such as proper manners, etiquette, and protocol. *Cambridge Dictionary* defines *manners* as "ways of behaving in accord with polite standards, or the socially correct way of acting"; *etiquette* as "the set of rules or customs that control accepted behavior in particular social groups or social situations"; and *protocol* as "the official procedure or system of rules governing affairs of state or diplomatic occasions."[13] The three norms display slight differences in meaning: "protocol" is more official and deals with global rules on the state level, while "etiquette" and "manners" are more social behavior rules, including concerns about standards of courtesy. The common ground, however, is clear that public relations students and practitioners should embrace social rules, standards, behaviors, and customs for the practice of public relations. Because the societal norms have been socially constructed throughout human history, breaking these social and global norms are not appreciated in the business world.

Business Manners/Etiquette Rules for the Practice of Public Relations

There are dozens of suggestions for business etiquette floating around, but here are the top ten most valuable guidelines to follow when practicing public relations in professional social situations. The guidelines are selected from Barbara Pachter's book *The Essentials of Business Etiquette*, which emphasizes the specific human relations skills professionals need to understand when presenting themselves in a business situation.

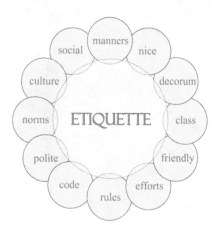

- *Use Your Full Name.* Exchanging full names provides an easier way for people to identify each other. It helps to start a connection between people and makes it easier for a conversation to begin (p. 4).

- *Shake Hands.* In the United States, the handshake is the standard business greeting. Your grip should be firm. If it is too firm or too weak, you may convey a negative impression. Two to three pumps are enough. Face the person and make eye contact (p. 16).

- *Stand When You Are Introduced to Someone.* Standing helps establish your presence. You make it easy for others to ignore you if you don't stand. If you cannot stand up, lean forward to indicate that you would stand if you could (p. 17).

---

12   Jacqueline Whitmore, "6 Ways to Make a Great First Impression," *Entrepreneur* Magazine, September 22, 2014, http://www.entrepreneur.com/article/237361.

13   "Etiquette," Cambridge Dictionary, https://dictionary.cambridge.org/us/dictionary/english/etiquette.

- *Use Verbal Prompts.* These are brief comments that let the person know you are paying attention. Don't overdo it, but an occasional "oh," "I see," or "okay" can be effective (p. 29).

- *Say "Thank You" Sparingly.* Say it only once or twice within a conversation. Otherwise, you may dilute its impact (p. 36).

- *Project Confidence with Your Posture.* Good posture projects confidence. Stand confidently: keep your legs aligned with your shoulders and feet, about four to six inches apart. Unless you are gesturing, keep your hands at your sides. Don't cross your legs or tilt your head (p. 51).

- *Suit Up for Formal and Less Formal Occasions.* Clothing is an important form of nonverbal communication. It can enhance or detract from a person's professional credibility. Send a professional message through your clothing choices (p. 76).

- *Ignore Your Cell Phone at Dinner.* Turn off your cell phone (or at least set it to vibrate) before you sit down—and no texting under the table. You need to give your full attention to the other people at your table. Do not place your phone on the table; if you do, it will look like you are more interested in your next call than in your dining companion (p. 104).

- *Schmooze with People.* Keep the conversation upbeat. Complaining about work or the economy is a downer. Parties allow you to mingle with people from different areas of the company. Talk to both people you know and ones you don't know. The person you meet at the party may turn out to be the person who interviews you for your next job (p. 131).

- *Stay Ahead.* Stay current with changes in your profession. You don't want to be left behind. Stay abreast of any trends in your field. Continue learning. Take advantage of any training your company offers. Stay up-to-date with technology, including social media (p. 187).

Protocol for the Practice of Public Relations

Protocol, as the official procedure for diplomatic occasions, requires the highest level of courtesy when conducting official business in the context of global relations. Protocols are designed to specify the proper, generally accepted behavior between states in diplomacy. Therefore, protocol, in sum, encompasses the principles of conduct expected of official representatives of nations and global organizations in the exercise of diplomatic functions. Activity based on proper protocol serves as a sign of official respect to a foreign country and its people.

Public relations practitioners travel around the world, often with their clients or bosses who operate global businesses or international events. They may have arranged meetings with foreign government leaders, high-ranking officials, and business leaders to discuss business agendas, such as investment and cooperation. Visiting foreign nations and doing business with foreigners from a public relations perspective requires more sophisticated etiquette and manners. The highest level of courtesy and politeness, along with a deep understanding of cultural practices, is central to foreign business practice. The diplomatic protocol guidelines, provided by the US State Department's Foreign Service Institute, serve as enlightening recommendations for the global practice of public relations, especially when it comes to building good relationships with prominent foreign audiences. The guidelines emphasize that "American casualness is often interpreted as rudeness in other societies," and "this can be taken as a personal or national insult."[14] The diplomatic guidelines offer details about how to conduct diplomatic public relations in other countries. The top 11 guidelines are as follows:[15]

1. *Introductions.* The purpose of making introductions is to exchange names between people so that a conversation can follow. For a formal occasion, the traditional "Mrs. Smith, may I present Mr. Jones?" is used internationally (p. 3).

2. *Recalling Names.* The best and most courteous way to handle recognizing someone without recalling his or her name is to mention your name again. For example, "Good evening, I'm Jim Smith. We met recently at the ambassador's home. I'm pleased to see you again." More than likely, he/she will reintroduce himself/herself. Starting from the assumption that he/she may also not remember your name could save both of you potential embarrassment (p. 3).

3. *Business Cards.* The exchange of business cards may follow a ritual. Notice how a person presents their card and accept it in a similar manner. If two hands are used holding the top corners face up so that you can read it as you receive it, accept it with two hands. Take the time to read the card before putting it away. As you present your card, take care that the print is face up and facing the receiver. Do not exchange cards while seated at a formal dinner; there is time before or after (p. 8).

4. *Hierarchy.* You should remain at any dinner party (United States or foreign) until all persons of all nationalities who outrank you have departed. Also, learn local social customs. For example, generally, the woman extends her hand first when shaking hands—except where she is not expected to shake hands at all (p. 11).

5. *Dress.* Dress varies according to country and event. Women should be particularly mindful of conservative dress rules, such as skirt length, low necklines, and having one's arms covered. Remember that "casual" in other countries almost never means jeans or shorts. It is always better to be too dressed up than too dressed down (p. 13).

6. *Gifts.* Even something as simple as bringing a gift to the host can be tricky. Many rituals and customs often surround the meaning of gifts. The type, color, and number of flowers you bring, for example, may have a hidden meaning. In Italy, mums are funeral flowers; think twice about bringing them to a dinner party (p. 13).

7. *Eating and Drinking.* To be polite, accept the food and drink that is offered. If unsure or a bit apprehensive, try a small portion. If you do not wish to drink alcohol, still take some to have in your glass for toasts (p. 13).

8. *Toasts.* When giving a toast, rise in place and speak to the entire room. Raise your glass to eye level and look toward the honored person and drink, making eye contact with the honored person. You should then nod and put your glass on the table and sit down. The person being toasted should never drink to themselves. A nod or smile of appreciation can suffice for a response, or the honored person can return the toast by rising afterward and offering a formal response (p. 20).

---

14   "State.gov Website Modernization," US State Department, June 3, 2019, http://www.state.gov/documents/organization/176174.pdf.

15   US State Department, "State.gov."

9. *Receiving Lines.* At formal receptions, a receiving line enables the host and hostess to greet each guest personally. Usually, the host stands first and the hostess stands second. However, the hostess may defer to guests of honor and stand after them in line (p. 20).

10. *Styles of Eating.* Hold the knife in the right hand and fork in the left to cut food, and then put the knife down and transfer the fork to the right hand to lift the food to the mouth, tines up. Lift the food into the mouth with the tines down. Cut no more than two pieces of food at a time (p. 22).

11. *Thank You.* There are often rituals involved in thanking someone. Without exception, thank your host before you leave. Tradition determines how you should thank the host the day after the event. If you feel the situation merits a more elaborate thank you, let local customs be your guide for an appropriate response (p. 14).

Practicing public relations in different countries and cultures employs the general rules of social conduct, as well as those customary instructions that are particular to the country. The practice of public relations, if aimed at creating and maintaining a good relationship with foreign audiences, is first linked to an understanding of those recommendations and instructions.

Future for Students in Public Relations and Related Fields of Communication

Public relations practitioners usually claim to be "people persons" who like to interact and communicate with every kind of person, regardless of age, gender, race, or nationality. They have a tendency to cooperate with other people. In short, public relations practitioners are the people who are trained and educated in communication and human skills. Basic communication skills (writing and speaking) must be cultivated by college students. They can enhance their human relations skills by networking with classmates, members of college clubs, and faculty members.

Using email as a professional form of communication remains an important way to communicate in today's business world. Getting familiar with formal email writing is a good way for college students to build relationships with people on and off campus. In addition, writing in AP style must be mastered by communication/journalism students before graduation. Investing a certain amount of time in writing news articles and reporting news stories according to AP style will bolster the skills of students who dream of getting a job in government, corporations, or any other organizations as public relations practitioners or strategic communicators. More importantly, an impressive demonstration of basic manners, etiquette, and protocol performed by job applicants will convince future employers to offer students their dream jobs.

CHAPTER SUMMARY AND REVIEW

1. Understand why email is an official communication tool for college students.

2. Identify the basic principles and practices of sending emails.

3. Study the rules of the *AP Stylebook*.

4. What are the differences between manners and etiquette and protocol?

5. Can you describe the ten fundamental practices of business?

PUBLIC RELATIONS IN PRACTICE

FURTHER READING

PR Week's Awards For **Best PR Integration**

Winner: Evereve and Carmichael Lynch Relate
Campaign Name: Turning "Dress Like a Mom" into the Ultimate Compliment

The team hosted a "dress like a mom" experiential event in New York City that introduced more than 30 editors and influencers to the brand and resulted in impactful coverage in key women's, business, fashion, and industry publications.

Read more at
https://www.prweek.com/article/1579436/prweek-us-awards-2019-winners

4

Careers in Public Relations for College Students

Becoming a public relations practitioner is a long journey that requires a bachelor's degree in public relations, journalism, strategic communication, marketing, English, or business communication. Students appeal to employers by building portfolios for their future careers through specialized college majors. Finding a job in public relations/communications probably is the most worrisome task for college students, just before they begin worrying about surviving at work. Fortunately, the academic preparation for a job in these fields has been extremely well organized nationwide with widely accepted curricula for public relations students.

Ideal Undergraduate Courses

The Commission on Public Relations Education (composed of public relations educators and practitioners from major professional organizations in public relations and related fields of communication) has identified six ideal undergraduate courses and two additional recommendations for broadening knowledge in public relations:

- *Introduction to Public Relations.* This course explains what public relations is, why it is needed, who needs it, and how it is practiced.

- *Public Relations Writing and Production.* This course helps students learn how to produce a press release, a pitch letter, speeches, and newsletters.

- *Case Studies in Public Relations.* Since public relations is a practical, real field of practice, this course offers an opportunity to learn about cases of success and failure in organizational performance.

- *Public Relations Research, Measurement, and Evaluation.* Public relations practitioners try to recognize an organization's issue and find a way of addressing or fixing it through the process of research and evaluation. This course, in short, teaches students how to conduct research.

- *Public Relations Campaigns.* This course teaches students how to apply basic public relations knowledge and skills to practical, real-world situations. Students learn how to work together as a team.

- *Public Relations Planning and Management.* Public relations is no longer confined to mere media relations. The practice of public relations has broadened to the organizational management level.

"I've been trying to get my resume around."

- *Directed Electives.* Colleges often encourage students to take courses outside their majors to build a wide range of academic course experience. Courses in psychology, sociology, political science, economics, marketing, and international business can be helpful in supplementing public relations education.

- *Internship.* After (or while) taking the courses noted earlier, students take an internship course or program as the last step to getting a job in public relations and related fields of communication. An internship at a public relations firm or in the public relations department of other organizations can be extremely helpful in getting a job as a public relations practitioner.

Entering the practice of public relations right after college provides former students with the opportunity to develop a career in corporations, government, education, public relations firms, communication agencies, and nonprofit organizations, as well as freelance opportunities. In other words, a person entering the public relations field will probably work at public relations/communication firms or within an organization's public relations/communication department. These are two major future employers for students, and honing the skills that employers expect from college graduates is key to completing a successful college experience for future employment.

Important Skills for Entry-Level Public Relations Practitioners

The demand for public relations practitioners is steadily increasing. "As business picks up and PR teams and agencies take on more projects and clients, employers recognize a need to bring in extra support," said Donna Farrugia, executive director of The Creative Group.[1] "We see continued demand for PR roles, which suggests that finding candidates with these skills remains a challenge." Although many jobs are available for public relations practitioners, employers have a difficult time finding good candidates with the needed skills. Candidates should hone the following ten skills to meet employers' expectations:

---

1   PRSA, In recovery: Recruiters say PR job market is improving, https://apps.prsa.org/Intelligence/Tactics/Articles/view/9639/1045/In_recovery_Recruiters_say_PR_job_market_is_improv#.XoPOMYhKiUk

1. *Speaking Skill.* Public relations practitioners regularly speak on behalf of their organizations and employers. They must be able to clearly communicate the organization's or employer's position to the target audience.

2. *Listening Skill.* Listening is as important as speaking in two-way communication. Public relations practitioners need to understand and find out the needs of their audience through listening.

3. *Media Savvy Skill.* Communication tools public relations practitioners use every day include television, newspapers, radio, magazines, webcasts, social media, and so on. As each medium has a unique system of operation, working with media personnel in each domain is essential.

4. *Writing Skill.* This is a must for public relations practitioners to produce engaging content that will get the attention of busy readers or listeners. Writing well organized, clear press releases and speeches is still a dominant task in the practice of public relations.

5. *Creativity Skill.* Employers expect fresh ideas and strategies to come up with new ways to promote businesses and approach new audiences. The practice of public relations must keep pace with the latest, newest thinking and perspectives.

6. *Problem-Solving Skill.* Public relations practitioners sometimes explain how an organization or client is taking care of sensitive issues. They need to understand these issues and how to implement the solutions.

7. *Research Skill.* Public relations practitioners have to keep track of rapidly changing marketplaces and be knowledgeable about what the audience wants and needs. Gathering and using information for the organization or client is the core element of public relations research.

8. *Organizational Skill.* Public relations practitioners are in charge of organizing events to raise awareness for the organization or client. Organizing events requires multiple processes: planning, instructing, implementing, and managing.

9. *Cultural Literacy Skill.* The practice of public relations requires meeting with all sorts of people in various industries. Broad knowledge of science, art, humanities, sports, and national affairs helps public relations practitioners build a fast relationship with an audience.

10. *Global Skill.* Globalization has led public relations practitioners to be interested in studying foreign languages and cultures to shape global mindsets, and global organizations and clients seek new business opportunities abroad.

A career in public relations will take more than these ten skills. However, it is worth noting that the skills always revolve around creating and promoting good images and reputations for organizations. A well-rounded candidate in public relations is one who demonstrates the valuable skills while performing public relations tasks as an intern or practitioner. The tasks include writing press releases, responding to information requests from journalists, coaching clients or bosses to communicate effectively with the target audience, organizing campaigns, promoting events, and generally maintaining good images of the organization and client.

Job Categories in Public Relations

The *Wall Street Journal* reported that many firms expect new college graduates to arrive job ready from day one. In an effort to cut costs, employers are reducing their training budgets.[2] The hiring trend for college graduates is changing rapidly. A decade ago, employers used to assure entry-level workers that they would receive occupational training from the first day of work, but nowadays, employers look for entry-level job candidates "who can immediately get in front of clients."[3] Rookie employees are not going to sit in a back office anymore. Organizations are assigning entry-level workers thinking roles, as opposed to "just following a checklist," according to David Vogel, a career development expert.[4] "It raises the bar on the types of work that can be done by the entry-level hire, as opposed to eliminating the need."

The *Wall Street Journal* has added two job fields that highlight the emerging trend in entry-level jobs: computer systems and public relations. It reported that "the number of entry-level jobs in computer systems and public relations are expected to grow over the next decade."[5] It is good news for students in these fields, but they have to get prepared to fulfill the expectations of employers who want first-timers to arrive job ready from day one. New hires in public relations are expected to arrive at work with sharp communication skills and acumen. In a nutshell, the job title "entry-level" is the same, but the responsibilities have shifted from novice to professional; requirements for skills and experience of first-timers have been raised.

According to Professor Ron Smith, five levels of job categories exist in public relations, including the entry-level position:[6]

1. **Technician.** As a first-timer at work after college, the entry-level technician in public relations typically begins work by maintaining files of material about an organization's activities, retaining relevant media articles, and assembling information for speeches and brochures. After becoming accustomed to the work, the first-timer is assigned to produce communication products by the supervisor. These include writing news releases, scripts, reports, speeches, and articles for publication or planning public relations programs. The first-timer may be asked to take photographs or perform other tactical assignments. To be promoted, the technician needs to develop skills in design, publishing, data gathering, and layout.

2. **Supervisor.** This position is responsible for developing and employing the skills and knowledge required to supervise projects and publications. The supervisor monitors staff activities while planning and coordinating workflow. Two of the most important tasks for this position are working with the media and training staff members.

3. **Manager.** At this level, the manager is responsible for all aspects of an entire department, including planning, organizing, directing and motivating staff members, budgeting, problem solving, and problem identification. The manager attends meetings in other departments and makes presentations or speeches to people outside the department or organization.

---

2   Lauren Weber and Melissa Korn, "Where Did All the Entry-Level Jobs Go?," *Wall Street Journal,* August 6, 2014, http://www.wsj.com/articles/want-an-entry-level-job-youll-need-lots-of-experience-1407267498.

3   Weber and Korn, "Where Did All the Entry-Level."

4   Weber and Korn, "Where Did All the Entry-Level."

5   Weber and Korn, "Where Did All the Entry-Level."

6   Ron Smith, Public Relations: The Basics (Routledge; New York), 2014.

4. ***Director.*** The director is involved in the design and implementation of the research programs and working on activities such as strategic planning, political action, and advocacy programs. Other obligations of this position include planning responses to evolving issues and developing organizational policies, in addition to directing the efforts of managers and their departments.

5. ***Executive.*** At this level, leadership is the most important principle. The executive is responsible for directing, motivating, and rewarding the performance of others, as well as developing the vision, mission, annual goals, and comprehensive systems for the organization.

A study published in the *Journal of Professional Communication* confirmed the existence of significant dissatisfaction among public relations supervisors in both the United States and Canada. Supervisors who have an immediate working relationship with entry-level public relations practitioners expressed their disappointment in technicians' levels of writing skills. The quality of writing performance by entry-level public relations practitioners in both countries was far below what supervisors expected. The study also found that entry-level public relations practitioners estimated their writing competency more highly than their supervisors did. Supervisors who have been in the field more than a decade viewed new college graduates entering the practice of public relations as incompetent at writing. In particular, supervisors gave failing grades for grammar, spelling, punctuation, and use of AP style. The study also found that public relations supervisors in the United States "judged recent college graduates least capable of writing in the persuasive-skill category identified as fundraising appeals and proposal copy."[7] Supervisors pointed out that, in an average 40-hour workweek, entry-level public relations practitioners in the United States spent most of their working hours on press releases and conversational emails. The study suggests a need for increased attention to writing training for future public relations practitioners in both countries.

Students in public relations and related fields who aim for a technician position must come prepared with the skills employers expect. They must be ready to work from day one with sophisticated communication skills and knowledge to keep up with the current market trends for entry-level job openings. Employers have set a higher bar for first-timers who wish to become not only communication technicians but also strategic communication supervisors. One thing students have to keep in mind when applying for an internship or a job is that the practice of public relations is still, and probably forever will be, evaluated according to the qualities of good writing.

Wages for Public Relations and Communication Majors

According to Chron.com, the website of the *Houston Chronicle*, college graduates with journalism and mass communication degrees in 2018 earned the following median salaries (Figure 4.1):[8]

Radio broadcasting announcers, **$30,310**

Newspaper reporters, **$35,130**

---

7   Jeremy Berry, Richard T. Cole, and Larry Hembroff, "US-Canada Study of PR Writing by Entry-Level Practitioners Reveals Significant Supervisor Dissatisfaction," *Journal of Professional Communication*, 1, no. 1 (2011): 57–77, https://escarpmentpress.org/jpc/article/view/86/41.

8   Ashley Adams-Mott, "Salary With a Mass Media Degree," Chorn.com, last modified August 16, 2018, https://work.chron.com/salary-mass-media-degree-23867.html.

Newspaper and print photographers, **$41,496**

Television broadcasting announcers, **$45,400**

Broadcasting reporters, **$45,420**

Television broadcasting video editors and camera operators, **$47,410**

Newspaper editors, **$55,680**

Public relations, business, **$61,740**

Advertising and public relations specialists, **$62,660**

Government public relations, **$63,530**

As the numbers show, careers in public relations are often the most lucrative, and public relations practitioners are "skilled professionals and often work in or near the C-suite in private corporations or with the executive staff in a governmental office."[9]

Salaries at advertising and public relations agencies or departments are higher than those in television, radio, newspapers, and magazines. The Bureau of Labor Statistics, a unit of the US Department of Labor, also announced that the median annual wage for public relations practitioners was $60,000 per year in 2018. The bureau estimated that employment of public relations specialists will expand by 9 percent through 2026: about as fast as the average rate for all occupations. The average pay for an entry-level public relations practitioner was $43,969, according to PayScale, an online salary information company.[10]

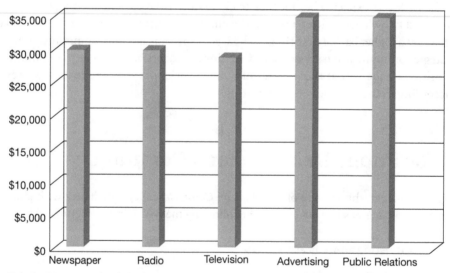

FIGURE 4.1 Salaries in communication.

9   Adams-Mott, "Salary With a Mass Media Degree."

10   "Public Relations Specialist," US Bureau of *Labor Statistics,* last modified September 4, 2019, www.bls.gov/ooh/media-and-communication/public-relations-specialists.htm.

It is apparent that skills in corporate and government communications are associated with high pay for a public relations job.[11] More specifically, specializations in corporate communication, marketing communication, government affairs, and event planning are correlated with higher pay in the practice of public relations.

A 2019 survey conducted by *PR Week*, a trade magazine for the public relations industry, illustrated current trends in public relations salaries. The survey, based on a poll of 1,213 public relations professionals across the United States, defined the hiring trend of 2019 as follows: "If communications practitioners are 'sellers' of capabilities and employers are 'buyers' of those skills, it is clearly a seller's market." The survey concluded that salaries in public relations and related fields of commutation were strong in 2019.[12] As the survey showed, public relations practitioners make a bit more money than those in related fields of communication. However, there exists a wage gap, depending on the public relations sectors practitioners work in.

Public Relations Firms or Public Relations/ Communication Departments in Organizations

Job offers in the field of public relations stem from two major players: public relations firms and organizations that have public relations/communication departments. When people are hired to work for such firms and departments, they are entitled to the job title of public relations practitioner. Several market terms describe the profession of public relations practitioner depending on which industry a person works in, including public relations specialist, communication specialist, media specialist, PR person, spokesperson, PR expert, and communication expert. Public relations practitioners pay close attention to what is happening to the client and organization, as well as what the audience and the public want and think about the organization and client. The process of practitioners doing their jobs in public relations begins and ends with the employer—either the public relations firm or the public relations department.

Public Relations Firms in General Practice

Like law firms, public relations firms provide services to clients. Clients of public relations firms include all types of industries: businesses, nonprofits, government agencies, and high-profile individuals. Public relations services range from crisis communication, marketing communication, media relations, public health, branding, public affairs, global cultural engagement, data analysis, to event management. Public relations firms, in general, manage communication strategies and fieldwork between an organization and the target audience in hopes of promoting favorable relationships and portraying a positive image in the media. Small businesses and start-ups that cannot afford to employ in-house public relations practitioners are likely to hire public relations firms.

---

11   "Average Public Relations (PR) Officer Salary," Payscale, last modified January 9, 2020, https://www.payscale.com/research/US/Job=Public_Relations_(PR)_Officer/Salary

12   Chris Daniels, "Evidence of Progress: 2019 Salary Survey," *PR Week*, https://www.prweek.com/article/1580188/evidence-progress-2019-salary-survey.

MAJOR PUBLIC RELATIONS TACTICS

As soon as the public relations firm accepts the client's request, it will work on raising awareness for the client by conducting market research, attracting media attention, organizing campaigns, and launching community activities. The public relations firm uses seven major tactics:

1. *Research on the Market.* The public relations firm will do research on the client company and its industry. The firm gathers data and analyzes market trends for the client while finding a way to create favorable perceptions in the minds of the target audience. The target audience can be customers, consumers, shareholders, investors, local residents, national residents, community activists, and the general public.

2. *Production of Local Press Releases.* Public relations practitioners at the firm make and tell the story of the client's brand or product through press releases. The story is designed to inform local people about the benefits of using the company's products and services. Local newspapers and TV stations will show their interest in the company, which is proud to be part of the community.

3. *Aiming for National Coverage.* The public relations firm serves as the voice of the client's brand and company in the media. While having achieved the goal of raising local awareness, the firm aims for national exposure of the client. National coverage of the client in the media will create a higher profile for the client. Press releases play a significant role.

4. *Pitch Articles about the Client.* Whereas press releases are delivered to as many journalists and media outlets as possible, pitch letters are used to narrow the journalist contact pool. The public relations firm crafts customized stories to grab the attention of a certain number of journalists who are willing to pay attention to the stories. Pitch letters are a great tool for the process.

5. *Special Events and Community Activity.* Where there is an event, there is a story. The public relations firm will organize an event for the client to connect with the audience. The event leads the audience to recognize the brand and company. It also becomes an effective means of attracting media coverage.

6. *Training the Client.* The public relations firm is behind media coverage. It focuses on helping the client receive good media attention and coverage with a positive public image. The firm prepared the client for media interviews, training the client on how to speak, what to say, and how to appear in the media. Preparing the client for press conferences, media interviews, and speeches is an important part of public relations tactics.

7. *Business Network.* The public relations firm has human and financial resources to help the client build good relationships with local and national industry leaders. The client will be advised to attend particular conferences and meetings to broaden the network in the community in which the client runs the business.

In the work with the public relations firm, the client expects positive outcomes that are directly linked to the existence of the brand and company. There is no doubt that hiring a public relations firm is a big investment for the client.

Public Relations Firms in Specialization

According to IBISWorld, a market research organization, more businesses will invest in public relations services to increase brand awareness and remain competitive because of an evolving digital media landscape.[13] Clients expect public relations firms to focus more on social media outlets, such as Facebook, YouTube, Twitter, Snapchat, Instagram, TikTok, and blogs as areas of growth for public relations campaigns rather than traditional mass media, such as TV, print, and radio. Based on the demanding social media use, IBISWorld forecast that the public relations industry is expected to continue to grow to $18 billion in the United States by 2023. As most of the public relations firms had fewer than ten employees, IBISWorld indicated that the largest public relations firms account for most of the industry's revenue, operating on both national and international levels.[14] Ranked by worldwide fees in 2019, the top-five public relations firms headquartered in the United States are Edelman (New York), W2O Group (San Francisco), APCO Worldwide (DC), Finn Partners (New York), and Zeno Group (New York).[15] Public relations firms are dropping the term public relations from their firm names—notice that none of the top-five firms use the term. This trend is probably due to the fact that public relations firms do not want to give clients the impression that they are limited to the traditional concept of media relations. Rather, they strategize to emphasize the consulting aspects of their services.

Although it's difficult to categorize the variety of reasons why clients knock on the doors of public relations firms, many firms introduce customized services by targeting a particular group of clientele. As different types of businesses and clients need different tactical approaches and fieldwork, public relations firms promote their customized skills for precisely divided industrial sectors. For example, Edelman, the largest public relations firm, offers public relations services to 18 categorized industries. The firm's website (http://www.edelman.com) explains how the firm specializes in strategies and fieldwork for industries in aerospace and defense, consumer packed goods, education, energy, financial services, and many more. The firm's fieldwork focuses on driving traffic to the industry, building engagement with the target audience, attracting media attention, and, ultimately, affecting the audience's purchasing decisions. Most public relations firms offer such services, and they require specialized strategies and skills.

Public relations firms operate worldwide. Whether it's to help American clients penetrate foreign markets or assist foreign clients in establishing relationships with American publics, public relations firms run foreign offices. APCO Worldwide, for example, has staff based "in major business, financial, political and media capitals throughout the Americas, Europe, the Middle East & Africa and Asia Pacific regions."[16] As APCO Worldwide also has five offices in the United States, a question about the operational structure of public relations firms arises.

In terms of operating physical offices, public relations firms have two simple categories: domestic and foreign. In a similar way, when structuring office workforces, public relations firms typically operate in two main structures: functional groups and account groups. The former operates with public relations staff members in various areas such as media relations, community relations, public affairs, and digital operations. The latter works as a team; its members include senior account executives, account executives, account coordinators, and interns.

When a new hire gets a full-time position at the firm, his or her job title is usually account coordinator. The account coordinator is expected to perform the same work as technicians do in PRSA levels of job categories. The account coordinator is responsible for writing press releases, media monitoring,

---

13   "Find the Industry & Market Research You Need Today," IBISWorld, https://clients1.ibisworld.com/reports/us/industry/currentperformance.aspx?entid=1434.

14   IBISWorld, "Find the Industry."

15   "Top PR Firms—2019 Firm Rankings," O'Dwyer's, https://www.odwyerpr.com/pr_firm_rankings/independents.htm.

16   "Middle East & North Africa," APCO Worldwide, http://www.apcoworldwide.com/about-us/locations/mea#focus.

maintaining contact lists, and updating databases. Account executives perform the same work as the supervisors do, and the duties of senior account executives are similar to those of managers.

The team's responsibilities and tactics for the client regarding customized public relations services are more specified and broader than the general services of public relations firms. Donald K. Wright, professor at Boston University, identifies seven trends of services at public relations firms:

- *Consumer Communications.* Consumer media relations, product promotion campaigns, brand positioning and awareness, grand openings, special events, and localized business/consumer programs

- *Corporate Communications.* Reputation management, crisis communications, corporate social responsibility, strategic media relations, public affairs, government relations, and employee communications

- *Creative Services.* Television commercials, B-roll packages, corporate training, videos, digital asset management, brochures, graphic design, logo development, media kits, online banner advertising, photography, illustrations, infographics, and trade show displays

- *Digital and Social Media.* Planning and implementation of social media campaigns, blogger outreach, social media training, auditing, monitoring, analysis, creation and distribution of online content, videos, polls, external website design and programming, mobile app development and search engine optimization

- *Media and Editorial Services.* Proactive and responsive media relations: local, regional, national, hyperlocal, and trade and specialty media; media materials; editorial content; speeches; presentations; major reports; corporate communications materials; organizational announcements; and influencer communications

- *Research and Insights.* Media tracking/evaluation, trend monitoring, polling, qualitative and quantitative research assessments, messaging, concept testing, employee and audience demographics, psychographics, legislative tracking, and analysis

- *Center for Training, Business, and Leadership Excellence.* Customizing training, webinars, online learning, group facilitation, strategy, and execution for annual planning meetings, individual/executive coaching, curriculum design/development, keynote speaking, and corporate retreats

Paul Holmes, CEO of Provoke Media, points out that public relations firms are increasing their investment in building digital media content, producing digital material, and managing social media communities. More public relations firms adapt and expand their service offerings to nontraditional assignments, which means that public relations practitioners should embrace the systems and functions of both traditional media and social media to generate optimal public relations outcomes.[17]

Departments in an Organization

The other player offering public relations jobs is public relations/communication departments in organizations. Organizations, as opposed to public relations firms, refer to corporations, nonprofit organizations,

---

17   "Paul Holmes: Founder & Chair," Holmes Report, https://www.holmesreport.com/authors/paul-holmes.

and local and federal governments. Degree holders in public relations tend to land jobs at public relations/communication departments in corporations such as business, manufacturing, sports, finance, media, insurance, travel, and entertainment. They also find jobs at nonprofit organizations, including nongovernmental organizations (NGOs), religious or educational institutions, advocacy groups, and humanitarian agencies. In short, public relations/communication departments in corporations, nonprofits, and governments play an important role in giving job opportunities to recent college graduates with communication skills.

Corporations usually call their public relations departments "communication departments," whereas governments prefer "public affairs departments." Nonprofit organizations commonly have media relations or media departments. Although the names are different, the principal functions of the departments are the same: creation of positive publicity for the organizations and enhancement of their reputations.

CORPORATE PUBLIC RELATIONS/COMMUNICATION DEPARTMENTS

Communication departments in corporations are inclined to incorporate practices of public relations, advertising, and marketing into communication strategies. The communication department is dedicated

Shareowner	Global Growth & Operations	John G. Rice	Vice Chairman President & CEO, Global Growth & Operations
	Capital	Keith S. Sherin	Vice Chairman Chairman & CEO, GE Capital
Corporate Executive Office	Appliances & Lighting	Charles Blankenship	President & CEO, GE Appliances & Lighting
	Healthcare	John L. Flannery	President & CEO, GE Healthcare
	Aviation	David L. Joyce	SVP and President & CEO, GE Aviation
Board of Directors	Transportation	Russell Stokes	President & CEO, GE Transportation
	Power & Water	Stephen R. Bolze	SVP and President & CEO, GE Power & Water
	Oil & Gas	Lorenzo Simonelli	President & CEO, GE Oil & Gas
	Energy Management	Mark W. Begor	President & CEO, GE Energy Management

(Jeffrey R. Immelt, Chairman & CEO, GE)

Corporate Staff	Commercial, Public Relations	Elizabeth J. Comstock
	Legal	Brackett B. Denniston, III
	Global Research	Mark M. Little
	Human Resources	Susan P. Peters
	Finance	Jeffrey S. Bornstein

FIGURE 4.2 GE company organization chart.
Source: General electric.

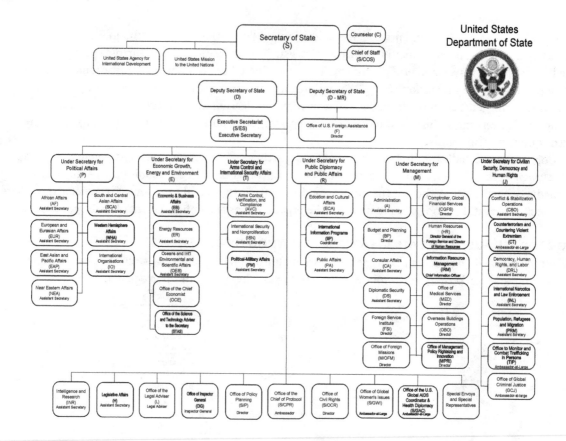

FIGURE 4.3 Structure of the US department of state.

to the production of information about the corporation, the distribution of the information to target audiences, the execution of corporate strategy, and the creation of messages for a variety of purposes, both inside and outside the corporation. The department serves as a main strategic management entity inside the corporation. The main functions of the communication department are to create and enforce communication strategy, maintain good media relations, deal with crisis communication, facilitate internal communication, organize reputation management, conduct corporate responsibility activities, support investor relations, and communicate with government affairs entities.

The communication department is generally divided into specialized divisions in large corporations (see Figure 4.3). The separate divisions carry out detailed tasks of media relations, investor relations, customer relations, governmental relations, and employee relations. For example, Anne Toulouse, senior vice president of communication at Boeing, the world's largest aerospace company, is responsible for facilitating "the company's global communications and brand activities, including media relations, brand development and management, digital, advertising, in-house creative services, and executive and employee communications."[18]

In order for staff members of the communication department to conduct the strategic management role, the first routine task is to write press releases and develop a good relationship with journalists, in

---

18   "Executive Biography of Anne Toulouse," Boeing, http://www.boeing.com/company/bios/anne-toulouse.page.

addition to monitoring 24/7 media sources, blogs, and social networking sites. Updating the corporation's comprehensive media web page is another important task. Most corporations have a "media" section on their websites. This section usually consists of press releases, articles, video footage, speech transcripts, event photos, company information, social media links, and blogs. The section includes all current information about the corporation, and it is managed by the communication department. Other assignments for the staff members include sharing the corporation's mission, products, and achievements with the media and stakeholders, along with producing newsletters, brochures, and other printed materials designed for the general public.

PUBLIC AFFAIRS DEPARTMENT IN GOVERNMENTS

Public affairs is associated with issues of which the public needs to be aware. The federal, state, or local government focuses on informing the public of policy, program, and safety information. This information is designed to raise awareness, gain public interest, and enhance public support for the government. A public affairs office or department in government is in charge of explaining governmental policies and views on public policy issues, assisting policy makers and legislators from a communication perspective and distributing information through press conferences or press releases. A person who does such a task commonly holds the job title of public affairs officer, communication advisor, or public affairs practitioner.

The public affairs officer in a government position engages in tasks of media relations, issue management, social responsibility, information dissemination, and strategic communication. The officer advises government agency heads, such as secretaries of federal or state departments, directors of bureau offices, chiefs of law enforcement departments, heads of congressional branches, and mayors of cities. In this setting, the officer aims to keep the public informed about the activities of government officials and agencies.

The US military is one of the largest entities that practices public affairs. The public affairs officer (PAO) is responsible for maintaining mutual working relationships with journalists, organizing robust community relations events, maintaining contact with other government agencies, and keeping military personnel and the public informed about military issues. The officer's job duties are similar to public relations practitioners in other fields. A U.S. Army PAO is expected to do the following:

- Provide media training for senior leaders.
- Respond to media queries.
- Plan and coordinate community events.
- Develop and execute communication plans.
- Evaluate the effectiveness of communication activities.
- Supervise photojournalists and broadcasters.
- Advise senior leaders on the implications of unit actions.
- Communicate news and information to the internal military audience.
- Gain the support of the American public.[19]

---

19   "TELLING THE ARMY STORY," US Army, https://www.army.mil/publicaffairs/

TABLE 4.1 Public Relations Firms versus Communication Departments

Public Relations Firms	Communication Departments
■ A variety of work	■ Consistent work
■ Many opportunities for networking	■ Good pay and benefit
■ A lot of experience	■ Laidback daily pressure
■ A variety of clients	■ Specialization in a certain public relations area
■ Supportive mentoring	■ Fast promotion

What the officer does is nearly identical to what the public relations practitioner does: training bosses for media interviews, responding to requests from journalists, developing communication plans, organizing events, evaluating outcomes of communication activities, producing media materials, and so on. One difference is the scope of people they want to inform and influence in hopes of gaining support. The military sees the American public as its target audience, while other civilian organizations view specific groups of people as their target audiences. If a person lands a public affairs job in the army, the military agency offers customized, hands-on training on how to develop communication strategies, oversee command information, build media relations, give public presentations, coordinate press briefings, and write speeches.[20] The duties and practices of public relations in corporations and government are aimed at informing, engaging, and creating good relationships with the audience.

MEDIA RELATIONS IN NONPROFIT ORGANIZATIONS

Nonprofit organizations conduct activities for the benefit of the general public without shareholders and without a profit motive. They are granted tax-exempt status by the Internal Revenue Service. Nonprofit organizations include NGOs, schools, colleges, hospitals, charities, churches, political associations, fraternities, sororities, and any independent institution that does not operate for profit.

Among the vast number of organizations qualifying for nonprofit status, the most representative entities are NGOs. A prime reason for NGOs to exist is to take on social problems. They aim to address or fight human rights violations, environmental damage, animal abuse, social injustice, and poverty. Public relations practitioners working for NGOs exclusively focus on media relations, as raising public awareness of what the NGOs do is immediately related to the existence of the NGOs. Since NGOs are not able to make profits, they depend heavily on contributions from individuals and organizations for their operation. Financial sustainability is key to their survival and bringing in more donations is in line with providing more essential information to the public.

Because of the lack of financial and human resources, NGOs focus on media coverage to promote their goals. They have either a media department, or media office, or media center. A public relations practitioner working for an NGO has the job title of spokesperson, communication expert, or communication officer. The practitioner is expected to launch public relations campaigns, organize protests or events, execute fundraising, train volunteers, distribute information to journalists, and ensure consistency of media coverage. For example, the Centre for Women in Governance (an NGO established in Uganda), posted a job opening for a communication officer who was capable of (1) building strong and active relationships with the media to increase the organization's profile in Uganda and internationally; (2) editing reports, articles, and proposals; (3) developing stories and blogs for external audiences; (4) ensuring that its communication strategy is adopted across the organization; and (5) raising public awareness of the

---

20   Ibid.

organization's grassroots activities and impact through traditional media, social media, websites, and multimedia.[21] Nonprofit organizations are likely to have fewer resources than corporations and governments. Hence they search for stable support from the public, and the practice of public relations plays a pivotal role in the operation.

In summary, college seniors and recent college graduates with degrees in public relations and similar fields often choose jobs at either public relations firms or communication departments in organizations. There are advantages in each sector (Table 4.1).

Public Relations Internships

Employers receive hundreds of applications for a single job opening. They choose the most skilled applicant who will arrive job ready from day one. In line with this hiring trend, college students are concerned about building skills and knowledge to be job ready, although they often point out that a college education is about building profound knowledge and developing academic interest rather than adapting to vocational skills. However, employers will continue to hire job ready candidates from the application pool while cutting the costs of entry-level training programs. It is apparent that there exists a reality gap between entry-level job seekers and employers.

Job applicants fresh out of college with bachelor's degrees are expected to have amassed experience elsewhere before applying for a full-time job. This experience can be gained through internship programs. In fact, the current hiring trend requires experience in internships. In response to the trend, more colleges include internships as part of the regular course curriculum. In the studies of public relations and communication, internships are considered a part of the popular curriculum before graduation. Although some say an internship is not fair to college students who sell themselves short to organizations, students can take advantage of the benefit of their internship experience with college credit and a taste of professional work. Employers sometimes promote valuable, hardworking interns to full-time regular staff members. Stuart Lander, chief marketing officer at Internships.com, stated,

> First and foremost, these results tell us that at a time when 54 percent of recent graduates are unemployed or underemployed, the best chance you have as a student not to be part of that statistic is to do an internship. You have a seven in ten chance of being hired by the company you interned with.[22]

Students can land full-time jobs through internships. A study found that "internships have become the 'new interview' in the job search process for students and employees, and 66 percent of employers view the new interview process as the most important factor in their hiring decisions—far more significant than strong academic performance."[23]

The top-five reasons that employers offer internship programs are to (1) find future employees, (2) support students, (3) increase productivity, (4) enhance perspective from the outside, and (5) use inexpensive resources. In thinking about entry-level employees as the future of a company, employers "get the opportunity to find the talent they need to help grow their business without relying on just a short interview."[24]

---

21 "Work with Us" Center for Women in Governance, https://cewigo.com/careers/

22 Jacquelyn Smith, "Internships May Be the Easiest Way to a Job in 2013," *Forbes*, December 6, 2012, http://www.forbes.com/sites/jacquelynsmith/2012/12/06/internships-may-be-the-easiest-way-to-a-job-in-2013/.

23 Smith, "Internships."

24 Smith, "Internships."

Internships at Public Relations Firms

During the summer, public relations firms offer internship programs. The firms prefer to hire interns who can assist with general office activities, monitor media stories, help research, and develop press materials. They also value interns who bring fresh perspectives. For example, Jill Schmidt Public Relations, a networking public relations firm, posted the following online internship announcement for students in public relations and/or communications:[25]

> The internship will begin mid-May. An outgoing personality, fantastic networking skills, extreme creativity, out-of-the-box thinking, multitasking abilities, proficient AP writing skills, and attention to detail in a deadline-driven environment are necessary. This is a fantastic opportunity to become directly involved with the Public Relations industry in Chicago and beyond. You will assist with setting up TV segments and developing articles with top editors and producers as well as with national media in high-level markets.

To get internships at public relations firms, students need to improve their writing skills, creative thinking, and ability to work cooperatively with others. The duties of interns include a wide range of activities, including copying and printing documents, assisting office work and event performances, drafting press releases, and planning social media campaigns. Students can learn and witness the kinds of jobs public relations practitioners do. There is a titanic difference between reading things in textbooks and observing things in real workplaces. A big advantage of public relations internships is learning things that are not being taught in the classroom. One college public relations student said that she learned how to compose accurate and useful reports, comprise a media list of contacts, and monitor media coverage for clients through her internship with a public relations firm in New York City. More importantly, she received instant feedback and advice on her work from her supervisor, which was the most valuable thing the student earned from her internship experience.

Internships in Organizations

Communication departments in organizations offer internship programs as well. The most well-known program for college students is the Walt Disney Company's summer internship program. The program claims students will have "a special opportunity to learn from and collaborate with Disney's creative, business, and technology teams."[26] Interns with Disney's communications/ public relations team can have the opportunity to join projects that enhance Disney's reputation, brands, and businesses around the world. The responsibilities of Disney's public relations interns include "managing Disney's reputation, developing strategic, cohesive external and internal communications, or managing large-scale, high-visibility projects."[27]

Whether students choose internships at public relations firms or communication departments, it is important that they have an interest in learning all practical aspects of public relations.

25   "Your Career Starts Here," WayUp, https://www.internmatch.com/internships/jill-schmidt-public-relations/ intern--2?show_location=280614.

26   "Jobs," Disney, http://disneycareers.com/en/career-areas/students-recent-grads/internships-co-ops/.

27   "Disney Professional Internships," Disney, http://profinterns.disneycareers.com/en/students-recent-grads/ corporate/communications-public-relations/.

Getting an Internship

Before applying for an internship, students tend to consider location, interest, payment, and brand. Completing a summer internship in Paris or Stockholm is cool for college students if the costs are covered. Unfortunately, *Forbes Magazine* found that "only 34 percent of all internships are paid, and paid positions get four times as many applicants as unpaid ones."[28] Since getting an internship (especially a paid one) is competitive, a strategic approach to the application should be planned.

Internship applications require a cover letter and resume. In the cover letter, students should demonstrate their education, coupled with experience that is relevant to the job description, according to Internships.com CEO Robin Richards.[29] After submitting the cover letter and resume, students hope an interview comes next. For the interview, dressing to impress interviewers at first sight is important. Overdressing is better than underdressing. For public relations students to handle interviews well, *PR Daily* offers these nine tips:[30]

- *Know the Public Relations Field.* Be able to exchange common public relations knowledge with an interviewer.

- *Know about the Company.* Read articles about it (including stock prices) until the day of the interview.

- *Read Up on the Company's Industry.* Know the company's competitors and industry trends.

- *Come Ready with Recommendations for the Company.* Give the interviewer a fresh perspective for the company.

- *Don't List Crucial Public Relations Skills as Weaknesses.* Instead, say verbal and writing skills are your strengths.

- *Have an Elevator Pitch.* Sell yourself with a brief pitch that emphasizes what you can bring to the company.

- *Ask Relevant Questions.* Ask how the company handles criticism and executes media strategy.

- *Send a Thank-You Email.* Thank interviewers for their time in a formal email format.

- *Even If You're Not an Expert, You Can Sound Like One.* Use information you prepared for the interview.

The internship has positioned itself as one of the core college courses necessary to land a dream job in public relations and related fields of communication. It is a long journey for college students to find a full-time dream job that they want to do for a long time. While taking academic courses, students need to build their own portfolios, including community engagement and voluntary work.

28   Jacquelyn Smith, "Nine Steps to Getting the Internship You Want," *Forbes*, May 21, 2012,.

29   Smith, "Nine Steps." http://www.forbes.com/sites/jacquelynsmith/2012/03/21/nine-steps-to-getting-the-internship-you-want/.

30   "Essentials for PR newbies," PR Daily, https://www.prdaily.com/14-essentials-for-pr-newbies/

The Professional Outlook for Public Relations and Communication Students

Hiring trends change quickly as the wide range of industries adopt new technologies. Not only do colleges try to correspond to the changes in job markets, but they also strike a balance by teaching in-depth academic knowledge and practical skills. The academic fields of public relations and communication also introduce new course curricula and adopt new communication technologies to guide students in keeping abreast of new challenges in the practice of public relations. According to the 2019 list from Career Research Institution, the best jobs for communications majors is public relations specialist, followed by meeting/event planner, college alumni, development officer, media planner, and social media manager.[31]

Public relations job descriptions are getting complicated and more challenging with the popularity of social media, in addition to traditional media. As a result, college students are expected to pay attention to emerging communication technologies and how to use them. It is worth noting that future employers look for applicants who are ready to contribute to organizations by skipping entry-level job training.

---

31   Mike Profita, "Best Jobs for Communication Degree Majors: Career Options for Communication Grads to Consider," The Balance Careers, November 18, 2019, https://bit.ly/3cWJs6H.

CHAPTER SUMMARY AND REVIEW

1. Take core public relations and communication courses.

2. Acknowledge the essential skills for entry-level public relations positions.

3. Understand responsibilities and job descriptions for public relations practitioners.

4. Explain what public relations firms do and how they are structured.

5. Identify the essence of getting and doing a public relations internship.

PUBLIC RELATIONS IN PRACTICE

FURTHER READING

PR Week's Awards For **Best PR Creative Excellence**

Winner: Anheuser-Busch/Bud Light and 3PM (Weber Shandwick, in partnership with PMK-BNC)
Campaign Name: Bud Light's Browns Victory Fridge

Working with the Browns' organization and Bud Light's wholesaler network, the brand coordinated strategic placement of the specially designed fridges at ten fan bars across Cleveland. To create buzz around the campaign, mini-victory fridges were seeded to mega-fan influencers.

Read more at
https://www.prweek.com/article/1579436/prweek-us-awards-2019-winners

5

Communication Models and Messages for Public Relations

Everybody is a communicator. People make conversation through speaking or writing or body language. They exchange their feelings, thoughts, opinions, and demands. What they are doing in the matter of social exchange is described as communication. They communicate with each other to get through a day or every second, although most of them do not consciously apply the action to the concept of communication. As a part of their daily routine, they talked, spoke, chatted, and wrote as acts of communicative. The term *communication* is synonymous with all human activities involved in expressing feelings, making meaning, and exchanging information.

Public relations practitioners are also communicators who talk, speak, and write. The practice of public relations requires them to listen to their clients or audiences for information exchange that gives rise to ideas and creativity for better work performance. Rather than simply talking and writing at work, public relations practitioners strategically communicate with their target audiences. They strategically characterize communication as a process of understanding, creating, and managing influential interaction with the audience. This is the difference between a common communicator and a public relations communicator. The difference stems from the knowledge of communication goals and models.

Goals of Communication

Communication in public relations is an organized and planned activity. This means that every communication has the following goals: (1) informing, (2) educating, (3) motivating, (4) persuading, (5) entertaining, and, eventually, (6) constructing mutual understanding.

■ ***To Inform.*** Public relations practitioners inform a target audience about products, services, or ideas. The target audience is informed to assist in possible decision making. For example, the US Centers for Disease Control and Prevention

(CDC) informs the American public of the danger of potentially spreading diseases, such as influenza and Ebola, whenever it is necessary. The CDC raises awareness of public health issues, providing a valuable information service. Spokespersons at the CDC serve as public relations practitioners, and its target audience is the public in the United States.

- **To Educate.** If the spokespersons at the CDC only alerted the public to the danger of spreading diseases, they would be involved in pure information transmission, but they do more; they advise how to protect the public from infectious diseases—, for example, getting a vaccine, wearing a mask, or using an alcohol-based hand sanitizer. They educate the public.

- **To Motivate.** Even after the public is informed of the danger and educated about how to prevent diseases, some people will not care about such information. In this case, the spokespersons tend to find a way to motivate people to pay attention to their advice. For example, to increase immunization levels for vaccine-preventable diseases, the CDC would offer some incentives to motivate the public to get vaccines. This is also a part of the management function in public relations.

- **To Persuade.** The most important goal of professional communication is to persuade the target audience. Public relations practitioners hope to persuade the target audience to act on their persuasive messages. For example, the spokespersons at the CDC could use all communication tactics to persuade the public to get vaccinated when a certain disease is expected to spread. The goals of informing, educating, and motivating the public eventually aim to persuade the public to take action.

- **To Entertain.** No one would reject being entertained. Communication exists in certain areas to make the target audience feel good and happy. The entertainment industry, for example, focuses on producing exciting and touching feelings in the audience with communication products, such as movies, television shows, and books. The CDC often entertains the public with stories of cured patients.

- **To Construct Mutual Understanding.** Public relations practitioners aim to communicate with the target audience. They are open to feedback from the audience. In a feedback process with a vital exchange of thoughts and opinions, both parties come to a better understanding of each other. It leads to the construction of mutual benefits, which should be the final goal of public relations practice.

Communication Models

As communication is used to achieve the goals of organizations or clients from a public relations perspective, public relations practitioners acknowledge the value in a communication process that illustrates how the practitioners and the target audience come to a mutual understanding. The following four communication models visualize the process of strategic communication.

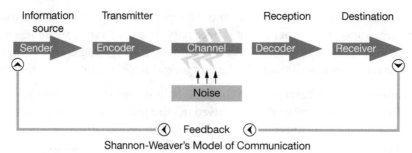

FIGURE 5.1 Shannon-weaver's model of communication.
Source: Claude Elwood shannon and warren weaver, "shannon and weaver model of communication," http://communicationtheory.
Org/shannon-and-weaver-model-of-communication/.

Shannon-Weaver Communication Model[1]

This model (Figure 5.1), designed to explain the communication process between sender and receiver, demonstrates how communication factors play an important role in completing one cycle of communication. "Sender" refers to the original source that initiates communication. Public relations practitioners are usually the sender in this model. "Encoder" is a form of message that sends and propagates communication ideas and subjects; public relations practitioners are responsible for taking the ideas of the source and putting them in a code that expresses the source's purpose in the form of a message. "Channel" refers to a medium that is used to send a message. When a message is formed, public relations practitioners need to find an effective way of disseminating the message to the "receiver"—the target audience. Television, radio, newspapers, and magazines are traditional media channels for spreading messages with "noise" as a means of sharing the message in written or spoken language.

"Decoder" refers to the reverse process of encoder. After the encoder forms communication ideas and topics into a message for the sender, receivers—the target audience—decode the meaning and purpose of the message. In other words, the message is being processed to be understood by the target audience. "Receiver" is the final destination in communication. Because there is a receiver, communication occurs and completes the flow of message exchange. Based on the decoded message, members of the target audience offer their thoughts and opinions about the message to the sender—public relations practitioners. This process is called feedback, to which the sender pays attention. Vital evaluation of feedback helps the sender improve the message creation and distribution process.

Berlo's Model[2]

Also known as the send-message-channel-receiver model, Berlo's model (Figure 5.2) includes the factors of communication in its four major sections. Communication skills, such as speaking, listening, writing, and reading, are essential components of human communication for both the source and the receiver in this model. When the source sends a message to the receiver, neither party will have an understanding of the message without these basic communication skills. Attitudes toward the receiver and the source

---

1   "Shannon and Weaver Model of Communication," CommunicationTheory.org., http://communicationtheory.
org/shannon-and-weaver-model-of-communication/.

2   CommunicationTheory.org, "Shannon and Weaver Model."

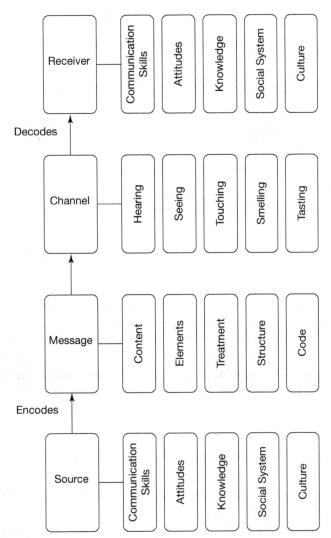

FIGURE 5.2 Berlo's model.
Source: "Communication models," tutorials point, http://www.Tutorialspoint.Com/management_concepts/communication_models.Htm.

encourage a desire for them to help each other. For example, when a public relations practitioner makes an effort to build a good relationship with the target audience, the practitioner's attitude toward the audience is already positive. In the same vein, if the audience has a positive attitude toward the practitioner, then the message sent from the practitioner is likely to be positively accepted by the audience.

Knowledge about a communication subject affects the outcome of communication. If both sides have the same knowledge of their particular communication subject, faster and more efficient communication can occur; they know what they are talking about. Social systems affect the process of communication as well. In a specific social environment, people have different values, beliefs, religions, and views. Public relations practitioners, when creating messages, contemplate how to customize the messages to appeal to the target audience's favorite social system. Culture is part of the social system, with the focus on a specific society in which communication takes place.

In the message section, content refers to whatever is transmitted from the beginning to the end of the message between the source and the receiver. Message elements include verbal and nonverbal language

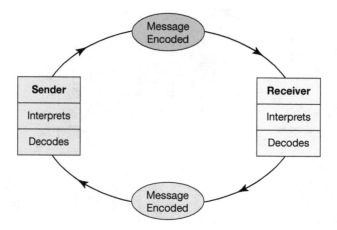

FIGURE 5.3 Schramm's model.
Source: Ricarl ramlagan, "schramm's communication model," https://www.Thinglink.Com/scene/623201146781040642.

and gestures. Such elements of the particular message accompany the content. Treatment is about how the source selects and arranges content and then how the source decides to deliver the message. Structure refers to the arrangement of messages into various parts, such as the beginning, the middle, and the end. Code means how the message is transmitted and in what format. The code can be body language, music, sign language, or oral language. Public relations practitioners use one or all of the codes to send messages in real-life settings.

Schramm's Model[3]

Schramm's model (Figure 5.3) emphasizes that both the sender and the receiver take turns playing the role of encoder and decoder in a circular fashion. After the sender as an encoder sends the message to the receiver as a decoder, the receiver responds to the sender's message with another message encoded by the receiver. The sender now becomes a decoder of the message. This circular process of encoding and decoding, including interpreting and transmitting, occurs simultaneously. Both the sender and the receiver put time and effort into the act of communication to maintain this process. The messages in this model are continuously created and exchanged until one of them stops sending messages.

Lasswell's Model[4]

This model (Figure 5.4) is simple but contains a significant description of communication that boils down to answering the following questions in a step-by-step fashion: Who says what, in which channel, to whom, and with what effect?

Lasswell's model explains especially the process of mass communication and public relations in society. For example, a public relations firm (communicator) launches a campaign shedding light on the notion that all women are beautiful regardless of their appearance (message). The campaign receives

---

3   "Osgood-Schramm Model of Communication," CommunicationTheroy.org, http://communicationtheory.org/osgood-schramm-model-of-communication/.

4   "Lasswell's Model," CommunicationTheroy.org, http://communicationtheory.org/lasswells-model/.

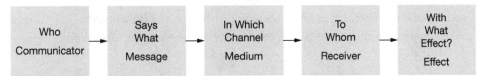

FIGURE 5.4 Laswell's Model.

heavy media coverage from television, newspapers, and radio (medium). Thanks to the media coverage, many women are exposed to the message (receiver), and, finally, they feel confident and comfortable with the shape of their bodies, even if commercial advertisements are flooded with slim models.

This model focuses on the messages presented in the media that can be conveyed to mass audiences. Public relations practitioners produce messages that are placed in press releases, news conferences, events, and social media platforms. Public relations practitioners are communicators who make titanic efforts to create powerful messages. They are adept at choosing appropriate, useful media to spread the message to their target audience. Without using the media, whether traditional or social, it is impossible for them to reach out to the target audience, usually numerous people. It means that public relations is associated with the principle of mass communication; the more people are informed, the better for the client or the organization. Public relations practitioners communicate with the target audience not because communication just spontaneously happens but because they aim to achieve their communication goals on behalf of their organizations or clients. Although Lasswell's model does not include the feedback process, it illustrates a vivid process of public relations communication.

The Message

The principal player in communication models is the message, defined as an "underlying idea or theme in an ad, or the central or primary content or information that passes from a communicator to a receiver."[5] A message is a verbal or written form of communication that communicators send to receivers. It communicates key points to the target audience. The main concerns public relations practitioners have about messages are threefold: (1) how to create an effective message, (2) how to disseminate the message, and (3) how to expose the message to the target audience. The most urgent and important concern is how to create powerful messages.

Words are the foundation of messages. Choosing persuasive and appropriative words is the first step to crafting key messages in public relations. As time goes by, words are subject to changes in meaning and usage. Messages need to contain socially unprovocative and less discriminatory words in current social settings. For example, gender-neutral words are commonly used in the practice of public relations: chairperson instead of chairman, firefighter instead of fireman, nurse instead of male nurse, workforce instead of manpower, the average person instead of the common man, a talkative woman instead of a gossiping woman, homemaker instead of housewife, salesperson instead of salesman, and actor instead of actress. Some phrases can also be changed: physically disabled instead of handicapped and mentally challenged instead of retarded.

Words are used to create key messages in public relations. According to Debbie Wetherhead, president of the Wetherhead Communications, well-crafted messages help public relations practitioners "(1) prioritize and crystallize information; (2) ensure consistency, continuity, and accuracy; (3) measure

---

5   "Message," Business Dictionary, http://www.businessdictionary.com/definition/message.html.

and track success; and (4) stay focused when speaking with media or stakeholders."[6] Key messages are a strategic and sophisticated entity that public relations practitioners prioritize. Wetherhead cited eight key message elements:[7]

1. *Concise.* Optimally, provide three key messages on one page, with each statement only one to three sentences in length or under 30 seconds when spoken.

2. *Strategic.* Define, differentiate, and address benefits/value proposition.

3. *Relevant.* Balance what you need to communicate with what your audience needs to know.

4. *Compelling.* Offer meaningful information designed to stimulate action.

5. *Simple.* Write in easy-to-understand language, avoid jargon and acronyms.

6. *Memorable.* Make the message easy to recall and repeat, avoid run-on sentences.

7. *Real.* Use the active rather than passive voice, no advertising slogans.

8. *Tailored.* Communicate with different target audiences effectively, adapting language and depth of information.

It is not easy to build influential key messages by including all the elements. In the process of building key messages, public relations practitioners include beneficial information for the target audience with real, memorable, and tailored key messages. The key message should convince the members of the target audience that they would be better off if they acted on the message. In other words, key messages should be able to touch the target audience members' hearts. Corporations are excellent players in tailoring key messages in catchy slogans toward target audiences. Some examples are as follows (Table 5.1):

TABLE 5.1   Examples of Corporations and Their Recognizable Marketing Phrases

Name	Messages
Harley Davidson	American by Birth. Rebel by Choice
Walmart	Save Money. Live Better
Toyota	Let's Go Places
Nikon	At the Heart of the Image
Subway	Eat Fresh
M&M	Melts in Your Mouths, Not in Your Hands
Nike	Just Do It
L'Oréal	Because You're Worth It
State Farm	Like a Good Neighbor, State Farm Is There
The National Lottery	It Could Be You
Motel 6	We'll Leave a Light on for You
Hallmark	When You Care Enough to Send the Very Best
Dunkin' Donuts	America Runs on Dunkin
eBay	Buy It. Sell It. Love It
Disneyland	The Happiest Place on Earth

---

6   Debbie Wetherhead, "Key Message Development: Building a Foundation for Communications," PRSA, http://comprehension.prsa.org/?p=4426.

7   Wetherhead, "Key Message Development."

The Objectives of Messages

Impressive and compelling messages are remembered and spread among the members of the target audience. The messages from Disneyland have a strong effect on the minds of children and their parents. When audiences happen to hear a message and think it is appealing, they accept the message and take action: visiting the place or buying the product. James Grunig, a professor at the University of Maryland, lists five objectives of public relations practitioners in terms of dealing with messages.[8]

1. ***Message Exposure.*** The target audience is exposed to messages in various forms via the mass media, controlled media, and social media.

2. ***Accurate Dissemination of the Message.*** The basic information, often filtered by media gatekeepers, remains intact as it is transmitted through various media.

3. ***Acceptance of the Message.*** The audience not only retains the message but also accepts it as valid.

4. ***Attitude Change.*** The audience not only believes the message but also makes a verbal or mental commitment to change behavior as a result of the message.

5. ***Change in Overt Behavior.*** Members of the audience actually change their current behavior or purchase the product and use it.

Creating impressive messages that represent an organization's or a product's characteristics is not as hard as making sure that the target audience has received the message and showed its interest in it. For example, the message of the National Lottery, "It could be you," triggers the subconscious desire of the members of the target audience to become multimillionaires, so the audience will not mind making a small-dollar investment in lottery tickets for fun. Even if some people characterized the lottery as a sinful game, they could change their attitudes toward the lottery because of the message. If they buy a lottery ticket because they were convinced by the message, then the influential effect of the message is clearly proven.

Good messages should be able to motivate the target audience and, further, the general public. In a similar vein, the public eventually can be the target audience. This is called multiple target audiences. A good example is the population that typically purchases lottery tickets.[9] While sending the message to particular areas where the target audience lives, the lottery organization aims to have another group of audiences exposed to the message. One of their tactics is to spread stories of people who bought scratch-off lottery tickets as gifts, and the recipients won. Some people who have never touched a lottery ticket could have a positive attitude toward playing the lottery as a gift. Not only does the message maintain its influence on the target audience, but it also attracts another layer of audiences with carefully planned stories that can motivate people to take action on the message: "It could be you." Therefore, the general public becomes synonymous with the target audience of the message.

Communication Tools for Messages

The final purpose of a message is to make the target audience act on it. The process of getting to this final destination requires hard work. Having the message exposed to the target audience depends on how

---

8   Dennis L. Wilcox. *Public Relations Writing and Media Techniques*, 6th edition, p. 97 (Berkeley: Peachpit Press, 2009),

9   John Wihbey, "Who Plays the Lottery, and Why: Updated Collection of Research," Journalist's Resources, July 27, 2016, http://journalistsresource.org/studies/economics/personal-finance/research-review-lotteries-demographics#.

TABLE 5.2 Five Unique Categories of Communication Tools

Communication Tools	Key Use	Examples
Public media	Build awareness	Newspapers, magazines, television, radio
Interactive media	Respond to queries Exchange information	Phone calls, audio text, email, bulletin boards
Controlled media	Promotion Provide detailed information	Brochures, newsletters, annual reports, books, direct mail, video, web pages
Events/groups	Motivate attendees Reinforce attitudes	Speeches, trade shows, exhibits, conferences, demonstrations, rallies, sponsorships, contests, awards
One-on-one	Obtain commitments Resolve problems	Personal visits, lobbying, solicitation

the public relations practitioner uses communication tools that transmit the message to the audience. What are communication tools? Although people generally regard them as the media, such as television, radio, newspapers, and social media, there are more communication tools, according to Kirk Hallahan, author of *Strategic Media Planning: Toward a Public Relations Model,* who lists five unique categories of communication tools (Table 5.2).[10]

A public relations practitioner can use all the tools in Table 5.2 to disseminate the message to the target audience. When the practitioner has a message to send out, she produces a press release in hopes of attracting the attention of journalists while posting any important information and messages on the organization's web page and social media platforms. In addition, she—if necessary—meets with journalists to persuade them to publish the message, and she organizes events such as sponsorships and speeches to get the message heard. Knowledge of the channels of dissemination is a basic skill for the practitioner to explore possible communication tools. She makes personal appointments with those who can affect the process of message dissemination. Ranging from using the media to sending out letters, to organizing events, to having one-on-one meetings, the practice of public relations uses any available communication tools to get the message out. This is a way to increase the chances that key messages will be transmitted to the target audience.

Understanding the Message

When the message is out, and the target audience acknowledges the existence of the message, it is time for the practitioner to ensure that the message has been understood by the audience the way the practitioner intended it to be. In the practice of public relations, tailoring the message with a certain intention is called framing. Framed key messages could result in positively positioning a product, a service, or an idea in the minds of the members of the target audience. For example, when abortion emerged as a social issue in the United States, the anti-abortion side framed its activities as the pro-life movement, recognizing the negative connotation of abortion. The pro-life movement disseminated the framed key message: an unborn child is a human person whose life has value and deserves to be protected by our society.[11] As the pro-life message gained support, the proabortion side also framed its activities as the

10   Kirk Hallahan, *Handbook of Public Relations,* p 461 (Thousand Oaks, CA: Sage Publications, 2001)

11   Sembi Bille Alfred, "Sharing the Pro-Life Message," Why Pro-Life, March 5, 2016, http://www.whyprolife.com/sharing-the-pro-life-message/.

pro-choice movement. The pro-choice movement came up with its own framed message: "Don't force your abortion views on my body."[12] This case demonstrates that the same issue can be understood in two different frames, depending on how the key messages are originally intended. Both sides attempt to persuade pregnant women and their families to act on their messages, asking them to choose either the pro-life or the pro-choice side. Both messages seem to be well understood and evenly attract public attention to support their messages; a Gallup poll found that the US public remained "divided on the abortion issue, with 50 percent of American adults describing their views as 'pro-choice' and 44 percent as 'pro-life.'"[13]

Message Credibility

There is a gap between a message that is recognized and a message that is acted upon. Even after the message was disseminated and understood, the target audience would not be sure whether they had to take action on the message. One compelling factor that bridges the gap is credibility. If the message was understood and the audience found it credible, they would not mind acting on the message. Public relations practitioners use three common devices to incorporate credibility into messages: news publication, source credibility, and statistics.

NEWS PUBLICATION

When a message is created for an organization, the organization can place the message in both advertisements and press releases. The message in an advertisement represents the organization's intention without filtering, while a press release has to go through journalists' evaluation process. Whereas an ad reaches out to members of the target audience directly by convincing them to believe in the message, the message in the press release is strictly scrutinized by journalists before it informs the target audience. For example, a food company introduces organic cookies for children, pitching the message that the product uses purely organic, healthy ingredients, such as honey instead of sugar, so parents should buy their kids the cookies. The message in the advertisement is copied and disseminated in the way that the organization intended. On the other hand, the press release containing the same message would not be able to serve as the same method for disseminating the message unless the claims of the organization are all truthful. When the message in the press release is examined by journalists, they check the facts about the product. In other words, they investigate if the message in the release is true and newsworthy. In this process, journalists serve as gatekeepers who are responsible for making objective judgments. If they find the message truthful, credible, and newsworthy, they will disseminate the message to the public in print or through broadcast. When the message is published or broadcast, the practitioner deserves a big round of applause because the public is likely to give higher credibility to the message in the news media than in the advertisement. When the target audience and the public are informed about the truthfulness of the message, they are likely to try the product. A message filtered by journalists or gatekeepers is a big element of vindicating credibility.

SOURCE CREDIBILITY

The second way to enhance message credibility involves source credibility. The target audience pays attention to a message by looking into which person or organization acts on the message. If the person

---

12   "Home Page," AbortionRights.org. http://www.abortionrights.org.uk/.

13   Lydia Saad, "Americans Choose 'Pro-Choice' for First Time in Seven Years," Gallup, May 29, 2015, http://www.gallup.com/poll/183434/americans-choose-pro-choice-first-time-seven-years.aspx.

or organization has authoritative expertise in the message while advocating its credibility, then the target audience will trust the message. For example, when a cosmetics company launches a campaign aimed at convincing teenagers to wear sunscreen every morning, the teenage audience will be more convinced to act on the message if dermatologists emphasize the importance of protecting skin at an early age. Public relations practitioners make efforts to find trustworthy people or organizations to integrate credibility into their messages. In general, nonprofit, academic, government, and research organizations are viewed as authoritative experts with a high level of credibility. If the CDC recommends using hand sanitizers to prevent the spread of germs, the public relations practitioner in the sanitizer industry gets busy disseminating messages about killing germs with antiseptic hand products, credibly justified by the government agency.

STATISTICS

The third device to increase message credibility is statistics, as numbers can add credibility to almost every message. The message gains credibility if the target audience is convinced by specific numbers and statistics. For example, if a university plans to encourage more high school seniors to apply for admission, then the university's public relations practitioner creates a message designed to persuade students to apply to the university. Simply sending a message that the university is the best for their future is less likely to convince them to apply than a message that statistically demonstrates that the university has lower college dropout rates and higher employment rates after graduation compared with other universities. Such statistics can strengthen the message's credibility. As a result, more high school seniors would apply to the university, eventually acting on the message.

Message Repetition

It is not over yet, even after the target audience responds to the message in a positive way. One more task is needed to create routine behavior in the audience. For a more successful result, the message needs to convince the target audience to repeat their action. If they bought a lottery ticket this week, the message serves as a reminder to buy another ticket next week. The target audience becomes loyal followers of the message. The practitioner does not forget to send the same message repeatedly since the message is likely to be more effective when repeated. Message repetition, according to many studies, is a means of convincing the target audience to believe in the message. For example, the messages "Got Milk?" and "Just Do It" have been repeated over two decades, guiding the audience to pass on their behavioral routines to their children and grandchildren. The audience and their family members drink milk and wear Nike products. In a short message, repetition helps the audience remember the message and stick to their decisions to act.

Thomas Smith's book, *Successful Advertising*, explains why message repetition is an essential part of achieving communication goals. Smith lists several steps for a message to be noticed through repetition. When the target audience and the public see the message, they just look at it instead of being aware of it. As they happen to run into the message more often, they begin to sense the existence of the message and pay closer attention to it. With more exposure to the message, they try to find more information about the message and even ask their friends and neighbors if they have acknowledged the message. As the message keeps hovering around in their lives, they start to believe that the message has value, and they feel like the product or service represented by the message is good to buy or try. They make a commitment at this point to get it. If they can't afford to buy the product or service, they blame their poverty, and, finally, they respond to the call to action by purchasing the product or service after saving money for a while. The message of GEICO Insurance Company is a good example: the repetition of "15 minutes could save you 15 percent or more on car insurance" continues with various icons in the message, such as the small tropical lizard, wee pigs, and cavemen. The 15/15 message repeats and repeats, sticking around the brains of the members of the target brains.

Forms of Messages in Connection

Messages themselves are intangible. Words and symbols make messages tangible. Messages are expressed, illustrated, connected, and symbolized through words and symbols, such as hand postures and logos. Organizations present marketing catchphrases or campaign slogans in words to enhance message connectivity. McDonald's "I'm lovin' it" catchphrase boosts the key message of the restaurant: fast and friendly. The catchphrase can capitalize on promoting synergy when combined with the symbol of the company: the golden arches. In a similar vein, Nike's symbolic "swoosh" plays a role in reminding the target audience of the message (getting into athletic activities—"Just Do It") without thinking too much.

Symbols are a unique means of representing an organization's identity and message. For example, BMW's propeller symbol represents a tribute to the company's aviation history—it built aircraft engines during World War II. In combination with its slogan, "The Ultimate Driving Machine," the symbol enhances the image of luxury and advanced technology for the company. Such forms of messages are designed to help the members of the target audience recognize and feel the essence of what organizations want to communicate to them.

A symbol without any words can also express a message. For example, the pink ribbon sends the message of solidarity and support for breast cancer patients and survivors. The pink ribbon symbolizes the important message of early detection and frequent checkups for the illness. The message has been spread and supported all around the world, as the pink ribbon represents the same advocacy for breast cancer survivors in different countries. Despite the fact that there are dozens of different types of cancer and thousands of survivors, the symbolic message of the pink ribbon, due in part to public relations campaigns, has functioned as a vehicle for a global movement in attracting more supporters. This case demonstrates the power of message.

Evaluation of Messages in Public Relations

The ideal goal of a message in public relations is to persuade the target audience to build positive attitudes that lead them to act on the message. For the audience to get to the action, many processes and communication tools are explored by public relations practitioners. Their efforts in creating and disseminating messages, as well as raising awareness and convincing the target audience, are evaluated by the following five questions:

1. Did the message reach the target audience and other multiple audiences?

2. Did the message play an important role in achieving the intended organizational objective?

3. Did the activities of message distribution and message influence fall within its budget?

4. Did the target audience understand the message?

5. Did public relations practitioners take the best steps to maximize message effectiveness?

A simple but popular approach to measuring message outcomes is to count stories in the media. Press releases, photos, and feature stories published in the media are known as press clippings. The practitioner can gather news articles, which contain the message content. Relevant television news clips and mentions on the radio are all considered media exposure for the message. Another approach is to count the number of people who notice and understand the message. As it is impossible to track down all people exposed to the message, media readership and viewership can be used. If the message is published in a local newspaper with a daily circulation of 10,000, then the practitioner assumes the same number of people were exposed to the message. Frequency is the third approach to measurement. The practitioner finds out how many times the audience looks at the message.

These three approaches to measurement are not able to reflect the high standards of public relations measurement requirements. Deborah Silverman, a professor at Buffalo State, pointed out that public relations industry groups, including the PRSA, adopted new techniques of public relations message/campaign measurement, which are named the Barcelona Principles. The seven principles serve as the foundation of public relations measurement.[14]

1. *Importance of Goal Setting and Measurement.* Goals should be as quantitative as possible, and traditional and social media should be measured.

2. *Media Measurement Requires Quantity and Quality.* Instead of overall clip counts, media measurement should account for impressions among audiences and quality, such as tone and credibility of source. More importantly, quality can be defined as negative, positive, or neutral.

3. *Advertising Equivalencies (AVEs) Are* **Not** *the Value of Public Relations.* AVE refers to the method of converting the value of stories in the newspapers and on the air into the equivalent advertising costs. This method is no longer effective.

4. *Social Media Can and Should Be Measured.* Just as evaluating quality and quantity is critical, measurement should focus on conversations and communities, not "coverage," in addition to data collection and tracking traffic.

5. *Measuring Outcomes Is Preferred to Measuring Media Results.* Outcomes include shifts in awareness, comprehension, attitudes, and behavior related to purchases, donations, brand equity, corporate reputation, employee engagement, and public policy investment decisions—in other words, measuring how the target audience took action as the message intended.

6. *Business (Organizational) Results Can and Should Be Measured Where Possible.* Models that determine the effects of the quantity and quality of public relations outputs on sales (or other business metrics) are preferred. If the message was aimed at increasing sales, then the sales amounts should be evaluated.

7. *Transparency and Replicability Are Paramount to Sound Measurement.* Measurement should be transparent and replicable.

---

14   "Key Message Development: Building a Foundation for Effective Communications," PRSA, https://prsay.prsa.org/2011/12/02/key-message-development-building-a-foundation-for-effective-communications/

Measurement of message effectiveness is complicated and sometimes arduous. On various occasions, it requires professional measurement services. But public relations practitioners try to make the process doable by focusing on how the target audience ended up being aware of the message. This process follows pure media coverage of the message. The practitioner can not only analyze if the message was portrayed positively or negatively in the media, but he or she can also interview the members of the target audience to see if they recall the media coverage of the message. In addition, the practitioner investigates the audience members' attitudes toward the message. The attitudes are measured before, during, and after the message was exposed to the audience. For example, the effectiveness of the message "Sign up for the Affordable Care Act for your health" can be measured by the following procedures: (1) media coverage tone, whether positive or negative; (2) the number of people who recognize the message; (3) changed attitudes toward the message; and (4) the actual number of people who joined the program based on the message.

Although the measurement process and principles are commonly applied to both traditional and social media, there are six specific categories for measuring social media message effectiveness. Nichole Kelly, president of SME Digital, listed them as follows:[15]

1. *Exposure.* How many people are listening to you or talking about the message? It is a combination of normal web analytics, Twitter followers, Facebook fans, and running a search for message mentions.

2. *Influence.* Public relations practitioners can get a report on the top influencers if they express their opinions about the message.

3. *Engagement.* Practitioners can count the number of clicks on the links they post and track the number of times the message is shared or retweeted, including how many direct comments they receive from the target audience.

4. *Action/Convert.* Practitioners measure the pieces of content that tie to their outcome process, in which there are people who visited social media sites of the organization to see the message.

5. *Sales.* How much money or outcomes are these messaging efforts generating? The final outcomes of the message are measured based on the objectives.

6. *Retain.* When the final outcomes of the message on social media are measured, the practitioners go back to the first step to repeat the activity with message repetition.

Messages are powerful, and they can be more powerful when reaching out to the right audience at the right time, in the right place, and through the right media.

15   Nichole Kelly, "Five Categories of Social Media Measurement," Folk Media, February 17, 2010, http://folkmedia. org/five-catagories-of-social-media-measurement/.

Public Relations Communication in the Future

By understanding the process and goals of communication, public relations practitioners propel their job performance. They never stop developing their skills of using communication tools to make messages available and influential to the target audience and other layers of audiences, including the public. Communication occurs in public relations when the sender creates and sends a message to the receiver, who understands what the message says and responds to the sender's message with a certain type of action. The receiver would either buy a product, advocate a cause, or vote for a particular candidate, depending on what the message was designed for. The message, of course, may have no impact at all.

At times, the effectiveness of the message "No Texting While Driving" has received mixed results, as some teen drivers end up getting themselves in car accidents while texting behind the wheel. The message is aimed at changing all drivers' attitudes if they think it is okay to send text messages while driving. The message is and will be repeatedly sent to the target audience until people see no more car accidents caused by the texting activity while driving. Making messages stronger and more powerful is what public relations practitioners see as an important but difficult part of their job. With the emergence and pervasiveness of social media, there are too many messages circulating around the world, and the public and target audiences do not have a chance to notice most of the messages. It has become the responsibility of public relations practitioners to boost message effectiveness in the most efficient ways.

CHAPTER SUMMARY AND REVIEW

1. Understand why communication is not a simple process.

2. Identify basic communication models.

3. Study characteristics of messages.

4. Explain effective ways of making messages influential.

5. Describe how the effectiveness of messages can be measured.

PUBLIC RELATIONS IN PRACTICE

FURTHER READING

PR Week's Awards For **Best PR Global Effort**

Winner: McDonald's and Golin
Campaign Name: Big Mac 50th Anniversary

Golin and McDonald's minted 6.2 million MacCoins with five unique designs celebrating the five decades of Big Mac and distributed the currency to more than 50 countries around the world. MacCoins debuted with a global piece of content shared in every participating country that showed them being minted and traveling through countries throughout the globe before eventually landing in the hands of an excited Big Mac fan.

Read more at
https://www.prweek.com/article/1579436/prweek-us-awards-2019-winners

6

Scholarly Research in the Field of Public Relations

The strategic process of public relations begins with research and ends with evaluation. It begins again with more research and repetition. One of the most famous public relations teachings is "know your audience first." How to know your audience? The answer is simple and clear: do research. Doing research is the first and most important step in completing a public relations assignment or campaign. It lays the groundwork for essential communication strategies. Research is the communication magic wand, which provides public relations practitioners with practical and useful strategic plans and executions.

Definitions of Research

What is research? Put simply, it is an attempt to understand (1) what is happening in the real world, (2) who is involved in a specific situation, and (3) how things can be resolved. More academically, research is a careful study conducted to find and report on new knowledge about a specific topic. Observing, reading, listening, and finding can be part of the research that people do every day. When people have something they are curious about, they find an answer either by asking their friends or searching online. This is research. Making an attempt to find an answer to the question is a clear way of describing what research is. Research usually needs a goal and an effort to discover things, but this isn't always the case. For example, if a person heard about new information while flipping through television channels and decided to use the information to reach a decision, then the person did research in an informal fashion. People gather information on purpose (or receive new information by chance) every day. They are all researchers in terms of acquiring information or discovering things to use in their lives.

An informal way of doing research is quick and spontaneous. People simply use Google. By contrast, formal research is usually conducted by professional researchers. Formal research uses two types of methods: one is formative research and the other is evaluative research. The former is carried out prior to any public relations project or campaign, whereas the latter is carried out after the campaign to evaluate outcomes for better strategies. These types are specifically used for public relations practitioners. Thus questions arise: Why do they conduct research, and what do they try to find out? Here are some examples:

- How effective is public relations on the Internet, radio, TV, or in print?

- How many journalists will find online press releases attractive and useful?

- What kind of corporate messages should CEOs communicate with the target audience?

- How many employees will think their company should improve inside communication, and what will be the best method to do so?

- How do we deal with criticism when a corporation makes a mistake or engages in misconduct?

- Which celebrity should be hired as a company's spokesperson?

- Which age group will be most affected by a new consumer service?

- How do we use social media to promote sustainable business products in the state of Montana?

- Why aren't more public relations interns included in the decision-making process?

Such questions demonstrate that public relations practitioners must investigate a wide range of people and issues in society. After conducting research to find answers to these questions, public relations practitioners, based on what they found, informed top managers (executives) of the research findings. Supervisors and CEOs reflected on the findings on organizational policy decisions and formulated new strategies to enhance performance and profits. For example, research by *PR Week* found that the web-sites of the top-100 companies listed on the London Stock Exchange were managed poorly in regard to communication effectiveness. According to the research, "One in three did not even state what their business did on the homepage, and only five percent clearly articulated their strategy business model."[1] The research also found that more than half of the websites failed to provide "a description on the positive reasons to work for the company." Thanks to such research findings, the companies acknowledged that they failed to make the most of their websites, although "the website is one of the few channels through which a company can tell its corporate story and should be seen as an opportunity to engage and influence their diverse stakeholder communities, to deepen their understanding of the business, and to build trust and confidence in their brand."[2] Research findings result in improving shortcomings in organizational management issues.

---

1   Michelle Perrett, "FTSE 100 Companies Do Not Communicate Well on Their Websites, Research Shows," *PR Week*, http://www.prweek.com/article/1339217/ftse100-companies-not-communicate-websites-research-shows.

2   Perrett, "FTSE 100 Companies."

Simple Research Procedures with the Possibility of Jeopardizing Credibility

There are five simple processes for doing research:

1. *Searching.* Finding basic information or investigating a matter through web search engines, such as Google, Bing, and Yahoo.

2. *Observing.* Identifying human behavior and behavioral patterns by watching and listening carefully.

3. *Generalizing.* Drawing a general conclusion from specific observations of humans or creatures in a given setting during a particular period of time.

4. *Reasoning.* Thinking about the general conclusion, drawn from the generalizing process in a logical, sensible way.

5. *Evaluating.* Concluding and deciding a systematic determination of a subject's merit, worth, and significance.

A public relations practitioner would conduct research with these processes. For example, if she hoped to investigate what kind of impression Hispanic college students in the United States have of cars, she would stop by several American college campuses to conduct research. First, she would google to discover which college campuses have many Hispanic students. After googling, she would choose one college campus and observe student parking lots to see what cars Hispanic students drive. In the process of observation, she would see many Hispanic students getting in and out of Dodge Challengers, Ford Mustangs, and Chevrolet Camaros on campus. She would generalize that Hispanic college students in the United States have good impressions of muscle cars. After seeing their cars with her two eyes, she would conclude that Hispanic college students are proud of their muscle cars because they believe the concept of "you are what you drive." In her reasoning process, she would also assume that their parents were wealthy and do not mind financially supporting their children studying at college. In sum, she would think that Hispanic students are proud of driving muscle cars with strong images on campus. With her research findings, she could recommend that muscle carmakers enhance promotional programs for catering to Hispanic students on college campuses nationwide.

Does her research represent a good quality investigation? When public relations practitioners do research, they need to find trustable, valid facts, not weak and easy guesses based on simple observations. On her way to the research conclusion, she made some errors. First, she reached the conclusion by observing only one college campus among thousands. How can one campus possibly represent all the campuses in the United States? Second, she generalized that all Hispanic college students and their families are strong and rich because they drive muscle cars. Do all Hispanic students drive muscle cars? What about those who do not have cars? Aren't Hispanic students from different countries, such as Mexico, Colombia, Honduras, Venezuela, and so on? What about Hispanic American students? Third, she assumed and reasoned that all Hispanic students have rich parents. What about their spouses or grandparents? And, finally, she thought all Hispanic students would believe the shallow stereotype of feeling superior by driving muscle cars. Such errors raise doubts about credibility in the research, which is categorized as informal and anybody's everyday research. The research ended up having flaws from the mere observation.

Professional Research Methods in Public Relations

A number of differences exist between informal research and formal research: formal research is more systematic, scientific, complicated, unbiased, and concerned about accuracy, validity, and reliability than informal research is. Formal research in public relations is based on the social scientific approach. This approach includes specific methods that can reduce the risk of inaccurate observation by using evidence and samples systematically. Public relations practitioners prefer to conduct formal research before setting any programs in motion.

Qualitative research and quantitative research are two formal methods of public relations research. Qualitative research, designed to discover a target audience's range of behavior and attitudes, provides an understanding of how the audience members think or feel about a particular topic or issue. It uses in-depth studies of the target audience to describe what they want and how they feel. In doing so, it achieves a detailed understanding of detailed information about the audience member's behavior and attitudes. In contrast, quantitative research is used to generalize a larger audience's behavioral patterns and thoughts. It analyzes data statistically for generalized results. While qualitative research is used to gain insights into the causes of issues and topics to find underlying reasons and motivations, quantitative research aims to generalize reliable results from a sample to a particular group of population.

Both research methods are derived from the foundation of database research techniques. Whether choosing qualitative or quantitative research, public relations practitioners also learn from already existing research information. Using the outcomes of existing research information from the media and electronic databases helps public relations practitioners design their research plan and choose one or both of the research methods. Popular sources for the database information technique in public relations include the following:

- Institute for Public Relations (www.instituteforpr.com)
- Council of Public Relations Firms (www.prfirms.org)
- Public Relations Society of America (www.prsa.org)
- Roper Center for Public Opinion Research (www.ropercenter.uconn.edu)
- National Newspaper Publishers Association (www. http://nnpa.org)
- National Center for Health Statistics (www.cdc.gov/nchs/default.htm)
- Center for Media and Democracy's PR Watch (http://www.prwatch.org/)
- The Institute for PR (www.instituteforpr.org)
- Survey Sampling, Inc. website (www.worldopinion.com)
- National Association of Government Communicators (www.nagc.com)
- Pew Research Center for the People & the Press (www.people-press.org)
- Society of American Business Editors and Writers (www.sabew.org)
- Social Media Association (www.socialmedia.org)
- US Census Bureau (www.census.gov)

Table 6.1 compares the two types of research.

TABLE 6.1 Qualitative versus Quantitative Research

	Qualitative Research	Quantitative Research
Objective	To offer an in-depth understanding of human behavior and attitudes, including underlying motivations and thoughts	To quantify data and generalize valid and reliable results to represent larger populations
Sample	Usually a small number of selected audience groups	Usually a large number of audience groups that represent the audience members' behavioral patterns and thoughts
Data Collection	Loosely structured techniques, such as in-depth interviews, focus groups, ethnography, and field observation	Structured techniques, such as surveys, content analysis, and telephone or Internet polls
Data Analysis	Researchers' subjective analysis	Statistical data, considered scientific and objective
Outcome	Exploratory explanation about why and how the audience has such attitudes and responds to the issue. The explanation offers an initial understanding for further public relations activity or programs	Valid and conclusive recommendation for organizations to implement activity or program

Public Relations Research Process

A public relations practitioner first decides to use either a qualitative or quantitative research method. If the practitioner decided to go with qualitative research, he will use in-depth interviews, focus groups, or ethnography. In contrast, if he chooses quantitative research, he will adopt the use of surveys, content analysis, or telephone/online polls. There are four important factors that have a great influence on choosing a public relations research method:

1. *Monitoring.* Define public relations issues and opportunities.

2. *Goal.* With the defined issues and opportunities, the next step is to set goals for public relations research operations. For example, if the organization's goal is to enhance sales of Greek yogurt among high school students, what kind of flavors and celebrity endorsements should be produced? The goal provides clear instruction on the research focus.

3. *Budget.* How much money will the research cost? How much can the organization afford? What percentage of the research budget is recommended? Public relations practitioners plan the scale of research depending on the size of the budget (e.g., whether they survey 10 students or 1,000 students).

4. *Timetables.* Any research should be done within targeted dates. The organization needs research findings to plan the next business operation. With the yogurt example, if it was found that high school athletes like more funky flavors of Greek yogurt, then the organization may develop barbecue- or wasabi-flavored yogurt endorsed by athletes.

After all factors are considered, the practitioner chooses one of the research methods.

Qualitative Research Method

If qualitative research is chosen, then the practitioner would do either in-depth interviews, focus groups (off-line and online), or ethnography.

- *In-Depth Interview.* Imagine what journalists do for a living. They find news sources, usually human beings, to report stories. Public relations practitioners also interview people to understand what they think and want. Public relations research interviews tend to take the form of an in-depth interview between the practitioner and the interviewee in an effort to gain more comprehensive information that cannot be usually obtained by observation alone. The in-depth interview needs a face-to-face relationship. One practitioner meets with one interviewee, who provides important knowledge and information. The practitioner can meet with as many interviewees as he wants until valuable information is obtained.

  In-depth interviews commonly include three items of preparation: time, place, and questions. The practitioner lets the interviewee choose the time and place, but the questions are created by the practitioner. While an interview is being conducted, the practitioner records or films the interview. As an in-depth interview lasts about an hour or more, the practitioner concentrates on getting more detailed and insightful information by trying not to get off track. Because the main purpose of the in-depth interview is to elicit high-level knowledge and information about a specific topic, the group of interviewees is normally limited to industrial or academic professionals.

- *Ethnography.* This is the study of the routines of a special group through close observation and interpretation. This research method is grounded in observation, but it requires public relations practitioners to assimilate themselves into the group's life, meaning that they need to become participants and observers. As a participant, the practitioner is one of the insiders in the group who tries to imitate members' routines. As an observer, the practitioner carefully records and interprets the group members' activities. In so doing, the practitioner is able to obtain information about what the group of people does in natural settings. For example, if the practitioner wants to conduct research on how members of an environmental group communicate with each other when they raise awareness about deforestation through provocative performances, the practitioner will join the group and function as one of the group members until the ethnographic research is over. The practitioner observes and participates in the activities while considering such questions as the following: (1) What motivates their activities? (2) How do they spread their messages to the public? (3) What are their main communication devices? (4) What's their decision-making process? (5) Who is in charge of instructing members' activities, and how do other members respond to the instructions? (6) How long does it take a message to be conveyed to all members? (7) What beliefs and attitudes do they have toward a certain subject?

  The practitioner aims to investigate and find out how a specific group of people communicate and what they pursue. The processes of ethnography are to (1) find a group that public relations practitioners are interested in; (2) observe the group members; (3) record observations, including their communication activities; (4) report the characteristics of the group; and (5) use the findings for the objective. The process can also be applied to investigating consumer behavior. Public relations practitioners can visit homes or offices of consumers to observe how they use products and to listen to consumers' complaints or compliments about the products.

In other words, ethnography allows the practitioner to view consumers' behavior in a natural setting. However, ethnography has some flaws in conducting public relations research. First, when members of the group recognize that they are being observed by the practitioner, they often change the way they usually behave. As a result, they tend to act in a different way. Second, the practitioner is prone to limited exposure to the entirety of group situations. Since the practitioner can hardly interact with all members of the group and participate in all activities, only some of the members and activities are observed to represent the group's entire situation. This can result in generating invaluable or partially biased research findings.

- *Focus Groups (Off-Line).* Imagine a group of people in a room gathering to discuss their thoughts and opinions about a particular product, service, or idea. The group traditionally consists of 6 to 12 people who have been selected to discuss their unfiltered opinions. Public relations practitioners view the people who join the focus group as research participants. Since participants should have something in common to represent similarity of attitudes toward a specific subject, the practitioner categorizes by age, gender, occupation, income, and so on. In a similar way, focus group participants can also be selected depending on their previous experience, current interests, consumption patterns, and family characteristics. In other words, focus group research is principally efficient in targeting certain demographic groups.

  For example, if the practitioner wants to investigate how consumers think about a laundry detergent container, participants of the group will be selected according to their laundry routines. Housewives or stay-at-home husbands are most likely to be qualified for the group. Another example is that ten female college students taking the same physical education class are asked to evaluate yoga pants to identify if there's anything to be improved in terms of fabric, fit, design, and length. The focus group research is also used for predicting political results. For example, college female students aged between 21 and 23 may be selected to express their opinions on the gubernatorial candidates in a state. A process of selecting and recruiting participants should be articulated, as the group can represent the entire specific population for a credible research outcome.

Guidelines for Organizing Focus Groups

Focus group research is popular among public relations practitioners and marketing professionals because it helps them refine reputation, image, and branding. There are seven guidelines for organizing focus groups, according to Glenn Blank, a professor at Lehigh University:[3]

1. *Define the Purpose (i.e., Objectives) of the Focus Group.* This has to be clear and specific. The more defined the objective, the easier the rest of the process.

2. *Establish a Time Line.* A focus group cannot be developed overnight. The planning has to start several weeks ahead of the actual session, experts say six to eight weeks realistically. Public relations practitioners take enough time to identify the participants, develop and test the questions, and locate a site.

---

3 Glenn Blank, "Conducting a Focus Group," Lehigh University, http://www.cse.lehigh.edu/~glennb/mm/Focus-Groups.htm.

3. ***Identify the Participants.*** Determine how many participants public relations practitioners need and how many to invite. Develop a list of key attributes to seek participants based on the purpose of the focus group. Using the list of attributes, brainstorm possible participants. Secure the names and contact information, finalize the list, and send invitations.

4. ***Generate the Questions.*** Because a focus group will last for little more than one or two hours, public relations practitioners will only have time for four to seven questions. They may include one or two introductory or warm-up questions and then get to the more serious questions that get at the heart of the purpose.

5. ***Develop a Script.*** Generating questions is a prelude to developing a more detailed script for the focus group. Plan on a one- to two-hour time frame. A minimum of one hour is recommended because the process requires some time for opening and closing remarks, as well as at least one or two questions. Be cautious not to exceed two hours.

6. ***Select a Facilitator.*** A focus group facilitator should be able to deal tactfully with outspoken group members, keep the discussion on track, and make sure every participant is heard. Public relations practitioners serve as facilitators in many cases.

7. ***Choose the Location.*** Public relations practitioners need a setting that can accommodate the participants where they will feel comfortable expressing their opinions. The final location can be chosen after asking the following questions: What message does the setting send? Is it corporate, upscale, cozy, informal, sterile, or inviting? Does the setting encourage conversation? How will the setting affect the information gathered? Can the space comfortably accommodate up to 15 people (6 to 12 participants plus facilitators)? Is it easily accessible (consider access for people with disabilities, safety, transportation, parking, etc.)? Once decided, reserve the location if necessary.

In essence, the group provides the practitioner with valuable ideas on how to develop, name, or package a new product or service.

Online Focus Groups

With the development of online communication, public relations practitioners tend to conduct online focus group research that can eliminate some traditional procedures. This method allows research participants to participate from anywhere as long as they remain online. The participants are connected through online communication software to express their opinions and attitudes toward a specific product, service, or idea. This online research helps the practitioner save lots of money in comparison to off-line focus groups, with no actual space required. Emma Borochoff, a marketing expert, explains the advantages of online focus groups:[4]

- As there is no geographic restriction, public relations practitioners can recruit even international participants.

- As there is no physical place needed, as many as 100 people can be invited to an online focus group.

- As participants are connected online, and they do not see each other, they can be more honest about their opinions and attitudes toward a specific subject.

- In an online environment, it's less likely that one person will dominate the discussion or influence others' reactions.

- If products or services are based online (such as online games and online shopping), then the participants feel more comfortable and savvier in giving feedback.

However, online focus groups also have weaknesses: a physical product cannot be touched, sensed, smelled, or felt unless all participants are given the product by mail. In addition, the identification of participants is relatively hard to be checked, as online anonymity remains.

Quantitative Research Method

Designing Surveys

Quantitative research uses structured techniques such as a survey (including telephone and Internet) to obtain more reliable, objective research outcomes. The most important part of quantitative research is to create a list of survey questions, also known as the questionnaire. Producing good survey questions means nearly everything in public relations research; it is a form of art. Surveys include two types of questions: open-ended and closed-ended. The former asks survey respondents to express their thoughts and opinions, whereas the latter asks them to choose answers provided by the questionnaire. In other words, open-ended questions allow the respondents to give short essay answers, while closed-ended questions ask respondents to answer from multiple-choice questions. The question, "How do you describe the packaging of iPhone 11?" is an example of an open-ended question. The question, "Who do you trust most: the Pope, Oprah Winfrey, Tom Brady, or Bill Gates?" is an example of a closed-ended question.

---

4   Emma Borochoff, "Online Focus Group," https://blog.remesh.ai/should-you-use-online-focus-groups

In constructing research questions, eight guidelines are suggested in the book *Mass Media Research: An Introduction.*[5]

1. ***Make Questions Clear.*** The question, "If you didn't have a premium channel, would you consider PPV?" is less clear than "if you didn't have a pay channel like Showtime, would you consider a service where you pay a small amount for individual movies or specials you watch?"

2. ***Keep Questions Short.*** Short, concise, and clear questions are best.

3. ***Remember the Purposes of the Research.*** For example, if the occupations of respondents are not relevant to the purpose of the survey, then the questionnaire should exclude that part.

4. ***Do Not Ask Double-Barreled Questions.*** The question, "How satisfied are you with your pay and job conditions?" requires two answers for pay and conditions. Ask a question seeking one answer.

5. ***Avoid Biased Words or Terms.*** The question, "Would you like to spend your time dating your spouse or just taking a nap?" contains a negatively biased tone with the word *just*.

6. ***Avoid Leading Questions.*** The question, "As everybody drinks coffee in America, do you drink a cup of coffee?" suggests that the respondent answer yes to be a part of the group.

7. ***Do Not Use Questions That Ask for Highly Detailed Information.*** The question, "Over the last three years, how much time did you spend on Internet surfing?" makes it impossible to receive a precise answer.

8. ***Avoid Potentially Embarrassing Questions Unless They Are Absolutely Necessary.*** The question, "How often do you fart?" will be answered with "none of your business."

Box 6.1 is an example of a public relations questionnaire.[6]

After completing the questionnaire, the public relations practitioner conducts a survey, which is viewed as a popular quantitative research form:

- Survey research is "a method for collecting and analyzing data via highly structured and often very detailed questionnaires in order to obtain information from large numbers of respondents presumed to be representative of a specific population."[7] In simple words, public relations practitioners who use the survey research method ask individuals things to collect information, known as data, through already-written questions for statistical analysis. Surveys are associated with the goal of getting information about certain groups of people—consumers or audiences—to ascertain the following: (1) What do people think and know? (2) What do people plan to do? (3) What do people believe in? (4) What are people's attitudes? (5) What do people want to possess in the near future? Although the survey research method seems unlikely to be different from other research methods regarding research questions and objectives, this method has several unique differences and advantages:

  1. The cost of surveys is relatively cheaper than other research methods, as public relations practitioners can use mail, telephone, and the Internet.

---

5 Roger D. Wimmer and Joseph R. Dominick, *Mass Media Research: An Introduction, p. 46* (Belmont, CA: Wadsworth Publishing, 2011),

6 Survey Monkey. "Public Relations Survey," https://www.surveymonkey.com/r/thcpublicrelationssurvey

BOX 6.1

Instructions: Check (✓) if applicable.

■ Gender
Female (   ) Male (   )

■ Age
21–30 (   ) 31–40 (   ) 41–50 (   ) 51–60 (   ) 61–70 (   )

■ Do you work in:
a PR firm (   ) an in-house PR department (   ) other (   )

■ Is your current role in
government (   ) NGO (   ) corporation (   ) other (   )

■ Which of the following activities do you perform in your current position?
monitoring press (   ) writing press releases (   ) lobbying (   ) other (   )

■ Rate, from 1 to 10 in order of importance, the characteristics needed for a successful career in public relations.
organization skills (   ) integrity (   ) team player (   ) creativity (   ) persuasiveness (   )

■ How acceptable are the following activities among your peers?
(1) totally unacceptable (2) practiced but ethically questionable (3) acceptable
Entertaining a journalist over drinks or dinner (   )
Exaggerating experience on a CV or application form to get a job (   )
Using personal relationships for professional gain (   )
Funding a bogus "grassroots" campaign (   )

■ Your highest academic qualification:
high school (   ) college (   ) graduate school (   ) PhD (   )

■ Do you have any industry-related qualifications?
Yes (   ) No (   )

2. The process of data collection is simpler than other research types. Survey research with the same questions allows gathering answers from a variety of people without categorizing participants by demographic differences, such as age, gender, race, education, and income.

3. Surveys are not limited to a particular region because they can be conducted all around the world with communication devices.

Surveys come in two popular forms: descriptive and analytical (explanatory). The descriptive survey attempts to offer the current conditions and attitudes of a group of people at a specific moment of time. For example, public relations practitioners conduct a survey to find out how satisfying or disappointing a customer's hotel visit was. Television companies use surveys to determine how popular their shows are and what content their viewers want to see more of. The analytical survey seeks to discover and explain why a current situation exists. This form of survey focuses on finding answers to the "why" question or examining the cause-and-effect relationship between certain kinds of behavior and characteristics of people. For example, public relations practitioners might attempt to discover if a corporation's $1 million donation to a children's hospital has something to do with an increase in the corporation's positive images. Both types of surveys attempt to understand the way people behave and examine any relationship in human behavior, which can be motivated by social, economic, psychological, political, and cultural reasons.

Sampling

For public relations practitioners to conduct surveys, they need to select a group of people who can represent a survey population. The representative group is called a sample, and it must represent the survey population; if not, then the survey results can hardly be credible. The process of finding a representative group of people is called sampling (Figure 6.1). As obtaining a sample is an important part of surveys, public relations practitioners commonly use two approaches: random sampling (also known as probability sampling) and nonrandom sampling (also known as nonprobability sampling).

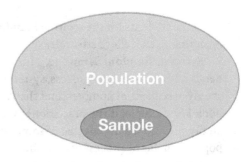

FIGURE 6.1 Sampling.

RANDOM/PROBABILITY SAMPLING

For public relations research involved in selecting a group of people for surveys, the process of selection is best done through random sampling. In other words, all members of a group have the same probability of being selected by chance to answer a survey. There are four different kinds of random sampling.

Simple Random Sampling. Each person in the group has an equal or known chance of being chosen. If a public relations practitioner wants to research occupations of those who go to see a baseball game, then the practitioner first has to decide how many people should be asked, and if 100 people are selected, the practitioner will choose seat numbers in his or her mind. For example, a list of seat numbers can be randomly chosen, such as No. 4, No. 19, No. 102, and the list goes on. With the randomly chosen seat numbers from the whole stadium, the practitioner goes to the seats and asks people about their jobs. In a similar sense, election polling uses the same sampling. As counting all voters is physically impossible, thousands of voters are asked about their favorite candidates. With simple random sampling, there is an equal chance (probability) of selecting survey respondents.

Stratified Random Sampling. All members of the group are divided into smaller groups (or strata) that are relevant to members' shared attributes or characteristics, such as age, gender, race, and experience. In stratified random sampling, the practitioner takes a random sample from each stratum. For example, if the practitioner wants to find out what dating apps college students use on their iPhones, the practitioner first needs to learn college enrollment rates by ethnicity. If the national enrollment statistics says that whites are 40 percent, blacks are 30 percent, Asians are 20 percent, and Hispanics are 10 percent, then the practitioner will choose 40 white college students, 30 black students, 20 Asian students, and 10

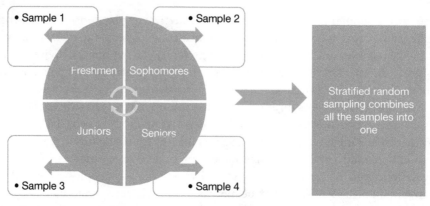

FIGURE 6.2 Stratified random sampling.

Hispanic students for the stratified random sampling (Figure 6.2) to list the most popular online dating apps among US college students.

Systemic Random Sampling. This is similar to simple random sampling, but instead of the spontaneous number-choosing process, systemic random sampling chooses every nth person. People in a group are given sequential numbers, and then the practitioner chooses every nth number to be in the sampling pool. For example, if the practitioner wants to research the favorite talk shows of 2,000 employees of an organization, a decent size of sampling—maybe 200 people—will be chosen to represent the entire population. In the process of choosing 200 people, the practitioner decides to randomly select every fifth name on the list of 2,000 employees.

Clustered Sampling. If large populations are spread out across a wide geographic area or among many different organizations, then the practitioner chooses clustered sampling (Figure 6.3). For example, if the practitioner wants to know how many times retired people shop for groceries nationwide, he randomly selects states, randomly selects cities and towns within those states, randomly selects retirement communities, and randomly selects retired people within each community.

All four types of random sampling allow every member of a group to have a chance of being selected equally. Thus random sampling is also called probability sampling, in which public relations practitioners

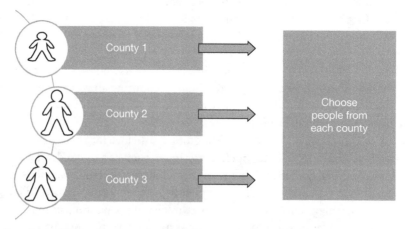

FIGURE 6.3 Clustered sampling.

rely on random choices or chances in selecting a sample like a lottery procedure. On the other hand, nonprobability sampling does not involve random selection and is known as nonrandom sampling.

NONRANDOM/NONPROBABILITY SAMPLING

When public relations research seeks speed and convenience and does not require a sampling frame, nonrandom sampling is chosen. The following are different kinds of nonrandom sampling.

Purposive Sampling. Public relations practitioners select a sample with a purpose in mind, and specific characteristics of people are carefully selected for research. The sampling is designed to focus on the specific people who are best able to answer the research questions. For example, if the practitioner wants to investigate where soccer moms buy lipstick and what color they like, the practitioner needs to go to the sideline of a soccer field to question soccer moms about their lipstick purchasing behavior. The soccer moms are purposely chosen for this research on two conditions: they are willing to talk, and they can be representative of soccer moms nationwide.

Convenience Sampling. Known as available sampling, people are selected because they are available for research. For example, a college professor asks her students questions in a classroom setting or observes their activities for her research. The students in the setting are an available sample. Journalists use convenience sampling when interviewing people who are available for a story. Some say convenience sampling is less likely to represent the population because of its lack of objectivity; respondents consist of only those who happened to be in the research venue.

Quota Sampling. Public relations practitioners choose a sample that represents certain characteristics in proportion to their prevalence in the population. This sampling is similar to stratified random sampling, but quota sampling is used to nonrandomly select the required number of members from each stratum. For example, if a public relations practitioner wants to research why people buy avocados, in a sample size of 100 people, 50 males and 50 females, will be selected in accordance with gender proportions in the United States. The practitioner will find any available 50 female and 50 male participants without considering their different characteristics.

Snowball Sampling. When public relations practitioners have a hard time finding an optimal sample of people, they contact a few people who can help find qualified participants for research. This sampling is useful for hard-to-reach or hard-to-identify populations, such as members of cult or Alcoholics Anonymous groups. Members in such a special setting can be reached through referrals. For example, once the practitioner has the chance to meet with a drug dealer through a friend or acquaintance, the dealer can invite the practitioner to a meeting with other drug dealers. The process of snowballing begins.

SURVEY DISTRIBUTION

After a sample is determined for a survey, the practitioners use telephones or the Internet to distribute the questionnaire.

Telephone Survey. Because of annoying telemarketers and telemarketing frauds, people do not want to talk to on the phone, especially when they are asked to answer several questions that are irrelevant to their lives. The skillful public relations practitioner, however, sets up strategies to convey the questions to respondents on the phone, such as (1) avoiding calls at busy times, (2) assuring that this is not a telemarketing call in the introduction, (3) reading the questions as worded, (4) repeating questions if necessary, and (5) thanking the respondent. Although many people tend to show their hostility on the phone, telephone surveys are still widely used in public relations research because the cost is likely to be lower and the response is faster, as opposed to sending questionnaires by mail, which is linked to low and slow response rates.

Internet Web Survey. According to the Pew Research Center, web surveys "use a host of multimedia elements such as having respondents view videos or listen to audio clips, which are not available to other survey modes."[8] This survey method has grown dramatically over the last 15 years, but "people with lower incomes, less education, living in rural areas or age sixty-five and older are underrepresented among Internet users and those with high-speed internet access."[9] To ensure a better result from online surveys, public relations practitioners send questionnaires via email or web survey links to chosen respondents. There is no doubt that online surveys have many advantages in comparison with other survey methods. Online surveys offer low costs, unlimited geographic access, 24/7 availability, and easy production. Online survey websites, such as SurveyMonkey, SurveyGizmo, Qualtrics, and eSurv, can help researchers create their own online surveys.

Research in Public Relations

There exists a variety of research types, methods, and kinds in public relations. Each of them has its advantages and disadvantages, but public relations practitioners make an effort to obtain accurate and credible research outcomes, which are used to offer profound strategic information for organizational operations. As noted, the practice of public relations always begins with research. Since most college students are required to take a research class at an upper level, they need to pay attention to the class for their future career practice.

Research in public relations offers new and fresh information about human behavior. This means research plays a critical role in making decisions that are directly related to organizational management. Top management acknowledges the importance of the research and makes informed decisions about how to proceed based on research findings. More importantly, new information provides public relations practitioners and their organizations with new opportunities for operational success. Research will never die in the practice of public relations.

FIGURE CREDITS
lmg. 6.1: Copyright © 2009 Depositphotos/ISergey.
lmg. 6.2: Copyright © 2014 Depositphotos/monkeybusiness.
lmg. 6.3: Copyright © 2020 by Haymarket Media Group Ltd.

---

8   "Internet Surveys," Pew Research Center, http://www.people-press.org/methodology/collecting-survey-data/internet-surveys/.

9   Pew Research Center, "Internet Surveys."

CHAPTER SUMMARY AND REVIEW

1. Understand why research is important in public relations.
2. Identify the basic processes of conducting research.
3. Study the difference between qualitative and quantitative research methods.
4. Explain random and nonrandom sampling.
5. Describe how to produce a survey.

PUBLIC RELATIONS IN PRACTICE

FURTHER READING

PR Week's Awards For **Best PR Consumer Launch**

Winner: IHOP and DeVries Global
Campaign Name: IHOb: The Day IHOP Flipped the Script

For a move that showed consumers how serious the chain was about its burgers, IHOP rebranded as IHOb and kicked off a two-month campaign with a tweet: "For 60 pancaking years, we've been IHOP. Now, we're flipping our name to IHOb. Find out what it could b on 6.11.18. #IHOb."

Read more at
https://www.prweek.com/article/1579436/prweek-us-awards-2019-winners

7

Ethical Issues of Public Relations

People make a living by participating in programs that are socially constructed. They try to find a job and keep it. They try to avoid unemployment to live a good life. Life requires action, which is part of everybody's daily decision-making process, leading to questions such as, "What do I do?" "Why do I have to do it?" and "How can I do it?" People deal with such questions to find the proper course of action for survival in societal settings. Why do they ponder, and why do they ask before making a decision? The answer to such questions is that every action has consequences. People are guided to make a living by not disobeying the law. They are aware of social norms telling them not to get involved in any ethical and legal wrongdoings. The society believes that they are bound to know what is right and wrong.

The law is enforced by the government, and a violation of law leads to punishment. The law clarifies what is wrong and right in human action. In other words, the law places human action in a black-or-white zone. If a wrongful act is committed in the eyes of the law, then the person goes through a sentencing process. However, the consequences of human action are not all about being judged or evaluated by the law. It is rather about how people make decisions about their actions based on their own beliefs, perceptions, opinions, and values. There exists a gray area between black and white, and the gray area is guided and enlightened, not by the law but by ethics.

Ethics and Public Relations

Sociologist Raymond Baumhart asked businesspeople, "What does ethics mean to you?" They answered:[1]

- Ethics has to do with what my feelings tell me is right or wrong.
- Ethics has to do with my religious beliefs.
- Being ethical is doing what the law requires.
- Ethics consists of the standards of behavior our society accepts.
- I don't know what the word means.

Public relations practitioners work with or for businesspeople who regard ethics as either socially or personally incorporated standards of behavior that guide their businesses. More realistically, few people, including public relations practitioners, can fully explain what ethics is and how ethics affects their business practices. They agree that the practice of public relations should always be ethical, but the gray area in public relations sometimes forces them to make difficult decisions to advocate for their clients' or organizations' wrong behavior. The gray area represents ethical dilemmas in the practice of public relations.

Public relations practitioners, while doing their jobs, are faced with occasions when they must make ethical decisions to meet their clients' or organizations' interests and goals. To achieve them, some of the practitioners would be inclined to go with unethical practices to keep their jobs, as well as to satisfy their self-esteem. They claim that the old expression, "the end justifies the means," is an unwritten rule in the business world, and public relations often belongs to that world. Do public relations practitioners really need to lie to hang on to their jobs? A survey of 1,705 public relations practitioners found that "25 percent of them had lied on the job, and 61.8 percent were compromised in their work by being told a lie," and 44 percent did not have a clear concept of ethics.[2]

Public relations practitioners, in some cases, are forced to manipulate facts or lie to journalists and the public. These cases occur

- when the CEO orders the practitioner not to reveal the side effects of a product,
- when the client pressures the practitioner to spread fake information,
- when the supervisor asks the practitioner to exaggerate and sugarcoat information before sending it to journalists,
- when the practitioner feels pressured to accomplish bigger outcomes to keep the job,
- when the practitioner finds that competitors perform unethical public relations practices with no consequences, or
- when other practitioners say it is a part of the long customary practices used by members of the public relations community.

---

1   Claire Andre and Manuel Velasquez, "What Is Ethics?," Santa Clara University, http://www.scu.edu/ethics/publications/iie/v1n1/whatis.html.

2   George Gunset, "PR Professionals Take Issue with Lying Survey," *Chicago Tribune*, May 10, 2000, http://articles.chicagotribune.com/2000-05-10/business/0005100332_1_pr-week-interior-decorator-lying.

Negative Perceptions of Public Relations

In such circumstances, Joe Marconi, a public relations veteran, explained that the practice of public relations has acquired two negative perceptions. "One is the overused term *spin*," Marconi explained. "What should be telling the story to show the client in the best light has become synonymous with lying."[3] The second is part of the shadows of the Watergate scandal. Marconi added, "It was said then that the White House was full of lying PR guys, and that gave public relations a bad image that has stuck for a long time."[4] Since then, journalists and the public have referred to public relations practitioners as spin doctors, spinmeisters, or flacks.

All these pejorative terms describe public relations practitioners who try to convert negative publicity by promoting a favorable interpretation of the words or actions of an organization or a client. Some journalists still say things like, "His title is Director of Communications, but he is just a spin doctor."[5] The main reason journalists have hostile attitudes toward public relations practitioners is that the two different professions have different ethical standards when it comes to maintaining their job performance. Journalists are responsible for being objective with the public, whereas public relations practitioners are bound to advocate for the interests of a specific group of people and organizations. In other words, journalists serve the public, and they are expected to fulfill obligations that are in the public's best interest. Public relations practitioners, in contrast, serve the particular client or organization that pays them to build positive attitudes and mutual relationships with the target audience.

Ethics for Journalists

Public relations practitioners consider their relationships with journalists significant since journalists are capable of conveying public relations practitioners' messages to a massive number of people. The practitioner needs to maintain a good relationship with the journalist. Understanding the journalist's ethical principles is a starting point to avoid offending journalistic pride rooted in ethical conduct. The practitioner should know that the derogatory terms describing public relations practitioners are derived from journalists' pride about their ethical job performance, although many of them often engage in biased and manipulative reporting, which is politically and personally motivated. The journalist believes that he

or she acts in accordance with personal and journalistic ethical standards to provide objective and unbiased information to the public. The journalist's ethical principles are found in the code of ethics proposed by the Society of Professional Journalists. The code has four principles:[6]

1. ***Seek Truth and Report It.*** Journalists should be honest, fair, and courageous in gathering, reporting, and interpreting information.

2. ***Minimize Harm.*** Ethical journalists treat sources, subjects, and colleagues as human beings deserving of respect.

---

3   Gunset, "PR Professionals."
4   Gunset, "PR Professionals."
5   "Spin doctor," Dictionary.com, http://www.thefreedictionary.com/spin+doctor.
6   "Code of Ethics," Society of Professional Journalists, https://www.spj.org/pdf/ethicscode.pdf.

3. ***Act Independently.*** Journalists should be free of obligation to any interest other than the public's right to know.

4. ***Be accountable.*** Journalists are accountable to their readers, listeners, viewers, and each other.

As the code suggests, the journalist is responsible for the public's right to know by providing objective and truthful information. The journalist's first loyalty is to the public, advocating accuracy and fairness.

Ethics for Public Relations Practitioners

As surveys found, many public relations practitioners and businesspeople confessed that it is hard to pinpoint what ethics is and how it is applied to their work. The Institute for Public Relations defines ethics in public relations as follows:[7]

> In the public relations discipline, ethics includes values such as honesty, openness, loyalty, fair-mindedness, respect, integrity, and forthright communication. This definition of public relations ethics goes far beyond the olden days of "flacking for space" or spinning some persuasive message, but this view is not shared by everyone.

Ethics signifies that humans conduct their behavior according to values, such as honesty, integrity, equality, and respect in the social environment. Ethics can only be embodied and realized by actual behavior when it is dictated by detailed guidelines for a specific field of practice. The public relations field, like journalism, has its own ethics guidelines to help public relations practitioners have a better understanding of the practice in the field. According to the Institute for Public Relations, ethics for public relations practice depends heavily on the major professional associations whose members agree to abide by a code of ethics. This means that there is a wide range of codes of ethics, introduced by many public relations organizations. These codes of ethics are written either to itemize a list of activities that public relations practitioners should not do or to enforce a set of ethical principles that they should obey in practice. Although there are no absolute, omnipotent guidelines that dominate public relations ethical standards, the ethical guidelines of PRSA and the code of ethics of the Council of Public Relations Firms are the industry's most widely used ethical codes.

PRSA states that ethical practice is the most important obligation of its members.[8]

PRSA MEMBER CODE OF ETHICS

This statement presents the core values of PRSA members and, more broadly, of the public relations profession. These values provide the foundation for the Member Code of Ethics and set the industry standard for the professional practice of public relations. These values are the

7   Shannon Bowen, "Ethics and Public Relations," Institute for Public Relations, October 30, 2007, http://www. instituteforpr.org/ethics-and-public-relations/.

8   "PRSA Code of Ethics," PRSA, https://www.prsa.org/ethics/code-of-ethics/.

fundamental beliefs that guide our behaviors and decision-making processes. We believe our professional values are vital to the integrity of the profession as a whole.

ADVOCACY
We serve the public interest by acting as responsible advocates for those we represent.
We provide a voice in the marketplace of ideas, facts, and viewpoints to aid informed public debate.

HONESTY
We adhere to the highest standards of accuracy and truth in advancing the interests of those we represent and in communicating with the public.

EXPERTISE
We acquire and responsibly use specialized knowledge and experience. We advance the profession through continued professional development, research, and education. We build mutual understanding, credibility, and relationships among a wide array of institutions and audiences.

INDEPENDENCE
We provide objective counsel to those we represent. We are accountable for our actions.

LOYALTY
We are faithful to those we represent, while honoring our obligation to serve the public interest.

FAIRNESS
We deal fairly with clients, employers, competitors, peers, vendors, the media, and the general public. We respect all opinions and support the right of free expression.

THE COUNCIL OF PUBLIC RELATIONS FIRMS' CODE OF ETHICS AND PRINCIPLES[9]

We adhere to the highest standards of ethics in the public relations profession.
Members and their employees will be honest and accurate when recording time charges and seeking reimbursement of expenses

We protect the integrity of client information.
Member firms will serve their clients by applying their fullest capability to achieve each client's business objectives.

We honor our role in society.
The professionalism and objectivity of our firms helps clients engage in that discourse, and clients turn to us for our counsel and assistance to vigorously pursue their organizational goals in educating or persuading audiences that matter most to them.

(Continued)

9   "THE PR COUNCIL CODE OF ETHICS AND PRINCIPLES," Council of PR Firms, https://prcouncil.net/join/the-pr-council-code-of-ethics-and-principles/

We are committed to accuracy.
In communicating with the public and media, member firms will maintain total accuracy and truthfulness.

We are conscientious stewards of taxpayer dollars.
Working for federal, state, and local governmental entities involves a unique responsibility, as it is paid for by taxpayers' dollars and, like the rest of our work, must uphold the public trust at all times.

We are committed to agency practices that increase society's confidence in the practice of public relations. We do not retain or compensate journalists to represent client interests in their media. We expect bloggers and other online influencers to be honest and accurate.

As the two codes of ethics demonstrate, public relations practitioners are expected to serve as advocates in an honest and accurate manner. Becoming an advocate requires a series of qualifications and skills.

Advocacy in Public Relations

An advocate refers to a person who supports a particular cause or policy on behalf of someone or some entities. In some countries, an advocate is used as the alternative term for "lawyer." In short, an advocate is obligated to promote the interests of a particular group of people or organizations. Public relations practitioners are advocates who serve those who hire or pay them. They are not civil servants or journalists, who are supposed to serve the public. Once they begin the role of advocate, the interests of the client or organization are valued above anything and anyone.

The practitioner first needs to listen to his client and organization to recognize what they want and need. The practitioner applies his knowledge to achieve his client's or organization's objectives while trying to maintain accuracy and truthfulness when communicating with the target audience and journalists. Considering these objectives, the practitioner's priority, like lawyers in the role of an advocate, is to protect his client's or organization's privilege, including personal or business secrets. In so doing, the practitioner provides productive and trustable advice that helps the client or organization make informed choices. After a certain decision or act has been taken, the practitioner monitors the responses of the target audience while being prepared to defend the client and organization against any possible criticism or attacks.

Today, it is essential for public relations practitioners to strike a balance between advocating for the client and engaging in fair and balanced communication with the public and media. Some unethical practices in public relations throughout its history have produced negative views about public relations because of the heavy emphasis on advocacy for the client over honesty and fairness to the public. To address such negative views, public relations practitioners take a balanced approach to the role of advocate. They try to find a way of achieving the client's objectives, which ultimately results in benefiting the interest of the public. The emphasis on advocacy for the client is supposed to be planned with the concern for the public interest.

Advocacy is the act of supporting a cause or policy, and it is linked with virtually every industry. Public relations practitioners are expected to have different skill sets that are customized for the industry they represent. If a public relations practitioner works for the in-house communication department of a construction company, the practitioner should know specific information about construction, such as industry terms, regulations, laws, systems, and any other detailed knowledge related to the company and industry. The practitioner was hired based on communication skills, but the practitioner's expertise should include the scope of the company's management and operational functions. In other words, the nature of advocacy is professional and accurate, so public relations practitioners need to hone their specialization in communication and the field they represent with dedicated knowledge and experience.

Advocacy in public relations has evolved to engage in the idea and practice of serving the public interest as well. Many public relations codes of ethics encourage the practitioner to inform the public of what's happening to the organization and to "provide an accurate picture of the organization's charter, ideals, and practices," in addition to "honoring their obligations to serve the interests of society and support the right of free expression."[10] The practice of public relations is responsible for serving both the interests of a client and the public. It is an emerging trend. Although it is not easy to fulfill the expectation of both sides regarding the difficulty of advocacy, Thomas Bivins, a professor at the University of Oregon, proposed four possible paradigms for public relations practitioners to satisfy both sides. He suggested that the practitioners have an obligation to improve the flow of information and open up issues important to the public in a transparent manner.[11] The four paradigms are as follows:[12]

1. If every public relations practitioner acts in the best interest of his or her client, then the public interest will be served.

2. If, in addition to serving individual interests, the practitioner serves public interest causes, the public interest will be served.

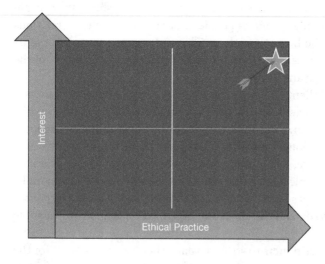

FIGURE 7.1 Ethical practice and interest.

3. If a practitioner assures that every individual in need of or desiring his or her services receives those services, then the public interest will be served.

4. If public relations as a practice improves the quality of debate over issues important to the public, then the public interest will be served.

The paradigms stress that, as long as public relations practitioners conduct their duties and responsibilities on behalf of the client or organization without deception and manipulation, the public will be served by truthfulness and will benefit from the outcomes of public relations advocacy. In the

10   "Global Principles of Ethical Practice in Public Relations and Communication Management," Global Alliance, https://www.globalalliancepr.org/code-of-ethics

11   Thomas Bivins, "Public Relations, Professionalism, and the Public Interest." *Journal of Business Ethics* 12.2 (1993): 117–126.

12   Ibid.

same vein, no public relations strategy should be planned without thinking about its influence on the public.

Effectiveness of Codes of Ethics

Public relations practitioners and public relations organizations are worried about their profession being denounced as "spinning" and "flacking." They suffer from the long-lasting negative image of public relations, even though the importance and practicality of the field are being significantly recognized by the public and major industries. Codes of ethics for public relations were created to change its image, and they are modified and redeveloped as new challenges and events that emerge in the practice of public relations. Some codes of ethics were adopted as early as the 1960s. For example, the code of ethics of the International Public Relations Association (IPRA) was adopted in 1965 and amended in 1968. The first code of PRSA ethics was written in 1950, and the latest amended one was introduced in 2000.

Although public relations ethics has been evolving, the issue of shaking off the bad image still remains salient. It can be understood that ethics has no enforcement authority. All codes of ethics in public relations are recommendations and guidance for public relations practitioners to stay out of trouble in their professional lives. Even if a public relations practitioner joined one of the public relations organizations as a member and made a pledge to its code of ethics, there would be no actual punishment for the practitioner's violation of ethics. Thus enunciating a code of ethics is more like a symbolic and educational gesture than an actual enforcement measure. Public relations practitioners deal with ethical questions and dilemmas while implementing their duties and responsibilities. A code of ethics is simply designed to encourage them to take the moral high ground when exercising for further action.

Ethical Dilemmas in Public Relations

The fundamental issue, which drags public relations practitioners into ethical dilemmas, is the pledge for the free flow of information. Myriad codes of ethics, including PRSA's, emphasize that the practitioner is obligated "to protect and advance the free flow of accurate and truthful information which is essential to serving the public interest."[13] As a result, the practitioner contributes to informed decision making in a democratic society. Journalists and the public have experienced some bad practices by public relations practitioners who disseminated half-truths and deceptive information. As a result, journalists label the practitioners as spin doctors or flacks, who show a lack of credibility. Journalists are unlikely to use information given to them by public relations practitioners until they check its credibility. This is why codes of ethics in public relations embrace the practice of free flow of information, which encourages public relations practitioners to maintain truthfulness and accuracy when communicating with journalists and the public.

When false or misinformation is disseminated, the codes urge a prompt correction with no hesitation. Public relations practitioners spread information and messages outside of their organizations, expecting that journalists will pick the messages up and deliver them to the target audience and the public. One uncomfortable truth about the information and messages is that public relations practitioners often have the propensity for being less concerned about "fostering the free flow of essential information in accordance with the public interest." That is why today's public relations practitioners and business communicators are determined to "uphold the credibility and dignity of the profession by 'practicing

---

13   "PRSA Code of Ethics," PRSA, https://www.prsa.org/about/ethics/prsa-code-of-ethics

honest, candid, and timely communication'" as they engage in disseminating "accurate information and promptly correct any erroneous communication for which they may be responsible."[14] Although many public relations practitioners agree that they use more ethical practices, it is still a long shot that the stigma of public relations held by journalists will be eradicated. According to a survey entitled "What Journalists Really Think of PR People," journalists in the New York area revealed their attitudes toward public relations practitioners by answering the following three questions:[15]

1. How much do you trust PR people?
   - Public relations practitioners embellish sometimes, but I sort of trust them (58 percent).
   - They're good people, and I have great working relationships with them (26 percent).
   - They're all liars—I trust them as far as I can throw them (16 percent).

2. Many journalists end up in PR. If something disrupts your current job, how likely would you be to consider a PR career?
   - I would rather dig ditches (56 percent).
   - I might consider it (40 percent).
   - It would be my first career choice (4 percent).

3. Has your relationship with a PR person ever crossed over into something inappropriate?
   - No (89 percent)
   - Yes (11 percent)

The survey found that journalists who expressed strong animosity toward the practice of public relations still need public relations practitioners, but they don't necessarily like the practitioners. Among those who answered "yes" to question number three, the journalists gave detailed information about the practitioners' unethical behavior:[16]

"One tried to get me fired when I wouldn't cover her client. Another showed up at a personal dinner, literally stalking me via my Twitter."

"Bribe in exchange for a story."

According to the journalists, public relations practitioners are involved in the practice of exaggerating, beautifying information; offering gifts; and making personal contact with them in hopes of getting the information and messages published on behalf of their clients or organizations. Such practices are considered unethical in modern public relations. In a similar vein, PRSA published several examples of ethical dilemmas that public relations practitioners might face:[17]

14   "IABC Code of Ethics for Professional Communicators IABC Code of Ethics," IABC, https://www.iabc.com/about-us/purpose/code-of-ethics/
15   Michael Kaminer, "What Journalists Really Think of PR People," *Observer,* November 19, 2014, http://observer.com/2014/11/what-journalists-really-think-of-pr-people/.
16   Kaminer, "What Journalists Really Think."
17   PRSA, https://www.prsa.org/about/ethics/prsa-code-of-ethics

- A public relations practitioner representing a ski manufacturer gives a pair of expensive racing skis to a sports magazine columnist to influence the columnist to write favorable articles about the product.

- A public relations practitioner spreads malicious and unfounded rumors about a competitor in order to alienate the competitor's clients and employees in a ploy to recruit people and business.

- A public relations practitioner deceives the public by employing people to pose as volunteers to speak at public hearings and participate in "grassroots" campaigns.

- A public relations practitioner declares publicly that a product the client sells is safe without disclosing evidence to the contrary.

- A public relations practitioner discovers inaccurate information disseminated via a website or media kit and does not correct the information.

Public relations practitioners question themselves about what to do when standing at the crossroads of an ethical decision. They are advocates and employees, as well as part of the public. They may have to confront a difficult situation as their clients or bosses order them to prioritize goal accomplishments. The practitioners are like many other people who are concerned about paying the mortgage and supporting their families while trying to keep their jobs. They know that making their bosses and clients happy is their priority. However, when they are ordered to do public relations tasks that embrace possibly unethical strategies and operations, they come up with such questions as the following: (1) Do I have to lie for my boss to promote a product if I am not certain about its safety? (2) Do I produce a press release while withholding information about all of the product's side effects? (3) Do I need to send gifts to the journalists and invite them over to dinner? (4) Can I present myself as an expert in my industry to have the journalists interview me? (5) Do I spread misleading information about my competitors? (6) Do I have to keep my job at all costs, even if it is against my morals?

Sometimes public relations practitioners are forced to be in tough ethical situations, and they are the ones who have to decide if they want to keep their jobs by pleasing their bosses or clients. One sure thing is that public relations practitioners can't avoid confronting a number of personal ethical decisions to make at work.

PRSA issues recommendations for public relations practitioners who struggle with ethical decisions. When they have an ethical problem in conducting their jobs, practitioners should do the following:[18]

- Be honest and accurate in all communications.

- Reveal sponsors for represented causes and interests.

- Act in the best interest of clients or employers.

---

18   "Ethics: Ethics for an Evolving Profession," PRSA, http://www.prsa.org/aboutprsa/ethics/#.VSbyR_nF9mU.

- Disclose financial interests in a client's organization.

- Safeguard the confidences and privacy rights of clients and employees.

- Follow ethical hiring practices to respect free and open competition.

- Avoid conflicts between personal and professional interests.

- Decline representation of clients requiring actions contrary to the code.

- Accurately define what public relations activities can accomplish.

- Report all ethical violations to the appropriate authorities.

These recommendations are purely based on the emphasis on ethics, urging public relations practitioners to decline any action against the PRSA code of ethics.

EXAMPLE OF ETHICAL DECISIONS IN THE NATURAL GAS INDUSTRY

Every industry in the United States encounters the moment of making ethical decisions. Public relations practitioners remain at the center of the decision-making process, as their job description says to communicate with the public and the media about what the industry does and how it plans to meet the public interest. A well-known event relevant to ethical practice is the natural gas industry's fracking development.

The U.S. natural gas industry has developed the new technology of extracting natural gas through hydraulic fracturing, or "fracking," which drills 6,500 to 10,000 feet below the surface to pump up natural gas (Figure 7.2). Within the past decade, thanks to the natural gas boom, large areas for drilling have been explored, and fracking unlocks valuable shale gas energy from oil shale reserves, mostly in Ohio, Pennsylvania, and Texas. The natural gas industry disseminated positive information on fracking, claiming it would generate hundreds of good jobs in America and establish American energy independence. Fracking companies highlighted the mutual connection "between safe natural gas production and jobs" and "between economic growth and greater energy security."[19] Stories of landowners on shale reserves were widely published in a positive light:

> Private landowners are reaping billions of dollars in royalties each year from the boom in natural gas drilling, transforming lives and livelihoods even as the windfall provides only a modest boost to the broader economy. In Pennsylvania alone, royalty payments could top $1.2 billion for 2012, according to an Associated Press analysis that looked at state tax information, production records and estimates from the National Association of Royalty Owners.[20]

Public relations practitioners working for the natural gas industry, fracking companies, and other organizations associated with the industry succeeded in creating positive images of fracking as great for the public interest. The practitioners spread the message that more fracking brings more jobs and stronger energy security for the public.

Drilling for natural gas does not come without problems. Many environmental activists and public health experts claim that fracking pollutes groundwater aquifers, destroys air quality, and endangers

---

19 "NATURAL GAS: AMERICA'S ABUNDANT, CLEAN ENERGY," API, https://www.api.org/oil-and-natural-gas/wells-to-consumer/exploration-and-production/natural-gas/natural-gas-americas-clean-energy
20 "Natural-gas royalties could top $1.2 billion in Pa.," The Philadelphia Inquirer, https://www.inquirer.com/philly/business/20130129_Natural-gas_royalties_could_top__1_2_billion_in_Pa_.html

the health of residents in the region. In fact, it causes several industrial hazards that negatively affect natural resources. A 2018 Duke University study found that "from 2011 to 2016, the water use per well increased up to 770 percent" for fracking, and "the water footprint of fracking could jump as much as 50-fold" in western states by 2030,"[20] which can deplete and contaminate freshwater sources in the region. An even bigger problem is the variety of chemicals used in the process of fracking that release cancer-causing chemicals into the air. Eight poisonous chemicals, including formaldehyde and hydrogen sulfide, were found near wells and fracking sites, according to Dr. David Carpenter, director of the Institute for Health and the Environment at the University at Albany–State University of New York.[21] It is not surprising that public relations practitioners advocating for the industry would have monitored and acknowledged all public concerns and frustrations. Since their loyalty belongs to the industry and its organizations, they focus on creating and maintaining good images of fracking through the dissemination of positive information and messages.

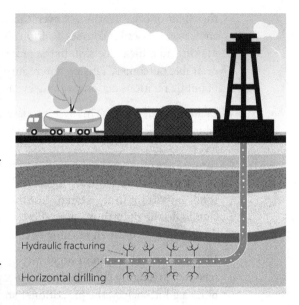

FIGURE 7.2 Hydraulic fracturing.

It is difficult to evaluate their job performance since two views exist: one is from the ethical perspective of environmentalists and people who are skeptical about fracking, whereas the other is from the perspective of the people in the industry who have jobs and financial benefits because of fracking. Some of the practitioners in the industry who view the promotion of fracking as an unethical business might quit their jobs. They could even work for environmentalists who warn about the dangers of fracking. Whether they work for the industry or the environmentalists, it is clear that the practitioners have to make individual ethical decisions. In short, ethics can belong to the individual practitioner. Departing from individual values and beliefs, the practitioner chooses what to prioritize. Ethics can be understood as a personal decision based on moral duties and responsibilities in the public relations profession.

Ethical Decision-Making Systems

Public relations practitioners agree that the practice of public relations should be ethical. Making public relations decisions, however, does not always produce the clear answer of being black or white; rather, a shade of gray exists. They may trust their guts and follow their hearts to finalize the decision, but the following four ethical systems are designed to help them make better decisions.

- **Teleological Ethics.** This system tells the practitioner to focus on the consequences of any action. The practitioner's morality originates in the duty and responsibility for what is good or desirable regarding the outcome. The practitioner is ethical if the outcome is good for

20   Joe Room, "Fracking Is Destroying U.S. Water Supply, Warns Shocking New Study," ThinkProgress.org, August 17, 2018, https://thinkprogress.org/fracking-is-destroying-americas-water-supply-new-study-9cb163923d24/.

21   "Toxic Chemicals, Carcinogens Skyrocket Near Fracking Sites," US News, October 30, 014, http://www.usnews.com/news/articles/2014/10/30/toxic-chemicals-and-carcinogens-skyrocket-near-fracking-sites-study-says.

the client or organization, or even the public. In order for the practitioner to make ethical choices, a particular course of action should be evaluated if it results in a positive outcome. Making an ethical decision in the practice of public relations counts on the prediction of desirable outcomes. This system requires the practitioner to think about the consequences of public relations actions, taking even the public interest into consideration.

- **Deontological Ethics.** This system instructs the practitioner to follow duty-based ethics in which ethical behavior is judged on whether the action is treated as right or wrong regardless of its outcome. The practitioner has a duty to do the right thing, and it is ethical because the essence of ethics begins with the right duty. The practitioner is not allowed to justify an unethical action by showing that the action promises good outcomes. The consequence is not important in the system, but the motivation is vital. In other words, the practitioner should do the right thing, even if it leads to more harm than doing the wrong thing. This system says, "Do the right thing because it is the right thing to do."

- **Virtue Ethics.** This system suggests that the practitioner is the focus, not the action, when it comes to judging the rightness or wrongness of the practitioner's action. As good people build a good society, the practitioner should be virtuous to prevent the bad practice of public relations. The practitioner should make an effort to become a virtuous person who will be able to make ethical choices in the practice of public relations. Therefore, this system provides guidance about the sort of characteristics and behaviors that the practitioner will seek to achieve. The practitioner should be someone who lives virtuously with the mission of becoming an ethical person rather than worrying about a particular action. As a result, the practitioner will develop good human traits that will lead to the production of ethical decisions.

- **Situational Ethics.** This system explains that rightness or wrongness depends on the situation. There are no universal ethics rules or truths because each public relations case is unique and deserves a different resolution. The practitioner should choose the best situational decision by monitoring and evaluating how the practice of public relations develops. The practice is conducted on a case-by-case basis. This system teaches that ethical decisions for the practitioner should follow flexible guidelines rather than absolute rules, depending on the situation the practitioner has to deal with. No matter what decision or action resulted, the situation was the key factor that drove the practitioner to take an ethical process to achieve the outcome.

The four ethical systems show that when public relations practitioners find themselves facing ethical decision making, they need to determine duties and responsibilities for their profession, clients, organizations, employers, and the public, in addition to the ethical principles of personal beliefs, occupational situations, professional consequences, individual traits, and social expectations. In the end, they need to make their own individual ethical choices.

Saying "No" to an Employer

No public relations practitioners want to lose their jobs. They strive to survive at work, even if they were ordered to get involved in unethical practice. It is a tough situation in which they feel pressured to fulfill unethical duties or responsibilities. To keep their jobs, they need to satisfy their clients' or organizations' goals, although they acknowledge that the process could include some ethical misbehavior. Several senior public relations practitioners, including Bruce Berger, a professor at the University of Alabama, summarized how to say "no" to a boss or client who asks a practitioner to do something unethical:[22]

- Use your organization's espoused values to legitimize your point of view (i.e., an organization needs to live its values, or they are meaningless).

- Demonstrate the "headline test." What if the proposed action becomes a headline? Prepare a brief fictional news story with the offending action in a bold, 60-point font.

- Make a rational or emotional appeal from the point of view of the affected public(s).

- Build a small coalition of like-minded individuals and say "no" collectively.

- Cite other companies and ethical examples in the news and review the unfavorable outcomes they experienced. Building a file of such cases may be quite helpful.

- Refer to the PRSA code of ethics, which provides a good framework for a response. The code should be used and cited in such cases.

All employees in the world have a hard time saying "no" to their bosses. When asked to do something unethical, public relations practitioners are advised to explain the anticipated consequences of the unethical request with factual evidence. They are professional strategic communicators with the extraordinary skill of persuasion

Public Relations Ethics in Foreign Countries

According to the IPRA, "'Cash for Editorial' and other unethical practices are widespread in the print and broadcast media of many countries around the world."[23] The IPRA conducted research in 52 countries, surveying 242 public relations and communications professionals to find out the most common problems in unethical relationships between public relations practitioners and journalists. The respondents listed the following common practices:[24]

- Editors and journalists asking for inducements to publish news releases or feature items

22 Bruce Berger, "Six Ways to Say "No" to an Unethical Assignment," *PR Week*, March 11, 2011, http://www.prweek. com/article/1264822/six-ways-say-no-unethical-assignment.

23 "Unethical Media Practices revealed by IPRA," StudyLib, https://studylib.net/doc/7761936/ unethical-media-practices-revealed-by-ipra-report

24 "Unethical Media Practices revealed by IPRA," StudyLib.

- Company news releases appearing in exchange for paid advertising elsewhere in the publication

- Advertisements disguised as editorial material appearing through influence or payment by a third party

- Publications asking for payment not to publish certain stories

The IPRA launched a campaign aimed at reducing the incidence of unethical practices in the relationship between public relations practitioners and the media. "As communications professionals, it is our goal to eliminate practices such as 'cash for editorial' which have been prevalent in certain countries," said Frank Ovaitt, cochairman of the campaign. "As long as the practice of illicit paid-for editorial continues in any marketplace, the local public can never have confidence in what they read."[25]

Ethical Public Relations Issues in the Future

Public relations ethics will evolve as more public relations practitioners make a pledge to the code of ethical conduct. They keep up with the ethical trend of assisting their client or organization, as well as the public, by benefiting from the ethical outcomes of public relations. They are advised to conduct public relations duties and responsibilities based on moral and ethical values by many leading public relations associations, including PRSA and IPRA. The dissemination of half-truths and misleading information is recognized as one of the most salient, unethical practices that journalists do not appreciate. Many journalists still see some public relations practice as the activities of spinning, flacking, and manipulating messages and information. The codes of public relations ethics are designed to assist practitioners in eradicating such negative perceptions. Effective public relations with the media should be built on credibility and accountability.

With the use of social media, public relations practitioners are inclined to rely less on journalists in disseminating information and messages; rather, they facilitate multiple layers of communication tools online. Social and digital media have provided more efficient tools for public relations practitioners to spread information and messages, but the overwhelming flood of information and messages with unverifiable sources distracts the target audience and public from paying attention to what the practitioners want them to hear and see. Social media as a communication tool requires higher ethical conduct in public relations because fewer people trust the flood of unfiltered and unidentifiable information online. Once credibility is lost, either online or offline, it is hard to restore it. Public relations practitioners should lead the way in representing the consciences of their clients and organizations.

---

25   "Unethical Media Practices revealed by IPRA," StudyLib .

CHAPTER SUMMARY AND REVIEW

1. Understand what ethics is and how it is adopted in public relations.

2. Identify codes of ethics for public relations practitioners.

3. Describe the natural gas industry's dilemma of modifying information.

4. Study the four philosophical systems of ethics for the practice of public relations.

5. Describe international ethical misbehavior in public relations.

PUBLIC RELATIONS IN PRACTICE

FUTHER READING

PR Week's Awards For **Best PR Content**

Winner: Wendy's and Ketchum
Campaign Name: We Beefin?

Wendy's created a five-song EP with dis tracks such as "Rest in Grease" and "Clownin'" as part of its ongoing public beef with competitors, such as McDonald's. The restaurant chain's goal was to earn a legitimate spot on hip-hop music charts, confirming Wendy's authentic voice with fans.

Read more at
https://www.prweek.com/article/1579436/prweek-us-awards-2019-winners

8

Formation of Public Opinion with Public Relations

When an individual or an organization does something wrong legally, the justice system takes action against the individual or organization. The system works under the court of law. On the other hand, when a high-profile individual (usually a celebrity or politician) or a large corporation is connected to a wrongdoing (whether it is a legal issue or not), the celebrity or the corporation will be judged in the court of public opinion, putting their reputation at stake. The court of public opinion takes place especially when the media caught and reported the wrongdoing. In a media-saturated environment, celebrities and corporations become sensitive to certain behavior that results in hefty consequences. Social issues that stem from the provocative or offensive actions of high-profile individuals, large corporations, and governments gain quick momentum and inform public opinion, which leads to the creation of negative images and reputations for such entities. Once public opinion on a specific issue is formed, the court of public opinion functions as an alternative system of justice, regardless of official rules of evidence, burdens of proof, and standards of admissibility, which the judicial process requires for a fair trial.

Frances Perkins, former secretary of labor, said public opinion is the leader in the United States; public opinion has the power to influence the courses of politics and business. With the recognition of the social impact of public opinion, public relations practitioners are committed to affecting public

opinion from the very beginning of its formation to its conclusion. The practitioners are called in on two occasions when it comes to public opinion. The first occasion is that an issue becomes problematic and attracts media attention. The second one is to build a type of wished-for public opinion on behalf of their clients or organizations before anyone else affects it. When an organization or a client is under the scrutiny of the court of public opinion, the practitioner declares it a public relations crisis. This is why the practice of public relations is inevitably associated with every step of public opinion formulation.

Concepts of Public Opinion

Public opinion is a sum of individual views and attitudes toward a particular issue or problem in society. To become public opinion, it needs to be expressed by many people who call on the issue-involved entity to take action or make a decision. As sociologist Charles Horton Cooley put it, "Public opinion is a process of interaction for mutual influence rather than a state of broad agreement." In the process, public opinion can turn into a vulnerable and possibly manufactured product. It can be established, altered, reshaped, dominated, and deceased, after all. A public relations practitioner, in an effort to build favorable public opinion toward an organization or an individual client, comes to the essential realization that it takes a heavy investment in time to build public opinion, but in a matter of seconds, a mistake can destroy it.

Once favorable public opinion is built, the practitioner focuses the organization's energy and time on maintaining it. Once favorable public opinion goes sour, the practitioner uses all resources to eradicate the roots of the problem. Unfavorable public opinion means a bad reputation that can threaten the existence of organizations; the same principle is applied to celebrities and politicians.

Opinions about social issues and noticeable behavior of celebrities become everybody's business in a culture where the media manufacture 24/7 news items, and the Internet allows the public to have access to an ocean of information. When the media highlight one specific issue, the public tends to give more attention to the issue, which leads to the initial creation of public opinion. This is a scandalized, traditional way of building public opinion with the media playing the lead role. However, members of the public, in a different vein, often express their comfort or discomfort toward a particular social issue through social media, even before the media pay attention to the issue. When the issue goes viral on social media, the media tend to pay attention to the issue and report it. Either way, public opinion is born in the collaboration between the media and the public.

Factors in Public Opinion

Public opinion is a product of human interaction through communication tools that convey an individual's opinion on a specific, controversial social issue to other individuals who agree or disagree with the opinion. Communication tools in this process offer a forum where the public exchanges beliefs and thoughts about an issue. It demonstrates that the nature of public opinion is interactive and changeable; people's beliefs and thoughts are interchanged to form a certain type of attitude toward public opinion. In a simple way, there are four conditions in the formation of public opinion:

1. There must be an issue.

2. There must be a significant number of individuals who express opinions on the issue.

3. There must be some kind of consensus among at least some of these opinions.

4. This consensus must directly or indirectly exert influence.[1]

---

1   W. Phillips Davison, "Public Opinion," *Encyclopedia Britannica*, March 17, 2017, http://www.britannica.com/EBchecked/topic/482436/public-opinion.

An opinion on a particular issue is expressed from an attitude of an individual, and such an opinion becomes public opinion in the sum of individual exchanges of beliefs and ideas. Public opinion calls for action at a given time in society. In short, attitudes lead to opinions, which encourage the sharing of individual beliefs, which creates public opinion that paves the way for verbal or behavioral action.

Public relations practitioners organize public relations programs that can either (1) motivate the public to have a favorable opinion on an issue for their clients or organizations, (2) reinforce favorable existing opinion, or (3) suggest a direction for an opinion. They understand the process of how public opinion is formed: from attitudes, to individual opinions, to public opinion, to action. In addition, they know how public opinion can be extremely polarized between two groups. For example, the Keystone Pipeline project, an oil pipeline system from Canada to the United States, stirred lots of public disagreement about whether the project is good or bad for Americans (Figure 8.1). People who have a favorable attitude toward the project believe that it creates American jobs and strengthens US oil independence. In contrast, those who have unfavorable attitudes toward the project believe that it destroys the natural habitats of wild animals and pollutes water sources. Both attitudes toward the same issue result in forming two sets of public opinion, and public relations practitioners, depending on which side they represent, try to persuade the public to believe that one side is better than the other. Therefore, their attitudes toward the project become strongly for or against the project while they participate in public opinion formation on the issue. If the majority of people were in favor of the project, then politicians and government officials would consider taking action to support it with advocating policies and financial aid. If the majority were not in favor of the project, no action would be taken. This example demonstrates the importance of public opinion and its impact on the entire public. As a result, corporations and governments tend to invest more and more in courting public opinion.

Attitudes

Public relations practitioners first initiate their public opinion formulation projects with the aim of building favorable attitudes in the public. The concept of attitude is grounded in social psychology. An

FIGURE 8.1 The contested keystone pipe.

attitude can be defined as a comprehensive way of thinking and feeling about a person, product, service, or idea. An attitude represents an individual's tendency to respond to a certain issue in a positive or negative light. It could be neutral as well, but an attitude has a predisposition as to whether it can influence the individual's choice of action. If an individual who follows stories about Kylie Jenner, who became the world's youngest self-made billionaire at 21 in 2019, was asked about his feelings about the billionaire's extravagant lifestyle, the answer would be either "I like it," or "I don't like it." If he likes her regardless of her controversial media exposure with the Jenner-Kardashian family, his attitude toward Kylie Jenner is defined as positive. His attitude toward her has an impact on his feelings.

However, an attitude is not everlasting but changeable, as the way humans feel and think about someone or something continues to adjust. Attitudes are changeable, and public relations practitioners take two strategic approaches to attitudes. The first approach is to reinforce the favorable attitude. This is an easy task because the individual already carries the attitude, which the practitioner hopes for. On the other hand, changing someone's attitude is a difficult approach. For instance, if individuals have negative attitudes toward a presidential candidate, the candidate's public relations practitioner tends to focus on switching the negative attitudes to positive ones. This process is hard but not impossible because attitudes are subject to change. At this moment, they don't like the candidate, but later they could like the candidate if the practitioner strategized an attitude-changing project through communication. Individuals' attitudes are likely to be modified when individuals deal with new social roles, adopt new behaviors, and live under new systems of society. There are seven elements that influence the shaping of attitudes:

1. *Family.* Families are generally the roots of individuals' attitudes toward something or someone. For example, if an individual was raised in a conservative family, she tends to vote for a Republican candidate. Her attitude toward politics is possibly influenced by her parents' and siblings' political affiliation.

2. *Religion.* Religious beliefs affect an individual's attitudes. If same-sex marriage emerged as a social issue, an individual would become a proponent or opponent of the issue according to his religious beliefs. For example, evangelicals remain among the most opposed to same-sex marriage, according to *Christianity Today*.[2] If an individual were evangelical, he would have a negative attitude toward the issue.

3. *Region.* When individuals grow up and reside in the same place for a long time, their attitudes are influenced by regional characteristics. For example, an individual who lives in California has a more environment-friendly attitude than those who live outside California. The Californian may strenuously advocate recycling and hybrid vehicles with such an attitude.

4. *Race.* Ethnicity leads individuals to shape attitudes. African Americans, for example, are more likely to have a positive attitude toward rap and hip-hop music than other ethnicities. In the United States, an individual can develop a particular attitude, depending on her racial status as a member of either a minority or a majority.

5. *Gender.* Living in society as a woman or a man has an effect on the formation of attitudes. Women in the United States tend to have a positive attitude toward equal payment and equal opportunity policies, as opposed to men. Male Americans tend to have a negative attitude toward the feminist movement. The gender difference particularly affects the process of political attitude formation.

6. *Education.* High school and college graduates can have different attitudes toward someone or something. For example, college-educated individuals may be more likely to consider the system of capitalism fairer than high school–educated individuals. In a similar example, a plan for

---

2   Tobin Grant and Sarah Pulliam Bailey, "How Evangelicals Have Shifted in Public Opinion and Same-Sex Marriage," *Christianity Today*, May 11, 2012, http://www.christianitytoday.com/ct/2012/mayweb-only/evangelicals-shift-same-sex-marriage.html.

free community college programs can attract more positive or negative attitudes between the two groups.

7. *Income.* The possession of wealth on a certain level leads individuals to have different attitudes. Rich people would favor a greater supply of organic foods, while poor people would worry about an increase in food prices if the government provided more subsidies to organic farmers. More money means people have a positive attitude toward luxury goods and services. Income levels also divide individuals into two groups: the haves and the have-nots. The Occupy Wall Street movement in 2011 gained more positive attitudes from the latter group.

Types of Attitudes

Individuals can have four different types of attitudes: (1) positive, (2) negative, (3) neutral, and (4) nonexistent. An individual likes or dislikes something or has a neutral mind on something. The individual can also not care about anything at all in a state of "no attitude." When an attitude is positive or negative, it becomes more fixed, meaning that the attitude can be barely influenced by any effort at communication. For example, if an individual is a vigorous activist for animal rights, she will never wear a fur coat. Her attitude toward the fur coat industry is negative, and the attitude is fixed. No messages would persuade her to change her attitude on the issue. In a similar case, if an individual raised in an "open-carry" gun advocacy family, he is likely to have a positive attitude toward the National Rifle Association. The positive attitude toward guns will hardly be changed by any gun control messages. Hence, public relations practitioners are likely to aim to influence neutral and nonexistent attitudes to develop a certain type of public opinion for clients or organizations.

When an attitude is neutral, it is like a wet lump of clay, which public relations practitioners can carve the way they hope. A neutral attitude refers to the state of an individual's decision not to make a judgment on an issue. The individual is seen as a spectator who takes one step outside of the issue and tends to wait to have a positive or negative attitude toward the issue until the matter emerges as a noticeable national issue. In other words, individuals with neutral attitudes toward an issue remain neutral until they begin to find themselves having favorable or unfavorable feelings or thoughts about the matter. People with neutral attitudes begin to more seriously embrace the issue if it becomes interesting and relevant to them before taking sides for or against the issue. Knowing the process of changing and forming attitudes, public relations practitioners endeavor to find a way to persuade people with neutral attitudes to have a positive attitude toward a specific issue, usually for the interest of their clients and organizations. A barrage of media campaigns portraying a political candidate in a positive light serves as a vehicle for persuading voters with neutral attitudes to change their attitudes to positive ones, which eventually lead to votes for the candidate. Neutral attitudes are an important source of establishing public opinion in a certain way.

Nonexistent attitudes are another specific state of mind. Some individuals refuse to be involved in the process of public opinion formation. They believe that an issue in society is not important to them, nor are changes necessary. They do not care about something or someone because other people besides themselves will get involved in any kind of issue and deal with it. Those with nonexistent attitudes think that society carries on issues without them, so the act of having an attitude remains less meaningful. They feel unemotional and detached from things occurring in society. Nonexistent attitudes are associated with the indifference and aloofness toward public opinion. In order for public relations practitioners to change nonexistent attitudes, they need to offer such a group of people inspiring, beneficial information and messages that encourage them to embrace the positive concept of social involvement. Not being excluded from social issues and not being a social outcast can enhance strong motivations for having an active interest and paying attention to something and someone in the environment. The four attitudes are summarized in the following points:

- I advocate the idea of raising the minimum wage—positive

- I don't like the idea of raising the minimum wage—negative

- I think an increase in the minimum wage can have pros and cons for our country—neutral

- I don't care about the minimum wage. Whatever. Who cares?—nonexistent

Whereas all attitudes—positive, negative, neutral, and nonexistent—coexist in society, most people have a fairly neutral or nonexistent attitude toward most issues, because the public is seen as separated and passive. A variety of interest groups can exist to represent diverse voices for people in specific areas such as human rights, environmental protection, religious freedom, small or big government, equality, immigration, education, and so on. Individuals are neither capable of embracing all issues as part of their lives nor willing to participate in raising their voices for or against all issues. More importantly,

social issues are actively moving and evolving in the process of forming public opinion. They wax and wane. As individuals cannot afford to keep up with all social issues, they prefer to selectively form attitudes in matters where their interests lie. If an individual had a part-time job at a fast-food restaurant, he would be more likely to form an attitude toward a minimum wage issue than those who have retired. Separated issues attract divided groups of people who feel related to the specific issues. The number of people involved in public opinion toward specific issues is relatively smaller than the entire population of the public. Society is passive in terms of participating in the process of forming public opinion.

Opinion Leaders

Individuals make a choice for every action when buying a product or using a service. They believe that they choose things they want based on their own volition. They, however, do not acknowledge that they bought the product or chose the service because their decision-making process was influenced by messages from organizations and opinions of other people. For example, if an individual made up her mind to buy a Prada handbag over Chanel, Louis Vuitton, or Gucci, her final decision could have been influenced by her friends, media exposure, fashion leaders, female celebrities, or Prada staff at the store. After she read an article in a fashion magazine, looked at a billboard, or saw her favorite celebrity carry the handbag, she ended up buying the Prada bag. This example shows that, although her purchase of the bag was her decision, the act of making the purchase was made because of opinion-based information from other people. People who are able to influence other people's decisions and actions are called "opinion leaders."

In the book titled *The People's Choice* (1948), sociologists Paul Lazarsfeld and Elihu Katz explained that "opinion leaders serve as filterers and interpreters of information, which the public seeks. An opinion leader is both knowledgeable and highly respected for his or her knowledge on a specific issue or subject."[3] For example, if a well-known journalist in the tech field applauds Samsung Galaxy Fold on her blog, the members of her audience who have been thinking about getting a new smartphone will buy it after reviewing what the journalist said. The journalist is considered an opinion leader.

Opinion leaders are commonly well-known individuals who have the ability to offer guidance to the public in making decisions. They can be community leaders, educators, Hollywood stars, doctors, politicians, journalists, media commentators, CEOs of large corporations, religious leaders, and high-ranking government officials, including the president. They are influential in forming public opinion in a certain direction. They have the power to sway people's attitudes to be positive or negative toward a specific issue. People with neutral attitudes tend to pick a side after they digest opinion leaders' guidance. Opinion leaders, however, should not necessarily be limited to people; an organization can serve as an opinion leader. For example, the United Nations can be regarded as an opinion leader of international human rights. Messages about the subject disseminated by the organization can have a strong impact on forming global public opinion.

Opinion leaders are everywhere. The *Washington Post* points out that "each industry, issue, interest and ideology has its own opinion leaders who are the filters of ideas and information."[3] There are four

TABLE 8.1 Adapted from Opinion Leaders: The Circle of Influence

Shaping Businesses and Industries (Section 1)

1. *Senior Executives and Business Leaders.* Their opinions are published, and their names become well-known as representing their business, their industry, and their industry's needs.

2. *Influential Constituents.* Influential constituents take up the concerns that affect local businesses and communities. Their goal is for these issues to be taken by opinion leaders onto the national and global stage.

Influencing Study and Debate (Section 2)

1. *Trade Associations and Business Coalitions.* Association members position themselves as opinion leaders in their specialty. More than 6,600 associations are headquartered in the Washington area to engage debate at the national level.

2. *Think Tanks and Research Institutions.* Think tanks conduct research focused on specific issues and points of view, whether industry-specific or policy-related. Opinion leaders monitor new research, discuss it, and promote it.

Spreading Ideas and Expanding the Conversation (Section 3)

1. *Journalists and Media.* Many journalists are opinion leaders in their own right, as they develop a following and recognized expertise on a particular topic.

2. *Independent Writers and Bloggers.* The Internet has spawned an (arguably) more literate society of idea exchange. The ideas of opinion leaders bounce around the Internet and are discussed by many.

Influencing and Setting Policy (Section 4)

1. *Lobbyists and Interest Groups.* Special interest groups influence government policy through lobbyists. Lobbyists interact directly with government leaders to communicate the issue they represent and influence the result of policy debate.

2. *Government and Leaders.* Government leaders tune into the debate and follow what opinion leaders are saying. Many government leaders are opinion leaders on issues important to them.

3 "Opinion Leaders: The Circle of Influence," *Washington Post.* http://www.washingtonpost.com/wp-adv/media_kit/wp/pdf/OpinionLeaderBook_MediaKit.pdf.

unique sections where public opinion leaders boast about their knowledge and expertise, according to the newspaper; each section contains two groups of opinion leaders (see Table 8.1).[4]

Opinion Leaders in the Process of Public Opinion Formation

When an individual hears about a new issue or idea, he does not have an instant attitude toward it. He might gather more information about the issue, but he usually does not form an attitude. In other words, he is either reluctant to make a judgment about the issue or is indifferent to the issue. For example, when the Patient Protection and Affordable Care Act, better known as Obamacare, was signed into law "to reform the health care industry by President Barack Obama on March 23, 2010, and upheld by the Supreme Court on June 28, 2012,"[5] many US citizens had no opinion about the program. They had no idea if it was good for their health or financial situations. As social issues such as Obamacare were becoming controversial and complex, many people began to pay attention and seek opinion leaders' guidance to understand and judge the issue. They believe that opinion leaders have the ability to interpret and give meaning to the issue. They would help individuals have a clear attitude toward the

issue. The process takes common steps: the media report a story, and opinion leaders pick up and interpret the story to help individuals understand the issue, which can have either advantages or disadvantages or both for society. This process of influencing the opinions of individuals can be visualized with "the two-step flow of communication" (Figure 8.2).

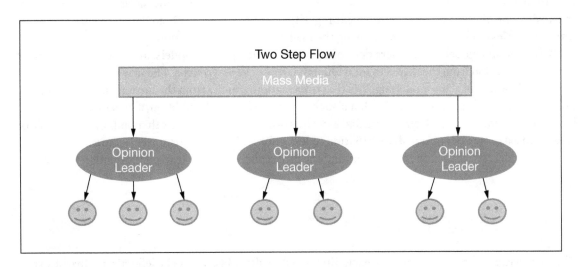

FIGURE 8.2   The two-step flow of communication.

---

4   *Washington Post*, "Opinion Leaders."
5   "Obamacare Facts: Facts on the Affordable Care Act," ObamaCareFacts.com, last modified May 11, 2020, http://obamacarefacts.com/obamacare-facts/.

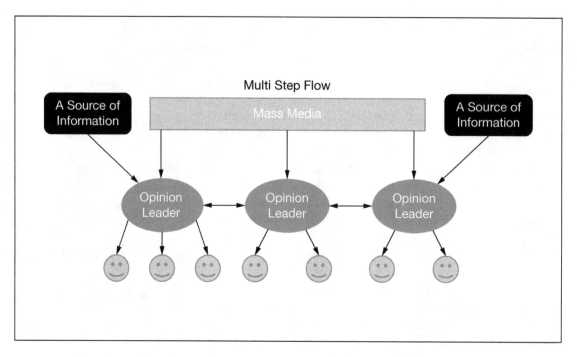

FIGURE 8.3 The multistep flow of communication.

The two-step model illustrates a public opinion formation process in which news stories first reach out to opinion leaders who actively collect, select, and interpret the meaning of messages conveyed through the media. The filtered and reprocessed meaning of the messages is disseminated to individuals who are less active or less informed in terms of using the media to gather information.

Based on this model, researchers developed more public opinion models, arguing that the actual flow of information from the media to individuals has more than two steps. The new model is called the multistep flow model. This model suggests that information, usually from the media, moves in multiple directions—not only to opinion leaders but also to media consumers. In addition, it explains that opinion leaders collect information from the media, as well as other sources, such as other opinion leaders. This creates an extra step of opinion dissemination to less informed media consumers (Figure 8.3).

Both models stress that opinion leaders and the media play a major role in public opinion formation.

The Power of the Media

The term *media* refers to mass media, excluding social media. Mass media is defined as a diverse array of media technologies that reach a large audience via mass communication, principally national newspapers, radio, and television. Mass media aims to reach out to the general public. The most astounding aspect of mass media is the ability to reach thousands or millions of people with specific information and messages every minute. With this systemic advantage, the media are capable of shaping people's ideas, values, perceptions, and behaviors in a certain way. Obtaining new information and being exposed to numerous messages in society has become a part of peoples' daily routine. They read, listen, and watch to gather information and messages conveyed by the media. Information is power, and messages are motivation for action.

The media tend to guide the public's attention to provocative and emerging social issues, leading the public to form opinions about them. The Occupy Wall Street protest in 2011, for example, was heavily covered by the media with two sides of the story. One side of the media portrayed the protest in a sympathetic light, suggesting that many poor workers and unemployed college graduates struggled to make a living on minimum wage as opposed to capitalist magnates who earn millions of dollars per year. The media interviewed and quoted protesters who were armed with the message, "We are the bottom 99%." The message referred to income inequality and one-sided wealth distribution in the United States between the wealthiest 1 percent and the rest of the public. The media showed their pain and disseminated their messages, calling for social changes.

The other side of the media, in contrast, focused on highlighting the protesters' political and racial bias toward the economic system of capitalism. The media also interviewed and quoted people who ran small businesses in the region. The owners of coffee shops and restaurants suffered from the protest, as they could not run their shops during normal business hours. The media did not fail to report the misconduct of protesters who smoked marijuana, urinated in the street, and broke windows in buildings. This example demonstrates that the same protest was reported from two different sides by the media, which led the public to shape their opinions for or against the protest. The media have the power to influence and even manipulate public opinion.

Media Manipulation

Manipulation is the act of influencing or controlling someone or something to one's own advantage, often without anyone knowing it.[6] Media manipulation is the act of creating a series of images and arguments that support the interests of specific groups of people who are usually behind the media operation. According to US Legal, Inc., media manipulation includes "the use of logical fallacies and propaganda techniques, suppression of information, or points of view by pushing them out, by making other people or groups of people stop listening to certain arguments, or by simply deviating attention elsewhere."[7] Media manipulation goes through three steps:

1. The media direct journalists to cover an issue by highlighting one aspect of the issue.

2. The media hire experts (commentators) who advocate the view of the media on the issue.

3. The media reinforce the issue in either a positive or negative light.

The public wind up shaping their opinions by following the media-intended direction.

The process of media manipulation is simple. For example, if a security corporation paid lots of money to a TV news station for advertisements, the station would be likely to cover a story related to the corporation's security products or services in a positive light. The news station broadcasts interview footage of the corporation's CEO as a security expert on a national home invasion issue. Other news coverage of home invasion incidents is reported, and the news emphasizes the importance

6   "Manipulation," *Cambridge Dictionary*, http://dictionary.cambridge.org/us/dictionary/american-english/manipulation.

7   "Media Manipulation Law and Legal Definition," USLegal, Inc., http://definitions.uslegal.com/m/media-manipulation/.

of installing home security systems. Viewers of the news story are likely to build positive attitudes toward the security system, and they would take action to contact the security company for further consultation. The TV station uses subtle tactics to have an effect on the viewers' conscious and subconscious minds and behaviors. In this process, the CEO played the role of an opinion leader about home security.

Media manipulation is orchestrated both by the media and powerful organizations, including the government. When the government needs undivided public support for a national issue, using the media is a conventional and effective choice for it. For example, if the government plans to wage war against terrorist groups headquartered in a foreign country, the administration first feeds information and intended messages to the media in hopes of attracting public support. Going to war results in relying on taxpayers to foot the bill. Without favorable public opinion toward the plan, the government might not be able to make the plan happen. The media serve as an effective tool for spreading messages and information to the public on behalf of the government. The media are able to manipulate the public with their own maneuvers and purposes, as well as to become a manipulative tool of promoting the interests of influential people and organizations.

Theories on the Media Shaping Public Opinion

Public relations practitioners use the media on behalf of their clients or organizations to build a certain type of public opinion. They need to maximize the effectiveness of the media and opinion leaders when it comes to achieving positive outcomes of public opinion. While the two-step flow and multistep flow models illustrate how opinion leaders are involved in the process of shaping public opinion, there are three media theories that illustrate how the media play an important role in forming public opinion. The theories are agenda setting, framing, and diffusion of innovations.

AGENDA SETTING

Communication scholars studying media effects argue that public opinion is created and shaped by the media, which supply an agenda for the public to consider important. Agenda setting theory, developed by Maxwell McCombs and Donald Shaw, explains that the media select important issues for the public to talk about. In particular, as newspapers and broadcast news programs have limited space or time for stories, they choose news items that editors or journalists find newsworthy and important. More media-chosen agendas can be reported on the front pages of newspapers or at the beginning of television news. When the public reads or watches the very important news stories, they believe the stories have something to do with their lives. The stories emphasized by the media become public issues for people to discuss. In other words, the media have a great influence on how people think about the news and what they think about it.

The agenda setting process occurs after journalists decide what to report and how to report news stories. This requires two levels of process: selecting general issues and interpreting aspects of the issues. For example, the media reported the O.J. Simpson case as a top story for many weeks in 1995, telling the public that the case carried huge public interest. The heavy coverage of the football star's trial, selected by the media, became a prominent national issue discussed by the public. As the public followed the trial through the media, journalists and media commentators also told the public how to understand the development of the trial because the trial itself and the verdict would affect the US public interest.

While agenda setting clarifies issues, media concentration on specific issues and powerful individuals leads the public to think of those issues and individuals as more important than others. This is the first step for the media in becoming an agent of shaping public opinion; the media select the news agenda.

The second step is linked to the way the public thinks about an issue; this becomes the public agenda. The third step is how the public agenda, in the form of public opinion, influences what policy makers consider important; this is the policy agenda.[8] In sum, the media have the ability to turn stories into important social issues by engaging members of the public, who are led to shape public opinion.

FRAMING

In reporting about special events or affairs of famous people, the media are able to determine and highlight particular aspects of reality in line with influential and powerful voices or media companies' policies. The media can frame stories in a certain light, depending on the way in which the media depicts the stories. Framing theory explains the following:

1. The media select certain facts and topics to shape a story.

2. Journalists engage in interpreting the story with a particular focus.

3. Additional supporting material is added to enhance the framed story.

Framing is the way the media define and construct a piece of reported information. Some media outlets are not afraid of framing stories by following their company policies. For example, Fox News (viewed as a conservative news channel) was very tough on Hillary Clinton, the Democratic candidate for president in 2016. Conversely, MSNBC (viewed as a liberal news channel) was even tougher on Donald Trump, the Republican candidate. Gallup Research found that, during the late stages of the 2016 presidential campaign, Clinton received far more negative coverage on Fox News, whereas Trump received even harsher coverage on MSNBC.[9] Fox framed Clinton as a crooked leader, while MSNBC framed Trump as a narcissistic and idiotic businessman.

Framing also occurs in international stories. Two international cases are frequently referred to as framing classics. The first is the downing of a Korean airliner (KAL) in 1983 by the Soviet Union, and the second is the downing of an Iranian aircraft (Iran Air) in 1988 by the United States. The US media framed the KAL incident as alleged criminality, while the Iran Air case was framed as a tragedy and technological mishap. In other words, the US media tend to hold different attitudes and contrasting frames toward similar issues. In sum, framing is realized as "a way as to promote a particular problem definition, casual interpretation, moral evaluation, and/or treatment recommendation for the item described," according to Robert Entman, a professor at George Washington University.[10]

DIFFUSION OF INNOVATION

Everett M. Rogers, a professor at the University of New Mexico, developed and popularized the diffusion of innovation theory in his prominent book *Diffusion of Innovations*. Rogers pointed out that diffusion is the process by which innovations are invented and distributed through communication channels over time. An innovation is communicated through certain channels among the public, and it embraces an idea or a practice that is perceived as interesting and new by the media and the public.

---

8   Stephen Littlejohn and Karen Foss, *Theories of Human Conditions* (Long Grove, Illinois: Waveland, 2010).

9   Frank Newport, "Trump's Image Slips; Clinton's Holds Steady," Gallup Research, June 21, 2016, https://news. gallup.com/poll/193043/trump-image-slips-clinton-holds-steady.aspx.

10   Robert Entman. "Framing: toward clarification of a fractured paradigm," *Journal of Communication* 1993, 43(4):51–58 .

This theory explains the adoption process being carried out from the media to the public. There are four main elements in the theory: (1) the innovation, (2) the communication channels through which the innovation is diffused, (3) time, and (4) the social system. The first step, innovation, determines how quickly or slowly journalists or individuals, such as opinion leaders of a social system, adopt issues that could influence people who are likely to show interest in accepting the issue. The second step, communication channels, shows the effectiveness of passing information about the issue through the media and interpersonal communication channels, such as peer networks. The third step, time, is important in the theory, as the public needs to know about the issue in order to pay attention and form an attitude toward it over time. And the last step, social system, refers to engagement in solving social issues to accomplish a common good. Therefore, throughout the process, issues spread successfully, and all members of the society will adopt and personalize opinions about the issues.

This theory also illustrates the five-step process of how the public adopts messages and participates in public opinion formulation:

1. **Awareness.** When a message is disseminated by the media, an individual knows that the message tells him or her something.

2. **Interest.** After being aware of the message, the individual makes an effort to search for more information about the message by doing web research, talking to friends, or reading news articles.

3. **Evaluation.** The individual tries to interpret what the message actually means. He or she determines whether the message is worth trying or not.

4. **Trial.** If the individual concludes that the message is worth trying, he or she goes through an experimental run. For example, if the message tells the individual to drive an electric car to help the earth breathe better, he or she will visit car dealerships to test-drive electric cars. The individual tests the cars to see if reality fulfills the message.

5. **Adoption.** The individual makes a decision to act on the message. He or she buys one of the cars.

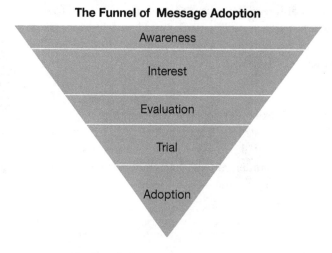

The Funnel of Message Adoption

FIGURE 8.4 The funnel of message adoption.

Although not every individual goes through all five steps to adopt or act on a message, the theory of diffusion of innovation illustrates the complicated process of adopting a message by the public whether people act on it or not.

In a nutshell, the three theories explain the functions and processes of media effects on public opinion formulation. Public relations practitioners are aware of these steps of finding and highlighting a specific agenda, framing issues, and diffusing messages through the media. In fact, they engage in such a process to influence media-driven opinion formulation.

Persuasion and Public Opinion

Public relations practitioners aim to shape positive public opinion from a target audience, the public, and policy makers to advocate for their clients or organizations. The practitioners use the communicative skill of persuasion to accomplish the goal of shaping public opinion in a certain direction. Persuasion is the act of convincing people to do or believe something, and it is part of the dominant technique of public relations to achieve good outcomes on behalf of their clients or organizations. If public opinion is hostile toward their organizations or clients, the practitioners need to engage in launching a program of changing or at least neutralizing public opinion. Any program to influence and change public opinion should be planned with the understanding of the "laws of public opinion" by Hadley Cantril, founder of the Institute for International Social Research. Cantril generalized some characteristics of individual opinion and public opinion:[11]

- Opinion is highly sensitive to important events.

- Once self-interest is involved, opinion is not easily changed.

- When self-interest is involved, public opinion in a democracy is likely to be ahead of official policy.

- Opinion does not remain aroused for any length of time unless people feel their self-interests are acutely involved or unless opinion—aroused by words—is sustained by events.

- At critical times, people become more sensitive to the adequacy of their leadership—if they have confidence in it, they are willing to assign more than usual responsibility to it.

- People have more opinions and are able to form opinions more easily about goals than they are about the methods necessary to reach goals.

- Public opinion, like individual opinion, is colored by desire (emotion), and when opinion is based chiefly on desire rather than on information, it is likely to show especially sharp shifts with events.

These characteristics show that the public pays sensitive attention and builds specific attitudes toward social issues that are related to their lives and interests. The public calls on the government and social leaders to take immediate action when the issue involves threats to the public's safety and livelihood. In this situation, the public tends to hold positive attitudes toward authority, and they support public opinion in favor of public safety enforced by the government.

Public opinion is formed and shared in society as a collection of individual opinions. Once an individual opinion toward an issue is established, the opinion can hardly be changed. For example, if a mother is an atheist who believes in the nonexistence of spirituality, she will not be easily persuaded to send her children to religious schools. If a public relations practitioner is hired to promote such religious schools by targeting atheist parents, the practitioner needs to use persuasive communication techniques

---

11   Michael B. Goodman, ed., *Corporate Communication: Theory and Practice, pp. 344–345* (New York: SUNY Albany Press, 1994).

to neutralize or change the mother's unfriendly opinion about spiritual existence. Psychologist Robert Cialdini cited six techniques for changing someone's opinion:[12]

1. *Reciprocity.* The rule of reciprocity requires that one individual try to repay, in return, what another individual has provided. To persuade someone, public relations practitioners give a little something to get a little something in return. For example, the practitioner gives away a new product to market experts hoping they will publish positive reviews for the product on their blogs—a little gift to get a positive review in return.

2. *Commitment.* The public wants their beliefs and behaviors to be consistent with public opinion. They hope to be seen as consistent with what they believed and did earlier. The practitioner plans to first get the target audience and public interested in a specific issue or product and then make them agree with what the practitioner points out. The audience will make a commitment to the particular product or issue.

3. *Social Proof.* People who use communication tools are likely to follow social trends. They hope to obtain the feeling of being integrated into what others are doing. The practitioner sends the message of "everybody is doing it" to persuade the target audience to participate in social trends, such as eating, buying, or using a particular product.

4. *Authority.* The public, in general, has a tendency to admire authority figures they want to copy in life. The public is also fond of complying with the requests of authority figures. The practitioner finds celebrities who can represent products and services on behalf of clients or organizations; for example, female Hollywood stars promote facial cream products as beauty authority figures.

5. *Liking.* The public likes other people who like them. It would be meaningful if someone shared ideas, thoughts, and experiences with those who have similar associations and tendencies. Liking is based on an individual's physical and psychological attractiveness to other individuals. The practitioner invites a group from the target audience to an event and offers the members a way to share their similarities and their likeability of products or services.

6. *Scarcity.* When the public is informed that only a special edition of a product is offered for a limited time, they are more convinced to buy the limited item. If there are fewer products or services and less time to purchase them, the public wants them more. The practitioners provide the target audience with a message about the great urgency: this is the last chance to acquire the item.

The six techniques of persuasion (Figure 8.5) are adopted in public relations to neutralize and change unfavorable opinions. Without the proper persuasion techniques, public relations practitioners would have trouble accomplishing the goal of shaping desired public opinion. It is important to note that public relations is involved in all kinds of social issues and events with a wide range of organizations and individuals, including the public.

---

12   Maurice Gilbert, "Effective Persuasion Through Good Communication," Corporate Compliance, December 24, 2010, http://www.corporatecomplianceinsights.com/effective-persuasion-through-good-communication/.

Public Relations and Persuasion in the Future

Public relations practitioners on behalf of clients or organizations influence the process of forming public opinion, and they use the media and opinion leaders, along with deliberate strategies of communication. As opinion leaders play an effective role in shaping public opinion, they are also a crucial target audience for the practice of public relations. They serve as catalysts for public opinion formation with their high interest in social issues or expertise in products or services. More importantly, since opinion leaders are believed to have greater knowledge and education than the average person, the public allows them to teach and interpret the meaning of public issues. Journalists and media commentators, such as Tom Friedman of the *New York Times*, Sean Hannity of Fox News Channel, and Rachel Maddow of MSNBC, are well-known leaders who give meaning to specific issues and shape public opinion about politics and global affairs. Celebrities such as Kim Kardashian and Jennifer Lopez spread more than enough images and messages about entertainment, fashion, and beauty trends in the field of social media marketing.

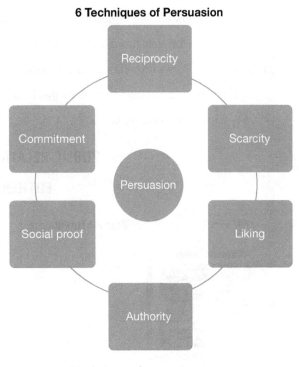

6 Techniques of Persuasion

FIGURE 8.5 6 techniques of persuasion.

By setting agendas and selecting issues, the media contribute to public opinion formation. In order for public relations practitioners to influence the process, they must serve as news sources for journalists. Journalists do not plainly accept and publish public relations sources; they check facts and filter news values as gatekeepers. A theoretical model of influencing public opinion suggests that public relations practitioners offer information to journalists for dissemination to the target audience and public, but the information can be recreated and framed in ways that journalists intend. Since social media serves as a powerful public relations tool to skip the gatekeeping process, the future of shaping public opinion associated with the practice of public relations hinges on how to capitalize on the effectiveness of social media in terms of forming public opinion.

FIGURE CREDITS

Img. 8.1: Copyright © 2014 Depositphotos/Faithie.

Fig. 8.1: Copyright © chesapeakclimate (CC BY-SA 2.0) at https://commons.wikimedia.org/wiki/File:Bill_McKibben_at_Stop_the_Keystone_XL_pipeline_rally.jpg.

Img. 8.2: Source: https://pixabay.com/en/identity-self-authentic-795295/.

Img. 8.3: Copyright © 2014 Depositphotos/Curvabezier.

Img. 8.4: Copyright © 2020 by Haymarket Media Group Ltd.

CHAPTER SUMMARY AND REVIEW

1. Study how an attitude can be formed and influenced.

2. Identify the elements of public opinion.

3. Understand who can become an opinion leader.

4. Identify the models and theories that lead to the formation of public opinion.

5. Explain why persuasion can or cannot be effective on a particular group of people.

PUBLIC RELATIONS IN PRACTICE

FUTHER READING

PR Week's Awards For **Best PR Healthcare**

Winner: Procter & Gamble (P&G) and MSL
Campaign Name: Always Combats Period Poverty with Donation Program

The campaign enabled the brand to donate tens of millions of pads nationwide to girls in need and gave P&G a 21 percent sales lift in Always purchases on Amazon within the donation period.

Read more at
https://www.prweek.com/article/1579436/prweek-us-awards-2019-winners

9

Media Relations and Publicity

T he practice of public relations relies heavily on media relations. In a similar way, the outcomes of public relations rely on publicity, which refers to attention from the media. Public relations practitioners send out customized information and messages to the media, hoping that outlets will publish what the practitioners want from the target audience and the public. The practitioners manufacture what the target audience and public need to hear and see in the form of publicity tools and techniques. Such tools and techniques incorporate the information and messages into various customized forms, which journalists can use as news sources.

The most commonly used public relations forms of publicity tools and techniques are as follows:

Publicity Tools

- Press releases
- Guest editorials
- Media advisories
- Pitch letters
- Video news releases (VNRs)
- Audio news releases (ANRs)
- Publicity photographs
- Media kits

Publicity Techniques

- Interviews
- Media briefings
- Media junkets
- Media tours

- News conferences
- Publicity stunts
- Talk show appearances
- Visits to an editorial board

These tools and techniques encompass the practice of public relations in terms of delivering customized information and messages to the media. The practitioners try to make sure that journalists will publish the customized messages in the press or broadcast on the air. When aiming to attract publicity, the practitioners need to strategize such tools and techniques in favor of journalists, who are more inclined to use the given information if it is formatted for the already standardized practices of the media community. Public relations—unlike advertising—prays for free space and airtime in the media to save money, and this free publicity makes an enormous contribution to the positive outcomes of public relations. The practitioners generalize their use of public relations tools and techniques in response to the needs and requests of the media community. This is critical to building good media relations, which maintains mutual collaboration between the journalists who produce the news and the practitioners who feed information and messages to the journalists. Media relations is an important task because it maximizes the probability of positive coverage in the media without paying for publicity, as opposed to advertising. Excellent media relations save money for clients or organizations represented by practitioners.

Publicity Tools

There are commonly used formats and components of publicity tools for public relations practitioners to use when they send their information packages to journalists. Such tools are written or recorded through a strategic planning process, including the purpose for informing and persuading the target audience. Popular publicity tools used by practitioners are press releases, pitch letters, op-eds, and media kits.

Traditional Press Releases

A press release, also known as a news release, is the most popular and commonly used publicity tool in public relations. The press release is a short, compelling news story that the practitioner sends to journalists or media outlets. It contains written information about a specific event in one or two pages. The information should be written in the form of an inverted pyramid, which includes the most important information and facts in the lead or first paragraph. Journalists do not want to waste their time selecting a newsworthy press release by reading every word of every page. The first paragraph is enough for them to decide whether they want to use the release for their news story. Therefore, the first paragraph must appear interesting and newsworthy, with the climax of the release at the beginning to grab the journalist's attention. To make a compelling press release, the practitioner should consider answering the following questions beforehand:

WHO?

The practitioner needs to define who the target audience is. The press release should contain information and messages that can benefit the specific audience that is likely to use the product or service or to attend the event. When the audience is defined and determined, the practitioner needs to emphasize why the product, service, or event is great for that audience and even the public, if necessary. For example, if the target audience is a group of patients struggling with hair loss, the press release should include medical information on hair rejuvenation.

WHEN?

Timing plays a significant role in getting the journalist's attention. If the press release offers information related to current social issues, then the journalist will take more time to review the release as a possible news source. For example, if the release introduces an organization's decision to increase its employees' minimum wage more than 10 percent at the time of national wage debates, the release will have a higher probability of being published in the media.

WHERE?

Depending on a press release's geographic angle, the practitioner needs to highlight the relevance of information and messages to the residents in the region where local media have great influence. If the release is about a fundraising event that will be held in a city to help its animal shelters, the release should be sent to the local media. In contrast, if the release is about an outbreak of E. coli bacteria in several states, then the release should be sent to all national media.

WHAT?

The practitioner should know what the goal and key message of a press release are. If the goal is to boost sales of a new product, then the release needs to contain messages about the benefits of using the new product. The messages should provide the target audience with the idea of newness and convenience in using the product. The message tells the audience about the merits and values of the product.

WHY?

A press release needs to show why it is important to the journalist and the target audience. The practitioner places important and interesting information in the release that grabs the journalist's attention. The journalist checks if the release is considered newsworthy. For example, if the release says that a cure for all cancers has been discovered, then the release has more than enough newsworthiness to be used and published by the journalist.

HOW?

The practitioner needs to decide how a press release is structured and organized. The release should have a strong title, a clear dateline, a compelling first paragraph, proper spacing (single or double), a specific writing style (usually the AP style), and a proper number of paragraphs. The release should include the practitioner's contact information. The "###" symbol must be placed at the bottom of the release, indicating that the release ends on that page.

After taking all these questions into consideration, the practitioner crafts a press release in the common format shown next.

FOR IMMEDIATE RELEASE
Date

Contact Person
Company Name
Telephone Number
Fax Number
Email Address

Organization
Logo

Headline

City, State, Date—The lead paragraph

Remainder of body paragraphs, including detailed information and quotes from experts in the industry or authorities in society.

The last paragraph repeats the key messages.

One additional paragraph about the organization's history.

# # #
(indicates this news release is finished)

After writing the press release, the practitioner sends it to journalists in various media outlets, such as newspapers, magazines, radio stations, and television stations, along with bloggers and professional press release distribution agencies, such as PR Newswire and Send2Press. In particular, to craft and send more customized press releases, the practitioner needs to categorize the media into four sectors: (1) local media (the area in which the organization is based), (2) specialized media (the organization's industrial sector), (3) audience media (the target audience's favorite news outlets), and (4) national media (the organization's product and service for the public).

The *Los Angeles Times* offers some tips on how to increase the possibility of getting the release published among thousands of news releases the newspaper receives in a week. The *Times* recommends that practitioners[1]

- keep releases short;

- double space;

- write clearly, addressing who, what, where, why, and when in the first two paragraphs;

- identify the organization or individual sending the release and include the name and daytime phone number (with area code) of someone we can contact if we have questions; and

- date the release and include whether the material is for immediate use or for release at a later date.

---

1   "Guidelines for Submitting a Press Release," *Los Angeles Times*, July 22, 2019, http://www.latimes.com/about/la-contactus-prguidelines-htmlstory.html.

From a journalist's perspective, the contact information is important in case he or she found the release interesting and newsworthy. The journalist will email or call the practitioner for more information about the release.

Online Press/News Releases

The basic format and principles of online press releases are the same as the traditional press release. Sending the release is easy via email; however, getting journalists' attention is even harder online. As journalists are inundated with press releases sent through email, they have less time to open them. Capturing their attention in today's digital world has become significant for raising the possibility of releases being used and published. Malayna Evans Williams, managing partner of PWR New Media, reveals "three secrets to capturing journalists' attention with precisely targeted, visually stimulating multimedia releases":[2]

1. *Journalists Are People Too.* They prefer to receive news releases with visually engaging content rather than only word content. Today's digital climate conveniently offers simple methods for placing photos, graphics, and images in the release.

2. *Journalists Like Great Stories and Engaging Content Too.* They want additional usable material that is connected to the content of the release.

   - Illustrated videos

   - Embeddable slideshows

   - Behind-the-scenes images and/or audio

   - Tweetable quotes

   - Social media sharing links

   - Infographics

   - Downloadable recipe/craft/pairing ideas

3. *Journalists Are Just as Addicted to Their Inboxes as You Are to Yours.* They want to receive news releases via email.

Email is journalists' favorite method for exchanging information and documents. When the practitioner emails a press release to a journalist, there are four principles affecting the likelihood that the journalist will open the email and read the release:

1. If the subject line is "PRESS RELEASE," the journalist will automatically delete it. Because the subject line is the headline in the email inbox, it should show the importance of the release. In fact, a valid subject line is essential.

2. In the email, the practitioner attaches the release and offers additional information and material that the journalist finds handy and accessible. Videos, photos, screenshots, and promotion codes are appreciated.

---

2 "3 Secrets to Getting Journalists' Attention with a News Release," *International Association of Business Communicators*, March 5, 2015, https://www.iabc.com/visual-storytelling-todays-news-releases-2/

3. The journalist can remove the release with one click in no time if the email does not get to the point in two sentences. Email releases should be short and compelling, as the journalist reads many emailed news releases every day.

4. Journalists don't like emailed press releases that are full of extraneous adjectives and adverbs or hyperbole. Email releases tend to contain exaggerated descriptions.

AVOID HYPERBOLE

Overused hyperbole in a press release diminishes the credibility of public relations. It is tempting to use extraneous adjectives and adverbs to demonstrate how the product or service is excellent and superior to those of other competitors, but the abuse of such hyperbole has been regarded as problematic by both public relations practitioners and journalists. Rob Burns, president and founder of prREACH.com, recommends ten words and phrases that practitioners should avoid when writing a press release: (1) solutions, (2) leading edge, (3) value added, (4) outside the box, (5) industry leader, (6) innovative, (7) disruptive, (8) world-class, (9) synergy, and (10) revolutionary.[3] Historically, news releases used cliché expressions: "We are the best! We are the most innovative company out there with synergistic, disruptive technology! We are the true leader of the industry! Our product is revolutionary and innovative! Our service comes with cutting-edge solutions." Now it's time to avoid such expressions.

Internet News Releases

Now that the competition to get press releases published in the media is tougher, public relations practitioners have created their own media outlets: websites. Corporations, nonprofit organizations, and governments operate media or communication sections on their websites. Press releases are updated on a regular basis whenever an organization introduces a new product, service, or event. Press releases on websites include photos, video clips, and hyperlinks to social media platforms. Some public relations practitioners email the web addresses to journalists, asking them to visit the sites for press releases.

Press releases are also posted on social media platforms. Social media releases are often embedded with blogs and online links that visitors can click to find press releases. Online media sections of websites and social media platforms are emerging trends in posting and publishing press releases, but online and social media releases have a limited or smaller number of visitors who read them. In other words, fewer people, such as employees, future job applicants, or competitors, are the main users seeking press releases about particular organizations on social media and websites. However, social media press releases have a variety of advantages in sharing opinions and accelerating online conversations.

Pitch Letters

A pitch letter is used to request that journalists attend a special event organized by a public relations practitioner. It informs journalists of the opportunity to cover a story. Unlike a press release, a pitch letter follows the regular business letter format, which doesn't require a particular writing style or compelling first paragraph. Rather, it is a teaser for possible media coverage that convinces journalists to come to the event. The pitch letter, of course, should demonstrate that the event is newsworthy.

---

3   Rob Burns, "Top 10 Words Not to Use When Writing a Press Release," BlogWorld, January 8, 2015, http://www.blogworld.com/2015/01/08/top-10-words-not-to-use-when-writing-a-press-release-2/.

Although a pitch letter is less formal than a press release, public relations practitioners have adopted a widely used style. A pitch letter is usually never longer than one page. It begins with the date and the receiver's name, job title, and the name of the media, including the media outlet's address on the top-left corner of the page. The content begins with "Dear Mr. or Ms." and the journalist's last name. In the first paragraph, the practitioner needs to get to the point, offering the journalist valuable information about why the upcoming event is a great opportunity for the media to cover. In the next paragraph, the practitioner gives information on where and when the event will be held, who is going to attend, why this event is relevant to the journalist's audience, what messages will be produced, and how the journalist will be assisted at the event.

The following paragraphs can include a testimonial or quote from the host of the event or someone important in the community. The testimonial needs to demonstrate how the event is related to a good cause or the benefit of news consumers in the community. In the next paragraph, the letter lists important interviewees for the journalist to use as sources. In the last paragraph, the practitioner places his or her contact information, assuring that the journalist will receive full support from the practitioner. The following is an example of a typical pitch letter:

Op-Eds

Date

Journalist's name
The title
The media's name
Address

Dear Mr. XXXXX:

Write about the event
Give detailed information about the event
Add a testimonial or quote.
Emphasize the newsworthiness.
Assure the journalist will receive support.
Provide the practitioner's phone and email information.

Practitioner's name
Organization's Address

An op-ed (opposite the editorial page) is a writing piece published by newspapers and magazines. Although there are some unconfirmed arguments about the origins of op-ed writing, the *New York Times* invigorated this publicity tool with its first inaugural op-ed page in 1970. Op-eds were created "to provide a forum for writers with no institutional connection" with the newspaper; views different from those of the newspaper have been expressed in the form of op-eds.[4] Op-ed pieces cover subjects that "have not been articulated in the newspaper's editorial space." They also focus on disagreeing with the newspaper's view on particular subjects. A good op-ed piece makes a strong argument in the form of an essay. Indeed, the piece should contain the elements of "timeliness, ingenuity, strength of argument, freshness of opinion, clear writing, and newsworthiness."[5]

Op-eds are the highest level of writing in public relations, and they are designed to argue for or against government policies, pending legislation, and current social and international affairs. The majority of people who read op-ed pieces are highly educated, wealthy, and influential in society. Many of them serve as opinion leaders and industry pioneers who want op-ed pieces to represent their causes and interests. In the same vein, contributors to op-ed pieces typically consist of politicians, corporate CEOs, celebrities, leaders of nonprofit organizations, and even presidents and kings. Famous and influential people—generally speaking—write op-ed pieces to argue about what should be done by the government, industries, or the public.

However, such powerful people are usually not able to write an entire op-ed piece without the help of their public relations practitioners. For example, if a car company's CEO writes an op-ed piece for the *New York Times*, the CEO and the company's public relations and marketing specialists put their heads together to produce a high-quality piece. If the op-ed is published in the newspaper under the name of the CEO, the public relations and marketing people serve as the by-liners. This is one of the highest achievements for public relations practitioners because op-eds are considered prestigious among powerful people.

When a public relations practitioner writes an op-ed for the CEO or president of an organization, the practitioner should include eight essentials:

1. *Have a Clear Editorial Viewpoint.* Pro or anti. There is no neutral attitude toward the subject.

2. *Don't Slowly Build to the Point.* Place the main point on top. In the first paragraph, the op-ed reveals the main argument.

3. *Concentrate on One Main Idea or a Single Point.* One themed argument with a fixed attitude is essential in making a strong point.

4. *Present Facts and Statistics to Build Credibility.* A strong argument is justified by scientific evidence and statistical data.

5. *Use Short, Firm, Strong Sentences and Paragraphs.* A good op-ed relies mainly on simple declarative sentences. Break long paragraphs into two or more shorter ones.

6. *Acknowledge the Other Side's Point of View.* Write that the opponent's view can be right but discredit the opposing argument by pointing out the superiority of the argument the practitioner's boss makes.

7. *Provide a Recommendation.* The purpose of an op-ed is not to inform but to educate people with professional insights. The argument should lead to recommendations for the target audience or public.

8. *Conclude with Repetition.* Summarize the main argument in a final paragraph by repeating the ideas from the first paragraph.

---

4   David Shipley, "And Now a Word From Op-Ed," *New York Times*, February 1, 2004, http://www.nytimes.com/2004/02/01/opinion/01SHIP.html?pagewanted=print.

5   Shipley, "And Now a Word."

Major U.S. newspapers that publish op-eds include the *New York Times*, the *Washington Post*, the *Wall Street Journal*, the *Los Angeles Times*, and *USA Today*. The commonly accepted length of a piece is between 600 and 1,200 words. As space is limited for all papers, the competition is extremely high; no op-ed is guaranteed publication.

Media Kits

A media kit, also referred to as a press kit, is a total package of information in a folder. Public relations practitioners are in charge of placing information about clients or organizations in the folder. This

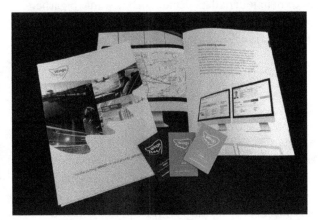

can include photos, CDs, DVDs, brochures, samples, documents, and USB flash drives. The folder, or media kit, is sent to journalists to encourage their interest in the comprehensive information package. Today, it has become the trend to send media kits to journalists online instead of by mail. Not only does the online media kit save money on printing and mailing costs, but it also allows journalists to have easier access to the information. The online media kit, like offline media kits, features comprehensive information with photos, videos, graphics, and downloadable documents. Both online and offline media kits should include seven sections:

1. *A Press Release.* As a media kit is a package of comprehensive information, the press release should be included in the folder or online media kit. It is supposed to contain the most recent information about the organization's special product, service, or event.

2. *Organization Overview Sheets.* A brief historical overview of the organization's performance and its people, including the CEO or head, is placed in overview sheets. The sheets give a time line of the organization's establishment, achievements, and major contributions to society.

3. *Biographies.* Key players in the organization should be introduced. The key players are investors, founders, and executives in the organization.

4. *Media Coverage.* If the media had reported any positive mentions or stories about the organization and its employees' performance, the stories should be included in the folder and online media kit. Reprints, clips, or screenshots of positive news coverage may impress journalists.

5. *Frequently Asked Questions.* Questions that journalists ask repeatedly should be answered up front. This can save time and energy for both journalists and public relations practitioners.

6. *Visual Content.* Photos of the organization, its products, and its key employees are offered. In addition, journalists look for videos, logos, and graphic images of the organization that can be used for reporting.

7. *Contact Information.* Clear information about how to contact public relations practitioners includes their names, email and mailing addresses, and office phone numbers. This section is placed on the back page of the media kit with the practitioner's business card.

Media kits of current organizations are mostly found online, which journalists and public relations practitioners find more convenient for sharing, in addition to being cheaper to produce.

Publicity Techniques in Public Relations

Whereas publicity tools are produced, controlled, and sent by public relations practitioners to journalists, publicity techniques provide journalists with more opportunities to be active in the news-gathering process. The practitioners use publicity techniques to help journalists decide if they want to gather further information on public relations events the practitioners promote. Popular publicity techniques that are used to invite journalists to events include interviews, news conferences, media tours, and talk show appearances.

Interviews

A primary reason for journalists to contact public relations practitioners is to ask for an opportunity to interview CEOs or heads of organizations. When a request for an interview is delivered to the practitioner, the organization's CEO needs to decide whether he or she will participate in the interview with the media. In particular, if the organization has a communications department, the department's staff will advise whether the interview is valuable for the CEO and the organization. If the organization does not have a communications staff, it hires a public relations firm to prepare for the interview. CEOs are commonly uncomfortable with interviews because journalists are inclined to ask tough, uncomfortable questions from an investigative perspective. When an interview occurs, the CEO and the journalist get together to talk. Although they are in the same environment, their goals are different. The journalist seeks a compelling story, while the CEO intends to promote his or her key messages and interests through the interview. The different goals often lead to conflict, and they may become less friendly to each other by the end of the interview.

There is no doubt that an interview is a great publicity opportunity for the organization. The practitioner needs to find a way of capitalizing on the opportunity by preparing the CEO for a smooth, productive interview. In fact, the practitioner trains and coaches the CEO before the interview, especially if it is for television. In a television interview, many CEOs appear anxious or frightened and wind up stumbling over their words. CEOs assume that they know what they want to say as industry leaders. However, appearing on television can be an incredibly daunting experience for anybody. They could end up just making themselves look bad. If this happens, the organization would have wasted a valuable publicity opportunity. The practitioner's main task is to coordinate the interview between the CEO and the journalist to meet their goals. Training the CEO through interview rehearsals is not an easy task, but a successful interview can be a promising opportunity for the organization.

Public relations practitioners and journalists agree that without the right preparation, "a media opportunity can quickly turn into a disaster, which can cause long-lasting reputational damage" to both the CEO and the organization.[6] Many media interview specialists follow ten dos and don'ts for a successful interview:

1. *Prepare for the Interview.* Preparing for media appearances is essential. The practitioner reminds the CEO of key messages that he or she needs to remember and convey.

---

6   Kirsty Walker, "Media Training: Five Tips for a Great Interview," The *Guardian*, July 24, 2013, http://www. theguardian.com/women-in-leadership/2013/jul/24/top-tips-media-training-interviews.

2. *Focus on the Journalist Asking the Questions.* The CEO can be distracted by lights and cameras while being interviewed. The practitioner trains the CEO to focus on what the journalist says, preparing to answer the questions, and making eye contact.

3. *Wear Something Professional.* Television viewers pay attention to what a CEO wears and says. If the messages are heavy and serious, dark-colored outfits are recommended. If the messages are entertaining and fun, more casual outfits with some accessories are recommended.

4. *Look Confident.* Appearing on television produces many butterflies in the stomach. The practitioner tells the CEO to lean forward when he or she talks and to stay calm when the journalist asks questions. In order for the CEO to look confident, the practitioner recommends not using too many "ums," "you knows," and "ahs."

5. *Stick to the Messages.* The practitioner emphasizes that the CEO's main goal is to relay messages during the interview. Regardless of the journalist's tough and embarrassing questions, the practitioner trains the CEO to stick to the task of conveying the desired messages.

6. *Make it Credible.* The CEO needs to convince the journalist that his answers are based on facts and credible sources. The practitioner supplies the CEO with facts, examples, and data that can support the credibility of the messages.

7. *Get Ready for the Worst.* The practitioner predicts worst-case-scenario questions from the journalist, and the CEO receives such questions in rehearsal. The CEO is trained not to look nervous under any circumstances.

8. *Don't Say "No Comment."* In preparing for the possibility that the journalist will ask the CEO unrehearsed and unexpected questions, the practitioner tells the CEO to explain why he or she is not answering a question instead of saying, "No comment," which makes it seem like the CEO is hiding something from the journalist.

9. *Don't Try to Be a Know-It-All.* The CEO is pressured to appear professional and trustable, in addition to feeling that all questions should be answered without hesitation. The practitioner advises the CEO that offering an "I don't know" answer is better than coming up with improvised answers during the interview.

10. *Don't Ignore the Training.* Interview training is the key to success. The practitioner plays the journalist in a simulated media setting, asking questions of the CEO. The training session is recorded and reviewed for improvement in terms of facial expression, body gestures, makeup, and outfits.

Interviews offer a great opportunity for the organization to achieve its goals. The practitioner uses various publicity tools to attract media coverage of the organization. In response to such tools, the journalist may ask for an interview with the practitioner or the CEO. When the interview is scheduled, the practitioner's number one priority is to train the CEO.

News Conferences

A news conference, or press conference, is a staged meeting that invites the media to the organization's location. In the meeting, journalists and public relations practitioners exchange messages and information related to the organization in a question-and-answer format. When there is a unique or newsworthy announcement from the organization, a news conference is arranged. The practitioner acknowledges that a news conference should not be abused as a publicity technique because journalists expect a truly big news story at the conference. If they don't get one, they will probably never show up to any conference organized by the organization again.

A news conference should be held when the organization has real, important news to announce. Frequent organizers of news conferences are corporations, government agencies, politicians, and sports teams.

- **Corporations**   When a new product that can change a market trend is produced, a corporation holds a news conference and invites as many journalists as possible. This type of news conference is also referred to as a promotional conference. The tech giant Apple has been an active user of such conferences since the birth of the iPhone. The founder of Apple, the late Steve Jobs, streamlined the trend of promotional conferences by introducing the corporation's new products in front of journalists while standing on a stage with big screens. The conferences became the market trend, as other smartphone corporations have implemented the same style of news conferences. Public relations practitioners organize such events.

- **Government Agencies**   The White House is one of the most active organizers of news conferences. The press secretary for the White House holds news conferences whenever important social and international issues emerge. Emergency news conferences are held in the White House as disasters or provocative social unrest spreads across the nation. Holding a news conference at a government agency attracts a whole host of journalists to cover the event since the media already assign designated correspondents to powerful agencies. By contrast, corporations normally invest a large amount of resources in asking the media to assign journalists to cover their news conferences.

- **Politicians**   When politicians announce bids for office, their public relations practitioners coordinate news conferences with the media and supporters. At the conference, the politician coveys the message of why he or she is entering the race and how the politician plans to make the country better. Political slogans and symbols are unveiled at the news conference. In 2015, the real estate mogul and TV reality star Donald Trump held a news conference at the lavish Trump Tower on Fifth Avenue in New York City to announce his candidacy for the White House. During the news conference, he stated, "So, ladies and gentlemen, I am officially running for president of the United States, and we are going to make our country great again."

- **Sports Teams**   Before big sports events are held, athletes or team owners hold news conferences to announce how they will play the game. Boxing news conferences are often seen as prefight public relations stunts. When boxers pose for pictures, they usually "happen" to get into a heated conversation or bare-knuckle confrontation.

The success of news conferences is associated with the number of journalists who attend. Public relations practitioners execute some strategies to increase journalists' participation in the conference. There are five steps to convincing journalists to attend:

1. ***Find a Newsworthy Story.*** Every employee and product should have a story to tell, but the practitioner needs to find the best newsworthy story to meet journalists' expectations. The CEO's story sounds more charming than an employee's story.

2. ***Find a Time and Location.*** In the media business, meeting the deadline means everything. Morning hours give journalists more time to attend and write about the conference. As the conference requires physical attendance, the conference location should not be too far from where journalists work.

3. ***Send an Invitation.*** Addressed to individual journalists, the invitation email or letter gives a brief explanation of the conference. As long as it's not an emergency conference, the invitation should be sent a week before the conference so the journalists can schedule to attend.

4. ***Arrange the People.*** The practitioner consults with the CEO about resource allocation for the conference. They need to decide who will announce the messages, who is going to be interviewed, who will escort the journalists, who will distribute the organization's samples, and what refreshments or gifts will be offered.

5. ***Assist the Journalists.*** The practitioner stays at the conference until the journalists leave, answering all questions and offering additional information about the conference. The practitioner needs to respond to any requests from journalists at the conference. Media kits can be provided.

A news conference as a staged public relations event requires some work, yet it is an effective publicity technique for reaching many journalists. As a result, the organization's messages can reach a large audience.

Media Tours

Public relations practitioners and journalists need each other to build a mutually beneficial relationship. They become partners at best or enemies at worst. They, as humans, want to build rapport before, during, or after work. Media tours are a good publicity technique for practitioners to build rapport and grab journalists' attention. Two types of media tours are commonly practiced: the junket and the newsroom tour.

1. ***The Junket.*** This is an all-expenses-paid trip for the journalist. The practitioner invites the journalist to a place where an event is held. For example, if the organization releases a new product in a foreign country, the practitioner invites the journalist to the country by picking up the tab for the flight and accommodations. In return, the practitioner expects a favorable article or reporting about the product. The junket also applies to an organization's factory tour. Journalists are invited to travel with the organization's executives to its manufacturing facilities across the country, with all expenses paid by the organization. The practitioner focuses on showing the journalist around the good parts of the facilities with the hope that the journalist builds trust in the organization's products, which leads to positive media coverage.

2. ***The Newsroom Tour.*** The practitioner and CEO can visit media outlets (in town or out of town) to build relationships with editors and journalists. As journalists work on tight, unpredictable schedules, the practitioner and CEO see these meetings as a good way to meet journalists and express appreciation. They can have lunch or dinner together while talking about the

organization's products or services, including upcoming events and conferences. Journalists may develop a story angle for the organization and schedule an interview. Newsroom tours combine the tasks of promoting the organization and building relationships with journalists. Although some journalists refuse to participate in newsroom tours, public relations practitioners often successfully invite journalists to the places where the events are going to impress them.

Talk Show Appearances

Some public relations firms try to maximize the benefit of using their media relations networks. These firms specialize in connecting a client with the media. When the client wants to promote his or her product, such as a book, music, movie, or food, the firm finds opportunities for the client to appear on television shows. Television talk shows are considered the best publicity technique in terms of generating instant and broad impact for the client. There are three types of TV talk shows that public relations practitioners use to promote different products to different target audiences.

1. *Early Morning Shows.* ABC's *Good Morning America* and NBC's *Today* are popular, influential morning television shows. These shows provide top domestic and global news, weather reports, and entertainment information. In addition, they conduct interviews with famous or rising figures, cover specific lifestyles of average people all around the world, and offer in-depth coverage on provocative social issues and touching humanitarian stories. In particular, specific segments of both shows are favored by public relations practitioners. These segments include issues focused on health, finance, cooking, and entertainment. During the shows, the hosts might participate in making fruit juice, following yoga poses, applying cosmetics, testing medicines, fixing quick breakfasts, wearing new clothes, learning new financial services, and watching clips from new movies. A wide range of new products and services can be introduced in the segments through the appearance of experts who are the clients of the practitioners.

2. *Daytime Talk Shows.* CBS's *The Talk* and ABC's *The View* are popular daytime TV talk shows with panels of four or five female cohosts who discuss trendy issues and news items. They talk about hot social and political issues from the perspective of women. Both shows often highlight the themes of parenthood, health, and beauty, in addition to interviews with celebrities or politicians who are the clients of the practitioners. These shows aim to represent stories of success and failure of working mothers, professional women, and female students. Controversial social issues, such as gay marriage, racial discrimination, equal payment, and freedom of expression, are often discussed during show hours. Public relations practitioners' favorite parts of these shows come when the hosts compliment specific products or public figures. As both shows target a female audience, products and services related to motherhood, health, romance, and beauty can earn a chance to be promoted on the shows.

3. *Nighttime Talk Shows.* Fierce competition has continued among nighttime talk shows throughout US television history. Unlike morning and daytime talk shows, nighttime talk shows severely compete for high ratings. Popular shows are *Jimmy Kimmel Live!* on ABC, *The Late Show with Stephen Colbert* on CBS, and *The Tonight Show Starring Jimmy Fallon* on NBC. These shows have almost identical traditional formats: (1) a male host gives an opening monologue; (2) the host has a brief conversation with the music players; (3) the host performs several skits; (4) the show invites a more famous celebrity as its first guest; (5) the show invites a less famous celebrity as its second guest; (6) a musical guest or comedy act ends the show. Nighttime talk shows are big fans of movie

stars, who have the power to increase ratings. Movie stars also view the shows as a publicity technique for promoting their new films (the same principle goes to musicians and book authors). When a movie star appears on one of these shows, he or she disseminates the message of how entertaining his or her movie is. In response, the talk show host plays a short clip of the movie and informs the audience of its opening day, often adding, "This is a great movie to see." The practitioners are behind the movie stars' appearance on the show.

A talk show appearance is a thoroughly organized publicity technique. It requires professional networking and assistance. Public relations firms and television companies orchestrate the appearance in hopes of promoting particular products, services, or people and boosting TV ratings.

Evolving Publicity Tools and Techniques

There are more tools and techniques for publicity. An ANR records the voice of an announcement, and the practitioner sends the recorded tape to radio stations. In a similar way, a VNR is used to produce a videotaped press release. As it requires the specialized skills of shooting and editing, the practitioner normally hires a production company. A VNR is produced

Cadidate Trump Talks With Jimmy Fallon

in a format that television stations use. The VNR is sent to the stations with B-roll footage that does not include sound. The footage allows the TV producers to insert voice or music to customize the VNR for its reporting. A satellite media tour (SMT), as a publicity technique, is a reserved interview with television programs. When a television journalist wants to interview a CEO or public spokesperson who is not physically able to appear on the program, the one-on-one interview is conducted via SMT.

Positive media coverage is a blessing for organizations and individuals. Free publicity is an even bigger blessing, although it takes a series of efforts and strategies. To improve their chances of garnering free publicity, public relations practitioners link their publicity tools and techniques to social media platforms and websites. In general, the practitioner needs to develop social media and digital skills to raise the chances of attracting media coverage.

CHAPTER SUMMARY AND REVIEW

1. Identify publicity tools.

2. Identify publicity techniques.

3. Study the core elements of those tools and techniques.

4. Understand how promotion works between practitioners and journalists.

5. Describe the best methods for catching media attention.

PUBLIC RELATIONS IN PRACTICE

FUTHER READING

PR Week's Awards For **Best PR Media**

Winner: HP and Edelman
Campaign Name: HP Bridging Political Divide with Togetherness

Working with award-winning director Lisa Rubisch, HP launched *Togetherness*, a short film about a family handling holiday tensions, with the help of a pocket printer to capture memories during the December 2017 holiday season. HP drove awareness of the film through the end of the holiday season, showcasing the brand's purpose. To amplify the message, the company partnered with ABC's *The View* to preview the spot, HP's president of print business Enrique Lores and CMO Antonio Lucio published thought pieces on the need for togetherness, and a behind-the-scenes interview from the film shoot was posted on HP's employee portal.

Read more at
https://www.prweek.com/article/1579436/prweek-us-awards-2019-winners

10

Corporate Relations

The term *public relations* used to be synonymous with media relations when Ivy Lee emphasized the importance of building a mutually beneficial relationship with journalists. It simply focused on responding to requests from journalists. Communication for public relations practitioners in the early twentieth century was confined to the dissemination of customized messages to large publics on behalf of clients or organizations. As public relations is positioned to play an important role in strengthening an organization's financial performance, this limited view of public relations as mere media relations has been redefined. Public relations is now incorporating a whole range of management functions, including image construction, crisis management, reputation management, and relationships with investors and government. Public relations has evolved into a decision-making process that results in managerial outcomes.

The management functions of public relations have grown especially in corporate operations. From the early 1900s, the business community began to realize that it would need something more than marketable goods or services to compete with competitors. Making a handsome profit is any corporation's number one priority, but simply selling goods or services was not enough to convince consumers to spend their money in pursuit of corporate profits. A number of new sales and marketing strategies have been added to many corporations' long-term goal of boosting profits, and public relations is invited to be center stage in planning and organizing strategies of corporate operations. Public relations for corporations focuses on the increase in profits, not with goods and services but communication and corporate social responsibility (CSR). There are two key components that explain what corporate public relations is and how it works: corporations and stakeholders (Figure 10.1).

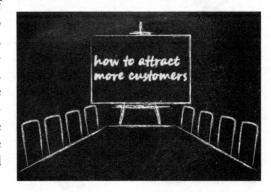

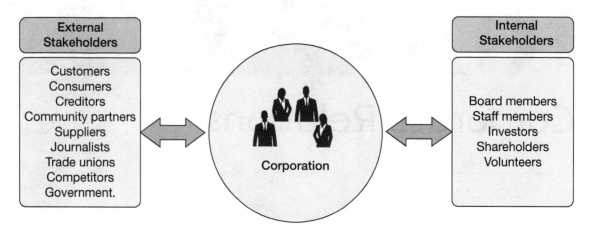

FIGURE 10.1 Stakeholders for corporations are divided into two groups.

Corporations

A corporation is a firm that is created by a group of shareholders who have ownership through stock. A firm is recognized as a corporation when it meets certain legal requirements that ask an independent legal entity to be separate from its owners. This means that shareholders, not the owners, elect a board of directors, and the directors appoint the CEO and oversee management of the corporation in the hope that the corporation provides a return for its shareholders. A corporation has three distinct characteristics:[1]

1. *Legal Existence.* A corporation can (like a person) buy, sell, own, enter into a contract, and sue other persons and corporations (and be sued by them). It can do good and be rewarded and commit offenses and be punished.

2. *Limited Liability.* A corporation and its owners are limited in their liability to creditors, only up to the resources of the firm, unless the owners give personal guarantees.

3. *Continuity of Existence.* A corporation can live beyond the life spans and capacities of its owners because its ownership can be transferred through a sale or gift of shares.

A corporation is a legal entity that embraces most of the rights and responsibilities to "enter into contracts, loan and borrow money, sue and be sued, hire employees, own assets, and pay taxes."[2] Shareholders of the corporation have the right to participate in the profits (through dividends and/or the appreciation of stock), but they are not held personally liable for the corporation's debts.[3]

---

1   "Corporation," Business Dictionary, http://www.businessdictionary.com/definition/corporation.html.

2   Will Kento, "Corporation," Investopedia, December 11, 2019, http://www.investopedia.com/terms/c/corporation.asp.

3   Kento, "Corporation."

Stakeholders

A stakeholder can be a group, an organization, or an individual who has a direct or indirect stake in a corporation. The stakeholder positively or negatively affects or is affected by the achievement of the corporation's objectives and policies. The stakeholder is interested in the activities of the corporation. The stakeholder with an interest or concern in the corporation can be identified as internal or external. Internal stakeholders are those who work directly within the corporation, whereas external stakeholders are those who do not work directly within the corporation. Internal stakeholders include board members, staff members, investors, shareholders, and volunteers. These people are directly connected to the activities of the corporation in terms of planning and implementing the corporation's operation. External stakeholders who affect the decisions of the operation from outside the corporation include customers, consumers, creditors, community partners, suppliers, journalists, trade unions, competitors, and the government. External stakeholders have a great influence on the corporation's decision-making process since they are the driving force that enables the corporation to survive in terms of producing goods or services, paying taxes, repaying debt, building a good reputation, buying raw materials, and negotiating conditions and terms of business operation.

Specializations in Corporate Public Relations

The corporation's success depends on its communication with internal and external stakeholders. It needs to know what shareholders and employees want, what consumers need, what the community expects, what journalists ask, and what the government requires. Corporate public relations deals with satisfying all the needs and wants of stakeholders by building a mutually beneficial relationship between the corporation and its stakeholders. In essence, corporate public relations as a management function aims to fulfill the expectations of stakeholders through communication. The mantra "happy stakeholder, happy corporation" calls for corporate public relations to take significant responsibility, divided into four major specializations:

1. Consumer/customer relations
2. Investor relations
3. Community relations
4. CSR

The four specializations of corporate public relations play an essential role in building good relationships with key shareholders. The management function of public relations continues to evolve to meet the expectations of rapidly changing business and social environments. Before the twenty-first century, many shareholders and corporations accepted the economic ideas of Milton Friedman, who argued that corporations exist to maximize profits, which would result in hiring more people and paying more taxes to support social programs that benefit the public. However, other corporations pursued nothing but handsome profits, regardless of any wrongdoing in business practices, although some economists and corporate professionals warned against the myopic pursuit of profits.

TABLE 10.1   How Americans Feel about Major Corporations[4]

	Very Satisfied (%)	Somewhat Satisfied (%)	Somewhat Dissatisfied (%)	Very Dissatisfied (%)	No Opinion (%)
2018	6	28	28	36	2
2016	5	30	31	32	2
2014	5	30	30	32	3
2012	4	26	28	36	5
2011	5	24	31	36	4
2008	6	29	28	33	3
2006	6	29	30	32	2
2003	6	37	33	21	3
2002	7	43	30	17	3

Source: "Big Business," http://www.gallup.com/poll/5248/big-business.aspx. Copyright © 2002 by Gallup, Inc.

In the early twenty-first century, corporations disappointed shareholders with financial scandals and government bailouts. The scandals of Enron, Tyco International, and WorldCom, along with the government bailout of the auto industry in the United States, crushed shareholders' trust and confidence in corporations. According to a Gallup poll (Table 10.1), more than 50 percent of Americans have been dissatisfied with major corporations' business practices since January 2003, a few months after the scandals received heavy media coverage. Since the corporate scandals, the negative opinions of major corporations soared to 67 percent while the United States struggled with the economic crisis after the 2008 bailouts. Negative views about corporations remained above 60 percent, even in 2018.

Shareholders call for transparency and corporate responsibility to build mutual benefits for corporations and themselves. Corporations understand that shareholders' and the public's negative views about corporations' unethical and illegal business practices will lead to their demise. They realize that shareholders' expectations must be fulfilled through transparent and responsible business practices. As a result, corporations attempt to inform their shareholders that they are implementing the right things to build trust and reinforce their corporate values. Corporate public relations uses communication channels to present evidence that the corporation sticks to its number one goal—making profits—in accordance with obeying laws and regulations while operating social charity programs that contribute to the public interest.

Consumer/Customer Relations

A customer purchases goods and services while a consumer uses them. However, the terms *consumer* and *customer* are often used interchangeably. Consumers and customers are the de facto force that allows corporations to do their business. They offer financial resources to corporations in exchange for goods

---

4   "Big Business," Gallup Poll, http://www.gallup.com/poll/5248/big-business.aspx.

and services. The economic activity allows corporations to reinvest in the cycle of production. Consumers/customers are the lifeblood of any corporation, so building and maintaining a positive relationship with them is a pivotal factor for corporate success. A successful business relies on how well consumers/customers are treated and how high their levels of comfort and confidence are in the corporation. Therefore, building good consumer/customer relations is one of the most important functions of corporate public relations. Now that public relations practitioners prefer the term *consumer relations* to *customer relations* (despite their interchangeability), the former is used to represent both terms.

Consumer relations refers to activities that establish consumer confidence; a corporation aims to achieve consumer satisfaction with the quality of its products and services. Consumer relations is about communicating with consumers, primarily focusing on addressing complaints, offering improved benefits, and updating information about the corporation. The main objectives of consumer relations are as follows:

- ■ *Knowledge Enhancement.* The corporation informs consumers of its products, services, and new developments. Sales increase when more consumers are informed and convinced about the specific products and services. Consumer relations is used to distribute new and updated information for sales promotion.

- ■ *Loyal Consumer Retention.* The corporation makes an effort to convince established consumers who have used the corporation's products and services to reuse or repurchase them through positive consumer relations programs.

- ■ *New Consumer Attraction.* For the corporation to make bigger profits, attracting new consumers is essential. The corporation develops programs that encourage consumers to try its products and services, in addition to conducting promotional campaigns.

- ■ *Favorable Consumer Opinion Promotion.* When consumers' attitudes toward the corporation are positive, there is a better chance of selling more products and services. Consumer relations is designed to give good impressions to consumers when they are in the process of buying, using, and reviewing the products and services.

- ■ *Complaint Handling.* No corporation is free from consumer complaints. As the consumer is king and always right, the corporation lets the consumer talk and file a complaint. Call centers play an important role in addressing consumer complaints and offering compensation for unsatisfied consumers. Since one dissatisfied consumer can inform thousands of people of his or her unhappy experience online, handling complaints is an important role in consumer relations. In fact, this is the number one priority for consumer relations in the digital age.

CONSUMER COMPLAINTS

Consumer relations is sensitive to complaints of unhappy consumers. As social media offers consumers a voice and a publishing tool, posting a complaint online is easy, free, and convenient; the complaint can be spread in no time and read by thousands of online users. The vast majority of dissatisfied consumers would turn into online commentators, expressing their anger and unhappiness about the malfunction of products and services. Worse, if a corporation failed to deal with such complaints, it could face organized resistance from a specific group of consumers. In a nutshell, alleviating one complaint can be worth more than attracting thousands of new consumers because one complaint establishes negative attitudes toward the corporation, and such attitudes would discourage new and even loyal consumers from using the corporation's products and services ever again. Many consumer relations experts advise customer service representatives on how to handle consumer complaints:

- **Listen.** In general, when a consumer complains, he or she is upset and angry. Let the consumer finish talking. Take the time to listen and let the consumer know that the representative has listened and understood what is driving the complaint.

- **Say You're Sorry.** As soon as the complaint is mutually understood, the representative apologizes. This does not mean an admission of the corporation's responsibility, but it rather shows good manners; this avoids the possible mishandling of the consumer's concerns.

- **Ask.** After saying "I'm sorry to hear that," the representative asks questions about the complaint. More information about the product or service helps solve the complaint.

- **Empathize.** Once the representative has gathered the information about the complaint, it is time to create a bond with the consumer by expressing empathy with his or her situation. The representative assures that the consumer has a valid point, and the corporation is always determined to resolve an issue.

- **Offer.** The representative tells the consumer what the corporation can do about the complaint. The representative offers a solution or compensation on behalf of the corporation, with the repeated mention of the corporation's dedication to customer service. Instant solutions are the best way to alleviate the consumer's unhappiness.

- **Thank.** This last complaint-handling process makes the consumer feel good about the right of consumers. The consumer will also thank the representative and the corporation's good consumer relations.

Although the offer of compensation might cost the corporation some money, it actually helped build a good reputation for the corporation by using good consumer relations techniques. More importantly, the consumer never turns to posting a complaint online. Consumer relations, especially when handling complaints, removes the uncertainty of potentially unhappy consumers.

Many corporations succeed in building and maintaining good consumer relations with effective complaint-resolution techniques. As an American chain of luxury department stores, Nordstrom's customer service is legendary. Some critics say customer service has become synonymous with Nordstrom. The department store's staff members regularly send thank-you notes to their customers and call to check if items sent by mail arrived. What makes Nordstrom the icon of consumer relations is its liberal return policy. It accepts any item back from any of its stores, for any reason, regardless of when it was purchased.[5] For example, a 36-year-old hiker from San Ramon, California, returned his 9-year-old backpack to the store and got his money back.[6] *Entrepreneur* magazine named Nordstrom one of the ten-most trusted brands in the United States.[7]

5   Kirsten Grind, "REI Nordstrom and the Perils of No-Questions-Asked Returns," *Wall Street Journal*, September 18, 2013, http://blogs.wsj.com/moneybeat/2013/09/18/rei-nordstrom-and-the-perils-of-no-questions-asked-returns/.
6   Grind, "REI, Nordstrom."
7   Paula Andruss, "Secrets of the 10 Most-Trusted Brands," *Entrepreneur*, March 20, 2012, http://www.entrepreneur.com/article/223125.

CONSUMERISM

Not every corporation has the luxury of enjoying a great reputation like Nordstrom. When a series of consumer complaints about a particular product or service arises and never gets resolved, consumerism is organized and promoted. Consumerism refers to an organized movement of individuals and groups asking for policies that protect consumer rights and promote fair business practices. Consumerism gained its popularity in the 1960s when activist Ralph Nader published his seminal book, *Unsafe at Any Speed*, exposing the US auto industry's attempts to appeal to consumers by emphasizing styling, comfort, speed, and power while cutting costs at the expense of safety. The book, published in 1965, cited General Motors' Corvair as an unsafe product, dubbing it a "death trap." As a result, in 1966, production of the Corvair was stopped. The action was enforced by the National Traffic and Motor Vehicle Safety Act, which empowered the government to establish safety standards for all automobiles sold in the United States. The act is regarded as a historical symbol of consumer advocacy. As Nader was gaining public celebrity status, he was followed by a private investigator hired by General Motors. The investigator was assigned to dig up dirt on Nader's personal life. Nader sued the company for invasion of privacy and received a $425,000 settlement. The money was used to establish several consumer advocacy groups, and Nader became an icon of consumerism.

BOYCOTTS

Millions of consumers are taking more direct action to handle their dissatisfaction with products and services. Social media is frequently used as a way to catch corporations' attention. When consumers' demands and complaints are not addressed, the unhappy consumers wind up organizing a boycott. The definition of a boycott is an agreement among public groups not to use or buy certain products or services. The boycott can also apply to particular events. It is a form of protest that pressures irresponsible corporations to respond to consumers' unhappy voices.

One of the largest boycott movements in the United States was Bank Transfer Day in 2011 (Figure 10.2). The boycott originated from Bank of America's new policy of charging debit card fees of $5 a month; Wells Fargo was charging $3 in its pilot program. The boycott encouraged customers to transfer their cash out of big banks to credit unions. Many angry bank customers closed their accounts in big banks and opened new accounts with credit unions. The boycott gained more support from the public and politicians as the media began to cover stories of angry customers. "Bank of America customers, get the heck out of that bank," Senator Dick Durbin (D-Ill.) said. "Find yourself a bank or credit union that won't gouge you for $5 a month and still will give you a debit card that you can use every single day. What Bank of America has done is an outrage."[8] In addition, President Obama advocated the boycott, saying, "Well, you can stop [the fee] if you say to the banks, 'you don't have some inherent right just to, you know, get a certain amount of profit if your customers are being mistreated.'"[9] Bank of America and Wells Fargo decided to eliminate the fees after public and political pressure from average customers reached all the way up to the president of the United States.

FIGURE 10.2 Bank transfer day poster.

---

8   Tim Max, "BoA Nixes $5 Debit Fee," Politico, November 1, 2011, http://www.politico.com/news/stories/1111/67339.html.

9   Max, "BoA Nixes."

Provocative social issues that catch activists' interest are often connected to boycotts. According to Brayden King, a professor at the Kellogg School of Management, the bigger the cause, the more likely the public is to hear of it and the more likely activists are to target a corporation in that category.[10]

Consumer relations for big corporations aims to nip a boycott in the bud before it attracts media coverage. Consumerism activists, in contrast, welcome more media attention, which enables them to gain public and political support. A boycott against certain products or services of bigger corporations with good reputation tends to receive more media attention, which leads to the higher possibility of public and political involvement in the activity. King advises how to deal with a boycott regarding consumer relations:[11]

- **Respond Quickly.** The more media attention that a boycott gets, the more damage it can do to the corporation's reputation. Here's one option: the corporation can just give in to whatever the activists demand.

- **Engage in a Dialogue.** A boycott can be hampered when the corporation and activists negotiate to resolve the situation. Dialogue prevents the boycott from gaining additional momentum.

- **Build Relationships.** The long-term solution for dealing with a boycott is to build good relationships with activists before they call for the boycott.

The most significant effect of boycotts is that corporations suffer from the long-term effect of damaged reputations. Consumer relations is an important specialization that is designed to provide swift and sincere solutions for dissatisfied consumers.

Investor Relations

An investor is a person who provides money or resources to a corporation with the expectation of financial return. Generally, the primary objective of an investor is the preservation of the original investment; he or she wants to minimize risk while maximizing return, as opposed to a speculator who is willing to take on high risks for high rewards. An investor expects a steady return on investment and capital appreciation. The investor expects updated information about the corporation's current financial situation and future earnings from the corporation's communications department. Public relations practitioners who specialize in building relationships with current and future shareholders, especially investors, are the highest-paid professionals in the public relations field.[12] They maintain and improve relationships between a corporation, its shareholders, and the financial community. Their specialization is categorized as "investor relations."

Investor relations is defined as "a strategic management responsibility that integrates finance, communication, marketing, and securities law compliance to enable the most effective two-way communication between a company, the financial community, and other constituencies, which ultimately contributes to a company's securities achieving fair valuation."[13] As the definition shows, investor relations includes

---

10   Brayden King, "How Do Activists Create Change?" KellogInsight, June 2, 2015, https://insight.kellogg.northwestern.edu/article/how-do-activists-create-change

11   Brayden King, "How Do Activists Create Change?" KellogInsight

12   Alexander Laskin, "Investor Relations," Institute for Public Relations, November 14, 2008, http://www.instituteforpr.org/investor-relations/.

13   "About NIRI," National Investor Relations, Institute. http://www.niri.org/FunctionalMenu/About.aspx.

both financial disciplines and communication functions, as well as an understanding of securities law. Practitioners in investor relations are required to have an in-depth understanding of financial systems and the current laws of the market.

Investors and the public expect corporations to stay away from ordeals like the corporate scandals and government bailouts, which occurred in the first ten years of the twenty-first century. Investors expect to hear transparent explanations about financial performance and nonfinancial information about corporations from investor relations specialists who are also responsible for helping investors and financial analysts understand the true value of the corporate business. The specialist helps investors "adjust their estimates no matter if it means decrease or increase in the stock price."[14]

BOX 10.1 THE ENRON SCANDAL

Founded in 1985, Enron Corporation of Houston, Texas, marketed electricity and natural gas, delivered energy and other physical commodities, and provided financial and risk management services to customers around the world. The corporation reached number 7 on the Fortune 500 list in 2000 because Enron's executives employed misleading accounting practices that inflated its revenues.

Enron adopted a variety of deceptive and fraudulent accounting schemes to glorify its financial information. These practices made the corporation look more profitable and created a more fraudulent cycle in which the executives had to create the illusion of billions of dollars in profit. The investors, of course, had no clue about the unethical and illegal practices. The manipulated profits helped the stock price reach new highs, and Enron executives began to sell their stock, thanks to insider information. Investors were fed rosy information about the great future of the corporation while it was actually losing money. Once the fraud came to light, the US Securities and Exchange Commission opened a formal investigation into Enron's financial performance in October 2001.

Enron admitted to the off-balance-sheet accounting frauds, which had inflated its income by $586 million since 1997. The corporation filed for Chapter 11 bankruptcy one month later. The filing left thousands of workers with worthless stock in their pensions and threw thousands of people out of work. Investors lost billions of dollars as Enron's shares shrank to penny-stock levels. Enron's stock price peaked at $90.75 in August 2000 and plummeted to $0.67 in January 2002, when the New York Stock Exchange suspended trading of Enron shares. Enron CEO Jeffrey Skilling was sentenced to 24 years and 4 months in prison in 2006. Critics say the energy business was deregulated by the government until the collapse of Enron. After the scandal, the government created the Sarbanes-Oxley Act of 2002, which tightened disclosure rules and increased the penalties for financial manipulation.

---

14   Laskin, "Investor Relations."

After the corporate scandals, the goal of investor relations shifted from gaining a high stock price to maintaining a fair stock price. In other words, investor relations used to focus on boosting stock prices regardless of bad financial situations, which could lead to off-balance-sheet financing, in which a corporation does not include a liability on its balance sheet. The Enron scandal historically served as a wake-up call for the financial community and led the government to change financial regulations and enforce harsh crackdowns that limit the use of off-balance-sheet financing (Box 10.1). Because of the Enron scandal—the first development to bring the use of off-balance-sheet financing to the public's attention—investor relations has become the most important specialization among all other specialized functions of public relations. Investors carefully look into balance sheets to evaluate a corporation's financial health.

Today's investor relations specialists acknowledge that investors are interested in understanding the corporation's financial health and corporate value. The understanding depends on detailed information delivered from the specialists. The detailed information to satisfy the investors' desire to know about the corporation should include the following five categories, according to Oliver Schutzmann, head of Investor Relations and Corporate Communications at SHUAA Capital:[15]

1. *Financial Performance.* Top- and bottom-line growth, with future-growth projections

2. *Corporate Strategy.* Long-term orientation on shareholder value with market trends

3. *The Corporate Dynamics.* How the corporation makes money

4. *Management Quality.* Management's ability to generate sustained earnings with credibility

5. *Corporate Governance.* Transparency regarding insider trading

Investors have the right to transparent and accurate information about the corporation. With this information, investors make the decision about whether to provide money and resources to the corporation. The main objective of offering corporate information to investors is to establish financial relationships that are linked to the corporation's value, trust, development, analysis, and stability.

- *Value.* The corporation through investor relations communicates its vision, strategy, and potential to investors.

- *Trust.* The professional reveals good and bad news about the corporation's financial health.

- *Development.* The professional develops investor materials; plans events, such as presentations with financial updates about the corporation; writes financial performance releases for the media; and conducts investor events to express the corporation's appreciation.

- *Analysis.* The professional tracks the corporation's financial performance and prepares quarter or annual reports that can serve as investors' guides for investment decisions.

- *Stability.* The corporation sends messages aimed at promoting the purchase and retention of the corporation stock so that its financial health is less likely to be swayed by the dramatic ups and downs of stock prices.

---

15 "Annual Report," Middle East Investor Relations Society, https://www.shuaa.com/media/23155/SHUAA-Annual-Report-2012.pdf

Investor relations specialists maintain close relationships with journalists and serve as news sources for the media. They are particularly sensitive to news stories reported by financial media. A survey conducted by Gorkana Group, a provider of media intelligence services, found that the *Wall Street Journal*, *Bloomberg News*, the *New York Times*, the *Financial Times*, and the news agency *Reuters* are the most influential media outlets in the eyes of US financial journalists.[16] In addition, the survey included two online-only media outlets—Yahoo! Finance and Business Insider—as influential online financial media. The specialists focus their energy and time on monitoring and responding to such influential media since financial media coverage can have a dramatic effect on a corporation's stock price. For example, in September 2008, one of the influential media outlets reported that United Airlines' parent company had filed for Chapter 11 bankruptcy protection, although the bankruptcy filing had happened six years before. An old article about the 2002 bankruptcy filing had apparently resurfaced, and it caused the company's stock price to fall as low as $3 from the previous day's price of $12.30 per share. As the price plummeted because of the false news article, NASDAQ halted trading of the company's shares for more than an hour, and a spokesperson for the company said about the article, "It's not true."[17] Although trading resumed and the price rebounded, it ended at $10.92 a share by closing (more than a 10-percent loss).

Community Relations

Community relations is another specialization of corporate public relations. The term "community" has several definitions:[18]

1. A group of people living in the same place or having a particular characteristic in common (the gay community)
2. A particular area or place considered together with its inhabitants (the Chinese community)
3. A body of nations or states unified by common interests (the African economic community)
4. The people of a district or country considered collectively, especially in the context of social values and responsibilities (the local community)

The local community is the focus of community relations from a corporate public relations perspective. Corporations strategize to build rapport with and gain support from the community. Community relations is designed to build mutual benefit for the corporation and the community with respect to responsible business performance and the social development of the community. Strong community relations bring high return on investment.

Community relations intends to create positive corporate interactions with the people living in the particular environment where the corporation operates. This is why community relations is regarded as a part of corporate relations at the local level. A corporation with a community relations program continues to foster mutual understanding, trust, and support. The key to success is engagement between

16 "Industry News," Gorkana Group, http://gorkana.com/news/corporate-and-financial/general-features/gorkana-survey-of-financial-journalists-in-the-us-2014/.

17 "How a Botched Web Story Wiped Out UAL's Shares," *Forbes*, September 8, 2008, http://www.forbes.com/2008/09/08/ual-tribune-bankruptcy-biz-media-cz_ja_tvr_0908ualstory.html.

18 "Community," *Oxford Dictionary*, http://www.oxforddictionaries.com/us/definition/american_english/community.

a wide range of people in the community and the corporation. In so doing, the corporation creates a pool of community supporters. This means the more community supporters, the higher the possibility of stable business practices in the community. Community relations requires designing and implementing community programs that include donations, philanthropic work, volunteerism, and partnerships. Such programs are aimed at improving the quality of the community environment and promoting the corporation's long-term business relationship with community members.

Building and maintaining a long-term relationship with the community is directly associated with the accomplishment of corporate community relations objectives. There are seven objectives of corporate community relations:

1. Informing the community of the corporation's business practices

2. Contributing to the community with corporate programs, such as free concerts, art exhibits, and food festivals

3. Fostering community understanding of all aspects of the corporation's operation.

4. Encouraging the employees of the corporation to participate in volunteer services for the community

5. Gaining positive attitudes through philanthropic work in the community

6. Informing the community of the corporation's facilities and services that the community can use

7. Promoting business cooperation with local government and small business owners to assist the community's economy

Corporations acknowledge the importance of being integrated into communities. Being a part of the community results in positively positioning themselves among members of the community. When the community accepts the corporation as a community member, the corporation can translate that into a boost for profits. Positive community acceptance can be derived from strategic community programs. For example, H-E-B Grocery Company, a privately held supermarket chain based in Texas, has a prestigious reputation because of its commitment and involvement in the community. The supermarket chain operates six noticeable community relations programs with the motto, "It's our way of saying thank you for allowing us to be your neighbor. We call it H-E-B's Spirit of Giving."[19] The programs are as follows:[20]

- **Excellence in Education Awards.** Each year, H-E-B gives away $600,000 in cash prizes to teachers, principals, and school districts.

- **Environment.** H-E-B recycles plastic bags and makes contributions in support of environmental programs, such as Keep Texas Beautiful, Earth Share of Texas, The Nature Conservancy, Hill Country Conservancy, and many more.

- **Community Events.** Among many events, "Feast of Sharing Dinners" celebrates the holidays with more than 250,000 free meals served annually.

- **Commitment to Diversity.** From employee recruitment to supplier registration, diversity is at the core of H-E-B's business principles. It sponsors and volunteers for cultural events, such as the Martin Luther King Jr. marches, Diez y Seis activities, and Juneteenth celebrations.

19   "Community Involvement," H-E-B, https://www.heb.com/static-page/Community-Involvement.
20   H-E-B, "Community Involvement."

- ***Read 3.*** H-E-B has donated nearly three million books (Figure 10.3) to children in need since 2011 with the catchphrase: "Grow Young Minds. Read 3 Times a Week."

- ***Apply for Support.*** H-E-B donates money to nonprofit organizations that specialize in hunger relief, health initiatives, social services, environmental programs, diversity, disaster relief, and the arts.

FIGURE 10.3 H-E-B read 3.

As a Texas-based corporation, H-E-B succeeds in building a connection with the community of Texas through its community relations programs.

Corporate Social Responsibility

Corporations in pursuit of profits are expected to do more. Rather than purely focusing on profits, they are expected to do something good for society. Since corporations have bigger impacts on society over time, stakeholders and the governments expect them to adopt a broader stakeholder perspective that is realized by CSR. Based on this expectation, the concept of corporate citizenship was introduced. Corporate citizenship, according to the World Economic Forum, refers to[21]

> the contribution a company makes to society through its core business activities, its social investment and philanthropy programmes, and its engagement in public policy. The manner in which a company manages its economic, social, and environmental relationships, as well as those with different stakeholders, in particular shareholders, employees, customers, business partners, governments, and communities, determines its impact.

Good corporate citizenship falls within the category of contributing to society through core business activities. While making money, corporations fulfill societal values, such as human rights, environmental protection, equality and, democracy in the twenty-first century. The process of delivering value is linked to the practice of CSR. CSR represents the relationship between corporations and society with which they communicate. It can be defined as a corporation's continuing commitment to integrate the social, economic, and environmental concerns of the society at large while improving the quality of life for the workforce and their families. CSR is becoming a mainstream business trend since forward-thinking corporations integrated social and economic sustainability into the core of their business operations. In essence, CSR provides a framework for creating shared values between the corporation and society.

Virtually every person on earth is directly or indirectly involved in CSR. Consumers are inclined to buy products from corporations that show high credibility and strong ethical performance; employees want to work for corporations with good reputations; investors tend to offer financial resources to corporations that are able to maintain sustainable social performance; governments like corporations that hire more employees; suppliers hope to build business partnerships with trust; nongovernmental organizations look for corporations that assist in solving social issues. Social values are increased if CSR, as an element of communication strategy, follows twenty-first-century trends at a global level.

---

21   Gardberg, N., & Fombrun, C. (2006). Corporate Citizenship: Creating Intangible Assets across Institutional Environments. *The Academy of Management Review*, 31(2).

Amy Bretherton, marketing and communication consultant at New London Communications, announced five CSR trends in 2019.[22]

1. *Focus on Gen Z.* As consumers, this generation will continue to pressure companies to be more sustainable and ethical.

2. *Broad Collaborations.* More corporations will cross industry lines to work together to address social issues, including government collaborations.

3. *Alignment between CSR and Procurement.* Corporations will dig deeper into what they buy and sell. Supply chain audits and ethically sourced product lines and packaging will become the standard.

4. *Authentic Communication.* Employees will become more involved in CSR initiatives by taking the lead and using social media platforms to share stories at an individual level.

5. *Tech Companies.* They have largely stayed in the environmental space, placing a greater focus on CSR. They concentrate on addressing important social issues, such as digital privacy and cyberbullying.

The trends demonstrate that CSR is mandatory for corporations to play a convincing role in tackling environmental and social issues in the world. Stakeholders, the public, and the government expect and demand more from corporations.

Theoretically, the practice of CSR is surprisingly simple: the corporation makes handsome profits in an ethical way and uses some of the profits to benefit the public. However, it takes strategic plans, thorough activities, and hierarchical steps to achieve good CSR in reality. Archie Carroll, a professor at the University of Georgia, introduced the four steps of effective CSR:[23]

1. *Economic Responsibilities.* A corporation should produce an acceptable return on its shareholders' investments.

2. *Legal Responsibilities.* A corporation carries a duty to act within the legal framework drawn up by the government and the judiciary.

3. *Ethical Responsibilities.* A corporation should do no harm to its stakeholders and within its operating environment.

4. *Philanthropic Responsibilities.* A corporation represents more proactive, strategic behaviors that can benefit the corporation or society, or both.

CSR has become a prominent specialization in corporate relations. Corporations realize that a responsible way of doing business leads to reputational advantages that help them achieve better financial performance. Thus many corporations view CSR as a way to build positive corporate images and reputations through communication. Communication strategies for CSR are realized through a variety of campaigns. The Loads of Hope campaign by Procter & Gamble is a good example (Box 10.2).

---

22   Amy Bretherton, "2019 CSR Trends Outlook," For Momentum, January 9, 2019, https://formomentum.com/2019-csr-trends-outlook/.

23   Carroll, Archie. "Carroll's Pyramid of CSR: Taking Another Look." *International Journal of Corporate Social Responsibility* 1, no. 1 (December 2016): 1–8.

BOX 10.2 LOADS OF HOPE BY TIDE

When a natural disaster strikes a community or a country, the expectation for corporations to engage in relief efforts increases. Although the government, relief agencies, and NGOs participate in helping victims of natural disasters, corporations also find ways of chipping in.

In the wake of Hurricane Katrina in 2005, Procter & Gamble Co. (P&G) launched the "Tide Loads of Hope" campaign. The corporation understood that, in times of disaster, victims seek the most basic of human needs, including clean clothes. When disaster struck, "Tide Loads of Hope" provided relief with the corporation's mobile laundromat—washing, drying, and folding clothes for families in need.

According to its campaign website, one truck and a fleet of vans housed more than 32 energy-efficient washers and dryers that were capable of cleaning more than 300 loads of laundry every day. The corporation also sold vintage-style t-shirts to raise money for the campaign, and all the profits went to charity. Since Katrina, the mobile fleet has traveled to communities afflicted by floods in Mississippi, Tennessee, North Dakota, Texas, New York, New Jersey, and California, washing more than 58,000 loads of laundry as of 2015.

The campaign has not been limited to displaced people in the United States. In the summer of 2010, P&G employees in Pakistan set up a system that washed 10,000 garments a day for a month in response to the flooding of the Indus River. After the earthquake in Haiti, profits from the sales of Loads of Hope t-shirts went toward rebuilding the laundry rooms at a hospital.[1]

In consultation with the Federal Emergency Management Administration and the American Red Cross, the corporation dispatches teams of CSR workers to places struck by hurricanes, floods, wildfires, and earthquakes. The team washes, dries, and folds clothes for free. This CSR campaign is closely associated with feelings of relief, help, and philanthropy. The corporation does not miss the chance to inform the public about their CSR activities: team members arrive in a giant orange truck and a fleet of orange vans, and their logo is printed on every washer and dryer. For example, the team of CSR workers in March 2019 was deployed to support relief and recovery efforts in the wake of the devastating flooding in Nebraska.

This CSR campaign offers a huge amount of help to those affected by natural disasters. More importantly, the name of the campaign successfully builds the identity of Tide laundry detergent, which creates the image of "hope" for people in need. Compared to other relief activities, this CSR activity could be considered small, but it offers a solution for a very basic human need during a time of chaos. This is an effective example of a CSR activity that built positive relationships with communities through disaster response. In sum, the CSR campaign makes a real and lasting impact on the lives of people in need.

---

1 Constance Casey, "The Spin Cycle," Slate, September 22, 2010, http://www.slate.com/articles/life/my_goodness/2010/09/the_spin_cycle.html.

TABLE 10.2   Ten Companies with the Best CSR Reputations of 2020

Rank	Corporation Name
1	The LEGO Group
2	The Walt Disney Company
3	Rolex
4	Ferrari
5	Microsoft
6	Levi Strauss & Co
7	Netflix
8	Adidas Group
9	The Bosch Group
10	Intel

CSR gives corporations the opportunity to build a good image and a strong reputation. As the example of P&G demonstrates, corporations capitalize on the activities of CSR. A survey found that 50 percent of American consumers intended to avoid purchasing a product or service from a corporation they considered not socially responsible.[24] Either through making financial donations, providing human resources or organizing philanthropic events, corporations make an effort to participate in CSR. Such participation is unlikely to go unnoticed since public relations practitioners are in charge of informing the media and target audiences about corporations' good deeds. The information commonly appears in press releases and the annual CSR reporting of corporations. In fact, more corporations compete for the best CSR reputations (see table 10.2).

The Reputation Institute, after surveying more than 230,000 individual consumers in the world, announced "The World's Most Reputable Companies for Corporate Responsibility 2020."[25]

Corporate Public Relations in the C-Suite

The practice of public relations, in general, aims to produce customized messages and stories and get them published in the media. Corporate relations from a public relations perspective, however, is more complex and demanding than the general practice of public relations. Specialized public relations practitioners are needed to conduct such complex duties for corporations. Their target audience is stakeholders who are deeply involved in a corporation's management. The audience is sensitive to every aspect of the business, including stock price, news reports, social responsibilities and rapidly changing consumer trends.

24   Robert L. Heath and Lan Ni, "Corporate Social Responsibility," Institute for Public Relations, September 25, 2008. http://www.instituteforpr.org/corporate-social-responsibility/.
25   "New Study from Reputation Institute Reports Across-the-Board Reputation," *Business Wire*, March 3, 2020, https://finance.yahoo.com/news/study-reputation-institute-reports-across-133000459.html.

Corporate public relations professionals seek to build mutually positive relationships with stakeholders while communicating with financial news outlets and investors.

The professionals are armed with knowledge about communication, finance, management, and legal systems. They can hardly survive unless they have a comprehensive approach to corporate operations. They have a seat among the members of the C-suite, a corporation's important senior executives. In other words, they participate in the corporate decision-making process in which sophisticated issues are discussed. The professionals advise CEOs and other executives to implement the practice of building a good corporate reputation, engaging with stakeholders, and maintaining a healthy corporate brand through CSR programs, community relations, consumer relations, and investor relations.

CHAPTER SUMMARY AND REVIEW

1. Understand the concepts of corporation and stakeholder.

2. Identify the historical public relations background of corporate relations.

3. Study investor relations, community relations, and consumer relations.

4. Explain why CSR is considered important in public relations.

5. Argue the importance of transparent management.

PUBLIC RELATIONS IN PRACTICE

FUTHER READING

PR Week's Awards For **Best PR CSR**

Winner: Michelin North America and Ketchum
Campaign Name: Teens Prove Their #StreetTread

The company teamed up with Vans for a limited edition #StreetTread sneaker featuring the Michelin Man. The launch was timed to Memorial Day weekend, the start of the 100 deadliest days during which teen driving deaths spike. The kicks could be had for a penny—as long as teens first used the coin to check for proper tire tread depth. The promo explained how to insert the penny to determine the amount of tread.

Read more at
https://www.prweek.com/article/1579436/prweek-us-awards-2019-winners

Employee Communication

An organization consists of individuals who are assigned to work on different tasks with the shared goals of producing products or services in pursuit of excellence. The individuals are members of the organization, and they are its greatest resource. The organization divides them into two inside groups: management and labor. Management refers to a group of executives and managers who have the authority and responsibility to oversee and manage the organization. They make crucial decisions for the organization's operations and policies. Labor is a group of individuals who work full- or part-time under an oral or a written contract of employment. They are hired to provide their effort, time, and energy to the organization on a regular basis, guided by the organization's instructions on how and what will be done at work. In return, they receive wages or compensation.

A wide range of factors can affect the achievement of organizational goals; these factors include consumers, communities, investors, NGOs, the government, journalists, and the public. However, the most essential factors are management and labor, which are the de facto engines that keep the organization moving. They agree to work with and for each other to achieve the organization's goals.

Since management and labor belong to the same organization, an organizational culture that minimizes and prevents workplace conflict is central to a successful business. Conflict in the workplace is commonly grounded in a lack of information or an abundance of misinformation. The most common conflict in an organization occurs between these two groups. If employees feel that management is hiding something from them, then feelings of distrust and disappointment toward the organization increase, and a conflict of trust arises. In general, the roots of organizational conflict can be found in the lack of communication between the two entities. Executives and managers with the power to make decisions realize that clear, timely, and honest communication with labor helps minimize, or even prevent, workplace conflict. This type of communication in an organization is called "employee communication." Any organization that aims to succeed in a specific industry needs to place value on positive employee communication. An organization's success depends on communicating the right content and information to its employees who are motivated to work for the common goals of the business. Building mutual relations between labor and management depends on the quality of communication between managers and employees. Employee communication as the dominant function of employee relations offers consultation, collaboration, facilitation, and resolution for workplace affairs.

Definitions of Employee Communication

Employee communication is often defined as the sharing of information, feelings, and ideas within an organization. This communication takes place between management and labor, and its aim is to ensure that both sides are committed to achieving organizational goals through stable collaboration and exchange of information. It motivates employees to implement the organization's strategy by supporting the company's beliefs, behaviors, and culture.

There are two ways of understanding the concept of employee communication. One is to see the organization as a container in which communication spontaneously occurs because management and labor have to communicate for the organization. The other is to see the organization as an essential force that imposes organizational meaning, culture, objectives, and values on its management and labor. This process flows from founders or CEOs who create missions, goals, and strategies for management and labor, who in return invest their resources in fulfilling the expectations of the founders or CEOs. Their resources combine time, energy, and effort.

Management plays a central role in fulfilling expectations by communicating with labor. In this communication setting, managers are required to have verbal, email, video and face-to-face communication with labor. Communication helps build strong relationships with employees and stimulates collaborative activities that create a better atmosphere in the workplace. Indeed, in many organizations, communications department staffers regularly educate managers about how to communicate better with their subordinates. The bottom line is that managers provide important information and advice about their subordinates' work performances and job security. This helps to create a more engaged, motivated, and satisfied workforce. Effective managers armed with communication skills establish a communication strategy that includes "keeping employees apprised of important developments, providing clarity on goals and priorities, and establishing a means to receive and respond to feedback."[1] Tom Fox, head of Partnership's Center for Government Leadership, suggested four strategies for communicating better with employees (Table 11.1):[2]

Generally speaking, employees appreciate management that makes an effort to keep them informed. Information about the organization varies. New information is produced and disseminated to employees every day through employee communication channels. Sometimes a flood of information distracts employees from recognizing the most important ideas and issues within the organization. A successful organization focuses on a few key messages to ensure that everybody within the organization understands the goals. The messages should be honest, motivating, and useful in building trust and facilitating openness in the organization's operation. The messages are aimed at empowering management and labor to do their jobs well.

1 "Tips for communicating better with your employees," *Washington Post*, August 8, 2014, http://www.washingtonpost.com/blogs/on-leadership/wp/2014/08/08/tips-for-communicating-better-with-your-employees/.
2 "Tips for communicating better with your employees," *Washington Post*.

TABLE 11.1 Four Management Strategies for Better Communication with Employees

Make communication a consistent priority.	There are multiple venues where employees can receive information from managers, ranging from quarterly call-ins to in-person and virtual town hall meetings. Managers can seek employee feedback through focus groups and surveys, customizing questions based on their immediate relevance to their job performance. Establishing effective communication requires long-term focus.
Communicate through multiple platforms.	To communicate with all employees effectively, managers should use multiple communication platforms. From more conventional means of employee communication, such as one-on-one discussions and emails, to more innovative communication methods, such as video conferencing and social media, managers should leverage a range of platforms to communicate with employees.
Maintain open lines between managers and employees.	Effective communication is only possible when those in top positions maintain open, direct lines with employees. Organizations can foster such communication by hosting office hours where employees meet directly with managers and by organizing webinars that allow managers to overcome geographical hurdles.
Implement employee suggestions.	Soliciting employees' opinions is an initial step toward improving employee communication. Simply collecting these ideas, though, does little to improve satisfaction if employees believe managers do not use their feedback. When managers implement ideas generated by employees, they receive a clear message that their voice is both heard and valued.

Source: Tom Fox, selection from "Tips for Communicating Better with Your Employees," *The Washington Post*. Copyright © 2014 by *The Washington Post*.

Vision First in Employee Communication

A study, conducted by the leadership development firm, Novations, found that a meaningful vision for the engagement of employees can have a positive effect on an organization when its employees can see how their work contributes to the organization's vision.[3] Great management engages employees in the journey of understanding the vision of the organization, which leads them to focus on achieving organizational goals. The study also found that employees who find their organization's vision to be meaningless are unlikely to care about its future success. In contrast, employees who find their organization's vision to be meaningful are likely to have higher engagement levels and are willing to do more than merely keep their jobs. The study discovered eight key factors that made a vision more meaningful to employees:[4]

1. ***The Vision Is Inspiring and Motivating.*** The best vision statements will be inspiring to both investors and internal stakeholders.

2. ***Employee Engagement and Satisfaction Is High.*** Creating a vision that employees accept and value creates engagement.

3. ***The Vision Is Communicated through Multiple Channels.*** The vision is communicated through sufficient channels to stay current and familiar to employees.

4. ***Innovation Is Used to Create Improvement.*** Excellent visions are aspirational and future focused.

5. ***Managers' Words Lead to Action.*** In organizations where words are rarely acted upon, vision statements become meaningless words with no reality attached.

---

3   Joseph Folkman, "8 Ways to Ensure Your Vision Is Valued," *Forbes*, April 22, 2014, http://www.forbes.com/sites/joefolkman/2014/04/22/8-ways-to-ensure-your-vision-is-valued/.
4   Folkman, "8 Ways."

6. ***Leaders Are Open and Honest.*** Leaders need to be trustworthy and demonstrate that they are willing to speak the truth.

7. ***The Company Is Quick to Respond.*** Because the vision is future focused, employees need to feel that the organization is agile, nimble, and able to make changes quickly.

8. ***People Can See the "Greater Good" the Vision Creates.*** Employees want to be part of something that creates positive outcomes and cares for the environment.

Management should feel responsible for communicating the vision to employees who can be inspired to do more for the organization. An organization's vision statement provides the foundation for employee communication. A vision statement can consist of a few words or long sentences. An example of a short vision statement is Oxfam's "A just world without poverty." An example of a longer vision is Coca-Cola's as follows:[5]

> Our vision serves as the framework for our road map and guides every aspect of our business by describing what we need to accomplish to continue achieving sustainable, quality growth.

1. ***People.*** Be a great place to work where people are inspired to be the best they can be.

2. ***Portfolio.*** Bring to the world a portfolio of quality beverage brands that anticipate and satisfy people's desires and needs.

3. ***Partners.*** Nurture a winning network of customers and suppliers; together we create mutual, enduring value.

4. ***Planet.*** Be a responsible citizen who makes a difference by helping build and support sustainable communities.

5. ***Profit.*** Maximize long-term returns to shareowners while being mindful of our overall responsibilities.

6. ***Productivity.*** Be a highly effective, lean, and fast-moving organization.

Coca-Cola's vision is very specific, and it represents the organization's goals to benefit its shareholders and people around the world. The vision also includes the elements of CSR and community relations.

Removing Barriers to Effective Employee Communication

Good employee communication is crucial to organizational success. Management used to merely focus on ordering and controlling labor. Organizational culture in today's workplace has changed: there are longer hours, heavier workloads, fewer employees, and higher expectations of outcomes. In addition, organizations emphasize high functional job performance. As management and labor understand and adapt themselves to the culture of the twenty-first-century workplace, today's good executives and managers

---

5   "Purpose and Vision," Coca-Cola, http://www.coca-colacompany.com/our-company/mission-vision-values.

place a high value on communicating with employees, which helps to build mutual trust. The trust functions as a vehicle for encouraging employees to contribute to the success of the organization. This is why management becomes more involved in supporting and assisting in the work of employees. Instead of dropping orders and controlling employees, managers share their knowledge, expertise, and insight with employees to achieve organizational goals. They know that the old era of insensitive management that tells employees what to do is long gone. The current era of considerate

management, which includes explaining why certain things need to be done, has become the norm for employee communication. The practice of considerate management even allows employees to engage in exchanging opinions during the decision-making process. Communication in the workplace is the central force in achieving organizational goals.

Management and labor agree that they want to work at a fun place where they can learn and grow while caring about each other. In contrast, they want to avoid an organization that does not allow them to speak up or express their feelings. They admit that barriers that negatively impact communication effectiveness exist. The major barriers are closed communication, private possession of knowledge, nonmotivational culture, biases, limited time, and individualism. Management that currently controls employee communication can remove such barriers with the following solutions:

- *Sharing Information.* Employees want to hear good and bad information about the organization they work for. As soon as they notice that management becomes secretive, their loyalty and trust in the organization weaken. Management should not avoid sharing bad news.

- *Giving Motivation.* Employees get into the same routine—come to work and go home. They get used to staying in their comfort zones. Management should have open discussions with them to offer reasons to boost outcomes.

- *Communicating Know-How.* Most managers used to be employees. Executives and managers know what employees struggle with and what they go through at work. Managers should be mentors and coaches for employees by giving them a great deal of advice and support.

- *Rejecting Biases.* Executives and managers tend to have personal biases toward employees. They might think that new employees don't have enough knowledge about a particular task or that female employees are more demanding and picky. Communicating with employees in a candid way removes biases and builds mutual understanding.

- *Teaming Up.* Employees focus on individual outputs and self-interest, whereas management sees the comprehensive performance of teams or departments. Structuring a teamwork-oriented assignment in which employees interact with management is a great way to overcome communication barriers. This enables management to understand employees' personal abilities and skills.

- *Allocating Time.* Managers are busy people, but they need to set aside some time to talk to employees in person. Executives and managers invest many hours in communicating with bosses, consumers, and other outside stakeholders. They often think less about employees when it comes to communication. Management should schedule time to listen to what employees care about.

The removal of communication barriers requires management to strive to build stronger relationships with labor. Management needs to recognize that employees will be more excited about and motivated by their work if they are heard and feel connected. They want to believe that they are great assets to the organization and that they make significant contributions to the achievement of organizational goals. In a similar vein, employees can feel valued when management offers mentoring systems, shares important information, develops new organizational strategies, and listens to their suggestions for the organization. They want to be included in the organization as important players.

Organizational Silence

If an organization is reluctant to remove communication barriers or does not want employees to be involved in the decision-making process, then it is stuck in the climate of organizational silence. Organizational silence refers to the collective-level phenomenon of doing or saying very little in response to significant problems or issues the organization confronts.[6] In such an environment, an organization discourages employees from participating through exchanging opinions on organizational performance. Rather than expressing their thoughts and opinions aloud, employees are, explicitly or implicitly, forced to withhold information about potential organizational issues or problems. They choose to shut themselves away from organizational decisions. When employees recognize the workplace's climate of silence, they decide to remain silent about organizational matters, believing that speaking up leads to nothing but negative consequences. Management, in turn, receives no information from employees. This means a broken connection in the communication within an organization (Figure 11.1). Employees will feel underappreciated and care less about what happens to the organization.

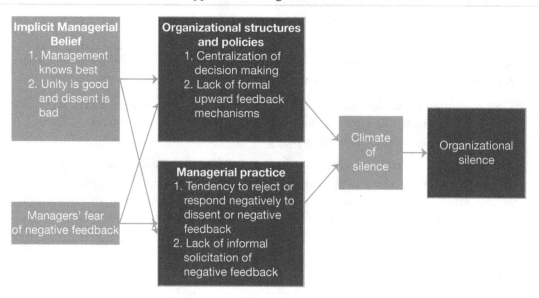

FIGURE 11.1 Organizational silence dynamics.

Adapted from Elizabeth W. Morrison and Frances J. Milliken, "Organizational Silence: A Barrier to Change and Development in a Pluralistic World," *Academy of Management Review*, 25 (2000): 709.

6   Kerm Henriksen and Elizabeth (2006). "Dayton Organizational Silence and Hidden Threats to Patient Safety" *Health Service Research*, http://www.ncbi.nlm.nih.gov/pmc/articles/PMC1955340/.

There are three types of organizational silence that negatively affect mutual understanding:

1. Acquiescent silence is an intentionally passive silent behavior that occurs when employees have no choice but to agree to something by being silent.

2. Defensive silence stems from the psychological intuition of self-protection, which results in the deliberate omission of work-related information based on personal fear of retaliation.

3. Prosocial silence is linked to conscious decision making by withholding work-related information out of concern for the benefit of others instead of personal fear.

Academic scholars Frances J. Milliken and Elizabeth W. Morrison introduced two factors that serve as virtual gag orders in terms of restricting employees from making comments or offering thoughts about organizational performance.[7] The first factor relates to managers' fear of receiving negative feedback from their employees. Executives and managers tend to feel threatened by negative feedback, especially from their subordinates. Although recognizing that the key to an organization's success is communication, managers prefer to avoid embarrassment, threats, and feelings of vulnerability or incompetence that are based on information from employees. The last thing managers may communicate are their weaknesses, especially to those below their own level of job ranking. Therefore, they are likely to avoid any negative information and negative feedback from the subordinates.

The second factor is associated with the belief that management knows what is best for the organization and how the organization's matters should be dealt with. In this mindset, employees are underexperienced, less informed, and less competent at finding the best ways of contributing to organizational goals. More importantly, managers believe that employees are self-interested and could not care less about what is best for the organization, so they cannot be trusted. As a result, the opinions and thoughts employees provide about organizational goals are not relevant to the pursuit of the goals to which management is committed.

These two factors demonstrate why many organizations find it difficult to abandon the top-down communication practice. With top-down communication, instructions and information from management filter down to employees, ensuring that the flow of information keeps employees focused on their relevant tasks and prevents them from being distracted by irrelevant information within the organization. This practice focuses on what is important (vision) and what is valued (goals), as information flows from the top. However, its primary disadvantage arises from the risk of not being able to gather diverse information and ideas from employees who are able to offer creative and fresh strategies for organizational performance. Moreover, employees have the ability to deliver direct messages from the organization's consumers or shareholders about what they want.

Good managers communicate with employees by thinking about how they can engage employees in decision-making processes with the free flow of information; in doing so, management engages in bottom-up communication practices. Communication from the bottom-up is likely to inspire loyalty and motivate employees to work harder for the organization. It educates how important it is for executives and managers to become good listeners. When employees' voices are heard, they feel a sense of strong morale and ownership. Indeed, they are more willing to be engaged in reaching organizational goals. An organization using the bottom-up communication model, however, can experience a logjam of ideas and

7   Elizabeth Wolfe Morrison and Frances J. Milliken, "Organizational Silence: A Barrier to Change and Development in a Pluralistic World," *Academy of Management Review* 25 (2000): 706–725.

opinions that slow the decision-making processes. Striking a balance between the two communication practices is a large task for management.

Breaking organizational silence relies on the willingness of management to do so. As organizational silence can lead to a missed opportunity to detect operational malfunctions and prevent further damage, a friendly communication climate that pays attention to employee feedback should flourish within an organization. The fear of dissent and negative feedback can be removed if executives and managers advocate a system that rewards employees with sensitive or challenging information in order to build an open and trusting communication climate. Rather than blaming employees for their self-interested and untrustworthy behavior, management needs to lay the foundation for supporting employees. In addition, managers' belief in unity, agreement, and consensus can create a strong organization with loyal and committed employees.

More organizations in the digital age have introduced programs to enhance employee communication and break organizational silence (see Box 11.1). They make an effort to invigorate the two-way flow of communication in pursuit of a better workplace, especially when organizations face tough times. Best Buy, the electronics retailer, is one of them.

BOX 11.1   BEST BUY EMPLOYEE COMMUNICATION IN THE FORM OF A TOWN HALL MEETING

During uncertain economic times, Best Buy began to focus on creating a communication channel with the company's 125,000 employees, who were spread out among 1,400 stores across the United States. In 2011, Best Buy received a series of criticisms from consumers and the media about the company's incompetence in competing with other more nimble competitors. Some media outlets predicted the company would go out of business within a few years.

As Best Buy's employees were well aware of such concerns, management at Best Buy set up a meeting that allowed employees and managers to talk about the company's present and future business issues.

Mike Voss, senior director of internal communications at Best Buy, created a live webcast meeting in which CEO Brian Dunn appeared on screens from the Consumer Electronics Show in Las Vegas. Employees of the company across the country were sitting in rooms where they communicated with the CEO through the screen. Two weeks before the meeting, the company's communication team sent out a call for questions to the company's employees, emphasizing that no topics were off limits.

"When we started it, it was eye opening. Employees really loved it. The comments were overwhelming, and over time, there became an expectation that our CEO Brian Dunn and all of our leaders would be just as accessible," said Voss. "The vehicle has done quite a bit for establishing credibility, with employees feeling they have trustworthy leaders with whom they can talk and pose questions."

It was critical to have an internal communication channel to reassure employees and help them understand the company's business strategies. "It's an inspiring event where people can feel good about the direction of the company and see that we're thinking through the issues they see and that there is work being done, even if they don't have visibility to it in their day-to-day jobs," Voss said. "As a result, they can get a sense of confidence regarding the direction of

(Continued)

the company and feel like they can be good ambassadors for Best Buy." The CEO assured the employees about the company's business model, saying, "It's always been important to provide a great experience when a customer walks into our stores or goes online. We have to create outrageously great experiences for our customers regardless of the capabilities we have to work with … that is the long-term, only sustaining advantage for us."

Although Best Buy's future seemed dark and headed to bankruptcy in 2011 in the media assumption, Best Buy is still in business, "standing up to Amazon and thriving," which is "certainly a big turnaround from almost a decade ago," Economics Professor Panos Mourdoukoutas declared in 2019.

Source: "Best Buy Internal Communications Promotes a Culture of Transparency during Challenging Times." Simply-Communicate Case Study, 2012. https://www.simply-communicate.com/case-studies/forum/best-buy-internal-communications-promotes-culture-transparency-during-challenging and Forbes https://www.forbes.com/sites/panosmourdoukoutas/#25096dca6650

As Mike Voss, senior director of internal communications at Best Buy, said, employees have the potential to serve as ambassadors for their organizations. When they are satisfied and feel appreciated at work, it is likely that employees will have a desire to demonstrate strong work performance. In short, employees want to contribute and be a part of the organization. This positive phenomenon is called organizational identification.

Organizational Identification

Employees feel a sense of pride and positive/negative emotions about organizations they work for. In fact, many of them spend more time at work than at home. The workplace is where they want to feel like family. When employees feel satisfied in the workplace, they are more likely to embrace the organization's unique goals and values as part of their views of what the organization should pursue. They identify themselves with the organization. Hence organizational identification can be defined as a psychological perception that is linked to employees' desire to belong to organizations and interact as one of their members. Fostering the perception of identification is beneficial to organizations and employees.

A stream of studies shows that employees are more likely to identify themselves with an organization when they are proud of it. Management is responsible for strengthening organizational identification in order to have committed employees with a strong sense of satisfaction and high morale. Organizational identification increases when the organization has a good reputation in the eyes of the public. A good reputation brings prestige to the organization; employees perceive the prestige with pride and identify more strongly with their organization. This strong organizational identification leads to higher self-esteem, consistently encouraging pride in employees who think about the organization as a prominent source of stability in their lives. Higher self-esteem, boosted by an organization's reputation and prestige, strengthens the sense of organizational identification among employees. When their organizational identification is high, the employees are inclined to tell outsiders the following:[8]

---

8 David Efraty and Donald M. Wolfe, "The Effect of Organizational Identification on Employee Affective and Performance Responses," *Journal of Business and Psychology* 3 (1988): 105–112.

- I like working for (name of organization) very much.

- I feel I am a part of (name of organization).

- The people in this community have much respect for (name of organization).

- This organization is always fair and honest.

- When I hear about someone criticizing the (name of organization), I feel as if I am being personally criticized.

- I feel a sense of pride in working for (name of organization).

- I would not want to work for any other organization.

- Personally, I share the goals of (name of organization), and I value its mission.

- I am a better man for having worked for (name of organization).

What the employees tell other people about their organization affects the public's view of the company. Employees with strong organizational identification serve as good ambassadors for the organization. Aanya Rose, a professional business consultant, listed four ways to strengthen organizational identification:[9]

1. ***Improve Organizational Communication.*** Management should allow employees to present issues to the organization freely and without hesitation. Employees should have a method of expressing grievances that is quick and easy, without a lot of hassle or confusion.

2. ***Build Positive Culture.*** Management can encourage interaction through corporate picnics or team-building contests while embracing individual differences as positive rather than negative. Differences of opinion in meetings might become opportunities for new ideas to emerge.

3. ***Make Work-Life Balance.*** Building an organizational culture that focuses on work-life balance will go a long way toward strengthening organizational identification. Management needs to provide health and wellness outlets or information that provides employees with healthy alternatives to reduce stress or boost dietary education.

4. ***Encourage Employee Participation.*** Providing stock options to employees and allowing them to participate in board meetings can build a rock-solid organizational identification strategy that will reduce turnover and build employee loyalty over time.

---

9   Aanya Rose, "How to Strengthen Organizational Identification," AZ Central, http://yourbusiness.azcentral.com/strengthen-organizational-identification-17022.html.

An organization must do several things to invigorate employee communication: (1) get rid of communication barriers, (2) reduce organizational silence, and (3) strengthen organizational identification. However, the best way for an organization to enhance employee communication is to build a culture of employee communication.

A Culture of Employee Communication within an Organization

A culture of employee communication refers to day-to-day interactions between management and labor. It occurs through freestyle communication that allows employees to talk without the fear of reprisal. Management should spearhead the establishment of the culture.

The culture begins with an organizational tradition that celebrates the major accomplishments of employees. This tradition often starts with casual meetings—getting together each morning to congratulate and encourage each other while exchanging new information about the organization. The morning meeting can be a simple yet effective way for employees to get information and messages from management. It also can help management gain information about market trends from labor. Managers and employees also talk about what they learned from the day before: what happened, what complaints and challenges they received, and what they can do to be a better organization. In short, it is all about small interactions that create a friendly climate for the exchange of information.

Organizations with cultures of robust employee communication are likely to achieve a better understanding between management and employees as follows:[10]

- High-performing organizations focus on communicating with and educating their employees.

- High-performing organizations do a better job of explaining change.

- High-performing organizations provide channels for upward communication and listen to what employees say.

EMPLOYEE COMMUNICATION CHANNELS

There are channels that stimulate employee communication if organizations are not fond of holding everyday meetings. Organizations adopt newsletters, bulletin boards, suggestion boxes, email, intranets, and blogs to exchange information.

Newsletter:

A Regular Organization-Wide Publication. A newsletter is designed to provide general information to all employees. The communications department in an organization is in charge of publishing a weekly or monthly newsletter that includes information and messages from all other departments. The department staff members act as journalists to find stories about management and labor and publish in the newsletter.

The newsletter is also seen as a newspaper for employees within the organization. Content is about feature-oriented, people-focused, light information. In other words, the newsletter highlights personal human stories about employees and management in addition to providing information about promotions, new hires, and transfers. A significant advantage of the newsletter is that it reports employee

---

10   "Communications Nova Scotia," Nova Scotia, http://novascotia.ca/cns/pubs/ItsNotRocketScience.pdf.

recognition, such as employee of the month, service awards, and special training, along with marriage and retirement announcements.

An effective newsletter might have several sections with a variety of topics: hot issues in the organization, the CEO's message, product promotions, consumer responses, an expert column, wellness programs, Q&A, new or modified organizational policies, and distinguished employees. The newsletter can be published in print and online with photographs and illustrations. It usually takes the format of a magazine. The communications department distributes a print copy to each employee or an electronic copy through email.

Bulletin Board:

Posting Information in a Way That Is Accessible to Most Employees. A bulletin board is a vehicle for routine news within an organization. Bulletin boards are situated in places where most employees have access—such as an in-house cafeteria, lunchroom, hallways, and elevators. Information on a bulletin board should be short, concise, and easily understood since employees who happen to walk past the board are less likely to pay close attention to information in a longer format. One advantage of a bulletin board is that it allows employees to post information. They might place postings to find people, sell items, or promote events related to their personal matters.

Suggestion Box:

Anonymous Suggestions from Employees for a Better Organization. Management wants to know what ideas and complaints employees have. Employees are often afraid to discuss their dissatisfaction with management or to speak up about poor policies within the organization. A suggestion box is designed to empower employees to offer honest recommendations and feedback. It helps improve the work environment for both management and employees. The key to a suggestion box is anonymity. The box should be picked up on a regular basis, and the suggestions should be used to address employees' complaints. Some organizations publicly post all suggestions, along with responses from management. Morale and productivity can rise when employees know that management is up to making a difference from the suggestions.

Email:

An Easy Way to Deliver Consistent, Timely Information to Employees. Information and messages from management can be repeatedly disseminated via email, which is a cheap and fast communication channel. All employees have an organizational email account, so management can send the same information to all employees at the same time. Information sent by management via email includes attachments or links for additional online information. Employees can send quick responses to management by replying to the email. It's easy and quick for both parties, although email can be abused when it offers too much information. One merit of email is that it helps an organization avoid printing costs.

Intranet:

A Computer Network That Uses Internet Protocol Technology within an Organization. An intranet is a collection of private computer networks that allow the exchange of information via Internet services that are available only to management and labor within the organization. As the intranet allows employees to have access to data and information about the organization, communications staff posts forms of organizational documents on the intranet that employees can download and fill out. For example, vacation applications, benefits enrollment, and resource bookings can all be done on the intranet. It also allows employees to finish online training and schedule organizational event participation.

The intranet houses data provided by employees, including phone numbers, home addresses, bank account information, emergency contacts, and email addresses. With the data, management knows where to send personal information to employees. In other words, each employee gets his or her own profile on the intranet. Since the intranet is only available to management and employees in the organization, some data and information about the organization are required to stay inside the organization.

Many organizations use the intranet to publish and share organizational policy and procedure manuals, as well as online directories to cut down on paperwork. The directory shows employee names, titles, duties, departments, and phone and fax numbers. Photos, videos, and colorful graphics are used to make an intranet friendly to employees. The intranet is useful when employees are located in different cities and countries. Although working in different places, they are connected through the intranet, which reflects the culture of an organization. The intranet makes employees feel more at home because it helps dispersed employees feel that they share the same space inside the organization.[11]

Blog:

A Frequently Updated Online Journal to Share Opinions and Information. A blog provides employees with an easy way of posting their opinions about an organization online. In a similar way, executives and managers use blogs to express their thoughts and post solutions to organizational issues. Employees either have an individual blog site that they use to discuss what is going on in their lives or use their organization's blog to share their knowledge and expertise. In using their organization's blog site, employees are likely to promote products or services for the organization in hopes of establishing themselves as experts in their fields. While blogging, they have a chance to expand their online social network to interact with other people in the same field of work and exchange current information.

In fact, blogs are also favored by management in terms of expressing opinions about organizational matters. CEOs and executives use blogs to feed information and messages to employees. For example, Bill Marriott, chairman and CEO of Marriott International, Inc., launched his blog in 2007 at the age of 75. Since then, he has been blogging about how he runs the organization and what he learns from his employees.

Employees find information about what management thinks from organizational blogs, and they leave comments on blog posts. These comments give management ideas for improving the way they exchange information online. It is worth noting that, with a blog, employees have a voice outside and inside the organization, and organizations strive to create their own blog culture (see Box 11.2).

Impact of Employee Communication on Organizational Performance

Many studies have found that employee communication directly affects the existence of an organization. The findings indicate the following:

---

11   "Intranet," Reference for Business, http://www.referenceforbusiness.com/small/Inc-Mail/Intranet.html.

BOX 11.2   IBM'S CULTURE OF BLOGGING FOR EMPLOYEES

International Business Machines, better known as IBM, published guidelines for corporate blogging on its employee intranet. These guidelines have historical value, as the technology service company, operating in more than 170 countries, pioneered them to give a clear understanding of blogging to its employees who were considered bloggers. In addition, the guidelines demonstrate how a global organization approached the matter of bloggers who were also employees of the company at the same time.

Management at IBM recognized that thousands of IBM employees would be the voice of the company, so it established a technology-friendly culture that enabled employees to become bloggers. According to IBM's website, "In 2003, the company made a strategic decision to embrace the blogosphere and to encourage IBMers to participate." In general, IBM has a long-established communication culture that lets employees talk to each other and the public without intervention from management.

The guidelines are as follows:

- Know and follow IBM's Business Conduct Guidelines.

- Identify yourself—name and, when relevant, role at IBM.

- Respect copyright, fair use, and financial disclosure laws.

- Respect your audience.

- Find out who else is blogging on the topic and cite them.

- Try to add value. Provide worthwhile information and perspective.

IBM bloggers are required to place a statement on each blog: "As they'll tell you themselves, the opinions and interests expressed on IBMers' blogs are their own and don't necessarily represent this company's positions, strategies, or views."

Source: IBM Bluemix, https://www.ibm.com/developerworks/community/blogs/jasnell/entry/blogging_ibm?lang=en.

1. Employee communication influences an employee's desire to stay with or leave an organization.

2. Organizations with engaged and committed employees were 50 percent more productive than organizations where employees weren't engaged.

3. A positive communication climate and effective employee communication strengthen employees' identification with their organizations.

4. Effective communication facilitates engagement and builds trust, which is a critical ingredient in strong, viable organizations; engaged employees enhance business performance because they influence customer behavior, which directly affects revenue growth and profitability.

5. A significant improvement in communication effectiveness in organizations was linked to a 29.5 percent rise in market value.

6. Employees' satisfaction with communication in their organizations is positively linked to organizational commitment, productivity, job performance, and other significant outcomes.[12]

These findings demonstrate that effective employee communication within an organization increases job satisfaction, morale, productivity, commitment, and trust; as a result, reputations and earnings of organizations increase.[13]

Employee Communication in Evolution

Management wants to connect with labor to achieve organizational goals. The connection is based on a business and human relationship. In today's organizational structure, management and labor build strategic partnerships rather than using a hierarchical ranking system of operation. Public relations practitioners or communications department staffers play a central role in connecting management with labor through employee communication channels. They strive to create and maintain a communication-friendly climate within an organization by being a messenger for both sides. The messengers are assigned to convey the needs and desires of management and employees. Newsletters, bulletin boards, suggestion boxes, and intranets are effective, useful employee communication tools.

New communication technologies help employees express their opinions and concerns about issues in their organizations. Management also benefits from communication technologies to address such issues for employees in a quick and easy way, acknowledging that decreasing employee dissatisfaction is crucial to productive organizational performance. Although employee communication is a complex and difficult process, organizations should take an honest and open communication approach. This approach can build employee trust, create shared identification, and encourage engagement. In sum, employee communication is the foundation for management and labor to make sense of their organization and share the understanding of what the organization means in their lives.

FIGURE CREDITS

Tbl. 11.1: Tom Fox, Selection from "Tips for Communicating Better with Your Employees," The Washington Post. Copyright © 2014 by The Washington Post.
Img. 11.1: Copyright © 2015 Depositphotos/gustavofrazao.
Fig. 11.1: Adapted from: Elizabeth Wolfe Morrison and Frances J. Milliken, "Organizational Silence Dynamics," Organizational Silence: A Barrier to Change and Development in a Pluralistic World. Academy of Management Review, vol. 25, no. 4, pp. 706-725. Copyright © 2000 by Academy of Management.
Img. 11.2: Copyright © 2014 Depositphotos/DragonImages.
Img. 11.3: Copyright © 2016 by MyHub.
Img. 11.4: Copyright © 2020 by Haymarket Media Group Ltd.

---

12   Bruce Berger, "Employee/Organizational Communications," Institute of Public Relations, November 17, 2008, http://www.instituteforpr.org/employee-organizational-communications/.

13   Institute of Public Relations, "Employee/Organizational Communications."

CHAPTER SUMMARY AND REVIEW

1. Describe strategies for better communication with employees.

2. Identify the elements of organizational identification.

3. Explain why organizational silence occurs.

4. Enumerate communication tools for employee communication.

5. Discuss the effective ways of building a culture of organizational communication.

PUBLIC RELATIONS IN PRACTICE

FUTHER READING

PR Week's Awards For **Best PR Internal Communication**

Winner: NBCUniversal
Campaign Name: Bring Your Parents to Work Day

The internal comms team organized panels and Q&A sessions with high-profile father and son teams from the company and recruited execs and NBCUniversal talent to give attendees updates about the business. To promote the event, the internal graphics team created an on-brand package featuring animated iconic characters that were displayed on screens across all six locations. Employees were emailed a save-the-date and invitation.

Read more at
https://www.prweek.com/article/1579436/prweek-us-awards-2019-winners

12

Crisis Communication

I n every minute, every day, and every place in the world, people are flooded with information because of modern digital media and social networking sites. Such information helps them assess risks and benefits that are directly relevant to their livelihoods. Based on the level of relevance, some information turns into recognizable personal issues in society. When a personal issue influences a considerable number of individuals within a community, it can become a social issue. Social issues are associated with poverty, discrimination, unemployment, environmentalism, political reform, public safety, drugs, war on terror, civil unrest, and the economy. All of these social issues provide both a direct opportunity and challenge for organizations when they strategize their operations in specific social surroundings.

No organization is free from socially constructed systems when they are required to follow laws and regulations enforced by the government while fulfilling public expectations. When the government or the public notices an organization's wrongdoing, the organization gets into trouble. Specifically, the organization is faced with a crisis. In the age of new communication technologies that keep the world connected, it takes only seconds for bad news about an organization to reach every corner of the world. Once a crisis breaks out, the organization exploits every resource to address the problem. Every resource includes financial, human, and knowledge assets. The practice of public relations provides communication resources for dealing with a crisis. The process is identified as crisis communication.

What Is a Crisis?

Every organization is vulnerable to a crisis in the era of the 24/7 news cycle of traditional and social media. Only about less than six decades ago, when television was not in everyone's living room and the Internet was not even invented, information about an organization's mistakes or wrongdoings might have been among a limited population. An organizational misdeed might have slipped past the radar of national media, but today's media environment barely allows any organizations' wrongdoings to go unnoticed by the public. A mistake or wrongdoing made by organizations, especially corporations, is unlikely to be confined to the mistake itself in the current media environment. Rather, it turns into a social issue from the standpoint of the media and the public. The social issue turns into a crisis, which the organization has to handle. As a result, a crisis calls for the organization to execute agile emergency management.

A crisis frightens organizations. Organizations recognize the term *crisis* as a catastrophic event that requires leadership to take decisive action. Such action aims to protect the organization and its employees from the distinct possibility of certain damage. A crisis can lead to tangible damage, such as the loss of lives or monetary value, as well as intangible damage, such as the destruction of an organization's reputation or credibility. A crisis is a serious moment in an organization's life cycle, and it can be predicted and prevented if organizations acknowledge the following five common characteristics of crisis:

1. *Surprise.* A crisis arises unexpectedly. Bad things can happen when an organization is not prepared for warning signs.

2. *Darkness.* Once a crisis breaks out, there is usually little information about it. An organization is kept in the dark in the first phase of a crisis until it receives more information.

3. *Swiftness.* A crisis spreads like wildfire as an organization tries to learn about it. The public and the media could know about the crisis even before the organization.

4. *Threat.* A crisis can threaten the existence of an organization. The threat of a crisis can destroy financial security, consumer relations, and the supply chain of products and services.

5. *Criticism.* When a crisis happens, and it is recognized by the media and the public, an organization will come under intense scrutiny and become a target of criticism.

A crisis is an unexpected, unplanned event that organizations want to avoid. Such an event should be handled in unique and, often, extreme ways, as opposed to the normal practice of business. Because a crisis surprises organizations, it creates uncertainty. However, this does not mean that organizations are helpless and hopeless when hit by a crisis. Organizations have accumulated knowledge and techniques by learning from each other's previous mistakes regarding crisis preparation.

Crisis Management

Most crises associated with organizations originate from human errors. Since a crisis caused by a human is likely to inflict direct harm on employees, consumers, suppliers, and the public, immediate action is essential to prevent further damage. Immediate action when dealing with a crisis is identified as crisis management.

Crisis management is a process (Figure 12.1) designed to prevent or diminish the loss that a crisis can bring to an organization. An organization must be prepared for a crisis to occur at anytime and anywhere. Expecting, thinking, and preparing are the keys to crisis management, which can be divided into three sequential steps: (1) before crisis, (2) during crisis, and (3) after crisis. The organization plans and prepares to confront a crisis in the before-crisis step. Once a crisis strikes, the organization responds in the during-crisis step, and lessons for how to address a crisis better will be discussed in the after-crisis step (Figure 12.2).

- ***Before-Crisis Step.*** An organization predicts a crisis that can, eventually, strike. In case it really happens, the organization prepares a crisis management plan by forming and training a crisis management team with exercises. The management team involves employees from the communications, human resources, legal, logistics, and finance departments. The Institute for Public Relations points out that organizations are better able to handle crises when they (1) have a crisis management plan that is updated at least annually, (2) have a designated crisis management team, (3) conduct exercises to test the plans and team at least annually, and (4) pre-draft some crisis messages.[1] The crisis management plan is designed to assign tasks and responsibilities to the team members during a crisis.

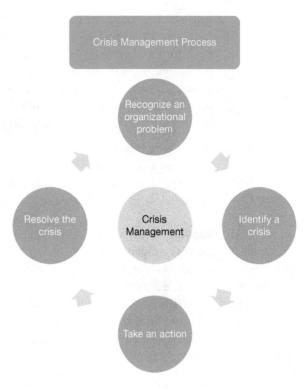

FIGURE 12.1 Crisis management process.

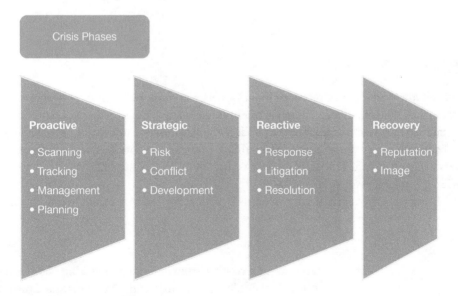

FIGURE 12.2 Crisis phases.

1 "Crisis Management and Communications," Institute for Public Relations, October 30, 2007, http://www.instituteforpr.org/crisis-management-and-communications/.

- **During-Crisis Step.** The crisis management team takes responsibility for responding to the crisis. The team members need to make decisions while sharing important and ongoing information as the crisis unfolds. Communications staff members or public relations practitioners should serve as spokespersons to respond to media requests. The media ask a barrage of questions, and the phrase "no comment" should be the last resort because it sounds like the organization is hiding something from the media and the public. Handling questions from the media is a key element in dealing with an ongoing crisis.

- **After-Crisis Step.** After a crisis is resolved, it is no longer the focal point of the organization's attention, although it still requires evaluation. The management team writes an analysis report to follow up on the process of dealing with the crisis. With the report, the organization and its employees learn not to make similar mistakes.

Crisis management is a specialized communication activity intended to protect the tangible and intangible resources of an organization from danger. Crisis management focuses on dealing with intense media scrutiny as soon as an organizational problem is exposed to public attention. When an organizational problem shows the potential to jeopardize the organization's operation, public relations practitioners identify it as a crisis and take action to minimize and resolve the situation.

Identifying and resolving a crisis is a contingency task in crisis management. The initial process is to organize contingency plans that help to prepare the organization with a range of technical and logistical responses. Contingency plans aim to ensure timely and effective resource operations. In other words, contingency plans are developed to facilitate responses to any requests from inside and outside the organization that may suffer from an unusual situation. These plans should contain information and strategies that are designed to help the organization restore normal operations. Contingency plans function as initial guidelines for organizations to train management and employees for crisis management.

Crisis Phases

Crisis responses are what a public relations practitioner or communications department does and says after a crisis strikes. The practitioner or department is in charge of developing responsive messages that are disseminated to the target audience or the public through communication channels. When responding to a crisis, the practitioner aims to control the damage to the organization. The practitioner is involved from the very beginning of the process of damage control. As a crisis commonly goes through four phases, the practitioner implements specialized tactics for each phase of a crisis to counteract it (Figure 12.3). These four phases were conceptualized by Dennis L. Wilcox, a professor at San Jose State University:[2]

Proactive Phase

This phase involves activities that can prevent a conflict from emerging or getting out of hand. In this phase, organizations will develop a general crisis plan to prepare for an issue to escalate into crisis proportions. The proactive phase consists of four steps.

---

2   Dennis L. Wilcox (2014). *Public relations: strategies and tactics.* Pearson; 11 edition.

1. **Environment scanning** involves constant monitoring for emerging issues relevant to the organization's interests. Public relations practitioners watch and listen to what the media and the public say about the organization, including activities of competitors.

2. **Issue tracking** is associated with the task of following specific and focused issues. Public relations practitioners gather and analyze news stories and public opinion, which can directly affect the organization's operation.

3. **Issue management** is a proactive early warning process that helps public relations practitioners inform and warn management of a possible threat to the organization. This step requires the practitioners to identify issues with which the organization should be concerned. As such issues have the possibility of escalating to crises, the organization analyzes every issue and displays strategic options to avoid catastrophic surprises. These surprises have a negative impact on reaching organizational goals, so management and the practitioners run simulation programs to prepare for a real crisis.

4. **Crisis planning** is designed to prepare for the worst event the organization could eventually face. The key to crisis planning is preparedness. Public relations practitioners create communication strategies to counteract public and media scrutiny. A crisis weakens the organization's normal operations, resulting in a political, legal, financial, and governmental threat to the organization. Furthermore, a crisis damages the organization's reputation and legitimacy.

Strategic Phase

Public relations practitioners identify a particular issue as an emerging conflict that needs attention and action. Three strategies take place in this phase: (1) risk communication, (2) the creation of conflict positioning strategies, and (3) the development of a crisis management plan.

Risk communication is an attempt to communicate dangers or threats to the public or society to prevent problems, such as personal injury, environmental damage, and health risks. The practitioners disseminate information to warn of the danger caused by the organization's operation. They strategize how to disseminate the information, when to communicate with the media and the public, what messages and information to communicate, and where to begin the process of communication. Risk communication is used to diminish the impact of a crisis by putting forth information about the organization in a positive light.

Conflict positioning strategies aim to create favorable attitudes toward the organization. The practitioners anticipate negative reactions from the media and the public amid a crisis. Therefore, the organization plans to organize strategic communication activities against boycotts, adverse legislation, and negative public opinion. In other words, the practitioners strive to create a positive reputation in the court of public opinion.

A crisis management plan includes setting up a crisis communication plan. While developing the crisis management plan, the practitioners focus on eradicating urgent threats, minimizing the disruption to organizational operations, removing the physical and financial damage, and implementing honest communication with stakeholders. In so doing, the organization expects to go back to its normal operations effectively and prevent the repetition of the crisis case. The ability to respond effectively to future crises increases.

Reactive Phase

When public relations practitioners find a specific issue disturbing to the organization's normal operation, the disturbing issue begins to be seen as a potential crisis to which the organization must react. This is when crisis communication takes place in terms of communicating with people affected by the organization's operation. It is the phase when management must make quick decisions to deal with the crisis. The organization establishes a dedicated crisis management team to stay focused on crisis response strategies. There are three pragmatic reactions for the organization in this phase: (1) responsive crisis communication, (2) litigation public relations, and (3) crisis resolution.

Responsive crisis communication is designed to answer questions from the media. The organization's crisis is the media's newsworthy event. The media inform the public about the crisis while calling on the organization to give statements or explanations regarding the origins of the crisis. Crisis communication should be fast and thorough, offering information about the crisis to the media before other news sources generate false information and rumors. If the organization is late in responding to the media's requests, there will be more negative coverage of the organization, and the public will begin to lose confidence in the company. In addition, social media plays an increasingly powerful role in spreading unidentified information. Responsive crisis communication includes the practice of generating timely communication, honest information, and interactive conversations with the media. As a result, the organization builds trust with the media and the public during the crisis.

Litigation public relations aims to support legal actions or trials and is used by an organization during the process of litigation if consumers or other people were harmed during the organization's operations. The core objective of litigation public relations is to diminish damage to an organization's reputation. Public relations practitioners acknowledge that litigation against an organization is only brought about when there is a strong suspicion of organizational wrongdoing. While lawyers argue in court to defend the wrongdoing of the organization, the practitioners communicate the defensive arguments to the media and the public.

Crisis resolution is executed by the dedicated crisis management team, which responds and reacts appropriately to resolve the issue at hand. The team consists of members from the human resources, finance, communications, legal, and logistics departments. The crisis is not over until the team declares an end to the crisis. The team members share their expertise in handling the crisis.

Recovery Phase

This phase happens during the aftermath of the crisis. Public relations practitioners focus on repairing the organization's damaged reputation and image—the damage done by the crisis. The organization concentrates on getting back to normal business. In this process, the practitioners follow up with stakeholders and keep the media informed of any updates on the situation. The crisis management team uses a chronological analysis to reflect on the crisis. The team communicates the aftermath's lessons and policies to executives and employees to avoid repeating the crisis. This phase includes two steps: reputation management and image restoration.

Reputation management includes systematic research to learn the state of the organization's reputation. After a crisis damages an organization's reputation, the company can launch campaigns that involve stakeholders to improve its reputation. The crisis can be used as an opportunity to upgrade the organization's reputation if handled properly.

Image restoration is used to undo defects that degraded the image of an organization. Public relations practitioners use special events to build positive images of the organization.

Communicating About a Crisis

When an organization neither detects nor deals with potential issues in a timely manner, such issues can escalate to a crisis. Most organizations do not suffer from a life-threatening crisis unless problems within the organizations are leaked to the media, the public, or the government. After the media covers the issues or problems taking place in an organization, stakeholders and the public are informed and become concerned about the organization. The person who responds to the media serves as a spokesperson in a time of crisis. The spokesperson—usually a public relations practitioner—explains what is happening with the organization and how the company is going to tackle the issue. Other public relations practitioners produce a press release that includes effective quotes from the CEO and other important staff members in the organization. The focus during a crisis is to convey key information and messages to the public and organize smooth communication with the media.

For example, Blue Bell, an ice cream manufacturer, recalled all of its products after listeria bacteria was found in two cartons of ice cream in April 2015. The outbreak infected five adults in Kansas, three of whom died. The CDC traced the outbreak to Blue Bell products manufactured in plants in Texas and Oklahoma. When the crisis was covered by the media, the company issued a press release that quoted CEO Paul Kruse, who said, "We're committed to doing the 100-percent right thing, and the best way to do that is to take all of our products off the market until we can be confident that they are all safe." Kruse added, "We are heartbroken about this situation and apologize to all of our loyal Blue Bell fans and customers. We want enjoying our ice cream to be a source of joy and pleasure, never a cause for concern, so we are committed to getting this right." The Blue Bell recall demonstrated that when an organization's problem affects other people's safety and well-being, the problem turns into a crisis, exacerbated by media coverage. Blue Bell issued the press release to minimize the damage, although it was already done.

After the press release, Blue Bell's crisis management team disseminated messages to assure consumers that the company would expand its safety procedures, including more cleaning and sanitizing of equipment and a daily sampling of specimens in a lab. The company's spokesperson said, "Blue Bell expects to resume distribution soon on a limited basis once it is confident in the safety of its product."[3] The company spread other information about product safety through the media. It promised to institute a "test and hold" system at its facilities for the time being; products would be tested and held for release to the market until after tests show they are safe.[4]

Blue Bell, without a doubt, experienced a crisis. Although the crisis might have surprised the organization and consumers, there is some evidence that the organization was not fully aware of the importance of being prepared for a crisis. According to news articles, the company was warned by health inspectors about some sanitary issues in its facilities. In September 2012, the inspector who monitored Blue Bell's production facilities wrote, "Crickets shall be removed, eradicated from milk storage rooms & evaporator room."[5] In November 2013, another issue was recognized by the inspector, who wrote, "Find source of

3   Schuyler Velasco, "Blue Bell Ice Cream Recalls All Products Amid Listeria Attacks, *The Christian Science Monitor*, April 21, 2015, http://www.csmonitor.com/Business/The-Bite/2015/0421/Blue-Bell-Ice-Cream-recalls-all-products-amid-listeria-outbreak-video.

4   Velasco, "Blue Bell Ice Cream."

5   "Crickets shall be removed, eradicated from milk storage rooms & evaporator room," NBC News, May 4, 2015, *https://www.nbcdfw.com/news/local/blue-bell-inspections-found-crickets-dirty-mop-buckets-no-towels-at-sinks/230100/*

mildew in 40-degree room."[6] Other inspections pointed out that the factory maintained rust on doorways, failed to close lids on various food containers, and placed no towels at hand-wash sinks. It is not clear whether Blue Bell took prompt action to address the issues before the bacteria crisis of 2015, but the issues were not considered to be a crisis because the media and the public had little information about the results of the inspections. After the inspection results were leaked in late April 2015, the company issued another statement, saying, "Blue Bell takes cleanliness in our production facilities very seriously and our top priority is always the quality and safety of our product for our customers."[7]

When an organization's issue or problem develops into a crisis, the company should take immediate communication action. There are eight stages to conducting an initial crisis communication response:[8]

1. Make public safety the number one priority

2. Be quick and try to have an initial response within the first hour.

3. Be accurate by carefully checking all the facts.

4. Be consistent by keeping spokespeople informed of crisis events and key message points.

5. Provide some expression of concern/sympathy for victims.

6. Remember to include employees in the initial response.

7. Use all of the available communication channels, including the Internet, intranet, and mass notification systems.

8. Be ready to provide stress and trauma counseling to victims of the crisis and their families, including employees.

The eight stages embrace the practice of supplying information, assurances, promises, expressions, and compensation. When a crisis jeopardizes someone's well-being, a public relations practitioner provides a response that tells the organization's side of the story to the media, which stakeholders and the public see as a key source of initial crisis information. While the crisis unfolds, the practitioner sends messages that justify the organization's efforts to address the crisis. As people want to know what to do during the crisis, the messages must be accurate, informative, and reasonably assertive. The practitioner continues to send the messages through the media and any other available communication tools. If there are actual victims as a result of the crisis, the practitioner needs to express sympathy for the victims and their families. The victims might have lost their lives, health, or money, and people expect an expression of sympathy from the organization. The practitioner should not forget to communicate with employees to discuss the crisis as well. They need to know what is going on in the organization, what they need to do during the crisis, and how the crisis will affect their job security.

6   "Crickets shall be removed, eradicated from milk storage rooms & evaporator room," NBC News

7   News Desk, "Texas TV Station Reports Past Health Violations at Blue Bell Plant," *Food Safety News*, May 1, 2015, http://www.foodsafetynews.com/2015/05/texas-tv-station-reports-past-health-violations-at-blue-bell-plant/#.VURLpSFVhBc.

8   Institute for PR, "Crisis Management and Communications," The Institute for Public Relations, October 30, 2007, http://www.instituteforpr.org/crisis-management-and-communications/.

Different Types of Crises

A crisis in an organization occurs when a mistake or wrongdoing is made by those who work for the company. Crisis communication experts classify organizational crises into ten different types:[9]

1. ***Natural Disasters.*** Tornadoes, earthquakes, hurricanes, floods, droughts, and severe storms

2. ***Malevolence.*** Product tampering, sabotage, kidnapping, terrorism, and malicious rumors

3. ***Product Recall.*** Misbranded, adulterated, or violent product in the market

4. ***Confrontation.*** Boycotts, picketing, protests, and ultimatums

5. ***Hazardous Materials.*** Spills, leaks, and buildup of toxic materials

6. ***Technological Breakdowns.*** Software failures, hardware failures, infrastructure collapse, and computer viruses

7. ***Human Error.*** Mistakes that cause significant damage or loss to the company

8. ***Workplace Violence.*** Violent actions against others in the workplace

9. ***Medical Emergencies.*** Heart attacks, broken bones, and lacerations

10. ***Organizational Misdeeds.*** Deception, management misconduct, misrepresentation, and illegal actions

Most organizations are vulnerable to one of the crisis types. For example, from February 14 to February 19, 2007, JetBlue made hundreds of passengers sit inside their planes on tarmacs for hours and forced thousands of customers to wait inside the terminal at JFK International Airport because of a snowstorm. The airline canceled 1,200 flights. Even though the crisis was caused by a natural disaster, the lack of crisis communication in dealing with angry passengers and customers led to a public relations crisis.

Another example of a crisis caused by a technological breakdown is the case of the discount retailer, Target. A breach of credit and debit card data at Target broke out in December 2013, affecting as many as 40 million shoppers who went to the store in the three weeks after Thanksgiving. Customers had to worry about using their credit and debit cards, and they were forced to go through the inconvenient process of getting new cards. The crisis, caused by a technical breach, cost Target the confidence and trust of its customers, who reacted with fury and frustration. Before the crisis, Target had a solid reputation for security and savvy communication about its brand.

A crisis is extremely hard to predict when it is connected to workplace violence. At a Lockheed Martin Aeronautics Company plant in 2003, an employee shot five workers to death and wounded nine before taking his own life with a shotgun. The gunman had gone through a bitter divorce and complained about a malfunctioning time card system at the plant. Despite the fact that the company had placed the gunman in anger management and threat assessment counseling, the crisis was not avoided, and it negatively affected the mentality of all employees.

---

9   RQA Inc., "Crisis Management," *Crisis Control Newsletter* U0110, no. 1 (January 2010): 1–2, https://www.rqa-inc.com/newsletters/Catlin_US_U0110.pdf.

Different Types of Crisis Responses

Many public relations practitioners and crisis communication experts believe that once a crisis hits, the organization should not waste any time and immediately focus on minimizing the impact of the crisis. The organization is expected to respond to any questions and requests from the media and to take quick action to communicate with stakeholders and the public. Press releases, media interviews, and online information can be today's standard approach to crisis communication. However, organizations have their preferences when responding to a crisis. W. Timothy Coombs of the University of Central Florida summarized six crisis communication response strategies that organizations can employ.[10]

- **Attack the Accuser.** A person who accuses an organization of wrongdoing is criticized as a false accuser by the company. The PepsiCo syringe case is a classic example (Case Study 12.1).

- **Reminder.** Once a crisis hits, an organization—rather than apologizing—tells the stakeholders and the public that the organization has a long history of credibility and trustworthiness. The organization reminds them of its past good works. Toyota used this strategy with its massive recall events (Case Study 12.2).

- **Denial.** An organization simply says that there is no crisis. A crisis can stem from a rumor or false information. Tommy Hilfiger's flat denial is an example of a crisis communication strategy of denial (Case Study 12.3).

- **Scapegoat.** A combination of internal and external issues can lead to a crisis. Such issues can be found in multiple organizations. One of the organizations in the situation blames other organizations. An example of the scapegoat strategy is the Dell battery crisis (Case Study 12.4).

- **Justification.** An organization has to minimize a crisis when it is under attack over a social issue. Justification is a strategy for downplaying the perceived damage caused by the crisis, which the National Rifle Association (NRA) prefers to use (Case Study 12.5).

- **Apology.** An organization takes responsibility for a crisis and makes a public apology to ask for forgiveness. An apology is a common strategy that organizations use to address a crisis. Domino's was quick to deal with its crisis with an apology (Case Study 12.6).

Case Study 12.1   The 1983 Pepsi Syringe Crisis

A syringe was allegedly found in a can of Diet Pepsi in Tacoma, Washington, by an elderly couple in June 1983. As the syringe story turned into a national media circus, new complaints poured in from other states. The following week, more than 50 consumers reported that they had found hypodermic syringes in cans of Diet Pepsi. The company's crisis communications team and the

(Continued)

---

10   "CRISIS MANAGEMENT AND COMMUNICATIONS," Institute for Public Relations, https://instituteforpr.org/crisis-management-communications/

US Food and Drug Administration gathered all of the reports from consumers in 23 states. While investigating the reports, the crisis team considered a voluntary recall, but company spokesperson Andrew Giangola insisted, "the FDA told us there was no need, that there wasn't a health risk." The company decided to take the stance that such accusations were a hoax and there would be no recall. The spokesperson added, "It would be highly unlikely for one needle to find its way into a can. It was absolutely ludicrous."

While the spokesperson denied the possibility of any wrongdoing by the company, Craig Weatherup, CEO of the company, went on television to explain and defend Diet Pepsi. He appeared on news programs, showing visual evidence of the bogus reports with the explicit support of the FDA. The evidence was surveillance camera footage from a supermarket in Colorado that showed a woman shopper who appeared to be inserting a syringe into a can of Diet Pepsi. Furthermore, FDA Commissioner David Kessler called a news conference in Washington and said, "This is a vicious cycle."

The crisis was quelled when multiple arrests were made by the FDA for filing false reports. After the crisis, PepsiCo launched a campaign with the message, "Pepsi is pleased to announce ... nothing." Also, on the fourth of July in 1983, Pepsi put out ads for its products, along with coupons that said, "Thanks, America." The company, instead of accepting blame, took a strong approach, calling the accusations hoaxes and disseminating the message about how the company was confident in its product quality. The crisis required an aggressive offense based on the belief in the company's high-quality production facilities. In a nutshell, the crisis was addressed effectively because of the counteraccusation.

Case Study 12.2   The 2009 Lexus Vehicle Malfunction Scandal

In August 2009, a Lexus vehicle suddenly accelerated after the gas pedal was caught under the floor mat, and the entire family inside the vehicle was killed. After a month, Toyota (Lexus's parent company) issued a safety warning to tell vehicle owners to remove driver's-side floor mats in seven Lexus and Toyota models. Toyota planned a recall to fix the problem in early November and began sending notifications to Toyota and Lexus vehicle owners about the issue.

The notification claimed that the National Highway Transportation Safety Administration (NHTSA) said, "No defect exists in vehicles in which the driver's floor mat is compatible with the vehicle and properly secured." When the NHTSA saw the notification, it released a statement, accusing the world's largest automaker of sending a message to owners with "inaccurate and misleading information." The agency viewed the unsecured mat as a defect. Toyota wasted no time responding to the agency by admitting that the NHTSA made a valid point. The company said in a statement, "We are in the process of developing vehicle-based remedies." In late November, Toyota recalled four million vehicles to reconfigure gas pedals because of the risk of floor mat entrapment. In January 2010, Toyota recalled additional millions of vehicles to correct a situation in which the gas pedal could stick without the presence of a floor mat. This was a different issue because Toyota found a defect in sticking accelerator pedals without floor mats. The company developed a fix for the sticking gas pedal issue the next month.

Before the crisis, Toyota enjoyed a stellar reputation that had been closely linked to safety and quality and served as the key to the company's success. During the crisis, Toyota received heavy criticism in the media. In reaction, the company launched campaigns that showed its dedication to fixing the problems and creating safer vehicles. The company capitalized on its excellent reputation, which had been built up over decades in the minds of the consumers. It reminded consumers of its history of making the most reliable vehicles, as well as the numerous American jobs Toyota created. The company took advantage of the fact that consumers were unlikely to criticize an organization with a favorable reputation.

Case Study 12.3   The 1996 Tommy Hilfiger Race Rumor

In 1996, there was a rumor that fashion designer Tommy Hilfiger said on *The Oprah Winfrey Show* that he wished that people of color would not wear his line. The rumor spread, and there was a call to boycott Hilfiger clothing and products. The company had to respond to the rumor, as there was gaining momentum for the boycott. Hilfiger simply denied the rumor. Winfrey herself denied the allegations on her show in 1999 and posted a statement on her website that Hilfiger had never appeared on her show. "For the record, the rumored event that has circulated on the Internet and by word of mouth never happened. Mr. Hilfiger has never appeared on the show. In fact, Oprah has never even met him." However, the rumor kept sticking to the company.

Hilfiger finally appeared on Winfrey's show in May 2007 in hopes of addressing the rumors that had plagued him for more than 10 years. He told Winfrey that he had enlisted the assistance of the FBI to find out where the rumor originated. The rumor was traced back to a college campus, but the investigators could not find anyone specifically. "It hurt my integrity, because at the end of the day, that's all you have," Hilfiger said on the show. "And if people are going to challenge my honesty and my integrity and what I am as a person, it hurts more than anything else. Forget the money that it has cost me."

Hilfiger laid the rumor to rest by appearing on the show. He denied and ended the rumor.

Case Study 12.4   The 2006 Dell Recall

In August 2006, Dell, then the world's largest PC maker, recalled 4.1 million laptop computer batteries because there was a danger that they could erupt in flames. Dell reported that there had been six documented instances in which laptops overheated or caught on fire; no injuries or deaths had been reported. While competing with other computer makers, such as Lenovo and Apple, Dell was losing profits and suffering from lower-than-expected sales. Its stock price was moving downward as well. Worse, the company had a longtime reputation for poor customer service. Amid the struggles, the recall became another big issue that caused the latest setback for Dell.

(Continued)

The media had previously reported that a Dell laptop had gone up in smoke and another had melted. Dell executives hoped the recall would prevent further damage to its operation. "We're getting ahead of the issue," said Alex Gruzen, senior vice president and general manager of the company's product group in an interview with the *New York Times*. "I don't want any further incidents to take place." The *Times* estimated that the cost of the recall could exceed $300 million.

In such a dire crisis, the company, hit by bad publicity that harmed consumer sales, guided media attention to the point that the cause of the explosions was batteries, not the entire laptop computer. More importantly, Dell did not manufacture the batteries, and they stressed that the explosion problems were a result of a manufacturing defect in batteries made by Sony. In most cases, the battery would shut down, but in rare instances, it could overheat and catch fire. In the end, most media criticism was aimed not at Dell, but at Sony. The media accused Sony of taking too long to accept responsibility and withholding information. Sony sold its batteries to most of the major computer makers.

Gruzen said, "We are absolutely confident that when we replace the [Sony] batteries that we are getting the at-risk batteries out of consumers' hands and that there will be no more incidents."

The scapegoat strategy, in the case of Dell, was effective in restoring the company's image as a computer technology company, not a battery manufacturer.

Case Study 12.5   The 2018 NRA Justification Strategy after School Shooting

In 2018, a 19-year-old gunman opened fire inside Marjory Stoneman Douglas High School in Parkland, Florida, on Valentine's Day, killing 14 students and 3 teachers. It was one of the ten deadliest mass shootings in modern US history. The gunman, Nikolas Cruz, used an AR-15 rifle, a semiautomatic weapon made for military use and seen in other mass shootings, including the 2016 Pulse nightclub massacre in Orlando, Florida. After the shooting, a movement for stricter gun control laws was formed by hundreds of the Florida high school survivors and thousands of teenagers nationwide. They used social media in hopes of changing gun laws to prevent other mass shootings, and mainstream media heavily covered the developments. For example, on February 22, from Arizona to Washington, students walked out of schools in support of demanding a ban on weapons, such as AR-15 rifles, and President Trump met with the group of survivors of the Florida shooting and parents of victims at the White House.

President Trump suggested stronger background checks and gun possession by teachers in schools. While national discussion and debate to prevent the next school massacre unfolded, a salient voice against the NRA gun lobby began to gain momentum nationwide. In early March 2018, the Florida Legislature passed a bill titled "The Marjory Stoneman Douglas High School Public Safety Act," which required an increase in the minimum age for buying rifles from 18 to 21, and a ban on bump stocks purchased by convicted criminals and certain mentally ill individuals. Florida Gov. Rick Scott signed the bill into law. However, in response to the law, the NRA immediately filed a federal lawsuit against Florida, arguing that "the age minimum section of the law violates the second and 14th amendments of the US Constitution." More importantly, the NRA sent out the repetitive message of justification for the use of guns to maintain a safer society: the only way to stop a bad guy with a gun is a good guy with a gun. The message is echoed every time a mass shooting incident occurs, and NRA spokesperson Dana Loesch justified the right to bear arms, pointing out that the person pulling the trigger is the problem, not the gun itself. Loesch appeared on a CNN town hall and said, "People who are dangerous to themselves and other individuals should not be able to obtain a firearm. ... Law enforcement could have done more to stop the Florida school shooting."

Case Study 12.6   The 2009 Domino's Social Media Crisis

A Domino's employee in North Carolina was filmed while preparing sandwiches for delivery in the restaurant's kitchen. He put cheese up his nose and nasal mucus on the sandwiches, which clearly violated health code standards. A coworker provided spoken narration as she filmed it. The video was posted on YouTube in April 2009, and it became a viral sensation with more than a million hits in a few days. After the video went viral, Domino's was alerted. Domino's, a pizza chain based in Ann Arbor, Michigan, organized a crisis communication team in response.

The video was posted on Monday night, and the company's first response to the crisis came out on Wednesday. It appears that the company made a quick response, but critics said it was too late in the social media environment. The crisis grew out of control in the social media world for less than one day, as opposed to Domino's reaction, which took two days. Instead of issuing a news release, the crisis communication team opened a Twitter account to respond to consumer inquires. The team also made a YouTube apology video that featured Patrick Doyle, president of the company, apologizing for the incident. "We sincerely apologize for this incident," he said. "We thank members of the online community who quickly alerted us and allowed us to take immediate action. Although the individuals in question claim it's a hoax, we are taking this incredibly seriously." The company shut down the store where the video was produced and fired the employees.

In just a few days, Domino's reputation was damaged because of the power of social media. It was a digital public relations crisis. The crisis team and management of the company decided not to respond to the social media frenzy at first, hoping the controversy would die down. That was a huge mistake. Many experts argue that the golden time to address a crisis being discussed on social media is less than 24 hours. Despite the late responses, the CEO's sincere apology turned out to be effective at engaging in dialogue with consumers. The company responded to all negative comments on Twitter, apologizing for the incident.

Organizations inevitably must deal with a crisis internally and externally. Many crises are kept and addressed inside organizations before the public and media recognize them. Depending on the situations and types of crises, organizations find that the best crisis communication strategy is to communicate with people in a sincere way. Public relations practitioners or communications department staff take the lead in responding to the crisis. They need to make a quick analysis of the issue, find the best communication channels, and implement the best crisis communication strategy.

The Cycles of Crisis Communication

Seven people were reported dead after taking extra-strength Tylenol capsules in Chicago in 1982. Johnson & Johnson, the manufacture of the medicine, faced a tremendous crisis. The incident is known as the Tylenol crisis, which is considered an American classic of crisis communication management. The deaths were caused by an unknown suspect who put deadly cyanide into Tylenol capsules. The company was not responsible for tampering with the product, but it recalled all their capsules from the market—31 million bottles of Tylenol, about $100 million worth. After the crisis, the company reintroduced Tylenol and restored consumer confidence with new triple-sealed, tamper- resistant packaging and a $2.50 off coupon. Johnson & Johnson also sent the message that the safety of the public was the company's most important responsibility. The media portrayed the company's decision to pull the product off the market and to engage in honest dialogue with the public in a positive light. The company saved its reputation. The Tylenol crisis is regarded as one of the most successful examples of crisis communication.

Since the Tylenol crisis, the concept of crisis communication and management has become a specialized discipline in the practice of public relations. Today's organizations have learned how to deal with a crisis from studying previous cases. They understand the value of maintaining a reputation when a crisis strikes. Managing a crisis begins with the development of crisis contingency plans and ends with the choice of crisis communication strategy. With the pervasiveness of social media, public relations practitioners must be prepared to strategize digital and online crisis communication, in addition to communication with the traditional mass media. Public relations practitioners guide organizations to avoid repeating the same crisis.

CHAPTER SUMMARY AND REVIEW

1. Explain how an issue can turn into a crisis.

2. Identify the phases of crisis management.

3. Discuss optimal ways of responding to the media in a crisis.

4. Find different types of crisis responses.

5. Study real cases of crisis communication.

PUBLIC RELATIONS IN PRACTICE

FUTHER READING

PR Week's Awards For **Best PR Multiculture Marketing**

Winner: Toyota and Republica Havas
Campaign Name: Juntos Somos Imparables

For Toyota and Republica, a Toyota US Hispanic AOR, Juntos Somos Imparables (Together We Are Unstoppable) was intended to inspire and celebrate Hispanic achievement and potential. The campaign centered on a license plate art installation, with each plate displaying a trait such as valiente (brave) or perseverante (persistent).

Read more at
https://www.prweek.com/article/1579436/prweek-us-awards-2019-winners

13

Integrated Marketing Communication

Organizations operate to fulfill expectations and demands from consumers, employees, investors, and the public. Organizations provide products and services for these audiences while looking for loyal support from them. Such support can be presented through product purchases, donations, steady demand for services, and high review ratings. High-quality products and services are the first components to receive support from the public or consumers. The second component for organizations to gain support is credibility with the people who use the products and services. Such credibility is built on a reputation of the organization's history of performance. If an organization boasted its long history of high product quality, and consumers found the company's products trustworthy, then the organization would be considered to have secured support from the consumers (Figure 13.1). This support leads to operational stability for the organization since consumers like to exchange their money for organizational credibility.

Credibility is defined as "how positively an organization and its products or services are perceived by its stakeholders," upon whom the organization depends for its success. Once stakeholders begin to build a negative perception of the organization, its credibility is diminished, and the organization will struggle to run its stable, regular business. Hence the organization makes every effort to prevent negative perceptions in the eyes of stakeholders. Maintaining credibility stems from the organization's promise to its stakeholders to deliver the products or services they expect. Keeping this promise, along with maintaining a good reputation, is critical for building solid credibility in an organization. Public relations has a great influence on building a good image and reputation for organizations by cooperating with other departments, such as marketing, human resources, and finance. Staff members from such departments collaborate to position the organization as credible in stakeholders' minds.

Before credibility, the team members plan to project the "positive image" of the organization, defined as an organizational identity. The organizational identity is created to maintain and protect a strong reputation for the organization. For example, a customer who is about to choose a pair of Levi's or Calvin Klein jeans tends to consider price and the quality of the jeans, including the image and reputation of the companies, before making a final purchase. This is why public relations and other relevant fields of business cooperate to achieve organizational goals, especially for-profit organizations or corporations. In particular, if they want to sell a specific product, then they focus on creating a positive brand identity to increase sales.

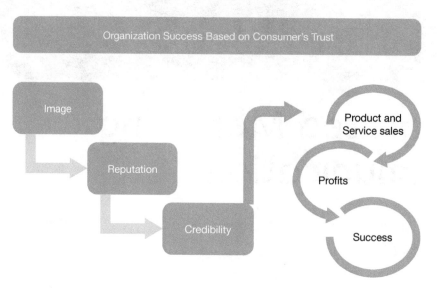

FIGURE 13.1 Organization's Success Based on Consumer's Trust.

The intersectional cooperation of public relations, marketing, advertising, and finance in pursuit of promoting sales and reputation is called integrated marketing communication (IMC). IMC aims to create and increase the organization's sales and its reputation at the same time. IMC facilitates sales and reputation promotion tools, including publicity events, advertising, sales promotions, endorsements, product placements, sponsorships, exhibits, and so on. All of these tools, in general, are used to enhance the outcomes of corporate IMC, which begins with building a unique identity and image for corporations.

Identity and Image

Corporate identity is the distinctive image of the corporation, positioned in the minds of stakeholders. This image can affect the specific corporation's reputation either positively or negatively. IMC's primary goal is to build and maintain a positive, distinct identity through the corporation's logo, package design, name, brand, symbol, uniforms, products, and services. For example, the golden arches of McDonald's, the "swoosh" of Nike, and the bite taken out of the apple of Apple's logo are recognized around the world as representatives of corporate identities. Financial services corporations, such as Goldman Sachs, AIG, and Bank of America, had negative public images because of their involvement in the 2008 financial crisis. Such images were a reflection of the corporations' identities. Apple, Google, and Samsung have their own identities as technology corporations with market-leading products. In a similar way, Amazon's identity allows it to be recognized as a leading online shopping corporation. In other words, identity helps stakeholders find or recognize the uniqueness of the corporation.

Corporate identity also enhances employee identification, which is founded upon the employees' image of the corporation. The identity asks them to think about who they are and what they need to do for their corporation, increasing a sense of alliance. Before a corporate identity is announced and recognized by other stakeholders, employees should be informed about the corporate identity because they are the driving force in successful implementation; employees are critical to the success of building a positive identity through a relationship with other stakeholders.

When employees deal with customers, their behavior and attitudes convey a corporate image to customers either good or bad. A corporation's identity can originate from its employees' practices at work. Dish Network, for example, has a bad image because of its poor customer service, which may be based on the employees' dissatisfaction with the company. According to the online financial news agency, *24/7 Wall Street*, the worst company to work for in America was the Dish Network in 2012.[1] Not surprisingly, the company was rated poorly in customer service in 2015.[2] Happy employees make customers happy, and happy customers create and maintain the distinctively positive image of the corporation. Dish Network ranked number six in the same category in 2017.[3] The *Street* pointed out that low employee satisfaction, "which can lead to poor customer satisfaction," explains the company's declining subscriber counts in recent years. In short, corporate identity is directly related to the performance of employees at work.

The first task in developing corporate identity is to make a visual statement about the corporation, which communicates its value and vision to stakeholders. In

FIGURE 13.2 IMC.

the beginning stage of developing corporate identity, corporations create a visual design that embraces symbolic meaning, which cannot be imparted through words alone. For example, the Starbucks logo is an image of a twin-tailed mermaid, or Siren, as she is known in Greek mythology. According to the company's website, the founder of the company searched "for a way to capture the seafaring history of coffee and Seattle's strong seaport roots, and Siren became the inspiration of the logo that represents Starbucks' identity."[4] The logo is intended to be recognized internationally as the welcoming face of

1   Caleb Hannan, "Dish Network, the Meanest Company in America," Bloomberg Business, January 3, 2013, http://www.bloomberg.com/bw/articles/2013-01-02/dish-network-the-meanest-company-in-america.

2   Michael B. Sauter and Thomas C. Frohlich, "Companies With the Best (and Worst Reputations)," Yahoo Finance, May 6, 2015, http://finance.yahoo.com/news/companies-best-worst-reputations-184332462.html.

3   Michael B. Sauter, "The 19 Worst Companies to Work For," MSN.com, June 12, 2017, https://www.msn.com/en-us/money/careersandeducation/the-19-worst-companies-to-work-for/ar-BBCompH?fb_comment_id=1572639576101938_1593710257328203#image=BBCocsU|15

4   Michelle Flandreau, "Who Is the Starbucks Siren," Starbucks, December 23, 2016, https://stories.starbucks.com/stories/2016/who-is-starbucks-siren/.

Starbucks, inviting customers "to explore, to find something new, and to connect with each other."[5] The company's identity evolved with the logo after Starbucks added three words around the head of the Siren logo: We Proudly Serve. Corporate identity provides visibility and symbolic meaning that remind stakeholders of the corporation's name and core business at the right time. Therefore, corporate identity contributes to corporate reputation.

Corporate Reputation

Corporate reputation refers to the overall perception of a corporation in the minds of stakeholders who have used the corporation's products or services or heard about them from others. Corporate reputation is built through a corporation's past actions and the probability of its future performance. It functions as a distinctive factor that makes the corporation superior or inferior to competitors. Therefore, the reputation of a corporation is essential to its survival. Stakeholders judge corporations "in a variety of ways—by what they do, by what they say they do, and by what others say they do."[6] Corporations acknowledge the importance of building a good reputation, learning from many studies that show corporations with better reputations are more likely to enjoy strong financial performance, attract and keep talented employees at lower costs, have lower capital costs, and receive support from government and other stakeholders in times of need.[7] More specifically, corporate reputation is estimated to be worth about 4 to 5 percent of sales per year.[8]

The greatest advantage of a good corporate reputation is that consumers may prefer the corporation's products or services when other competitors' products or services are available at a similar price on a comparable level of quality. A good reputation enables the corporation to differentiate its products or services from competitors, thus encouraging consumers to choose the corporation over others. It also offers the corporation the power of placing premium pricing. A prestigious reputation for corporations is not built overnight, nor can it be achieved with a single product or service. With so many factors in play, building a strong corporate reputation needs comprehensive strategies and long-term practices. There are ten components of corporate reputation:[9]

1. **Ethical.** The corporation behaves ethically, is admirable, is worthy of respect, and is trustworthy.

2. **Employees/Workplace.** The corporation has talented employees, treats its people well, and is an appealing workplace.

3. **Financial Performance.** The corporation is financially strong, has a record of profitability, and has growth prospects.

---

5   Starbucks, "Who Is the Starbucks Siren."

6   Rosa Chun, Rui Da Silva, Gary Davies. *Corporate Reputation and Competitiveness* (Routledge: London. 2003)

7   Rosa Chun, Rui Da Silva, Gary Davies. Corporate Reputation and Competitiveness

8   Rosa Chun, Rui Da Silva, Gary Davies. Corporate Reputation and Competitiveness

9   Kim J. Harrison, "Why a Good Corporate Reputation Is Vital to Your Organization," Cutting Edge PR, n.d., http://www.cuttingedgepr.com/articles/corprep_important.asp.

4. ***Leadership.*** The corporation is a leader rather than a follower; it is innovative.

5. ***Management.*** The corporation is well managed, with a clear vision for the future.

6. ***Social Responsibility.*** The corporation recognizes social responsibilities and supports worthy causes.

7. ***Customer Focus.*** The corporation cares about and is strongly committed to its customers.

8. ***Quality.*** The corporation offers high-quality products and services.

9. ***Reliability.*** The corporation stands behind its products and services and provides consistent service.

10. ***Emotional Appeal.*** It is a corporation that people can feel good about; it is kind and fun.

As the ten components clearly demonstrate, corporate reputation involves a wide range of corporate operations that satisfy stakeholders in an ethical and reliable way.

Once corporations establish a good reputation, they develop operational strategies and corporate programs to maintain it. According to *24/7 Wall Street*, several corporations have built good reputations through their particular corporate operations. For example:[10]

- **Kraft Foods** dropped the use of preservatives from its kids' table and dorm room favorite, macaroni and cheese. The announcement boosted the company's reputation as a trustworthy food company, especially for children.

- **Costco**, the wholesale warehouse store, is shoppers' favorite membership-based company. Its customers are more satisfied than those of any other specialty retail company, and it has a membership renewal rate of 91 percent. Customers look upon the company favorably, largely because of its good relations with employees and customers.

- **L.L. Bean**, the outdoor clothing retailer that has operated for more than a hundred years, has a reputation as one of the best retail apparel companies. L.L. Bean's customer satisfaction rate is always high, due in part to the company's return-anything policy.

- **Google** is known for being the best company to work for, offering on-campus amenities, such as exercise facilities, as well as free legal advice and reimbursements for further education. In addition, Google users are satisfied with its offerings, such as Google Search, Map, Gmail, Play, and Drive, compared to other Internet portal competitors. Employees and customers are both happy, so the company maintains a high reputation.

- **Amazon.com**, scoring as the top company for customer satisfaction among Internet retailers, has an indisputable reputation as one of the best online sites providing products and services for consumers.

- **Samsung** has built its reputation by competing with several major competitors, including Apple and LG, in the smartphone and tablet markets. The company's Galaxy series is a stunning success, driving some customers away from Apple's iPhones and iPads. Its vision and leadership as an innovative tech company with strong financial performance helps to maintain its good reputation.

Corporations with good reputations never stop developing systems that satisfy stakeholders.

---

10 Sauter and Frohlich, "Companies With the Best."

Corporate Branding

Along with corporate identity and reputation, IMC specialists add one more strategy to increase the value of corporations—branding. From the IMC standpoint, branding is the process of creating a unique name and image for a corporation, product, or service—one that represents the corporation's particular personality in consumers' minds. Simply put, branding promotes a corporation by linking it with a particular brand.

Corporate branding promotes the brand name of a corporate entity, attempting to create greater credibility for a new product or service by associating it with the already-established company name. If a corporation has a successful brand name, consumers view its products in a positive light. Regardless of what products or services the corporation provides, the name of a corporate brand has an effect on consumers' behavior. Coca-Cola, for example, has a strong corporate brand name with high credibility that leads to loyal purchases of its products.

A good corporate name is vital for successful corporate branding. Corporations often change names to represent new identities or reflect new objectives. The following are five examples of successful corporate branding with new names.

1. **Google.** The world's most popular search engine was created in 1996 under the name "BackRub," but in 1997, Google.com was registered as the trademark. The name Google—a play on the word "googol," a mathematical term for the number represented by the numeral 1 followed by 100 zeros—reflects the founders' mission to organize a seemingly infinite amount of information on the web.[11] The trademarked company name even became a popular verb.

2. **LG.** This South Korean consumer electronics manufacturer's original name was Lucky Goldstar. The name was shortened to "LG" in 1995 to create a corporate identity aimed at expanding the corporation's global market. LG launched its new brand-name campaigns with the tagline, "Life's Good," aiming to make a connection with consumers' enriched quality of life (Figure 13.3). Consumers think the name of LG stands for "life is good," which sounds Western.

3. **KFC.** The fast-food giant, founded in 1952 by Colonel Harland Sanders, changed its name in 1991 to KFC from Kentucky Fried Chicken. Because of the social dieting trends in the 1980s, consumers regarded "fried" as a fatty word and the company banished the word from its name. The word "Kentucky" also signaled a limited area, so the company decided to abbreviate the name to KFC while boosting the profile of Colonel Sanders, their familiar brand icon.[12]

4. **Altria.** Few people know the original name of this company was Philip Morris, the tobacco industry giant. In 2003, the CEO announced its new name, saying that the change was an important milestone in the evolution of the company. The new name was a part of corporate branding efforts to disassociate the company from the negative image of smoking, although critics of the tobacco industry said the name change was "a PR maneuver meant to distance the corporation's image from its deadly business practices."[13]

11   "The History of Google," itspoon, https://www.iteaspoon.com/single-post/2017/11/03/The-History-of-Google

12   Seth Stevenson, "Alphabet Soup: Now What Does KFC Stand For?," *Slate*, May 3, 2004, http://www.slate.com/articles/business/ad_report_card/2004/05/alphabet_soup.html.

13   Reuters, "Philip Morris Changes Name to Altria," *USA Today*, January 27, 2003, http://usatoday30.usatoday.com/money/industries/food/2003-01-27-altria_x.htm.

5. **Sprint.** In 1983, Southern Pacific Communications Company and General Telephone & Electric Corporation entered merger negotiations, and they merged under the name "GTE Sprint." After several more mergers and acquisition processes, the corporation called "Sprint" is known as one of the major wireless network operators in the United States.

FIGURE 13.3 LG's Life Is Good Branding.

As these examples illustrate, corporations can differentiate themselves to increase their corporate branding with new names that signal their business philosophies and new identities in the marketplace.

Corporate branding has a positive correlation with familiarity and favorability for consumers. Familiarity refers to how well the brand is known; favorability refers to how positively felt the brand is. To increase familiarity and favorability, corporations strategize their corporate branding with three different types of brand architectures:

1. **Monolithic Brand Architecture.** This structure integrates all products and services, communication and marketing tools, and employees and business operations under the same company name in hopes of emphasizing a single master brand. For example, vehicles produced by Mercedes-Benz carry the same corporate name, distinguished simply by different segments such as A, C, E, and S Classes. This architecture embraces the single identity of the corporation.

2. **Endorsed Brand Architecture.** This structure is designed to stand entirely on a specialized brand identity, applied in different market segments. General Motors (GM) is an example of operating under this brand structure. GM, as the parent company of Chevrolet, Cadillac, Buick, and GMC, allows each brand to develop its own marketing and communication strategies to fulfill the different demands of customer segments. The four brands are endorsed by the parent company name, even though each brand takes a stand-alone approach to its products. This structure is considered an umbrella brand or a family brand.

3. **Individual Brand Architecture.** This structure lies between monolithic and endorsed brand structures, making a corporate brand seemingly unrelated to its parent company's name. This structure aims to allow a company to present its own work in concert with the other, with no particular connection between the parent and sister companies. For example, the Japanese carmaker Honda is known for its monolithic brand structure with its Accord, Civic, CR-V, and Pilot segments. However, the company has another high-end brand, Acura, but the company does not widely advertise the relationship. This structure is designed to enhance an individual brand's ability to carry its own name in the marketplace.

Although the three architectures of corporate branding are adopted and practiced all around the world, today's trends are moving toward the monolithic model. Monolithic corporate branding offers advantages when it comes to IMC campaigns and high corporate values. A monolithic corporate brand saves financial and human resources, promoting products and services to all stakeholders instead of promoting each brand's independent products and services to separate segments. Because consumers are inclined to purchase particular products and services based on corporate identity, one consolidated entity can be helpful in operating the business as an entire organization. Johnson & Johnson provides a good example of this trend (Box 13.1).

"The World's Most Valuable Brands" in 2019, ranked by the *Forbes* Index, demonstrates the effectiveness of monolithic brand structure: most of the "top-ten brands" adopt the monolithic corporate branding strategy.[14]

IMC Strategies

Corporate branding is a component of IMC strategies that is used to strengthen a brand and is viewed as the personality of a corporation. Placing a good perception of corporations in stakeholders' minds is a hard task that requires time, resources and strategic planning. Reputation, corporate brand, and identity can hardly be built overnight or achieved through luck; however, that does not mean there are no methods to achieve quicker, effective results. IMC specialists practice the following four IMC strategies to bring quicker, effective results in the short term.

BOX 13.1   THE FIRST CORPORATE BRANDING CAMPAIGN FOR JOHNSON & JOHNSON IN MORE THAN 10 YEARS

In 2013, Johnson & Johnson launched its first corporate branding campaign in a decade. The campaign's message "For all you love, Johnson & Johnson" was disseminated through television commercials and print advertising. It emphasized the positive impact of caring for loved ones every day.

This campaign, aimed at promoting the company's monolithic branding, was created after the company faced a series of challenges in the US market since 2010. Johnson & Johnson's McNeil Consumer Healthcare unit had recalled more than 280 million packages of over-the-counter medications like Motrin, Children's Tylenol liquid, and Benadryl. In addition, its DePuy Orthopedics unit recalled two popular artificial hip replacement models. According to the *New York Times*, since 2010, about 10,000 lawsuits were filed involving those artificial hip devices, and a Los Angeles jury ordered the company to pay more than $8.3 million in damages to one Montana man.

During such product recalls and lawsuits, the campaign focused on returning the company to its roots of love and family, celebrating the people who do the selfless work of caring for others. Michael Sneed, vice president for global corporate affairs, said the company wanted to "continue to reconnect with all of the people who come into contact with J.& J. in their daily lives."

The campaign shed light on love and caring by creating a sense of trust with the brand, signaling a desire to reestablish the company's core principles. "Corporate branding which tries to instill a sense of trust in the company and for J.& J., given the kind of products it makes, that trust is very, very critical," said Kapil Bawa, a marketing professor, in an interview with the *Times*.

Source: "Trying to Burnish Its Image, J.&J. Turns to Emotions," *New York Times*, April 24, 2013.

---

14   "The World's Most Valuable Brands," *Forbes*, n.d., https://www.forbes.com/powerful-brands/list/#tab:rank.

TABLE 13.1   Most Powerful Corporate Brands

Rank	Most Valuable Corporate Brands 2019	Industry
1	Apple	Technology
2	Google	Technology
3	Microsoft	Technology
4	Amazon	Technology
5	Facebook	Technology
6	Coca-Cola	Beverages
7	Samsung	Technology
8	Disney	Leisure
9	Toyota	Automotive
10	McDonald's	Restaurants

Source: "The World's Most Valuable Brands," *Forbes*, n.d., https://www.forbes.com/powerful-brands/list/3/#tab:rank.

Public Relations Advertising

Advertising is the activity of producing information to lead the public's attention to products or services. Advertising is usually done through various forms of paid media, including television and radio commercials, newspaper and magazine ads, and Internet or online ads. Corporations pay millions of dollars to the media in order to reach out to a large audience. Simply put, they use advertising to maximize the consumption of products or services.

Advertising provides commercial information to existing and prospective consumers. Corporations use this expensive communication form (1) to introduce consumers to their new products or services, (2) create a desire for products or services, (3) strengthen the image and identity of corporations, (4) secure the loyalty of existing consumers, and (5) remind them of commercial messages. Now that the marketplace is changing rapidly, consumers tend to quickly forget commercial information and messages. However, competitors do not quit advertising. Hence, corporations have little choice but to use advertising, which is somewhat essential to survival and growth. One of the concerns corporations have about advertising is that if they stop advertising, consumers will begin to forget about their products or services. As a result, the initial financial investment in advertising becomes lost, and greater advertising expenses are needed to recreate consumer awareness of products and services. Advertising is an investment that increases the likelihood in which more consumers will know what a particular corporation's products or services are.

Public relations advertising can be considered an IMC tactic to build better corporate branding. It is used to create and maintain a good corporate reputation as a whole rather than promoting its products or services alone. In other words, the primary purpose of public relations advertising is to promote the corporation's name, brand, image, and reputation. Similar to traditional advertising, public relations advertising has four objectives: (1) creating the consumers' awareness of the existence of the corporation, (2) projecting a good image of the corporation among consumers, (3) sharing a sense of belonging with employees, and (4) increasing sales of the products or services with a reputation. Since public relations advertising focuses on creating and maintaining the image and reputation of the corporation (rather than a product or a service), larger corporations with more revenue tend to use this IMC tactic. In short, there is a positive correlation between the size of corporations and the use of public relations advertising.

By focusing on building the corporation's image and reputation through advertising, specialists in public relations advertising attempt to brand the corporation in ways that have a positive impact on consumers. When producing public relations advertising, the specialists use advice, announcement, or occurrence. These forms are embodied in three types of public relations advertising:

1. **Image Public Relations Advertising** Image public relations advertising is meant to create a favorable perception of the corporation by associating the corporation with its business philosophy and values. For example, leading American frozen-food corporations, including ConAgra, General Mills, Nestle, Heinz, and Hillshire, together launched a new advertising campaign that sought to revive sluggish frozen-food sales in 2014. The advertising, called "Frozen. How Fresh Stays Fresh," was designed to portray freezing "as nature's pause button."[15] The corporations aimed to fight and eliminate the negative frozen-food images: "If you are using a frozen vegetable you have taken a shortcut and you are not trying to help your family."[16] The image advertising, informing consumers of the benefits of freezing, which is capable of pausing "just-picked, just-baked and just-crafted foods," was announced through TV, digital and print ads. The "Frozen. How Fresh Stays Fresh" advertising was a three-year, $30-million-per-year effort.

2. **Advocacy Public Relations Advertising** Corporations have taken to advocacy public relations advertising because they want to be seen as the promoter of the public interest. Advocacy public relations advertising, as opposed to commercial advertising, is designed to support a particular cause or a matter of public importance. For example, Kellogg launched "No Kid Hungry," a national public relations campaign to end childhood hunger in the United States in 2018. Kellogg, on a mission to give more kids access to school breakfast, served numerous students at the beginning of the school day while raising awareness of the importance of breakfast for kids with its donation of $1 million. Celebrating National School Breakfast Week (March 4–8) of 2019, the corporation also hosted school breakfast pop-up events across the nation while spreading the messages via social media platforms and press releases.[17] Kellogg also experienced a successful advocacy campaign in 2011 with the name of "Share Your Breakfast" by teaming up with Action for Healthy Kids, a national nonprofit organization. Kellogg set the goal of donating a million breakfasts to children in need for the 2011–2012 school year.[18] Kellogg's marketing executive explained the intention of the advertising: "We just felt like as the breakfast leader, we should do something about that."[19]

3. **Cause-Related Public Relations Advertising** Corporations understand that their sales might be linked to charitable activities or other public causes. Instead of simply giving corporate money to charities (corporate philanthropy), corporations use this type of advertising by expecting a return. A common way of initiating cause-related advertising is to build a mutually beneficial collaboration between a corporation and an organization for a specific social cause, and then they can communicate the shared values to consumers. This advertising is meant to develop goodwill, increase consumer loyalty, differentiate from the competition, and promote employee morale.

---

15   E. J. Schultz, "Frozen-Food Makers Launch $30 Million Image Campaign," *Advertising Age*, May 13, 2014, http:// adage.com/article/see-the-spot/frozen-food-makers-launch-30-million-image-campaign/293201/.

16   Sarah Nassauer, "Food Processors Address Frozen Produce's Image Problem," *Wall Street Journal*, December 30, 2013, http://www.wsj.com/articles/SB10001424052702304483804579282520637682840.

17   No Kid Hungry. https://www.globenewswire.com/news-release/2019/03/06/1748799/0/en/No-Kid-Hungry-Launches-National-Powered-by-Breakfast-Campaign-to-Raise-Awareness-of-the-Importance-of-Breakfast-for-Kids.html

18   *New York Times.* http://www.nytimes.com/2011/03/08/business/media/08adco.html.

19   Ibid.

For example, Starbucks took a step in 2008 to address the global issue of climate change by developing a strategic alliance with Conservation International, a major international environmental nonprofit organization. This advertising campaign was targeted at promoting the coffee-growing practices of small farms, which would protect forests and restore degraded landscapes in Mexico and Indonesia. The company made a five-year commitment, spending $7.5 million. Another example is the partnership between Hanes and the Salvation Army. The apparel company donated 2.4 million pairs of socks to the Salvation Army from 2013 to 2019 for the homeless and others in need. The Salvation Army distributed the socks to homeless shelters in New York and California. Such cause-related advertising was published through both organizations' social media platforms.

Public relations advertising promotes the interests of corporations by enhancing their images and assuming a position on a special issue or promoting a certain cause.

Product Placement

Product placement is another popular strategy of IMC that generates awareness of corporate brands, which can lay the foundation for a great reputation. Product placement is defined as a form of advertising that subtly promotes products or services within film, radio, and television, usually without explicit reference to the product or service. The vast majority of paid placements are in television and film, but video games, music performance, and YouTube videos also offer space for corporations to place their products or services. Not surprisingly, the United States remains the world's leading product placement market, thanks to its global entertainment industry.

Corporations are likely to use more product placement as a major IMC tactic amid today's consumer trend of avoiding advertisements. According to PQ Media's "Global Product Placement Spending," "the U.S. product placement market expanded 13.7% to $8.78 billion in 2017 and is surging toward a ninth consecutive year of double-digit growth in 2018"; such a trend is fueled by the increased value of brand integrations in live and on-demand television, digital video, and recorded music.[20] Because more consumers control their media content consumption with digital and wireless technologies that help them skip commercial ads, corporations view product placement as an alternative solution for obvious advertising. Product placement has become a multibillion-dollar business as more media audiences avoid television commercials; it is an effective and less intrusive way to get brands exposed to the audience. Product placement commonly occurs when a corporation funds a media program. The media company, in turn, places the corporation's product or service in the program. The product or service is expected to be used, displayed or mentioned in the program. There are three basic types of product placement:

1. *Visual.* When a product, service, or logo is shown or placed in a virtual environment, such as a television show or movie, the audience recognizes it with their eyes.

2. *Spoken.* When actors or commentators talk about a particular product or service in a movie or television/radio show, the audience recognizes it with their ears.

3. *Usage.* When characters in a movie or television show use a particular product or service, the audience recognizes it with both their eyes and ears.

The history of product placement goes back to the early 1900s. The concept was popularized when Will Hays, the first president of the Motion Picture Producers and Distributors of America, praised the

---

20   PQ Media, https://www.pqmedia.com/wp-content/uploads/2018/06/US-Product-Placement-18.pdf

benefits of placing American-made products in films. "Motion pictures perform a service to American businesses by creating an increase in demand for our products," Hays said in a radio speech.[21] "The motion picture carries to every American at home, and to millions of potential purchasers abroad, the visual, vivid perception of American manufactured products."[22] Since then, corporations have used movies and television shows to place their products or services. However, it was not until the 1980s that the practice of product placement emerged as a popular IMC tactic. Film and media companies began to establish in-house divisions to deal with corporations' requests for product placement during this time. The following are five historical examples of product placements.

1. *E.T. the Extra-Terrestrial*: **Reese's Pieces** This movie is considered an American product-placement classic. During the production of *E.T.*, Director Steven Spielberg contacted Mars, Inc. about a possible tie-in between M&Ms and the film for a scene where a boy lures the shy little alien from his hiding place by leaving a trail of M&Ms. Mars did not like the idea of its product being eaten by such an ugly alien, so it turned Spielberg down. Spielberg turned to Hershey, which said, "Yes." A product placement deal was made in which Hershey agreed to promote *E.T.* with $1 million of advertising. Hershey, in return, could use *E.T.* in its own ads.[23] The trail scene was covered with Reese's Pieces. The deal turned out to be a huge success for the company after *E.T.* was released in 1982. The sales of Reese's Pieces shot up 65 percent.[24] This case has been heralded as the most successful one throughout American product-placement history.[25]

2. *You've Got Mail*: **AOL** This romantic comedy portrays the early era of email communication. The dial-up sound from the America Online (AOL) modem when Tom Hanks and Meg Ryan logged on reminded people of how exciting it was to hear "you've got mail!" chirping from the computer. AOL's copyrighted catchphrase became universal in 1998 when the movie was released. In fact, the world's leading instant-messaging service company at that time used the "you've got mail" sound to alert its users to the arrival of a new email. According to Jean-Marc Lehu's book, *Branded Entertainment*, the movie's title was initially *You Have Mail*, but AOL convinced the movie's director, Nora Ephron, to change the title to *You've Got Mail*. The movie title achieved noticeable mutual benefits.[26]

3. *American Idol*: **Coca-Cola** This show, which finds new solo singing talents, debuted on the Fox Network in 2002, and it has since become one of the most popular reality shows in the history of American television. Coca-Cola got a $10-million product-placement deal in the first season of the show. The deal rose to $35 million in season Seven. The multimillion-dollar deal required the show to prominently feature cups bearing Coca-Cola's logo on the judges' table. In addition, contestants and the host of the show were shown gathering between songs in the "Coca-Cola

21   Tanya Nitins, *Selling James Bond: Product Placement in the James Bond Films*, P.3 (United Kingdom: Cambridge Scholars Publishing, 2011).

22   Nitins, *Selling James Bond*. P.3.

23   Snopes Staff, "Did M&Ms Turn Down 'E.T.'?, Snopes.com, July 24, 2001, http://www.snopes.com/business/market/mandms.asp.

24   Claire Suddath, "Hollywood's New Product Placement Is in the Plot," Bloomberg Business, August 22, 2014, http://www.bloomberg.com/bw/articles/2014-08-22/relativity-medias-new-ad-agency-takes-product-placement-farther.

25   Suddath, "Hollywood's New Product."

26   Erik, "Top 40 Product Placements of All time: 30–21," Brands and Films, January 7, 2011, http://brandsandfilms.com/2011/01/top-40-product-placements-of-all-time-30-21/.

Red Room." The deal has been called one of the most successful TV product placements. "Wow, you couldn't ask for better TV. If you look at ratings, it's got universal appeal—everything from kids to 35 to 64-year-olds," said David Raines, Vice President of Integrated Communications for Coca-Cola. "It's hard to find something that is that universal."[27]

4. *Tomorrow Never Dies*: **Many Corporations** The 18th film in the James Bond series holds the record for the largest product placement deal in history. Filmed in France, Thailand, Germany, Mexico, and the United Kingdom, the movie attracted global corporations seeking to make product placement deals. Indeed, the fame of the 007 series played an important role in generating a record-breaking deal for $100 million. Eight major corporations made tie-ins with the movie: Avis rental cars, BMW cars and motorcycles, Ericsson mobile phones, Heineken beer, L'Oréal makeup, Omega watches, Smirnoff vodka, and Visa credit cards. The corporations, in fact, covered the movie's entire production budget.

5. *Academy Awards*: **Samsung Galaxy** While hosting the Oscars in 2014, Ellen DeGeneres handed a Samsung Galaxy Note 3 to actor Bradley Cooper for a celebrity-filled selfie shot (Figure 13.4) that included Meryl Streep, Jennifer Lawrence, Kevin Spacey, Julia Roberts, Brad Pitt, and Lupita Nyong'o. DeGeneres posted the selfie photo on her Twitter account during the show, and in less than an hour, it set the record for the most retweeted tweet of all time—more than one million retweets for a single Twitter post. Soon after DeGeneres's selfie broke the record, Samsung tweeted, "Record-breaking selfie taken on #TheNextBigThing! Noted."[28] "We crashed and broke Twitter, We made history," DeGeneres said during the broadcast from the stage. A marketing expert explained, "That was a social media home run. It really was."[29] No doubt, the selfie made the picture worth every dollar Samsung paid for the placement. Although Samsung did not disclose how much it paid for the product placement, it announced the next day that it would donate a total of $3 million to two charities picked by DeGeneres as a way to thank her.[30]

Third-Party Endorsements

A corporation sends a message to stakeholders and the public about the corporation itself or its products or services through the media. To make the message more credible, IMC specialists use the third-party endorsement strategy, employing outside individuals or groups to promote customized messages to the media. Since the younger generation seems less tolerant and unlikely to believe messages from direct corporate advertising, IMC specialists place the outside individuals or groups between the corporation and its target consumers to increase the credibility of the message. The outsiders are assigned to pass along the message from the corporation, relying on the consumers' perception that the message comes from an independent, unbiased, and credible source. The consumers believe that the message displays their best interest, whether the corporation is behind the message or not.

There are three types of third-party endorsements that IMC specialists commonly use to gain credibility:

27   Erik, "Top 40 Product."

28   Chenda Ngak, "Ellen DeGeneres Takes Selfie with Samsung Onstage, iPhone Backstage," CBS News, March 3, 2014, http://www.cbsnews.com/news/oscars-2014-ellen-degeneres-selfie-samsung-onstage-apple-iphone-backstage/.

29   Jessica Guyan, "For Samsung, Ellen DeGeneres' Oscar Selfie Is a Triumph," *Los Angeles Times, March 3, 2014*, http://articles.latimes.com/2014/mar/03/business/la-fi-samsung-oscars-20140304.

30   Guyan, "For Samsung."

FIGURE 13.4 The Oscar Selfie.

1. **Expert Endorsement** An expert is selected to endorse the corporation and its products or services. The expert is expected to express a positive opinion about a specific product or service. Consumers believe the opinion because the expert is an authority with vast experience and knowledge in the specialized industry. Typically, medical doctors, nutritionists, dieticians, gadget experts, designers, engineers, bloggers, or other category specialists hold authority as endorsers. For example, when a corporation claims its product is "clinically proven," consumers are inclined to trust the quality of the product. The corporation should present the expert who tested the product in the media to support the use of the product. In particular, expert endorsement is a favorite tactic for infomercials. An infomercial is a TV or online feature program, usually 15 or 30 minutes long, which is presented more as a talk show than a promotion. It aims to demonstrate a product's use and benefits with experts. For example, since 1995, Proactiv acne cream has been considered a success with endorsements from dermatologists Dr. Kathy Fields and Dr. Katie Rodan.

2. **Media Endorsement** Journalists or media outlets can be selected as endorsers. In this type of endorsement, credibility is added to the corporation's message as a result of being endorsed by reputable journalists or influential media outlets. They have the power of third-party endorsement because consumers tend to believe that information about a product, service, or even a corporation is objectively produced and disseminated by unbiased media or journalists who have used or evaluated the product before reporting the information. Indeed, consumers trust journalists more than direct corporate advertisers. The credibility of journalists and media outlets is vital for convincing consumers to buy or use the product or service.

   One important fact about this type of endorsement is that it is made without explicit reference to a product, service, or corporation; instead, journalists place the endorsement in their stories. For example, CNN's "On Money" segment published a story of the father who bought $1,000 of Disney stock in 2003 for each of his two daughters. The stock, as of May 2015, was worth nearly $5,000 for each girl. The story goes on to shed light on the good investment value of Disney stock, displaying the company as a good wedding and family vacation place, along with other customers' happy experiences.[31] Furthermore, the title of the article is "Why I Love My Disney Stock." CNN endorsed a clear message for Disney and its stock.

3. **Public-Figure Endorsement** Famous people, such as celebrities and sports stars, are selected as endorsers. Public figures can influence consumer behavior, thanks to their fan bases. Corporations prefer to employ famous people with clean images and good reputations to represent their products or services. For example, Oprah's Book Club was a book discussion segment of *The Oprah Winfrey Show* that debuted in 1996. Winfrey selected a new book and asked the viewers to read and discuss it. Whenever Oprah selected a book, it became an instant bestseller. As viewers believed that Oprah's free will and unsolicited opinion would lead to the selection of good books, the book club gained wide popularity. Eckhart Tolle's *A New Earth* was recorded as the best seller (with five million copies sold) among the 70 books that Oprah selected.

Third-party endorsements build credibility for corporate messages. In particular, they validate the benefits of a product or service in the consumer marketplace because a credible endorser speaks positively about it.

Corporate Sponsorship

Corporations with the goals of increasing their images and reputations adopt corporate sponsorship as their IMC strategy. Corporate sponsorship refers to financial support for public interest programs as a solution of enhancing corporate image and reputation. A corporation pays for all the program's costs. In return, its logo and brand name are guaranteed to be displayed alongside the program, including a specific mention that it has provided the funding for the public interest program. Business writer Harvey Meyer pointed out that corporations with sponsorship can achieve the following advantages:[32]

- Enhancing a corporation's visibility
- Differentiating the corporation from competitors
- Helping develop closer relationships with current and prospective consumers
- Showcasing products and services
- Unloading obsolete inventory
- Boosting sales, both long term and short term
- Allowing the corporation to compete more effectively against bigger firms that have much larger advertising budgets

Corporate sponsorship, like product placement, can be cost-effective, providing corporations with a unique opportunity to position their brands in the marketplace. For example, Rolex, the world's most famous luxury watch manufacturer, is one of the biggest sponsors of sports in the world, especially for

---

31   Patrick Gillespie, "Why I Love My Disney Stock," CNN, May 8, 2015, http://money.cnn.com/2015/05/08/investing/disney-stock-shareholders/index.html?iid=HP_LN.

32   "Corporate Sponsorship," Inc., n.d., http://www.inc.com/encyclopedia/corporate-sponsorship.html.

the three major tournaments in the world of tennis: Wimbledon, the Australian Open, and the French Open. The company uses its sponsorship to promote its unique pledge as the "Official Timekeeper," which signals the message: "As time passes, history is made." Rolex is present at the most prestigious events in golf, sailing, tennis, and motor sport, as well as equestrian tournaments as the main corporate sponsor. Sponsoring such prestigious events can subconsciously enhance a sign of success and personal accomplishment. Ariel Adams of *Forbes* magazine explains that Rolex has successfully spread its core message through sponsorship which communicates the brand values: "Rewarding yourself and celebrating success."[33]

IMC—Then and Now

Corporations acknowledge the importance of corporate reputation. The higher the reputation, the more likely they are to achieve their goals. While providing good products and services to consumers, corporations explore new strategies for enhancing sales and profits. They have found IMC effective in supporting sales. IMC aims to create and maintain a positive image and reputation for corporations. Several key factors play important roles in strategizing the use of corporate resources and tactics. In the long term, a corporation wants to build a unique identity, associated with good images, while trying to maintain an influential brand name and secure a stellar reputation.

To achieve such a long-term goal, a corporation implements IMC strategies, such as product placement, sponsorship, third-party endorsements, and public relations advertising. IMC strategies focus on increasing the awareness of the corporation for the media and consumers. Social media, of course, plays a big part in IMC tactics these days. In the online community, corporations are able to create a buzz in less than an hour, as the Oscar selfie proved the power of social media for IMC. In addition, the expression "going viral" has emerged as a new online IMC tactic when corporations use social media to promote a particular product or service. As an IMC expert said, "The most important element remains that customers want and expect a consistent experience across all of their touch points with companies and products," and social media plays the role of keeping consumers in touch with corporations.[34]

FIGURE CREDITS

Img. 13.1: Source: https://commons.wikimedia.org/wiki/File:Starbucks_logo_evolution.JPG. Copyright © 2011 by Starbucks Coffee Company.
Fig. 13.3: Source: http://www.lg.com/global/about-lg/corporate-information/at-a-glance/our-brand. Copyright © by LG Electronics.
Tbl. 13.1: Source: CoreBrand, "The 25 Most Powerful Corporate Brands," http://www.marketingprofs.com/charts/2014/24798/the-25-most-powerful-corporate-brands. Copyright © 2014 by MarketingProfs LLC.
Fig. 13.4: Source: https://www.youtube.com/watch?v=GsSWj51uGnl. Copyright © 2014 by ABC Television Network.
Img. 13.2: Copyright © 2020 by Haymarket Media Group Ltd.

33   Ariel Adams, "Why Rolex Watches Are the Most Reputable Consumer Products in the World According to Industry Study," *Forbes*, April 14, 2014, https://www.forbes.com/sites/arieladams/2014/04/14/why-rolex-watches-are-the-most-reputable-consumer-products-in-the-world-according-to-industry-study/#5bc14ff4a593.
34   Steve Olenski and MarketShare, "Integrated Marketing Communications—Then and Now," *Forbes*, May 31, 2012, http://www.forbes.com/sites/marketshare/2012/05/31/integrated-marketing-communications-then-now/2/.

CHAPTER SUMMARY AND REVIEW

1. Understand what communication fields IMC can include.

2. Identify how identity, identification, and reputation are related.

3. Study why brand and image play an important role in sales.

4. Find out how product placement and endorsement are being organized.

5. Distinguish public relations advertising from commercial advertising.

PUBLIC RELATIONS IN PRACTICE

FURTHER READING

PR Week's Awards For **Best PR Corporate Branding**

Winner: Aflac, FleishmanHillard, KWI, Marina Maher Communications, and Carol Cone On Purpose
Campaign Name: Aflac CSR—A Well Hatched Plan

After Aflac found that children's emotional needs are sometimes unmet, it created My Special Aflac Duck. The social robot, which helps patients understand their condition and communicate with their parents and doctors, was unveiled at the 2018 Consumer Electronics Show.

Read more at
https://www.prweek.com/article/1579436/prweek-us-awards-2019-winners

14

Government Relations

Every organization uses public relations functions. Corporations, associations, nonprofits, firms, and governments employ the practice of public relations to establish a positive climate for their operations. Public relations practitioners who are obligated to generate publicity and build a stellar reputation for their organizations are expected to fulfill their organizational goals in accordance with the interests of their target audience. Depending on which public relations fields they practice, public relations practitioners specify their target audience, such as customers, consumers, voters, investors, employees, clients, and the public. The audiences can be even more distinctly classified by their gender, age, education, income levels, beliefs, attitudes, and interests. Among audiences, the largest is the public. The public can be any organization's or practitioner's target audience. In particular, the public is the priority for national, state, and local governments to serve; governments exist to fulfill the public interest, and the public is their target audience.

By definition, governments should respond to the expectations and requests of the public by offering security, freedom, and sustainability for their lives. The public, in return, pays taxes and provides labor to help governments exist and succeed. The relationship between the public and governments is built on credibility and mutual understanding, in which they trust each other to survive and share the common interest of prosperity and well-being. Such an understanding and credibility can be accomplished through the process of communicating national and local information to the public. The public, in response, forms public opinion toward governments. For governments, informing the public is the fundamental principle of public relations. Federal, state, and local governments are responsible for disseminating information about their daily activities, which are aimed at serving the public. Public relations practitioners working for governments are required to practice a wide range of communication activities, including writing press releases and speeches, as well as holding press briefings and meetings with the public and media on behalf of government employees, such as the president, high-ranking officials, agency heads, governors, and mayors.

To communicate with the public, governments engage in the practice of public relations, day in and day out. The focus of public relations in government is the public information activities. Governments disseminate important information about policies and the work of agencies to the public. Information produced by the government is expected to raise public awareness and compliance. The practitioners in charge of disseminating public information for governments hold job titles such as public information

FIGURE 14.1 President-Elect Donald Trump and His Wife, Melania, Arrive at the White House After Their Inauguration Church Service at St. John's Episcopal Church in 2017.

officers, public affairs officers, or communication officers. Ironically, since 1913, governments and agencies in the United States have been banned from using the practice of public relations. Because of the policy, US federal, state, and local governments keep a distance from the term *public relations,* so they come up with alternative terms such as *public information* and *public affairs* to communicate with the public. In this practice, governments make an effort to inform, educate, and persuade the public in hopes of resolving social disturbance, conflict, and danger, as well as developing new government policies and activities with feedback from the public. In essence, governments implement the practice of public relations like other organizations, but they simply do not use the term *public relations* publicly because more than a century ago, lawmakers were concerned with the power of public relations used for promoting government interests. Therefore, it is important to understand how the practice of public relations in US government has evolved from a historical perspective.

A Brief History of Public Relations in Government

In the United States, the federal government is responsible for informing its citizens of what the government does for the public, but it is illegal to persuade the public by using taxpayer dollars to promote the government's political interests with the aid of public relations campaigns. The guideline was introduced in 1913 when Congress and political activists were concerned about government agencies involved in the practice of public relations. Between the late 1800s and early 1900s, legislators and civic and political groups wanted to stop the government from influencing legislative decisions by manufacturing or

FIGURE 14.2 George Creel.

manipulating public opinion in favor of government affairs. People outside of the government at the time feared government public relations turning into a propaganda machine.

Congress, as a result of the fear, enacted the Gillett Amendment in 1913, which simply stated, "Appropriated funds may not be used to pay a publicity expert unless specifically appropriated for that purpose." This meant that Congress would hold the power to allow the government to spend the government's budget for public relations purposes. The amendment limited the government and its agencies to spending on any public relations activities while only allowing the government to inform the public with no obvious promotion of its own agendas or interests. In fact, the amendment made the government back away from using the term *public relations* in its affairs. "That is why many government agencies today use such titles as information officers, press office, public affairs experts, communications specialists and press secretaries," said Joseph J. Carvajal, former president of the National Association of Government Communicators.[1]

During World War I, President Woodrow Wilson established the Committee on Public Information (CPI) to convince the American people that US military intervention in Europe was necessary. The CPI was ordered to find a way of gaining public support for America's entry into the war. Headed by journalist George Creel (Figure 14.2), the CPI recruited businesspeople, journalists, professors, professional writers, and artists to produce press releases, speeches, and films while even enforcing media censorship to influence public opinion. For example, a volunteer group of thousands of men, known as patriotic speakers, was dispatched nationwide to give pro-war speeches at meetings in public places. Films with pro-war messages were produced to reach out to the public, who did not read newspapers. The CPI also distributed more than 6,000 press releases in a week, and "more than twenty thousand newspapers carried information provided through CPI propaganda."[2] Clearly, the CPI served as the US government's propaganda and publicity agency by opposing the antiwar sentiments of the American people and defying enemy propaganda. Edward Bernays, with his profound understanding of human psychology in public relations, was one of the members of CPI, crafting propaganda strategies and disseminating fearful images that invoked the threat of the Germans. In particular, the CPI using psychological public relations techniques focused on creating anger and fear across the nation to illustrate "how terrible life would be if America and its allies lost the war to the Germans" through various communication tools, such as leaflets, movies, photographs, cartoons, pamphlets, booklets, magazines, posters, and billboards.[3] The CPI engaged in advertising by securing "millions of dollars' worth of free advertising space" from newspapers.[4] Such activities show that the CPI used propaganda tactics, which violated the Gillett Amendment. As a result, the CPI was formally disestablished by an act of Congress in 1919. In the same year, Congress developed

1   "Based on an article by Joseph J. Carvajal, 1977, NAGC President," National Association of Government Communicators, https://nagc.com/page/history

2   Propaganda Critic, http://www.propagandacritic.com/articles/ww1.cpi.html.

3   "Committee on Public Information Facts," American Historama, http://www.american-historama.org/1913-1928-ww1-prohibition-era/committee-on-public-information-facts.htm.

4   American Historama, "Committee on Public."

an amendment to the gag law, which prohibited the government and its agencies from influencing, in any manner, members of Congress in regard to legislation, policy, or appropriations.

As history shows, the use of public relations, technically, is banned in government. According to the Government Accountability Office—an independent agency that provides Congress with audit evaluation and investigative services—the use of funds for "publicity or propaganda" by the government and its agencies is strictly prohibited by Congress. This does not mean all communication acts by public information/affairs officers are illegal. For example, they are allowed to produce press releases highlighting the successes of their agencies and to be interviewed by the media for stories, as long as it is an act of information. However, if they pay money to citizens or individuals to influence lawmaking processes for their agencies' interests, it falls into the category of an illegal communication act. Generally speaking, it is understood that any communication act of the government, other than purely informing the public, is banned, according to the laws and regulations.

Public Information/Affairs Officers in Government

It is a civic duty for the government to inform the public, while the law prohibits using taxpayer money to promote its interest and manipulate the public. Informing the public is an official task conducted by public information officers, who are government employees. They are primarily responsible for facilitating communication between government agencies and the public. As such agencies produce important information, the officers disseminate the information mainly through the media in the form of press releases, news conferences, news briefings, and interviews. The media convey the government information to the public.

Similar to what public relations practitioners do in private sectors, government public information officers plan communication strategies and respond to requests from the media. One unique difference between government public relations and private public relations is the classification of target audiences. Government public relations is designed to serve the public with public information, as opposed to advocating a specific group of people with customized messages. Public information officers spend much of their time answering questions from journalists and the public. They, of course, issue press releases, hoping that journalists publish the information from the releases. Like public relations practitioners, public information officers are expected to manage a government crisis with quick and effective responses to the public and media. In addition, they strive to build solid reputations for their government agencies with strategic communication techniques. Compared with public relations practitioners, public information officers are likely to receive more calls and emails from journalists who prefer to use the officers as their main news sources. Journalists rely on the officers for accurate and trustable public information. The officers, in turn, expect journalists to report their agencies in a positive light.

Government agencies depend on public information officers to manage their images in a way that the agencies want to be depicted. Positive depictions (in terms of good work for the public) mean stronger public support, as opposed to negative depictions, which can lead to a public relations nightmare. For government agencies that don't have permission to use publicity and propaganda, positive media coverage is the backbone for boosting their operational morale. They need to attract attention for their not-for-profit work from the public, which pays taxes for their operations. The media also play an important role in the process as public information officers are located at the heart of the process. For example, when Hurricane Katrina (Figure 14.3) ravaged three states and disrupted hundreds of thousands of lives in 2005, the disastrous failures of the Federal Emergency Management Agency (FEMA)

FIGURE 14.3 Hurricane Katrina: New Orleans.

were vehemently highlighted by the media. The media reported that FEMA was useless when dozens of people were desperately asking for rescue for days on rooftops without food and water, and hundreds of people were waiting for medical supplies in shelters. The media mocked the agency by reporting that even journalists were able to do both, providing supplies and rescuing the victims while covering the disaster. Such media criticism led to public outrage against the agency and offered a reason for a deeper review of the agency's malfunction.

The media were persistent in exposing the agency's lack of ability to respond to disasters. Deeper problems within FEMA were exposed, and heavy criticism targeted the agency's director Michael Brown, who took the position in 2003. The media stressed that Brown, despite his lack of experience in disaster work, was appointed by President George W. Bush because Brown was a friend of the then-FEMA director who hired him. The director was Joe Allbaugh, who was President Bush's 2000 campaign chairman. After coming under fire over his qualifications and for what critics called "a bungled response to Hurricane Katrina's destruction," Director Brown resigned about two weeks after the disaster hit.[5] In FEMA's defense, there were two reasons for its weakened preparedness for natural disasters: (1) in 2003, it came under the Department of Homeland Security's control, which shifted FEMA's main function to responding to terrorist attacks over natural disasters and (2) more than 75 percent of the agency's preparedness grants were targeted to state and local readiness for terrorism, not for disasters.[6] Not surprisingly, the media

5   John King and Suzanne Malveaux, "FEMA Director Brown Resigns," CNN, September 12, 2005, http://www.cnn.com/2005/POLITICS/09/12/brown.resigns/.

6   "Exposed by Katrina, FEMA's Flaws Were Years in the Making," *USA Today,* September 7, 2006, http://usatoday30.usatoday.com/news/opinion/editorials/2005-09-07-our-view_x.htm.

rarely reported these reasons. This public relations nightmare resulted in publishing FEMA's booklet, titled *Basic Guidance for Public Information Officers*, in 2007.

The booklet serves as prominent guidance for modern public information officers and teaches what duties to perform and how to prepare for crisis communication. It states that public information officers are responsible for "communicating with the public, media, and/or coordinating with other agencies, as necessary, with incident related information requirements," as well as for "developing and releasing information about the incident to the news media, incident personnel, and other agencies and organizations."[7] The core statement of the booklet is that coordinated and timely communication is critical to effectively help the community since efficient and accurate communication can save lives and property, with the aim of ensuring credibility and public trust.[8] Public information officers are required to deal with information requirements, mainly from the media and public, in an accurate and timely manner to gain credibility and public support. The booklet instructs public information officers on how to prepare for an effective response to an incident or planned event.

Once an incident occurs, the officers are responsible for gathering accurate and timely information about the incident's cause, size, and current situation; they need to make sure that resources are committed; and they check other matters of general interest for both internal and external use. The booklet offers a checklist of responsibilities for the officers, in case any incident related to crisis management requires a response to the media:[9]

- Determine from the communication director if there are any limits on information release.
- Develop material for use in media briefings.
- Obtain the director's approval of media releases.
- Inform the media and conduct media briefings.
- Arrange for tours and other interviews or briefings as required.
- Evaluate the need for and, as appropriate, establish and operate a joint operation team.
- Disseminate accurate and timely incident-related information.
- Maintain current information summaries and/or displays on the incident.
- Provide information on the status of the incident to assigned personnel.
- Manage media and public inquiries.
- Coordinate emergency public information and warnings.
- Monitor media reporting for accuracy.
- Ensure that all required agency forms, reports, and documents are completed.

The checklist is a great manual for crisis communication. The officers should be ready to follow the instructions in terms of communicating with the media and public in case of such an incident.

---

7   FEMA, "Basic Guidance for Public Information Officers (PIOs): National Incident Management System (NIMS)," FEMA 517, November 2007, http://www.fema.gov/media-library-data/20130726-1623-20490-0276/basic_guidance_for_pios_final_draft_12_06_07.pdf.

8   FEMA 517, "Basic Guidance."

9   FEMA 517, "Basic Guidance."

They are hired to inform the public of specific action the public should take in a crisis, and their responsibilities will be completed when the victims return to the way of life before the incident.

The Executive Branch in Public Relations

According to the White House, the power of the executive branch is vested in "the President of the United States, who also acts as head of state and Commander-in-Chief of the armed forces."[10] Under the leadership of the president, there are 15 executive departments. More than four million Americans are employed in this branch, including members of the armed forces. Every department and agency has its own public information/affairs officers to communicate with the public and media. Some departments and agencies receive more media attention than others, depending on the relevance and importance of their relationship with the public. The White House, the Department of State, and the Department of Defense (DoD) are considered the top three US government organizations to which the media pay most attention for news stories.

The White House

The president and his staff receive heavy media attention every day. Every move the president makes and every word the president says, or tweets, are recorded and informed to the public. Journalists observe the president's behavior and record every word. The US president often receives the most media coverage in the world. The president, from the viewpoint of media attention, has the status of the bully pulpit. The term *bully pulpit* refers to a prominent public position of authority that allows a person to expound his or her views to a wide audience. The bully pulpit has the power of speaking out and being listened to on any issue he or she wants to talk about. Hence, the media are always attracted to the bully pulpit, which has a great influence on social issues that the public wants to know how the government handles. The media strive to get the president's attention. The president has the most famous bully pulpit to spread his or her messages to the public. In other words, the US president is one of the public information officers, maybe the most powerful public relations officer in the world.

Pushing a message is relatively easy for the president. Major broadcast television networks, newspapers, and wire news services report what the president says on the evening television news, on online news sites, and in the morning papers. The public receives the message coming from the president. All US presidents have taken advantage of the bully pulpit due in part to the intense media attention. The president uses it by explaining why he makes such hard decisions, defending his failures, seeking public support for his agendas, and spreading his preferred messages. President Ronald Reagan, known as "The Great Communicator," used his Hollywood looks and voice to disseminate his messages in simple speeches. He had the ability to focus the nation's attention on his victories in economic and international policies. His most famous message came with an important historical event—the fall of the Berlin Wall, which marked the end of the Cold War. "Mr. Gorbachev, tear down this wall," Reagan declared in Germany in June 1987. His simple and symbolic message was transmitted all around the world, signifying that American-led freedom and peace dominated the value of human life in the world.

---

10 "The Executive Branch," The White House, n.d., https://www.whitehouse.gov/1600/executive-branch.

President Bill Clinton used his bully pulpit to defend himself from criticism. His most famous message was "I did not have sexual relations with that woman [Monica Lewinsky]," in front of the press corps. Clinton strenuously denied his affair with the White House intern Monica Lewinsky, and he ended up emphasizing the message, which later turned out to be a lie. His defensive message is regarded as one of the two most unfortunate political one-liners alongside President Richard Nixon's "I am not a crook."[11]

Three days after the September 11 attacks in 2001, President George W. Bush visited Ground Zero, where the twin towers of the World Trade Center were still smoldering. As he conducted his tour, Bush suddenly climbed atop the rubble and used a bullhorn to speak with his arm around an elderly fire fighter. He made perhaps the most iconic impromptu speech of his presidency when he said, "The rest of the world hears you. And the people—and the people who knocked these buildings down will hear all of us soon." The crowd at the scene chanted, "USA! USA! USA!" His speech embraced the clear message of retaliation. His approval ratings peaked at 90 percent because of his strong message from the bully pulpit.

President Barack Obama used the bully pulpit to push his gun control message. Standing in front of mothers of gun victims invited to the White House in 2013, Obama, after reminding the nation of the Sandy Hook Elementary School gun shooting with 26 deaths, said, "Shame on us if we've forgotten. I haven't forgotten those kids. Shame on us if we've forgotten." He pushed his message through the bully pulpit to generate public pressure on Congress to take action on strong gun control policies.

President Donald Trump arguably best used the presidency as a bully pulpit to raise awareness of his political agendas in media coverage. Unlike previous presidents of the United State of America, Trump prefers Twitter to traditional media outlets in terms of communicating with the public. Trump explained that Twitter offers direct and unfiltered communication with the public as a substitute for traditional media. The president argued that critics and other media personalities heavily focus on criticizing his behavior via traditional media. His outspoken animosity toward the media resulted in the production of harsher coverage of his agendas. The Committee to Protect Journalists, an American independent nonprofit NGO, found in 2019 that from the beginning of his candidacy announcement for the 2016 presidential election to the end of his second year in office, Trump sent 1,339 tweets insulting or criticizing "journalists and outlets, or condemned and denigrated the news media as a whole."[12] In turn, the media obsessively focused on reporting "gossip, trivia, and hostility" toward Trump instead of important national and global issues.[13] It is understood that the media and President Trump, in fact, use each other to promote their agendas and interests.

The president cannot afford to give speeches or hold press conferences to address national or global issues on a daily basis. To assist the president in communicating with the media and public every day, the White House press secretary acts as the chief public relations spokesperson. The press secretary is responsible for communicating the president's thoughts, remarks, and opinions on particular issues to the public through the media, as well as providing information about the performance of the White House and the president's administration. The press secretary informs the media of current events by holding daily press briefings and press conferences in front of the White House press corps.

---

11   "Top 10 Unfortunate Political One-Liners," *Time*, n.d., http://content.time.com/time/specials/packages/article/0,28804,1859513_1859526_1859514,00.html.

12   Stephanie Sugars, "From Fake News to Enemy of the People: An Anatomy of Trump's Tweets," The Committee to Protect Journalists, January 30, 2019, https://cpj.org/blog/2019/01/trump-twitter-press-fake-news-enemy-people.php.

13   Newt Gingrich, "New Gingrich: the World Is Fraying—But American Media Is too Busy Criticizing Donald Trump," Newsweek, February 28, 2019, https://www.newsweek.com/newt-gingrich-world-politics-america-criticizing-donald-trump-opinion-1346839.

FIGURE 14.4 President Trump and the Press Corps.

Although the first spokesperson to officially hold the post of press secretary was George Akerson (who served President Herbert Hoover from March 1929 until February 1931), Stephen T. Early, President Franklin Roosevelt's long-serving press secretary, is considered American's first modern press secretary.[14] Early took charge of getting the president's message out to the press corps and crafting Roosevelt's image of trustable, beloved authority during the dramatic years of the Great Depression and World War II. Early also recommended that Roosevelt hold twice-weekly presidential press conferences, creating a line of communication with the press, which was applauded as informal and informative.[15] The White House press secretary is expected to act as the official spokesperson and media liaison for the president. A good relationship between the president and the press corps can be managed by the press secretary. The press secretary needs to be an advocate for the freedom of the press and the public's right to know what is happening inside the White House while also serving the president's interest. Former press secretary for Bill Clinton's administration, Mike McCurry, who pioneered the practice of televising press briefings, explained the importance of maintaining the president's amicable relationship with the press corps: "The modern presidency cannot work effectively if it is constantly at war with the media. It helps the president to have a channel of communication available to the press."[16] The press secretary is also expected to act as a mediator to resolve any conflict between the president and the press corps.

---

14   Mark Jurkowitz, "7 Facts about White House Press Secretaries," Pew Research Center, June 19, 2014, http://www.pewresearch.org/fact-tank/2014/06/19/7-facts-about-white-house-press-secretaries/.

15   "The Life and Presidency of Franklin D. Roosevelt," The White House Historical Association, https://www.whitehousehistory.org/the-life-and-presidency-of-franklin-d-roosevelt .

16   "What is it like to be the White House Press Secretary?" The White House Historical Association, https://www.whitehousehistory.org/questions/what-is-it-like-to-be-the-white-house-press-secretary

The Department of State

The United States of America is the most influential country because of its dominant economic and military power. The country, whether intended or not, is often viewed as the world's policeman. Faced with a cascade of global problems, the US government has engaged in resolving international conflict and crises since its entrance into World War I. The State Department plays the lead role in resolving diplomatic global issues. The department, as the lead US foreign affairs agency, is responsible for "promoting peace and stability in areas of vital interest to America and helping developing nations establish stable economic environments."[17] The department is assigned to communicate with foreign countries and global citizens to develop international security in favor of US national interests. It uses communication techniques to inform and educate global citizens about US foreign policy in hopes of building good relationships with the approximately 180 countries with which the US government maintains diplomatic relations.

Within the department, the Bureau of Public Affairs takes charge of the department's communication activities. Public affairs officers in the department are assigned to inform the American people and global audiences in a variety of ways, and their work includes the following functions:[18]

- Strategic and tactical communications planning to advance America's foreign policy interests
- Conducting press briefings for domestic and foreign press corps
- Pursuing media outreach, enabling Americans everywhere to hear directly from key department officials through local, regional, and national media interviews
- Managing the State Department's website at state.gov and developing web pages with up-to-date information about US foreign policy
- Using social media and other modern technologies to engage the public
- Overseeing the State Department's six international Regional Media Hubs, which serve as overseas platforms for engagement of foreign audiences via the Internet and broadcast and print media
- Answering questions from the public about current foreign policy issues by phone, email, letter, or through social media
- Arranging town meetings and scheduling speakers to visit universities, chambers of commerce, and communities to discuss US foreign policy and why it is important to all Americans
- Producing and coordinating audiovisual products and services in the United States and abroad for the public, the press, the secretary of state, and department bureaus and offices

These functions demonstrate that public affairs officers are obligated to employ a wide range of media platforms to communicate timely information to foreign audiences. More trendily, the department's website offers a variety of social media links, including Twitter, Facebook, YouTube, Flickr and Instagram. The department, like the White House, holds daily press briefings and issues press releases, focusing on activities of the secretary of state.

---

17   "What We Do," The Department of State, n.d., https://careers.state.gov/learn/what-we-do.

18   "BUREAU OF PUBLIC AFFAIRS (PA)," The Department of State, https://fam.state.gov/fam/01fam/01fam0320.html

One important challenge the department confronts currently is to find a means of undermining the communication ability of terrorist groups, especially the Islamic State, also known as ISIS. With the rise of ISIS and terrorism, the department is burdened with the task of "analyzing and countering terrorists' messaging around the world."[19] The Center for Strategic Counterterrorism Communications, designed to counter the appeal of violent extremism, was established within the department in 2011. The center concentrates on counteracting ISIS's effective social media tactics; the department regards social media as a powerful recruitment tool for terrorist groups. The center produced a YouTube video entitled *Welcome to the Islamic State Land* in September 2014, showing ISIS "blowing up mosques with Muslims inside, crucifying and executing Muslims, and plundering public resources."[20] While launching a social media campaign called "Think Again, Turn Away" to counter violent extremism, the center posts its mission to "expose the facts about terrorists and their propaganda" on the campaign's Facebook page.[21] The communication encounters between ISIS and the State Department are viewed as a new propaganda war in social media. Under the Trump administration, the bureau engages "domestic and international media to communicate timely and accurate information with the goal of furthering US foreign policy and national security interests as well as broadening understanding of American values."[22]

The Department of Defense

The DoD is a major government employer of public affairs officers. The Office of Assistant Secretary of Defense for Public Affairs (OASD(PA)) consists of the principal staff in charge of public information, internal information, community relations, information training, and audiovisual matters. The Defense Department takes charge of the military and civilian forces as the nation's largest employer; it has more than 1.4 million men and women on active duty and more than 710,000 civilian officers, and 1.1 million serve in the National Guard and reserve forces.[23] Similar to the Bureau of Public Affairs of the State Department, OASD (PA) carries out public information activities as follows:[24]

- Be the sole release authority to news media representatives for official DoD information.
- Be the principal spokesperson for the DoD.
- Develop communications policies, plans, and programs in support of DoD objectives and operations.
- Coordinate public affairs support of defense support to public diplomacy.
- Establish a formal media analysis function to build greater awareness in developing new trends, alerts to breaking news, and media coverage of DoD policies and views.

19   Judson Berger, "State Department Enters Propaganda War with ISIS," Fox News, September 9, 2014, http://www.foxnews.com/politics/2014/09/09/state-department-enters-propaganda-war-with-isis/.

20   Elise Labott, "State Department Releases Graphic Anti-ISIS Video," CNN, September 8, 2014, http://www.cnn.com/2014/09/05/world/state-department-anti-isis-video/.

21   Labott, "State Department Releases."

22   "Bureau of Global Public Affairs," Bureau of Public Affairs, n.d., https://www.state.gov/bureaus-offices/under-secretary-for-public-diplomacy-and-public-affairs/bureau-of-public-affairs/.

23   "ASSISTANT TO THE SECRETARY OF DEFENSE FOR PUBLIC AFFAIRS (ATSD(PA))," The Department of Defense, https://fas.org/irp/doddir/dod/d5122_05.pdf

24   "MEMORANDUM FOR DEPUTY SECRETARY OF DEFENSE SECRETARIES OF THE MILITARY DEPARTMENTS," Department of Defense Directive, https://fas.org/sgp/othergov/dod/media.pdf

FIGURE 14.5 US Pentagon.

- Prepare speeches, public statements, congressional testimony, articles for publication, and other materials for public release by the secretary of defense.

As the information activities show, the White House and the departments of defense and state conduct similar public information functions and systems in the government. They inform the media and public, mostly on a daily basis, of what their policies and programs are aimed at and what they achieved.

For the Defense Department, there was a turning point that changed its information strategy: the September 11 attacks of 2001. Just days after the attacks, the Bush administration and the Pentagon (see Figure 14.5), which is the headquarters of the DoD, came to realize that the country's super military power had failed to make the world like America and its people. In other words, they agreed that America would not win the "war on terror," or anything else, merely with military power. The Pentagon, in response to the realization, laid the foundation for the new communication strategy of shaping international public opinion in favor of the country. The Pentagon, teaming with the White House, felt the urge to spread a positive image of the United States around the world and combat anti-Americanism through global communication. The new global communication initiative was enforced to deliver the military's messages to citizens in specific foreign countries where the Bush administration had declared war on terrorism, such as Iraq and Afghanistan.

The Pentagon instructed American forces abroad to engage with empathy and understand foreign nations and their people while focusing their attention on gaining support from the citizens. As a result, then-secretary of defense Donald H. Rumsfeld established the Office of Strategic Influence (OSI) in October 2001 to respond to the fear that the United States was losing public support overseas for its war on terrorism, particularly in Islamic countries.[25] OSI was assigned to implement the practice of public relations toward foreign target audiences and was headed by Air Force Brigadier General Simon P. Worden, who began "circulating classified proposals calling for aggressive campaigns that use[d] not only the foreign media

---

25   "Office of Strategic Influence," Sourcewatch.com, last modified August 27, 2007, http://www.sourcewatch.org/index.php/Office_of_Strategic_Influence.

and the Internet, but also covert operations."[26] However, misinformation and rumors about OSI began to circulate around the Pentagon and media outlets at the same time of its establishment. For example, OSI was accused of planning to provide "news items, possibly even false ones, to foreign media organizations as part of a new effort to influence public sentiment and policy makers in both friendly and unfriendly countries."[27] In addition, critics accused the secretary of setting up OSI as a propaganda tool. Such allegations led to negative publicity and heated debate, causing Rumsfeld to shut down OSI in February 2002.

Even after OSI was shut down, the Pentagon did not stop its efforts to transform US wartime communication to create positive attitudes toward American soldiers and the country itself in foreign audiences. More importantly, the Pentagon did not ignore the fact that American public opinion would be the fundamental backbone for its wartime communication. The Pentagon understood that, without American public support, it couldn't achieve the goals. Between 2003 and 2008, the Pentagon dramatically increased—by 63 percent—the money it spent on winning hearts and minds, attempting to shape positive national and international public opinion while the support for the war on terrorism dropped considerably both at home and abroad.

In 2013, the US Army released its new communication field manual, called "Inform and Influence Activities (IIA)." IIA refers to "the integration of designated information-related capabilities in order to synchronize themes, messages, and actions with operations to *inform* United States and global audiences, *influence* foreign audiences, and *affect* adversary and enemy decision making."[28] The US Army is responsible for informing both US and foreign audiences, but it is limited to influencing only foreign populations to get them to support US objectives and stop supporting terrorists. As noted, any government communication activity to influence or persuade the American public in the form of propaganda is illegal.

The Legislative Branch

The legislative branch (Congress), which includes the House of Representatives' 435 members and the Senate's 100 members, makes the laws. Each member of Congress has a press secretary. The press secretary for a congressional representative has seven specific responsibilities to assist in media relations. The press secretary is obligated to: (1) act as the formal spokesperson and media liaison; (2) develop and implement public relations strategies; (3) evaluate current events and media reports for their impact; (4) provide advice on the effects of the congressperson's actions and legislative activities; (5) oversee the creation and distribution of newsletters and questionnaires; (6) maintain good working relationships with the congressperson, staff, media, and constituents; and (7) remain abreast of current legislative and nonlegislative issues about which the congressperson may be questioned. [29]

The press secretary in the legislative branch is required to multitask in a wide range of legal, personal and, media matters. The press secretary needs to arm himself or herself with professional knowledge of social and legislative issues, district voters' tendencies, and media strategies, in addition to professional relationships with all individuals associated with the congressional representative. In fact, the most important task of the press secretary is to inform the congressperson's constituents of how diligently and ethically he or she represents them so they can vote for the congressperson again. Whereas public relations practitioners work

26   Sourcewatch.com, "Office of Strategic Influence."

27   Sourcewatch.com, "Office of Strategic Influence."

28   Steven Aftergood, "Army Manual Highlights Role of 'Inform and Influence Activities,'" Federation of American Scientists, February 1, 2013, https://fas.org/blogs/secrecy/2013/02/inform_influence/.

29   "Recent Updates," Congress Foundation, n.d., www.congressfoundation.org.

for an entire organization and its employees, the press secretary mainly focuses on assisting one person, the congressperson, with strong communication skills and thorough knowledge of the legislative process.

The Judicial Branch

This branch, headed by the Supreme Court, enjoys the sole power of interpreting the Constitution and the meaning of laws, reviewing laws, and ruling on how a law should be applied. The Court's main public relations practice is consolidated into the Public Information Office, which is the central communication office for the Court and its nine justices. The office staff is in charge of responding to media inquiries. The staff has "the best contacts for information on what has been filed and when, as well as for updates on status," according to the Court's guidelines for reporters.[30] The staff offers one press copy of all case filings that may be copied in the pressroom during business hours.[31]

The Court remains the least covered of all Washington institutions because of its conservative and supreme status quo in the closed system.[32] If journalists are assigned to cover cases at the Court, they have to call the office ahead of time to secure a seat in the first two rows of the press section. The rows are reserved for journalists with permanent Supreme Court press passes, and reporters are not allowed to have tape recorders—no electronics of any kind are permitted in the courtroom.[33] Although the Court appears to have no interest in media relations, the office provides a press packet, "a thick folder with a sample term schedule, a past opinion, and some guidelines" for journalists.[34] It is extremely rare for the justices or any Court employees to be individually interviewed or quoted in the media about cases because the guidelines clearly state that no one in the Court may speak on camera or agree to be recorded regarding a Court decision.[35] Any communication matter in the Court has to go through the Public Information Office.

Each state has its own Public Information Office in their state supreme courts. For example, the Supreme Court of Ohio's Public Information Office manages five main tasks: (1) maintaining the Court's website, (2) publishing the Court's print publications, (3) corresponding with media inquiries, (4) distributing news releases, and (5) publishing articles about Court cases.[36] The office divides the staff into two groups: a news and information staff and a publications work staff. The former is responsible for working with the media, drafting oral argument case previews and publishing news articles about Court activities; the latter is responsible for managing the Court's website, along with the design and development of the Court's publications.[37] Because of sensitive legal issues and consequences, all courts in the United States are cautious about communicating with the media and the public. Therefore, the Public Information Office takes charge of consolidating all communication affairs.

---

30 "Supreme Court Guidelines for Reporters," Supreme Court of the United States, n.d., http://www.supremecourt.gov/publicinfo/reportersguide.pdf.

31 Supreme Court, "Supreme Court Guidelines."

32 "Structural Reforms to the Federal Judiciary," National Press Foundation, https://www.americanprogress.org/issues/courts/reports/2019/05/08/469504/structural-reforms-federal-judiciary/

33 "Structural Reforms to the Federal Judiciary," National Press Foundation

34 "Structural Reforms to the Federal Judiciary," National Press Foundation

35 Supreme Court, "Supreme Court Guidelines."

36 "Office of Public Information," The Supreme Court of Ohio, n.d., www.supremecourt.ohio.gov/PIO/.

37 Supreme Court of Ohio, "Office of Public Information."

Corporate Lobbying in Government Relations

Federal, state, and local governments make efforts to communicate with the public. They need to inform the public of policies and warnings to maintain stable government operations. There is no doubt that governments have a great effect on the public, and the public in general expects better public services and protection from their governments. When the public is disappointed in or frustrated with what governments do for them, the voting system works to replace government officials and form better governments.

The relationship between governments and the public can be built based on mutual benefits. In contrast, federal, state, and local governments appear to have a superior and controlling position over the business community since governments have regulatory power over how corporations operate. Corporations place government activities and policies on the radars of government relations specialists. Corporations are afraid of new regulations on their operations, and the government relations specialist closely monitors and assesses any movement of governments. Since governments have the power of regulating business practices, the specialist is expected to represent the corporation's voice to influence the government's process of creating regulations. The specialist has five objectives:[38]

1. To influence public policy in support of the corporation's business objectives

2. To enhance the corporation's reputation by building coalitions with government and congressional officials

3. To interact with state governments, manage local community activities, and handle emergency responses on a local level

4. To build partnerships with other corporate people in the same industry

5. To develop policies and educate key players in legislation about the policies in favor of the corporation's interest

To achieve these objectives, the specialist meets with officials at all levels of governments, discussing what the corporation and business community want. Such work is commonly viewed as lobbying, and the specialist is called a lobbyist. Lobbying is controversial and often viewed as a corrupt maneuver used by greedy interest groups. However, it is a legitimate act that informs and educates government officials about what policies and enforcements are beneficial for all sides. Lobbying can be one of corporations' numerous communication activities, and lobbyists are activists and advocates who seek to persuade members of the government and Congress to enact legislation and enforce laws that would benefit their organizations. The range of organizations can include corporations, labor unions, universities, environmental groups, religious institutions, and foreign governments.

In 1995, the Lobbying Disclosure Act took effect, requiring individuals who work for a third party at the federal level to register with the Senate and the House. Under the act, lobbying firms, self-employed lobbyists, and corporations employing lobbyists must file regular reports of their lobbying activity.[39] In

---

38   Jill E. Fisch (2005). "How Do Corporations Play Politics?" University of Pennsylvania Law School, https://scholarship.law.upenn.edu/cgi/viewcontent.cgi?article=2043&context=faculty_scholarship

39   Tom Murse, "What Does a Lobbyist Do?," About.com, last modified January 15, 2020, http://dc.about.com/od/jobs/a/Lobbying.htm.

lobbying, frequent topics with government and congressional officials include whether laws and policies need to be revised or enacted to protect corporations and the business community from economic shocks or foreign competition.[40] Sometimes a group of corporations partner up to fund their own lobbying activities in a particular industry. Thus, some industries are more inclined to lobby policy makers than others. For example, in 2019, the top five industries spent the following amounts: (1) pharmaceuticals and health products—$85 million, (2) insurance—$41 million, (3) electronics—$39 million, (4) oil and gas—$34 million, and (5) business association—$32 million. [41]

One main reason for rich industries to invest millions of dollars in lobbying is to pay fewer taxes. According to the financial organization, NerdWallet, the ten most profitable US companies, including Exxon Mobil, Apple, Microsoft, and JPMorgan Chase, paid an average federal tax rate of just 9 percent.[42] In addition, many of the corporations that have seen their tax rates fall since 2010" are among the biggest spenders "when it comes to lobbying."[43]

Corporate lobbying, despite its reputation, does work in the US tax system. For example, General Electric famously did not pay a penny on taxes to the US government in 2010 by using a "series of deductions to report a $408 million loss in America, even though its international business made $10.8 billion."[44] General Electric was named the most direct lobbying corporation, spending $134 million from 2009 to 2014.[45] A business writer accused US corporate lobbying of hampering a movement for fixing tax loopholes.[46] More recently, Amazon paid $0 in US federal income tax on more than $11 billion in profits in 2018; it also received "a $129 million tax rebate from the federal government."[47]

Although lobbyists still struggle with negative perceptions of their jobs, they are known for their thorough analytical, interpersonal communication skills. Many of the lobbyists have advanced academic degrees. They can be viewed as corporate communication and government relations specialists. While there is no formal training required to become a lobbyist, the Association of Government Relations Professionals offers a lobbying certificate program, aimed at strengthening "the skills and effectiveness of government relations personnel in lobbying firms, corporations, and not-for-profit organizations."[48] By the end of 2019, 11,862 lobbyists were registered in the Washington, DC, area

40   Evangeline Marzec, "What Is Corporate Lobbying?," *Small Business Chronicle*, n.d., http://smallbusiness.chron.com/corporate-lobbying-11729.html.

41   "Industries," Open Secrets.org, n.d., https://www.opensecrets.org/lobby/top.php?showYear=2019&indexType=i.

42   Maxime Rieman, "NerdWallet Study: Top Companies Paid 9% U.S. Tax Rate," Nerdwallet.com, July 24, 2012, http://www.nerdwallet.com/blog/investing/2012/corporate-taxes-only-9-percent/#.UB-zQshYu9c.

43   Alexander Eichler, "10 Most Profitable U.S. Corporations Paid Average Tax Rate of Just 9 Percent Last Year: Report," HuffingtonPost, August 6, 2012, http://www.huffingtonpost.com/2012/08/06/most-profitable-corporations-tax-rate_n_1746817.html.

44   Jesse Solomon, "Top 10 Companies Lobbying Washington," CNN, October 1, 2014, http://money.cnn.com/2014/10/01/investing/companies-lobbying-10-biggest-spenders/.

45   Solomon, "Top 10 Companies."

46   Mark Gongloff, "U.S. Companies Lobbying Furiously to Save Corporate Tax Loopholes: Study," HuffingtonPost, June 18, 2013, http://www.huffingtonpost.com/2013/06/18/companies-lobbying-corporate-tax-loopholes-study_n_3461044.html.

47   Andrew Davis, "Why Amazon Paid No 2018 US Federal Income Tax," CNBC, April 4, 2019, https://www.cnbc.com/2019/04/03/why-amazon-paid-no-federal-income-tax.html.

48   "About the Lobbying Certificate Program," Association of Government Relations Professionals, http://grprofessionals.org/events-education/lobbying-certificate-program/about-the-lcp

FIGURE 14.6 Lobbying in DC.

(Figure 14.6), and they spent more than $ 3.4 billion for their lobbying activities.[49] The number of unregistered lobbyists and the amount of money they spend can be far higher than the publicly known figures.

Government Relations for the Public

Ideally, all federal, state, and local governments exist to serve the public. The information governments produce and disseminate is supposed to be valuable and important to the public. Because of the Gillett Amendment, the government avoids the practice of public relations; instead, its communication officers conduct public affairs/information practice, excluding the acts of persuasion and influence on the public. The officers carry out communication activities that are quite similar to what public relations practitioners do. Press releases, news briefings and responses to journalists are part of the officers' routine tasks. They focus more on enhancing the public interest than on advocating for a specific audience's interest.

Lobbyists are a different story. They are paid to achieve the objectives of those who hire them by using sophisticated communication and legislation skills. Lobbyists are armed with knowledge of national and international government affairs, political and legislative programs, and opinion research.

Whether lobbying is seen as a part of problematic public relations practice, or whether government communication activities are separated from the core practice of public relations, public relations is a central communication function when it comes to an information exchange in pursuit of mutual benefits. Government relations is another function of public relations in which governments disseminate information and the members of the public respond to the information with their feedback. In a similar vein, corporations provide information and opinions through lobbying, and governments respond to corporations. Government relations is used to communicate with the public, media, and corporations.

---

49   "Trends in Spending," Open Secrets.org, n.d., https://www.opensecrets.org/federal-lobbying/trends-in-spending.

CHAPTER SUMMARY AND REVIEW

1. Understand why there is no public relations in government.
2. Identify what public information officers do.
3. Discuss how the president and press secretary communicate with the media.
4. Find similar public relations job descriptions for government departments and Congress.
5. Argue why lobbying is necessary or unnecessary for the public.

PUBLIC RELATIONS IN PRACTICE

FURTHER READING

PR Week's Awards For **Best PR Public Affairs**

Winner: National Safety Council, Ketchum, Energy BBDO, m ss ng p eces, Flare, The Mill, and PHD
Campaign Name: Prescribed to Death

To turn the focus of Americans and their public health policy makers onto the urgent need to address the problem and combat misinformation and misconceptions surrounding opioid addiction, the National Safety Council created a traveling memorial wall that depicted the faces and stories of 22,000 victims of opioid overdose—successful student athletes, loving and hard-working mothers, or active grandfathers taking prescription opioids. Every 24 minutes, a machine etched another victim's face on a new pill, adding to the death toll.

Read more at
https://www.prweek.com/article/1579436/prweek-us-awards-2019-winners

15

Nonprofit Organizations in Public Relations

Every organization performs the practice of public relations to survive in a highly competitive society. For organizations to maintain their existence, public relations is an essential device to achieve organizational goals from the viewpoint of reputation and image. Public relations is used for a wide range of organizations, such as corporations, government agencies, political associations, foundations, religious institutions, hospitals, colleges, and interest groups. These organizations use public relations to inform, educate, entertain, and persuade their target audiences in hopes of developing mutually beneficial relationships. One of the core functions of public relations is to build a positive reputation and image in media coverage and in the minds of the target audience. As a result, organizations can secure the target audience's support.

Most organizations see public relations as an imperative instrument to increase their financial security because public relations makes a significant contribution to sales. These organizations are categorized as for-profit organizations. On the other hand, some organizations are not established to seek profits. They exist for social causes and the public interest (the welfare or well-being of the general public). They conduct their operations in society without having actual products or services to sell in exchange for money. These organizations are known as not-for-profit organizations or simply NGOs (see Figure 15.1). NGOs exist because government can neither be everywhere nor do everything for the public. Most NGOs provide valuable services for social causes that range from human rights, environmental protection, and health care to education. Such services keep a great distance from the concept of making a profit to survive, and many people assume that public relations can be less important to the NGO community than the business community; on the contrary, NGOs view the practice of public relations as a primary activity of existence. To understand this view, the characteristics and roles of NGOs should be discussed first.

The Characteristics and Roles of NGOs

An NGO is not a government agency. It is not even a for-profit business. An NGO can be defined as any nonprofit or voluntary group that is formed by task-oriented people in pursuit of a common interest for the public. NGOs can be organized on a local, national, or global level. One important characteristic

FIGURE 15.1 NGOs.

of NGOs is their independence from governmental influence, even though some of them may receive government funding. They are generally established by and for a specific community (with or without intervention from the government). They aim to improve the quality of life for a group of people who struggle with social, economic, cultural, or environmental issues.

Based on their purpose of improving life, NGOs act as the backbone of civil society's attempt to change or correct a host of problematic issues on behalf of the poor, the oppressed, and the marginalized in a nation or the world. Their activities include human rights, foreign policy, environmental protection, political and social movements, economic development, animal advocacy and many other issues. In essence, NGOs promote social equality, political justice, and environmental stability by playing a critical role in increasing the standards of living for people in need. NGOs can virtually represent every cause in society.

Because their primary purpose is not about making money, NGOs, in order to achieve their goals, seek financial and voluntary support from the public; this is where public relations plays a vital role in persuading the public to support NGOs. Receiving public support begins with information dissemination and is finished with strong public participation in NGO activities.

Approximately 1.5 million NGOs operate in the United States to serve the public interest.[1] Although the government generally does not offer direct financial aid to NGOs, it provides NGOs with a special policy: exemption from state and federal taxes. To gain the tax benefit, NGOs must be incorporated and registered as not-for-profit organizations under the laws of any of the 50 US states in which "anyone can

---

1   "Non-Governmental Organizations (NGOs) in the United States," US State Department, https://www.state.gov/non-governmental-organizations-ngos-in-the-united-states/

incorporate an NGO in just a few days at the state level."[2] According to the fact sheet published by the US Department of State, any group of individuals can be allowed to establish an NGO as long as they complete the process of providing a short description "of the organization, its mission, name, the address of an agent within the state, and paying a modest fee" in a few days.[3]

Establishment is not as hard as maintenance for NGOs. Maintaining and conducting NGO operations is the hardest part of achieving an organization's goals of helping nationally and internationally marginalized people. In order for NGOs to implement activities, they do need sources of finance and humans. They have to pay their expenses, spend money on their programs and pay employees. Raising money for stable operations is the largest challenge for most NGOs since they are faced with budget shortfalls every year in a competitive environment.

Sources of finance mostly come from donations from individuals, philanthropic foundations, for-profit organizations, or grants from the government. There is no specific enforcement code that prohibits NGOs from receiving donations from foreign entities such as foreign corporations and governments. NGOs, technically, are allowed to welcome any kind of donation without asking questions about the source. However, NGOs struggle with the reality that they compete with one another for donations and employees.

Securing the sustainable flow of finance through donations is the priority of NGO operations. Since donors have difficulty deciding which NGOs to give their dollars to, NGOs initiate strategies to find donors by informing people about what they do, which group of people they help, what issues they address, and why they are involved in particular activities or demonstrations. More importantly, NGOs strategize to convince donors that their money would be used for protecting "human rights, human dignity, and human progress."[4] Again, the practice of public relations is aimed at gaining the attention of potential donors.

Because most NGO activities are associated with humanitarian work, NGOs have traditionally enjoyed one advantage over for-profit organizations: credibility. As they are perceived as committed to protecting and advancing the public interest, the public in general trusts and supports what NGOs do. The good work of NGOs can attract more donors and volunteers who stimulate NGO activities.

NGOs have four primary roles in advancing modern societies. Professor Scott T. Young at DePaul University has discussed these roles:[5]

1. *Social Development.* NGOs maintain institutional independence and political neutrality. Free from political and government pressures, NGOs shed light on social issues that government or politicians are reluctant to address. For example, when they believe a government policy is not fair to the public, they organize rallies, demonstrations, or boycotts to raise public awareness and garner public support.

2. *Sustainable Community Development.* Because of their particular ideology and nature, NGOs are good at reaching out to and mobilizing poor, remote communities. NGOs especially aimed at the reduction of human suffering offer counseling services for households, legal aid, and microfinancing. The long-term aim for these NGOs is to assist in sustainable community development through activities such as capacity building and self-reliance.

---

2   US State Department.
3   US State Department.
4   US State Department.
5   Scott T. Young and Kanwalroop Kath, *Sustainability: Essentials for Business,* p. 19 (Los Angeles: Sage, 2007).

3. *Sustainable Development.* NGOs that focus attention on the social and environmental impacts of business activity pressure the business community to conduct their business in an ethical manner to achieve sustainable development. Labor issues and environmental or human rights records of corporations are monitored by NGOs, which take action if any violations are detected. In response, corporations make an effort to operate their businesses without hurting consumers, communities, or the public. This is a stakeholder-centered approach that cares about customers, employees, communities, and other interested groups instead of merely focusing on profits.

4. *Sustainable Consumption.* NGOs team up with corporations to encourage consumers to use ecofriendly products and services. Some NGOs specialize in ranking products and services based on CSR to inform consumers about the products or brands they purchase. NGOs also lead corporations to develop or design products that will minimize the environmental effects of consumption.

As the characteristics and roles show, NGOs act as community organizers, advocacy groups, environment protectionists, and watchdog groups.

Public Relations for NGOs

NGOs are different from corporations in terms of their operating systems and organizational structures, although they both facilitate the practice of public relations. So, we can ask, How different is public relations in NGOs from corporate public relations? And what are the reasons for the difference?

Both corporations and NGOs take advantage of public relations to garner positive media coverage. Whereas corporations use communication tools and techniques to persuade consumers to use their products and services, NGOs use communication programs to persuade individuals to participate in NGO activities voluntarily to promote social values and public goals. NGOs commonly cannot afford to pay for expensive advertising, so public relations programs that generate media coverage lie at the heart of their success. Most NGOs create public relations programs or campaigns to persuade the public to join their activism. Such programs are aimed at cultivating public awareness, stimulating financial support, and increasing involvement in their activities. As a result, public relations programs of NGOs tend to engage heavily in building relationships with the public. In this vein, public relations for NGOs has five distinctive functions that separate them from for-profit organizations:

1. To spread messages explaining what activities, initiatives, and projects are related to philanthropic and solidarity activities.

2. To develop and implement policies that can benefit vulnerable people by pressuring decision makers such as government officials and lawmakers.

3. To advocate ideological accomplishments such as credibility, transparency, reputation, and equality.

4. To promote environmental protection that discourages corporations from adopting measures that damage nature.

5. To educate the public about what actions should be taken about a social problem that jeopardizes the public interest.

Communication in NGOs is used to promote voluntary participation in problem solving and developing better conditions by empowering the public. To empower them, organizing public relations programs that respond to the public is essential. More public support means more shared feelings between NGOs and the public. NGOs need to grab public attention to further their activities and causes. Public attention in many cases is the product of sophisticated, thorough strategies of public relations programs that can interest journalists. Like for-profit organizations, NGOs seek positive media coverage. Most NGOs acknowledge that a low-cost method of gaining public attention is connected to how media relations is practiced. NGOs implement popular media relations tactics, such as press releases, news conferences, special events, interviews, and Internet sites, in the hope that the media will disseminate the information about their existence. The more people are informed, the better a chance that NGOs will receive support.

NGOs hire public relations practitioners to perform a wide array of tasks: media relations, program creation, reputation management, event planning, employee relations, and fundraising. The practitioners are expected to maximize their communication skills and techniques to create awareness among the public about NGO activities, raise funds from funding bodies, attract volunteers, network with other NGOs, work with policy makers, educate the public about the cause, and bring about attitudinal change.[6]

Letting the Public Know about the NGO

There are famous NGOs and others that are less known (Box 15.1). Regardless of the level of fame, NGOs take action in a number of ways to promote their names and existence to the public. They need to share what they believe and how they operate for the public while expecting more support to come in. Informing the public of the existence of the NGO is a significant first step to gaining public support.

There are more than a million NGOs officially registered in the United States. Most of the public would unlikely know their names, functions, or activities; however, some names such as Oxfam, Wikimedia Foundation, PETA, Greenpeace, and the Susan G. Komen organization (or simply Komen) are well-known to the public. Departing from the differentiation of famous or unknown NGOs, two questions arise: (1) What makes the public aware of the existence of more popular or less popular NGOs? (2) How do practitioners raise public awareness of the existence of an NGO? There are four players to better inform the public of the existence of an NGO:

1. **The Media.** By working with the media, an NGO and its workers can spread its message by holding press conferences, issuing press releases, being interviewed, or even setting up online information centers. No doubt, the media are a great help for an NGO in informing the public of what the NGO does, where it is located, what it needs, and whom it helps. For example, Oxfam receives a great deal of media coverage, as the NGO offers media support packages, such as press releases, press kits, activity reports, and videos. More importantly, the NGO makes media officers available for any inquiries from journalists who tend to cover more stories about NGOs if they receive quick and abundant information from the organizations' representatives. Making information available for journalists is important.

2. **Local Outreach.** Most NGOs have limited geographic areas for activity unless they have enough resources to operate globally. Reaching out to the people in the community where the NGO

---

6   Anshu Bhati, "Role of Public Relations for Effective Communications in NGOs," *International Journal of Scientific Research,* Volume: 2, Issue : 11 (2013), pp. 338-340. https://www.worldwidejournals.com/international-journal-of-scientific-research-(IJSR)/fileview.php?val=November_2013_1493276278__107.pdf

operates can be an initial step to inform people about the existence of the NGO. If the NGO shows the community how determined it is to help the people, community support for the NGO is strengthened. With strong community support, the NGO can expand its reputation and activity beyond the community. For example, in 1983, the Susan G. Komen organization started with $200 and a shoebox full of potential donor names when it launched its first race for a breast cancer cure in Dallas, Texas. Eight hundred participants joined the race.[7] In 2019, the Komen race events hosted 140 races globally with the aid of corporate sponsors.[8]

3. *Visual Activity.* Visual representations of NGO activity can be a very strong asset in informing the public about the existence of the NGO. In addition, a strong visual representation invites more media coverage. For example, Greenpeace, arguably the most visible and well-known environmental NGO in the world, provides many examples of the effective use of visuals to raise public awareness. It has launched many public relations campaigns with visual evidence since its foundation in 1972. The NGO launched a campaign in 1975 when the Soviets harpooned whales off the California coast.[9] The NGO deployed a rubber boat with professional photographers and cameramen to visually capture the cruelty of the Soviet whaling vessel. Films and photos containing bloody scenes of Soviets killing whales were published around the world, and the NGO raised global awareness of its existence.

4. *Corporate Partnership.* More corporations want to get involved in CSR. Whereas some of them conduct their own programmed CSR, others seek an opportunity to team up with NGOs to generate better CSR outcomes. Choosing the right NGO partner paves the way for a successful partnership, as both sides recognize and respect the differences between profit and social causes. For example, when Kodak planned to expand the photography market into a rural area in China, the company approached NGOs to build a CSR partnership before displaying its products. Kodak sought a credible global NGO with a strong reputation in the country. The Nature Conservancy, with its long-standing relationship with China, agreed to team up with Kodak. The NGO was also looking for a company that could help an innovative program that "would provide cameras and film to remote villagers in order to learn about local priorities and needs in southwestern China."[10] The program was called Photovoice, an integral part of the Nature Conservancy's effort with local government agencies "to establish nature reserves, protected areas, and other conservation objectives."[11]

NGOs make efforts to tell the public that they exist and conduct specific work to help animals, wildlife, or people in need. The media play an important role in helping NGOs to inform the public about their work. Small NGOs tend to focus at the community level to promote their names and reputations. Some NGOs produce a series of visual content that attracts more media attention, directly relating to an increase in public awareness of the existence of NGOs. Other NGOs team up with corporations to conduct their activities since the NGO-corporate partnership helps "to enhance business understanding of social and environmental issues."[12] In any way possible, NGOs need to tell the public that there are NGOs seeking public support. Several of them decide to choose more provocative, dramatic measures to inform the public of their existence.

7   "Race for the Cure," Susan G. Komen Organization, n.d., https://ww5.komen.org/RaceForTheCure/.

8   Susan G. Komen, "Race for the Cure."

12   "How Can Corporate-NGO Partnerships Create the Long-Term Change? Live Chat, *The Guardian*, n.d., http://www.theguardian.com/sustainable-business/2014/nov/10/corporate-ngo-partnerships-long-term-change-live-chat.

BOX 15.1   PEOPLE FOR THE ETHICAL TREATMENT OF ANIMALS (PETA) PUBLICITY STUNTS

As the largest animal rights organization in the world, according to its website (http://www.peta.org), PETA focuses its attention on the four areas in which the largest number of animals suffer the most intensely for the longest period of time: on factory farms, in the clothing trade, in laboratories, and in the entertainment industry. The NGO highlights the human cruelty of animals while emphasizing the health benefits of vegan foods and showing the vulnerability of animals in laboratories and circuses.

Most of the public agrees with the core philosophy of PETA, believing that many animals should be protected from abuses by greedy or insane humans. However, many members of the public disagree with PETA's campaign strategies of grabbing the public and media attention to raise awareness. Here are two examples.

In February 2009, the animal rights group staged a protest at the Westminster Kennel Club Dog Show, having two of its members dress in Ku Klux Klan (KKK) garb outside Madison Square Garden in New York City. The members handed out pamphlets with catchy messages, such as "The KKK and the American Kennel Club (AKC): BFFs?" to dog show exhibitors and fans from across the country. Their goal, according to a post on the PETA website, was to draw a parallel between the KKK and the American Kennel Club. "Obviously it's an uncomfortable comparison," PETA spokesman Michael McGraw told the Associated Press.

Another example is the "McCruelty" campaign against the fast-food giant McDonald's in 2009. PETA dramatically took on McDonald's for the company's treatment of chickens by displaying almost-naked women, as well as a tweaked catchphrase, "I'm hatin' it." Considering PETA's provocative history of public performance, it is no surprise that the unconventional, attention-seeking demonstrations were conducted on the streets in broad daylight. As PETA pointed out on McCruelty.com, chickens killed by McDonald's suppliers were slaughtered using an outdated method that results in extreme suffering. The NGO's protest methods have been seen as extreme, but PETA, with such provocative demonstrations surely attracts media attention from a public relations perspective.

More recently, PETA hosted an event (Figure 15.2), "Sexiest Vegan Next Door" in 2019, which recognized a man and a woman who were enthusiastic about their vegan lifestyles and displayed sexy bodies as a result. The event was open to the public to determine the winners by vote counts. The female winner was Jasmine, a licensed vocational nurse, and the male winner was Kevin, a firefighter.

FIGURE 15.2 PETA Event.

Sources: *Los Angeles Times*, http://latimesblogs.latimes.com/unleashed/2009/02/akc-kkk.html.
USA Today, http://usatoday30.usatoday.com/sports/2009-02-09-peta-westminster-kkk-protest_N.htm.

Media ITE, http://www.mediaite.com/online/petas-most-controversial-publicity-stunts/#0.

PETA, https://www.peta.org/features/sexiest-vegan-next-door-2019/winners/

Donors

Financial insecurity is the scariest reality for NGOs. Paying the bills is a monthly challenge. NGOs rely on a variety of sources to fund projects, operations, salaries, and other overhead costs. Such sources include membership dues; philanthropic foundations; grants from local, state, and federal agencies; and private and corporate donations.[13] If the sources steadily give a certain amount of money every month or year to NGOs, none of the NGOs will worry about their financial situations. In reality, NGOs have to make strong efforts to motivate the sources to donate more money. In order for NGOs to survive, fundraising strategies and practices are developed by people such as public relations practitioners, marketing specialists, and nonprofit experts.

Individuals, corporations, and charity foundations are the main donors to NGOs. In 2018, *Business Insider* named the top ten US companies that give the most donation (Table 15.1):[14]

TABLE 15.1   Top Ten Cash Donations via Corporate Giving Programs

Corporation	Total Cash Donations
Gilead Sciences	$388 million
Wells Fargo	$287 million
Goldman Sachs Group	$280 million
Google	$255 million
JPMorgan Chase	$250 million
Johnson & Johnson	$227 million
Pfizer	$210 million
ExxonMobil	$204 million
Bank of America	$181 million
Microsoft	$169 million

Forbes revealed that the largest individual donation came from Warren Buffett (Figure 15.3) in 2019, followed by Bill and Melinda Gates, Michael Bloomberg, the Walton family and George Soros.[15]

The third type of main donors for NGOs is charitable foundations. Charitable foundation connotes an organization that donates funds to NGOs, deriving its money from a family, individual, or corporation for charitable purposes. According to the FundsforNGOs website, charitable foundations have been long-term suppliers of funding to NGOs around the world, and they serve as important sources for

13   Jean Folger, "How Do NGOs Get Funding?," Investopedia.com, February 5, 2020, http://www.investopedia.com/ask/answers/13/ngos-get-funding.asp.

14   Chelsea Greenwood, "10 of the Companies That Give the Most to Charity in the US," *Business Insider*, November 14, 2018, https://www.businessinsider.com/companies-that-give-the-most-to-charity-in-the-us-2018-9#10-microsoft-corporation-works-with-more-than-200000-nonprofits-10.

15   Jennifer Wang, "America's Top 50 Givers," *Forbes,* November 20, 2019, https://www.forbes.com/top-givers/#277e4c4666ff.

new partnership opportunities, especially for small grassroots NGOs in low-income countries.[16] These foundations not only donate their money to NGOs, but they also work with NGOs worldwide to address global issues together. In fact, they partner up with NGOs if necessary. They play an important role in funding NGOs that wrestle with developing nations' issues, such as public health systems, child abuse, and women's rights. Some of the top ten foundations (Table 15.2) contain familiar family or corporate names in their NGO partnerships.[17]

FIGURE 15.3 Warren Buffett and Bill Gates.

TABLE 15.2 Top Ten Foundations That Donate to NGOs

Name	Focus Area
The Bill and Melinda Gates Foundation	Health-care problems
Open Society Foundations	Business development
The Ford Foundation	Freedom and democracy
The William and Flora Hewlett Foundation	Social and environmental problems
The Children's Investment Fund Foundation	The lives of children
The United Nations Foundation	Global health
The John D and Catherine T Macarthur Foundation	Global conservation and security
The Conrad N. Hilton Foundation	Human rights
The Rockefeller Foundation	Ecosystems
The Gordon and Betty Moore Foundation	Innovation

Fundraising

Even though numerous individuals, charitable foundations, and corporations donate billions of dollars to NGOs annually, these amounts are not enough for tens of millions of NGOs all around the world to share. It's up to each NGO's ability to raise money through fundraising when it comes to securing funds for stable operation. Public relations practitioners or nonprofit fundraising experts take charge of fundraising. They have specialized skills of fundraising and in-depth knowledge of the NGO funding process, aiming to bring more money into the NGO they represent. First of all, they investigate their

16 "The Top Ten US Charitable Foundation," Funds for NGOs, n.d., http://www.fundsforngos.org/foundation-funds-for-ngos/worlds-top-ten-wealthiest-charitable-foundations/.

17 Funds for NGOs, "The Top Ten."

target audience: donors. Donorbox.org, a fundraising expert website, points out that the way donors give their money away changes as time goes by. The major donor fundraising trend for 2019–2020 can be categorized into five characteristics:[18]

1. *Mind the Gen Z.* They're sometimes also called "iGen," a term that denotes the digital and cloud natives that make up this generation. Gen Z makes up a quarter of the US population and will account for 40 percent of all consumers.

2. *Email Is Not Dead.* Emails aren't as distracting as social media and are easier to control. Email will be the way to reach those young people who are taking a break from social media. In addition to that, emails are cost-effective and easy.

3. *The Growth of Corporate Giving.* Corporations and their philanthropic arms want to invest more in socially and environmentally responsible initiatives. This has largely been driven by the rise of conscious consumerism but also conscious employees.

4. *It's All About Communities.* In the nonprofit world, there's been a lot of focus on community-led and community-driven development. These approaches involve a community working together on a shared vision to govern and learn from local action to achieve social change objectives.

5. *Artificial Intelligence Is Rising.* Artificial intelligence can help nonprofits gather more data and use it better to advance their missions and solve societal problems. For example, a nonprofit that helps youth at risk of self-harm and suicide can use AI (as well as psychology and machine learning) to label content on social media to see which young people are at risk.

With public relations practitioners or NGO fundraising experts knowing the characteristics of donors, NGOs can plan several fundraising programs and implement them.

Fundraising Tools

The three major players in donations for NGOs are individuals, charitable foundations, and corporations. People might think that corporations are the largest donors for NGOs (by cash amount), followed by foundations and individuals. Surprisingly, the largest amount of money donated to NGOs has come out of individual pockets. The National Philanthropic Trust revealed in 2018 that the largest source of charitable giving came from individuals at $286.65 billion, or 70 percent of total giving, followed by foundations ($66.90 billion/16 percent), bequests ($35.70 billion/9 percent), and corporations ($20.77 billion/5 percent).[19] NGOs and their public relations practitioners develop fundraising tools, such as direct mail, special events, telephone solicitations and online links to raise money from the target donors.

- *Direct Mail.* This fundraising tool requires an initial investment of time and money. The traditional direct-mail format includes an envelope, brochure, solicitation letter, and postage-paid return envelope. Now that many potential donors have become less impressed with direct-mail appeals, NGOs should not send a letter every month. Most NGOs use year-end direct-mail appeals during the holidays, and direct mail by itself has an average

18   Ilma Ibrisevic, "8 Fundraising Trends Your Nonprofit Needs to Know for 2019," Donorbox, January 1, 2019, https://donorbox.org/nonprofit-blog/fundraising-trends-2019/.

19   "Charitable Giving Statistics," National Philanthropic Trust, n.d., https://www.nptrust.org/philanthropic-resources/charitable-giving-statistics/.

response rate of 2 percent on a prospect list.[20] It is important to send thank-you letters and holiday postcards after donations are received.

- **Special Events.** Fundraising events should be fun and rewarding. Such events contain particular activities that attract the attention of potential donors living in the region. Common NGO events are dinners, fashion shows, dancing parties, and sporting tournaments. Every NGO event typically involves a lot of volunteer effort and staff work. They need to plan and implement the event in a thorough manner. Although the event is difficult to prepare, it functions as a great way to build community relations with donors who feel included in charity work. In addition, it makes the NGO more visible in the region.

- **Telephone Solicitations.** Effective telephone fundraising occurs when a well-written script includes "introductory comments, bullet points on why the support is needed, where the money will go, and information on the urgency of the gift."[21] Since potential donors do not like to receive telephone calls asking for money out of the blue, NGO callers have to build quick rapport with the people they contact. As telephone is a two-way communication medium, only reading the script without listening is directly linked to failure.

- **Online Links.** An increasing number of potential donors can be reached online. NGOs understand the changing landscape of communication and strategize how they can use online tools to raise funds. Creating an NGO website is a profound way of raising funds from all around the world, as almost every potential donor these days looks at the website before donating money. Most NGO websites display a "Donate" button on their homepages to encourage donors to click on it. If a potential donor clicks the icon, it takes the donor to a new page that asks how much the donor wants to give with payment method options. It's simple and convenient for the donor to make a contribution to the cause. As a result, the online fundraising tool is effective and efficient for NGOs to raise funds. NGOs do not limit their online fundraising tools to websites. They create social media platforms to facilitate modern online fundraising tools. Many NGOs operate Facebook, Twitter, YouTube and Instagram platforms to connect with potential donors from all around the world. NGOs post videos, pictures, or fact sheets that support their causes so potential donors can be convinced to give. NGO websites and social media platforms, while offering the "donate" button, serve as a vehicle for highlighting news stories, developments, and information about NGO activities.

Volunteers

After NGOs have succeeded in securing a certain amount of donations, alleviating their fears of financial insecurity, another operational challenge is waiting for them: getting volunteers. Whereas donors give their money, volunteers offer their time and labor to NGOs. Many NGOs seek volunteer help to fulfill their goals, welcoming any people who can donate skilled or unskilled labor. Some NGOs try to recruit volunteers with expert skills such as computer, accounting and marketing knowledge, but most NGOs

---

20   "10 Tips for Successful Phone Solicitations," Richard Male and Associates, n.d., http://richardmale.com/10-tips-for-successful-phone-solicitations/.

21   Robert Male and Associates, "10 Tips for Successful."

invite volunteers who are willing to do any work, such as sending letters, cleaning offices, and working at the reception desk. In other words, volunteers provide vital support for both the frontline work and the back-office tasks of many NGOs, and in some smaller organizations, "the volunteers are the staff."[22]

Volunteers, directly or indirectly, represent the NGO. They need to be trained and educated about the NGO. In many NGOs, public relations practitioners are in charge of educating volunteers about the basics of NGO work and functions, including the training of how to communicate with people inside and outside the NGO. After these basic training sessions, volun-

FIGURE 15.4 Online Donation Site.

teers can be assigned to specialized NGO tasks such as fundraising, event planning and office management.

Public relations practitioners focus on keeping volunteers engaged in the NGO work by offering support and growth opportunities. The volunteers should always be assigned something to work on and should feel that they are doing it for a good cause.[23] The practitioners acknowledge that volunteers tend to quit quickly unless they are motivated by their NGO work. For the volunteers to stay motivated, the practitioners offer constant "feedback, positive reinforcement, and recognition of their work," making them feel appreciated and part of the NGO.[24] Volunteers play an important role in saving operational costs.

Other Organizations with NGO Characteristics

There are two types of organizations that can be characterized as NGOs, even though the public might not view them as NGOs. These are not-for-profit hospitals and not-for-profit educational organizations. These hospitals and educational organizations, like NGOs, look for donations to operate their facilities. They engage in the practice of public relations to garner public support.

Hospitals

There are 6,146 hospitals in the United States in 2020, according to the American Hospital Association.[25] Of these, 2,937 hospitals are not-for-profit, and 965 are owned by state or local governments. Although hospitals make money through what is called fee-for-service billing of insurance companies and government medical programs, most not-for-profit hospitals make an effort to raise donations and receive

22   "How to Train Your Non-profit's Volunteers Fundraising Authority Team," The Fundraising Authority, n.d., http://www.thefundraisingauthority.com/volunteers/train-your-volunteers/.

23   The Fundraising Authority, "How to Train."

24   The Fundraising Authority, "How to Train."

25   Health Forum LLC, "Fast Facts on U.S. Hospitals, 2020," American Hospital Association, January 2020, https://www.aha.org/system/files/media/file/2020/01/2020-aha-hospital-fast-facts-new-Jan-2020.pdf .

grants in order to provide better medical services. Public relations practitioners try to build a hospital's reputation to attract more donors.

All hospitals have a communications department to communicate with the media and the public. As hospitals deal with life-or-death situations every second, there are newsworthy stories to be shared. The public relations practitioner communicates such stories both inside and outside the hospital; this task includes the responsibility of writing internal publications, handling media requests, and creating various materials that attract more donations for the hospital. The practitioner also issues press releases, organizes media briefings, arranges interviews, and launches special events, all aimed at raising funds. In essence, the practitioner focuses on providing information to the public and building relationships with the media and government agencies.[26] The number of donations an organization receives are often correlated to the touching stories hospitals produce. Every news outlet runs health/medical stories on a daily basis, and hospitals have new and miraculous stories to offer to journalists.

The practitioner ensures that journalists are given stories that show the hospital's excellent treatment capacities and doctors' life-saving skills on the local or national level. For example, after a team of doctors at Texas Children's Hospital (Figure 15.5) successfully separated ten-month-old conjoined twins during a 26-hour surgery in 2015, major national media, including CBS, NBC, ABC, *USA Today,* and the *New York Times* reported the story. The doctors who undertook the long, difficult surgery were interviewed by the media outlets, and the name of Texas Children's Hospital and its faculty were depicted in a favorable light to news consumers. The media highlighted nervous and pleasant moments of the twins' parents before and after surgery, as well as the greatness of the doctors. The media published what the twins' mother said: "We know how much planning and time went into this surgery and we are so blessed to be at a place like Texas Children's where we have access to the surgeons and caretakers that have made this dream a reality."[27]

Hospitals in general produce "amazing human stories," which lead to the media's favorite type of coverage. It motivates potential donors to give their money to hospitals. The practitioner serves as the facilitator, transmitting hospitals' stories to the media and to donors, while managing fundraising activities, such as maintaining the donation webpage, mailing reminder letters to previous donors, and organizing special events.

Educational Organizations

Whereas hospitals focus on sharing human stories of miracles, educational organizations, especially universities, shed light on the importance of higher education for students' futures. Every university operates an office that handles public and media relations. For example, Yale University has its Office of Public Affairs and Communications that serves as a public relations source for local, national, and international media. The office also manages the university's official social media channels.[28]

Universities employ public relations practitioners who aim to promote university brand and reputation. They issue press releases, disseminate information about university affairs to students and faculty, respond to media inquiries, and organize campus events. Their activities for universities are no different than what other public relations practitioners do in different industries. However, there is one special task for public relations practitioners in the academic community: building strong alumni relations.

26   Lisa McQuerrey, "Job Description for a Public Relations Officer in Health Care," Chron, July 20, 2018, http://work.chron.com/job-description-public-relations-officer-health-care-27000.html.

27   CBS News, "Conjured Texas Twins Separated in 26-Hour Operation," CBS News.com, February 23, 2015, http://www.cbsnews.com/news/conjoined-texas-twins-separated-in-26-hour-operation/.

28   "For the Yale Community," Yale University, n.d., http://communications.yale.edu/faculty-staff.

As state and federal funding declined after the financial crisis of 2008, alumni donations are needed more than ever for universities. Alumni fundraising is considered crucial for university revenues, and public relations practitioners are assigned to build alumni loyalty, relating it to increasing funding; alumni are an institution's most loyal supporters and fundraising prospects.[29] Alumni are the group of people who are most likely to donate their money to the university because they have a sense of gratitude and want their university to succeed.[30]

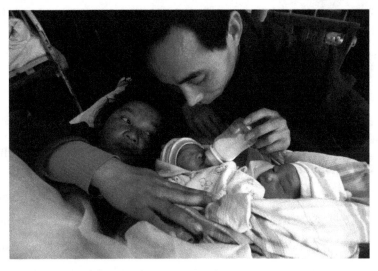

FIGURE 15.5 Conjoined Texas Twins in Media Coverage.

To manage strong alumni relations, public relations practitioners make alumni feel included in university affairs through university communication channels. Practitioners can also invite alumni to art and sport events on campus by sending them free tickets. More importantly, the practitioners strategize to spark alumni's old, beautiful memories of their college days. For example, in Stanford University's effort to appeal to the nostalgia of its alumni, the university's fundraising website noted:[31]

> What did you get from your time at Stanford? A mentor? A new way of looking at the world? A partner? The chance to study overseas? A best friend? A chance to help others? A job? It's very likely that The Stanford Fund supported many of the experiences that mattered most to you. And even if you graduated just a few years ago, it's not too soon to think about giving back.

The practitioners attempt to increase the alumni participation rate and raise more dollars than the previous year. The pressure gets greater as universities face the tougher challenge of finding new ways to pull in potential givers. According to the *Wall Street Journal*, colleges and universities received a record $37.5 billion in donations in 2014, and of that amount, alumni giving accounted for $9.85 billion, an increase of 9.4 percent.[32] The newspaper explained the reason for the increasing number of alumni donations: "As schools get better at tracking down alums due to the growth of social networks such as Facebook and LinkedIn, they're able to tap those graduates for targeted gifts to support student scholarships and new buildings, among other things."[33] In 2019, *Fortune* magazine reported that three universities brought in

29   "Engaging Alumni to Increase Charitable Donations to their University," University of Oregon Applied Information Management Program, https://scholarsbank.uoregon.edu/xmlui/bitstream/handle/1794/19635/Whitinger2015.pdf

30   "Engaging Alumni to Increase Charitable Donations to their University," University of Oregon .

31   "Young Alumni and the Stanford Fund," Stanford University, n.d., giving.stanford.edu/the-stanford-fund/programs/young-alumni.

32   Melissa Korn, "Harvard, Stanford Lead Record Year for College Gifts," *The Wall Street Journal*, January 28, 2015, http://www.wsj.com/articles/harvard-stanford-lead-record-year-for-college-gifts-1422421261.

33   Korn, "Harvard, Stanford."

more than $1 billion each from donors in the fiscal year of 2018 : Harvard University $1.4 billion, Stanford University $1.1 billion, and Columbia University $1 billion.[34]

NGOs in Social Media Practice

It is an irresistible trend for NGOs, hospitals, and universities to use online communication to stimulate the public's interest and promote their causes. Many social media experts classify the revolutionary use of online communication for NGOs into three steps:

- *Web 1.0.* The computer web on which NGOs create their websites
- *Web 2.0.* The social web on which NGOs use social media
- *Web 3.0.* The application web on which NGOs build smartphone apps

It has been the universal public relations practice for every NGO to manage its website and several social media platforms. Social media for NGOs offers them an opportunity for conversation with their current and potential supporters while allowing NGOs to publish messages, stories, and other public relations material about their real-world actions at low cost. In addition, NGO websites and social media platforms feature the "donate" button, which is considered effective in soliciting financial support from individuals.

NGOs should try to keep up with the trend of communication evolution to survive. Today's online communication for NGO public relations revolves around the Internet world, and the younger generation, like Gen Z, has migrated to the smartphone community. Although NGO websites and social media sites are still accessible on smartphones, they need to develop more smartphone-friendly apps.

---

34   Natasha Bach, "U.S. Colleges Raised a Record $47 Billion Last Year," *Fortune*, February 11, 2019, http://fortune.com/2019/02/11/college-university-fundraising-record-2018/.

CHAPTER SUMMARY AND REVIEW

1. Understand characteristics of NGOs.

2. Identify why NGOs use the practice of public relations.

3. Study the difference between hospitals and universities in regard to donations.

4. Explain how corporations team up with NGOs and why.

5. Describe major players that make NGOs more visible to the public.

PUBLIC RELATIONS IN PRACTICE

FURTHER READING

PR Week's Awards For **Best PR Nonprofit**

Winner: The Ad Council, the Brady Center to Prevent Gun Violence, Droga5, and Sunshine Sachs
Campaign Name: End Family Fire

The Brady Campaign and Center to Prevent Gun Violence, an advocate for gun control and against gun violence, set out to shift the perception that having a gun in the home makes us safer by creating the phrase "family fire" to describe the danger of an unintentional shooting with an unsecured or misused gun in the home.

To seed the term and educate the public about what it means and how to prevent it, the organization launched a mass market campaign, grounded in research with the target audience, as well as expert input. The campaign included a national public service announcement element and robust comms plan, including press and influencer outreach.

Read more at
https://www.prweek.com/article/1579436/prweek-us-awards-2019-winners

16

The Internet and Social Media

I t took the radio 38 years to acquire 50 million listeners and the television 13 years to have the same number of owners.[1] Television served as the most popular medium to entertain the public and influence target audiences until the late 1990s, when a new medium of communication was introduced to the public—the Internet. Only four years were needed for the Internet to reach 50 million users as the latest revolution of communication technology. The Internet has changed the way people around the globe communicate by creating a new culture of communication—online communication. The new communication culture accelerated by the Internet stimulates people to express opinions, exchange information, give feedback, and share knowledge without the limitations of time and distance. The online community never sleeps and is always active in creating and sharing new information. The Internet has brought freedom of access to information all around the world, except for several countries where use of the Internet is restricted and monitored by authorities.

Throughout history, communication technology has evolved with many revolutionary inventions and discoveries. Writings on stone as a means of communication were replaced by the invention of the printing press, which enabled people to circulate information and knowledge to other places. Books and newspapers became the main communication devices in the seventeenth and eighteenth centuries. The 1900s witnessed an incredible revolution of communication technology, beginning with electronic waves and signals that introduced the era of radio and television. Radio and television opened the door to mass communication, in which an individual or organization is empowered to disseminate information and messages to a large group of people or the public. Mass communication embraces the use of traditional media, such as television, radio, newspapers, and magazines. The disseminator of information and messages through traditional media is regarded as a strategic communicator representing an organization or individual. Information and messages in mass communication reach out to the public through the forms of news and campaigns.

---

1   Maya Kamath, "To Reach 50 Million Users Telephone Took 75 Years Internet Took 4 Years However Angry Birds Took only 35 Days!!," TechWorm, March 13, 2015, http://www.techworm.net/2015/03/to-reach-50-million-users-telephone-took-75-years-internet-took-4-years-angry-birds-took-only-35-days.html.

Strategic communicators still see the traditional media as an inevitable tool to communicate with the public and target audience, but they admit that social media has outpowered all traditional communication tools in terms of planning and implementing communication strategies in the digital age. Social media empowered by the Internet technology has evolved into the most dominant communication tool both for organizations and individuals.

History of the Internet

Concerned about what might happen to the United States after the 1957 launch of the Sputnik satellite by the Soviet Union, American scientists and military experts collaborated to invent efficient long-distance communication tools without wires and lines. They created the Advanced Research Projects Agency Network (ARPANET), which delivered its first message from one computer to another in 1969.[2] More computers were connected from California to Hawaii to London to Norway through ARPANET in 1973. The term *Internet* was born, and Queen Elizabeth II hit the "send" button for her first email in 1976. As more researchers and scientists used it to send files and data from one computer to another in the 1980s, the domain name system established the ".com" era, including .edu, .gov, and .org.

In 1989, "The World" (world.std.com) became the first company to provide Internet access (through dial-up) to the public. In 1991, a computer programmer in Switzerland whose name was Tim Berners-Lee introduced the World Wide Web, "an Internet that was not simply a way to send files from one place to another but was itself a web of information that anyone on the Internet could retrieve."[3] At the same time, the White House, United Nations, and universities went online by creating websites, followed by commercial sectors, such as banks, motor companies, energy corporations, and media companies after Congress approved legislation that allowed private organizations to use the World Wide Web for commercial purposes.

Nearly every organization has a website that contains information about what the organization does, what it offers or produces, what events it plans, who the employees are, and how online visitors can communicate with the organization. Online content is visually developed with graphics, videos, and photos in a colorful format to inform and impress visitors. Organizations spend more money on visually attractive websites after they learned that the average visitor spends about 10–20 seconds on a webpage before they decide whether to leave or stay.[4]

---

2   History.com Editors, "The Invention of the Internet," History.com, last modified October 28, 2019, http://www.history.com/topics/inventions/invention-of-the-internet.

3   History.com Editors, "The Invention."

4   Nielsen Norman Group, "How Long Do Users Stay on Web Pages?" Jakob Nielsen on September 11, 2011, https://www.nngroup.com/articles/how-long-do-users-stay-on-web-pages/

Creating a website for an organization is considered the first generation of the Internet, better known as Web 1.0. The major characteristics of Web 1.0 are summarized as publishing general information about the organization, advertising the organization's products or services, and promoting the organization's goals. There was little room for online visitors to interact with the organization since Web 1.0 focused on developing a static information portal in the late 1990s. Web 1.0 offers organizations the opportunity to open a new communication channel that they can own and manage themselves.

Whereas Web 1.0 uses the Internet as a simple online platform to offer information to online users, Web 2.0 facilitates online interaction between users and websites, allowing users to offer feedback and post comments. The interaction has been accelerated, growing exponentially since the rise of social media made a historical shift from producing information to sharing information via feedback. Web 2.0 is synonymous with participative web and read-write web, where users could influence web content; social media platforms provide such web-based forums of online communication. Web 2.0 enables online users to contribute skills, edit written content, generate visual content, and network with each other through four types of social media platforms (Table 16.1).

In today's online world, Web 3.0 has been popularized at a fast pace. Although there is no absolute definition or clear concept of Web 3.0, it can be understood as a new phase of the Internet that replaces social media with a personalized online connection for "more effective discovery, automation, integration, and reuse across various applications" in the world.[5] In Web 3.0, computers, tablet PCs, and smartphones can interpret individual use of online data by users, websites, and applications (apps).

Web 3.0 is able to adjust to meet the needs of users, based on their online activities. For example, if a user visits a news website and reads articles or watches videos about the Dow Jones Industrial Average and the Nasdaq Composite Index, the user will receive more advertisements related to financial investment,

TABLE 16.1   Examples of Web 2.0 Platforms

WIKIS	Collaborative websites that allow users to edit, delete, or modify content. Online users are encouraged to contribute and collaborate in order to update more information for any visitors. Wikipedia is the most popular wiki-based site.
USER-GENERATED CONTENT (UGC)	The words, videos, and photos that unpaid contributors create and provide to publications, particularly web properties.[1] UGC is created by individuals outside of organizations to express their personal feelings or thoughts with online content that is open to the public. Blogs are a good example of UGC.
SOCIAL CURATION	Collaborative sharing of web content organized around one or more particular theme or topic.[2] Pinterest and Instagram have been popularized by photos that demonstrate users' expertise in particular topics.
SOCIAL NETWORKING	The use of Internet-based social media sites to build relationships with friends, coworkers, consumers, and clients. Social networking is used by individuals or businesses to expand new personal or business contacts. They communicate with each other by posting information, linking to other websites, and exchanging short messages. Depending on their interests, livelihoods, or purpose, users make an effort to find and connect to other people through social networking sites such as Facebook, LinkedIn, Google+, Instagram, and Twitter. These sites are used to create and maintain relationships in the online world.

[1]Tech Target, http://searchcio.techtarget.com/definition/user-generated-content-UGC.
[2]WhatIs.com, http://whatis.techtarget.com/definition/social-curation.

---

5. Tim Berners-Lee and Eric Miller, "The Semantic Web Lifts Off," *Ercim News*, no. 51, para. 5 (October 2002). http://www.ercim.eu/publication/Ercim_News/enw51/berners-lee.html.

as well as information about stock markets. In other words, Web 3.0 analyzes the pattern of the user's Internet routine and delivers information the user is about to seek. The information is customized for the specific individual by the technology of Web 3.0.

The inventor of the World Wide Web, Berners-Lee, refers to Web 3.0 as the "semantic web," in which users' needs are automatically served because of the intelligent and intuitive analysis of online data stored in computers, smartphones, and tablet PCs (CST). The semantic web teaches CST what the data means to users and when to deliver customized information to users. Hence, Web 3.0 is all about personalization to incorporate real-time data into the real lives of users. If computers were the main Internet device for Web 1.0, then computers and tablet PCs, such as the iPad, were mainly used for Web 2.0. With Web 3.0, smartphones with bigger screens make computers and tablet PCs less popular in terms of maintaining online communication. Users interact with apps on their smartphones to find out how to solve problems, where to shop, and where to go for entertainment. Based on long-stored, analyzed personal data, smartphones respond to users with customized information. Web 3.0 is an ongoing process, whereas Web 4.0 is about to introduce a new era of communication technology. Web 4.0, the active web, will integrate all functions of robotics, artificial intelligence, and machine learning into "the Internet of Things" that will build "a smart planet where everyone and everything is connected and communicating non-stop."[6] Although the concept and dimensions of Web 4.0 are still in development, the combined agents of artificial intelligence, virtual reality, machine learning, and big data are bound to spearhead human-machine connectivity.

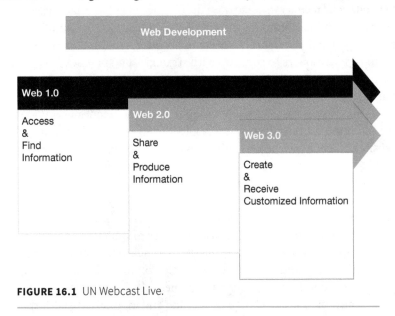

FIGURE 16.1 UN Webcast Live.

Public Relations and the Internet

The Internet has revolutionized the way people communicate and build relationships with each other. Organizations are busy taking advantage of the Internet as a dominant communication tool. They create websites and social media platforms to inform audiences and promote their products or services.

---

6   Chris M. Skinner, "Web 4.0, the 2020s and the Internet of Things," The Finanser, February 17, 2017, https://the-finanser.com/2017/02/web-4-0-2020s-internet-things.html/.

In essence, online communication has become an inevitable method for organizations to interact with their audiences. Organizations can update information, and audiences can offer feedback to the organizations without time or space limits.

Online communication is fast and cheap. The Internet offers organizations the tools to disseminate messages without fees for printing, transportation, or delivery. Audiences benefit from the Internet, which allows them to find the information they need. As more and more audiences are armed with in-depth knowledge of products and services due to the Internet, they become wiser and smarter about accepting information or messages from organizations. For example, when a consumer plans to buy a new car, research on the web is naturally considered the consumer's first step before walking into a dealership. The consumer compares cars, prices and even reputations of dealerships online to find the best deal. In response, car dealerships use their websites and social media platforms to upload videos and photos of cars with detailed specifications, including prices. In general, the Internet is convenient and cost-effective for both audiences and organizations to exchange information.

Public relations swiftly reacts to the digital age, connecting organizations with a large audience. From a public relations perspective, online audiences for organizations are divided into journalists, the target audience, and the public, all of whom visit the websites or social media platforms of organizations. In particular, organizations use the Internet for different purposes: corporations use it for business; government agencies use it for public service; nonprofit organizations use it for educational or social purposes.

As the Internet and social media evolve, so does the practice of public relations. Public relations in the online world incorporates online communication skills and techniques to fulfill the needs of organizations and audiences. Now that the Internet has become a powerful tool of communication, organizations expect public relations practitioners to come up with strategies and practices to maximize the benefits of new communication technologies. No practitioner can imagine that today's public relations could survive without using the Internet.

Traditionally, the most important audience for public relations practitioners is journalists. The practitioner in the age of online communication is responsible for maintaining and developing his or her organization's website content to provide organizational information to journalists. Because journalists are usually assigned to work on numerous stories at one time, they find easy access to online information convenient. According to a survey conducted by Arketi Group, 81 percent of business journalists visit corporate websites and watch webinars "when looking for story ideas, breaking news, or seeking a corporate spokesperson."[7] The survey found that the journalists looked for contact information, search capabilities, text documents, PDFs, and publication-quality graphics or photos on the websites they visit. To capture the interest of journalists, the practitioner incorporates newsworthy information and documents into an online newsroom or media room section on the website as part of a communication strategy. The online newsroom should include a list of media items, as noted in Table 16.2.

Public relations practitioners are in charge of creating and maintaining both the online newsroom and the entire website for their organizations' online content. Organizations do not expect the practitioners to have skills like web designers or webmasters who create or systemize fancy visualization for websites, but the practitioners are required to work with web designers to develop better looking and functional websites in regard to visualization and content richness. Corporations, among all types of organizations, make the heaviest investments in improving their websites.

7   "81 percent of journalists use corporate websites, survey finds," Ragan, https://www.ragan.com/81-percent-of-journalists-use-corporate-websites-survey-finds/

TABLE 16.2   Media Elements of an Online Newsroom

PRESS RELEASES	The practitioner posts and updates press releases frequently in reverse chronological order, as journalists seek the most recent information about the organization. Press releases older than a year should be archived on an individual basis. Press kits can also be posted if necessary.
MEDIA CONTACT	When journalists can't find information they seek in the newsroom, they want to get in touch with the organization's public relations practitioner or media specialists. The name, job title, email address, and phone number of the practitioner must be included in the newsroom. If a journalist contacts the practitioner, interviews or meetings can be arranged.
MULTIMEDIA GALLERY	Journalists can look for photos, graphics, or video clips that portray the characteristics of the organization. Such material should be downloadable and usable for journalists. The practitioner should pick good-quality visual images and post them right after they are produced.
RESEARCH AND STATISTICS	The online newsroom should be trusted and include scientific and compelling evidence that promotes the organization's products or services. Journalists love to use statistics and research results to make their reporting credible. The practitioner needs to include not only the organization's research findings but also any relevant statistics in the industry.
SEARCH FUNCTION	Providing a search function in the newsroom helps journalists to find content more quickly and easily. They can locate information about the organization by typing words, finding direct information produced by the organization. Google or Bing can be added to the organization's website as well.
SOCIAL MEDIA INTEGRATION	The newsroom needs to include links to the organization's social media sites. Links to the organization's blog sites, Facebook, YouTube, Instagram, and Twitter should be featured in the newsroom.

Corporate Websites

The website for a corporation serves as an online hub for consolidated corporate information to be provided to consumers and the public. The corporate website is designed to attract people and sell products or services while building a relationship with the target audience. The practitioner and web designer focus on making the website easy to find and navigate. It should allow visitors to find the information they are looking for with no obstruction. Important messages and information are displayed on multiple pages so the website grabs their attention, which can lead them to take action. A survey by Gartner Research found that business people rank the corporate website as the most important tool for a successful marketing campaign, defeating "both social media marketing and online advertising."[8] According to Bill Gassman, Gartner Research's director, the survey demonstrates that corporations "continuously invest in testing and optimizing their websites, paying attention to all aspects—from customized landing pages to compelling content that encourages visitors to be engaged" with corporate services and products.[9]

---

8   Helen Leggatt, "Gartner Survey Reveals Corporate Websites Rank Most Important for Marketing Success," *Biz Report*, March 18, 2013, http://www.bizreport.com/2013/03/gartner-survey-reveals-corporate-websites-rank-most-importan.html.

9   Leggatt, "Gartner Survey."

Five Reasons Why Corporations Maintain and Develop Their Websites

1. *Credibility.* Today's consumers, before making a final choice to purchase something, often try to find information about the corporation online first. If consumers can't find it online, they are unlikely to trust the corporation and are more likely to be skeptical about the products or services from the corporation. Consumers believe virtually all corporations have websites, and they like to visit them to get more information.

2. *Brand.* Websites give unlimited freedom to corporations, like the ability to control content and design. On corporate websites, information about products, services, events, CSR, and consumers' satisfied reviews can be displayed 24/7. Good images of corporations, thoroughly organized on websites, encourage consumers to have positive attitudes toward corporate brands.

3. *Engagement.* Consumers are more engaged with corporations when they can share their thoughts and opinions on corporate websites. They express their satisfaction, frustration, or recommendation about particular products or services they use, expecting employees of corporations to respond to their online expressions. An exchange of online messages or comments between consumers and corporations enhances consumer engagement.

4. *Advertising.* Websites are the centerpiece of corporate online presence, providing information about products or services with low advertising costs or no cost at all. Once a corporate website is established, driving as many visitors as possible to the website is a top priority of the corporation.

5. *Accessibility.* Websites allow consumers to find information about corporations any time at their convenience. Consumers can find corporate websites accessible 24 hours a day from anywhere around the globe. Websites are a great source of easy-to-access information with no problems of time and distance.

A corporate website lays the foundation for the online existence of the corporation, the first public relations step to communicating with consumers in the online world. It is clear that the Internet and corporate websites have added more tasks to the practice of public relations and have changed the way public relations is evolving.

More Tools for Online Public Relations

A website is an important tool for the practice of online public relations, but there are more tools to galvanize the effectiveness of public relations in the online world. Webcasts, podcasts, blogs, social media platforms, and smartphone apps are widely used by public relations practitioners to promote organizational interests online.

Webcasts

Webcasting is Internet broadcasting. By using the Internet to broadcast live or recorded programs, webcasting includes the content of visual images shown on websites. Press conferences, interviews with corporate CEOs, speeches, and online meetings are popular subjects for webcasts. Such content is recorded and edited, if necessary, by organizations before being broadcast on websites. Some are broadcast live. All webcasting programs are particularly aimed at providing information to online audiences.

Public relations practitioners, collaborating with camera and video editing professionals, are involved in the whole process of making webcasts. Several webcasting programs are known well and viewed by many online users.

- ***The United Nations Web TV (http://webtv.un.org/).*** The largest international organization broadcasts its web video programs, which are available 24 hours a day. Selected UN meetings or events are broadcast live on the web, and prerecorded video clips and documentaries are posted, showing how people in the world discuss and act to address global issues, including poverty, war, natural disasters, and human rights.

- ***Johnson & Johnson Webcast (http://www.investor.jnj.com/).*** Video and audio clips are posted on the website. Meetings with investors, scientists, shareholders, and people in the pharmaceutical industry are recorded and broadcast online. Many of the programs are published as audio clips.

- ***Georgetown University (https://www.georgetown.edu/news/webcasts.html).*** Live and recorded webcast programs are offered on the website. The university streams campus events, lectures, and speeches by famous figures on the website, such as Bill Clinton, Tony Blair, Barak Obama, and United Nations Secretary-General António Guterres.

Podcasts

A podcast is a digital audio file that is distributed on the Internet. Podcasts are downloadable to a computer, smartphone, or portable media player. Because most podcasts are audio files, they are regarded as portable radio programs to which people can listen anywhere and anytime. Podcasting allows audience members to select their own content, as opposed to television and radio programs, which the audience needs to tune in to. Podcasting is considered an alternative to commercial radio; thousands of podcasts are tailored to entertain a particular group or audience who has "specific niche interests."[10] A podcast is produced through three steps: (1) an audio file is saved as an MP3; (2) it is uploaded to the creator's website; (3) audiences visit and download the file. Anybody can be a podcast creator, but market and industry experts earn more credibility as podcasters by providing insight about specific topics. Some corporations also have podcast websites. For example, IBM (https://www.ibmbigdatahub.com/podcasts) provides downloadable audio podcast files on the corporation's website that discuss how mobile devices and software change industries and human lives. The following are three podcasting sites, most popular in 2019, according to *Digital Trends* magazine.[11]

- ***The Daily (https://www.nytimes.com/spotlight/podcasts).*** The *New York Times'* podcast provides all the news that's fit to listen to in a tidy format.

- ***Comedy Bang! Bang! (https://www.earwolf.com/show/comedy-bang-bang/).*** Hosted by man-of-many-nicknames Scott Aukerman, Comedy Bang! Bang! is the pinnacle of comedy podcasts.

---

10   Daniel Nations, "What Is a Podcast?," About Tech, last modified February 13, 2020, http://podcasting.about.com/od/basics101/a/whatis.htm.

11   Digital Trends Staff, "The Best Podcasts of 2020," *Digital Trends*, March 16, 2020, https://www.digitaltrends.com/mobile/best-podcasts/.

- ***This Week in Tech (https://twit.tv/shows/this-week-in-tech).*** Hosted by tech enthusiasts Leo Laporte and Patrick Norton, this is one of the premier tech podcasts discussing trending tech.

Blogs

A blog is a frequently updated online diary by an individual. It offers an online space to tell the world what the individual thinks and promotes. Personal thoughts and interests are expressed by a blog, so a blog is a website for an online user. However, it does not mean that blogs are limited to the use of individuals. Blogs are embraced by organizations, media outlets and interest groups as well. Multiple studies have discovered who uses blogs and why they blog; findings have been summarized in the following bulleted points: [12]

- Most bloggers are younger than 30 years old.

- Teenagers are much more likely than adults to have blogs and read other people's blogs.

- The majority of bloggers come from four countries: the United Kingdom, Germany, Japan, and the United States.

- Bloggers are more racially diverse than the general online population.

- Blogs are a more trusted source of information than advertising or email marketing.

- Bloggers receive great credibility, power, and influence as sources of information for everything from news to corporate reputations to product purchasing.

Since 1994, when the very first blog (Links.net) was born, there may have been more than 200 million blog posts, which are created throughout the world every second. Although it is hard to pinpoint why each individual wants to blog, some common reasons are (1) blogging lets an individual express what he or she thinks about certain issues; (2) blogging helps the individual connect with people who think alike; (3) blogging helps an individual maintain psychological stability by venting anger or boasting happiness; (4) blogging is used to promote the individual in the field of his or her expertise or interest; (5) blogging can offer comfort or sympathy to people who go through the same pain the individual experiences; (6) blogging motivates the individual to keep studying and posting new content on his or her field.

Public relations practitioners use blogs to achieve the goals of their organizations. From a public relations perspective, the practitioners acknowledge the effectiveness of blogs as follows:[13]

1. Businesses that update their blogs 20 times a month (i.e., four to five times per week) generate five times more traffic than those that update their blogs fewer than four times a month.

2. Businesses that own and regularly update their blogs generate four times more leads than those that do not own a blog.

3. Blogs help to influence consumers' buying decisions and purchases.

---

12 "WHO BLOGS?," *Advertising Age*, http://adage.com/article/digital/blogs/116998/ & AdAge.com Blog PDF, http://adage.com/images/random/0507/blogs.pdf.

13 WP Virtuoso, "How Many Blogs Are on the Internet," WordPress Directory, November 20, 2013, http://www.wpvirtuoso.com/how-many-blogs-are-on-the-internet/.

Because of the importance of blogging in the business world, the practitioners are assigned to manage blogs for their organizations, especially for corporations. Corporations blog because their competitors and consumers are involved. Corporate blogs, similar to corporate websites, seek to humanize corporations and build credibility. Corporate blogs are mostly used to inform consumers of current corporate events and new products or services in the format of visualized stories. More importantly, addressing urgent issues directly relevant to corporate operations is a great advantage of using blogs. For example, Walmart, the world's largest company by revenue, runs its blog, Walmart Today (https://blog.walmart.com). The corporation publishes a wide range of information, including organizational stories about employees, customers, and innovations, which display photos and videos of people and their relevant activities at Walmart stores.

Social Media Platforms

A social media platform refers to an online venue for people to create and maintain communication by posting photos, videos, comments, messages, and opinions to share their interests in the form of a public profile. It enables people to increase online social interactions and build personal relationships. By using social media platforms, such as Facebook, Instagram, YouTube, LinkedIn, Snapchat and Twitter, people can expand their business and social contacts through online connections. Such platforms commonly require users to create an online profile, including biographical data, photos, and any background information. When users post their thoughts or photos, exchange messages, or respond to other users' social media activities, the practice of social networking is conducted. Social networking migrates from personal use to business use. Organizations view social media platforms as promising media channels to reach target audiences to advertise products or services, enhance brand recognition, or gain public support.

An online site called Six Degrees is considered the first social media platform, launched in 1997. Sixdegrees.com was based on the idea of six degrees of separation, which explains that anyone in the world can be connected to any other person through chains of acquaintance, so an individual is just six introductions away from any other person on the planet. In other words, everyone in the world is separated from everyone else by six links online. Researchers confirmed in 2008 that the idea of six degrees of separation stands up in the online world after investigating 30 billion electronic messages among 180 million people in various countries. Microsoft researchers announced that any two strangers are, on average, distanced by precisely 6.6 degrees of separation.[14] Putting fractions to one side, an individual is "linked by a string of seven or fewer acquaintances to Madonna, the Dalai Lama, and the Queen."[15]

The first social media platform did not live long, although it had millions of users, because of the lack of people connected to the Internet. While the Internet's infrastructure was improving to catch up with the demand for online communication, two other social media platforms, Friendster in 2002 and MySpace in 2003, opened a true age of social networking. The latter became extremely popular and was acquired by News Corporation for $580 million in 2005. It was named the number one social media platform in 2006 and was valued at $12 billion.[16] The fame of MySpace was eclipsed by Facebook,

---

14   David Smith, "Proof! Just Six Degrees of Separation Between Us," *The Guardian*, August 2, 2008, http://www.theguardian.com/technology/2008/aug/03/internet.email.

15   Smith, "Proof!"

16   "Then and Now: A History of Social Networking Sites," CBS News, n.d., http://www.cbsnews.com/pictures/then-and-now-a-history-of-social-networking-sites/7/.

FIGURE 16.2 Popular Social Media Sites in 2020.

launched by Mark Zuckerberg in 2004 when it was only available to Harvard University students. Since Facebook rolled out to the public in 2006, it has taken the title of the most popular social network on the web. According to a Pew Research Center survey conducted in 2019, Facebook and YouTube are the clear leaders in the social media usage battle, followed by Instagram, Snapchat, LinkedIn, Twitter, and Pinterest.[17] The survey also found trends in the use of sites:[18]

- Instagram and Snapchat remain especially popular among those ages 18 to 24

- Majority of Facebook, Snapchat and Instagram users visit these sites daily

- Sixty-eight percent of Facebook users are between 50 and 64 years old, and nearly half of those are older than 65

- Roughly seven in ten American adults (69 percent) say they never use Facebook or YouTube (73 percent)

- Pinterest remains substantially more popular with women

- LinkedIn remains especially popular among college graduates and those in high-income households

17   Andrew Perrin and Monica Anderson, "Share of U.S. Adults Using Social Media, including Facebook, Is Mostly Unchanged since 2018," PewReserach, April 10, 2018, https://www.pewresearch.org/fact-tank/2019/04/10/share-of-u-s-adults-using-social-media-including-facebook-is-mostly-unchanged-since-2018/.

18   Maeve Duggan, Nicole B. Ellison, Cliff Lampe, Amanda Lenhart, and Mary Madden, "Social Media Updated 2014," Pew Research Center, January 9, 2015, http://www.pewinternet.org/2015/01/09/social-media-update-2014/.

Visiting a social media platform or multiple platforms is a daily routine for many users. Some of them go to the platforms to update information about their personal lives and to be entertained with information about their friends, in addition to finding specific information relating to their interests. Others use them to seek online word-of-mouth advice or vent about unfortunate experiences with products or services of organizations. An important characteristic of social media from a public relations standpoint is that consumers are using social media to share their personal experiences in evaluating products or services. As consumers tend to rely on recommendations from friends and family over all forms of advertising, word-of-mouth communication is essential for public relations, especially in the social media community, where users are inclined to make informed decisions that lead them to feel empowered and relieved. Social media users, when engaging in conversations beyond personal life, expect a meaningful interaction to learn from each other.

It is easy and quick for consumers to share information about a product or service or an entire organization through social networking, which plays a significant part of today's word-of-mouth communication. Consumers used to have in-person conversations to exchange information about a specific topic, but social media enables them to spread a wide range of word-of-mouth opinions to a large audience. Recognizing the power of social media, any organization that can encourage users to post or mention positive information about a product, service, or the organization itself should make an enormous effort to capitalize on online word-of-mouth communication.

To achieve a positive outcome with this type of communication, public relations practitioners concentrate on reaching out to consumers by giving the social media community something to talk about. For example, Crest, a brand of toothpaste made by Procter & Gamble, unleashed a series of online-only videos, photos, and educational articles to show how yellow teeth can be fixed with its new whitening products. The brand's public relations practitioners exclusively used social media to prompt discussion, acknowledging that consumers stay in social media. Public relations practitioners are using social media in a lot of ways to "either supplement or add on to existing communication strategies."[19] More importantly, they strive to engage with consumers in the social media community, seeking a continuous conversation for ongoing relationships. As a result, more content for public relations, advertising, and marketing campaigns is produced only for social media users.

The ultimate goal of using social media for public relations practitioners and other communication professionals in marketing and advertising, is to make their social media campaigns "go viral." "Going viral" means that online content spreads quickly and widely on the Internet through social media; an image, video, article, or link is shared with a huge number of users who forward or repost it. Popular topics that go viral online are "strong political content, celebrity news, news of disasters, America's funniest home videos, and crude sexual humor."[20] Public relations practitioners using social media as a powerful device for raising public awareness and engagement aim to drive more traffic to their social media platforms, where visitors can view and subscribe to the content of organizations and eventually become followers. The interaction between the practitioners and followers continues. Therefore, creating viral content requires the following commitments:

- *Investment in Time and Resources.* "Going viral" does not just happen. To attract more audiences, the practitioner keeps an eye on current news and trends to develop online content, trying to read online consumers' minds.

---

19   Christina Warren, "How PR Pros Are Using Social Media for Real Results," Mashable.com, March 16, 2020, http://mashable.com/2010/03/16/public-relations-social-media-results/.

20   Cheradenine, "Go Viral," Urban Dictionary, November 12, 2009, http://www.urbandictionary.com/define.php?term=go+viral.

- *Visual Items.* Dry and boring content with no personality kills the interest of the audience. In order for content to go viral, entertaining photos and videos are likely to be shared in a short time period.

- *Events.* An audience likes samples or gifts. Contests or biddings have the power of attracting and engaging them. With a vote or photo contest, audiences take action to interact in social media. Winners should receive prizes.

- *Hashtags.* The mission of keeping conversations together can be secured with a hashtag—a pound sign (#) in front of a relevant key word, phrase, or string of letters. The "hashtagged" key word or phrase generates a series of conversations on the given topic and encourages an audience to spread messages.

- *Participation.* After content is created, monitoring the audience's reaction is a pivotal follow-up activity. When an audience forwards, reposts, or links to content in social media, public relations practitioners are expected to respond to the audience with new content or comments to keep the conversation going and the audience engaged. Being recognized by each other is the lifeblood of online interaction.

- *Connection with Influencers.* A public figure tends to have millions of followers. Building an online relationship with a public figure is hard, but once the public figure shares content with a massive number of followers, the interaction goes viral.

Case Study 16.1   TheBestMenCanBe Social Media Campaign

The men's razor brand Gillette debuted a short social media campaign, " We Believe: The Best Men Can Be," that seeks to redefine masculinity in 2019. The campaign with #TheBestMenCanBe was released in a form of a short video on Twitter (Figure 16.3). The campaign video begins by invoking the company's 30-year-old slogan, "The Best a Man Can Get," and turns it into an introspective reflection on negative aspects of masculinity, including bullying, sexism, and sexual misconduct. The video made direct reference to the #MeToo movement. A voiceover in the video asks, "Is this the best man can get?" The answer is no, and it shows "how men can do better by actively pointing out toxic behavior, intervening when other men catcall or sexually harass and helping protect their children from bullies."[21] The voiceover narrates, "We believe in the best in men: To say the right thing, to act the right way, since the boys watching today will be the men of tomorrow." As a result, the original slogan is reworked to reinforce this message, becoming "The Best Men Can Be."[22]

21   Emily Dreyfuss, "Gillette's Ad Proves the Definition of a Good Man Has Changed," Wired, January 16, 2019, https://www.wired.com/story/gillette-we-believe-ad-men-backlash/.
22   Alexandra Topping, Kate Lyons, and Matthew Weaver, "Gillette #MeToo Razors Ad on 'Toxic Masculinity' Gets Praise—and Abuse," The Guardian, January 15, 2019, https://www.theguardian.com/world/2019/jan/15/gillette-metoo-ad-on-toxic-masculinity-cuts-deep-with-mens-rights-activists.

(Continued)

The campaign was aimed at challenging the stereotypes and expectations of what it means to be a man in the United States in hopes of preventing any toxic masculinity that can influence young boys' future behavior. Gillette also created TheBestMenCanBe.org and promised to donate "$1 million per year for the next three years to nonprofit organizations executing programs in the United States designed to inspire, educate, and help men of all ages achieve their personal best and become role models for the next generation."[23]

The Twitter campaign immediately went viral with more than 2.3 million Twitter mentions and 4 million views on YouTube in 24 hours. In three days, it has had more than 11.5 million views on YouTube and 4.1 million views on Facebook (with 24,000 comments and nearly 150,000 shares) with a 214.9 percent increase in mentions for the brand compared to the previous 24-hour period.[24] The driving forces that made the campaign go viral on social media were the negative and positive responses from consumers and the media. Parents across social media shared the Twitter link and applauded the campaign in their Facebook posts with touching and moving emojis:

However, some men argued that the campaign was anti-male, both generalizing all men in together as "sexists," and demeaning "traditional masculine qualities."[25] Regardless of the campaign's good or bad intentions, it is important to note that Gillette created the successful social media campaign, which went viral, by tapping into a growing consumer consciousness for corporations that take stances on political and social issues. Public relations expert Mark Borkowski evaluated the outcome of the campaign: "It is no longer enough for brands to simply sell a product as customers are demanding that they have a purpose—that they stand for something. Masculinity is a huge part of Gillette's brand, and there is a recognition in this campaign that the new generation is reworking that concept of masculinity, and it is no longer the cliché is once was."[26]

"Boys will be boys"? Isn't it time we stopped excusing bad behavior? Re-think and take action by joining us at TheBestMenCanBe.org. #TheBestMenCanBe

31M views   0:38 / 1:49

FIGURE 16.3   Gillette Campaign Tweet.

23   Gillette. https://gillette.com/en-us/the-best-men-can-be

24   Amy Gesenhues, "Gillette Sparks Emotions, Controversy, Possibly Gold with 'We Believe: The Best a Man Can Be' Video," Marketing Land, January 16, 2019, https://marketingland.com/gillette-sparks-emotions-controversy-possibly-gold-with-we-believe-the-best-a-man-can-be-video-255429.

25   Dreyfuss, "Gillette's Ad."

26   Topping, Lyons, and Weaver, "Gillette #MeToo."

Influential Social Media Platforms for Public Relations

It is unclear how many social media platforms exist on the Internet. However, it is apparent that people spend a significant amount of time on social networking activities by "liking, tweeting, subscribing, pinning, sharing, and linking." Popular platforms include the following:

Facebook

Worldwide, there were over two billion monthly active users on Facebook in 2019. Facebook is considered the most influential social media platform, providing users with social networking sites to share information, exchange private messages, and communicate with friends and family. Every 60 seconds, 510,000 comments are posted, 293,000 statuses are updated, and 136,000 photos are uploaded.[27] Organizations use Facebook pages to place basic contact information and their logos to incorporate their brands into sales and promotion.

Consumers are inclined to view Facebook as an active communication venue for organizations, while viewing websites of organizations as static places for background and archived information. Organizations operate their Facebook pages to receive active and fast opinions from consumers, as well as to advertise their products and services. From a management standpoint, it is cheaper and easier for organizations to manage Facebook pages, compared with websites, which require professional web design and technology skills. Organizations can export their Facebook events so that they appear in Outlook, iCal, and Google calendars. More importantly, a page allows organizations to use Messenger as a way to connect with consumers. According to Social Media Stats, 78 percent of American Facebook users have discovered something to purchase via this platform, the most popular social network for small businesses in 2019.[28] Although Facebook is considered the most powerful social media site, it struggles with one big issue: millennial users leave Facebook, and younger teenagers prefer other social media platforms as Facebook becomes the parents' favorite digital playground.

Twitter

Many people use their smartphones to connect with one another in the Twitter community. Twitter allows them to follow various brands and news outlets to receive new information every second. With a limit of 280 or fewer characters, this microblogging platform is a unique social media tool for organizations to send instant messages as a distribution platform. Organizations use Twitter to break the latest news, update information about ongoing events, issue apologetic statements, and refute rumors. An organization's Twitter page is branded with its logo or symbolic image and biography. Managing a brand on Twitter for a public relations practitioner is straightforward. The practitioner monitors what people say about the organization on Twitter and interacts with them by tweeting or retweeting content. Sports

27   Dan Noyes, "The Top 20 Valuable Facebook Statistics," *Zephoria*, modified January 2020, https://zephoria.com/top-15-valuable-facebook-statistics/.

28   Kris Spisak, "2019 Social Media Trends & Statistics," Business 2 Community, January 2, 2019, https://www.business2community.com/social-media/2019-social-media-trends-statistics-02156179.

teams and professional athletes use Twitter to communicate with the fans who want to be informed about games. Twitter is a good place to seek immediacy. Twitter's daily active users grew 9 percent between 2017 and 2018 with over 300 million monthly active users, due in part to President Trump's active use, but it lost users to other social media platforms and was not proving to be attractive for new users in 2019.[29]

LinkedIn

As the leading professional network, LinkedIn helps college students and professional workers build their personal brands, associated with their expertise. LinkedIn users browse profiles to find professionals and build relationships, especially for job opportunities. Users can join groups with shared interests. In other words, LinkedIn is a great platform for those who seek to find a new job or join a professional group. Organizations also have LinkedIn pages with information about their status updates.
On LinkedIn, users can network with other people by adding them as "connections," similar to how Facebook users make a friend request. It offers specialized features, such as the company page, which is viewed as a great place to drive business results, raise brand awareness, and promote career opportunities. On the company page, users can add a cover image and logo, create a company description, and fill in the company details with the contact information of page administrators. To enhance business opportunities, users are encouraged to post articles or company updates on a regular basis, including other social media links. One advantage of using LinkedIn is that being an active participant in a LinkedIn Group can help individuals and companies build networks with other professionals and businesses in the same field. Participating in a group discussion also attracts views to the company page.[30] As of 2019, over 260 million users with at least bachelor's degree are active on LinkedIn monthly, and 40 million are in "decision-making" positions."[31]

YouTube

Founded in 2005 and owned by Google, YouTube is the most popular online video platform today. It is also the world's second most popular search engine, after Google. Millions of users around the world upload videos that anyone can search and watch. YouTube has become an archive for storing favorite video clips, video tutorials, songs, and movies, as well as a marketing social media platform for corporations to promote
their products or services. Using YouTube as a public relations tool is simple: create video content and upload it with the aid of YouTube's caption and subtitle functions. As YouTube provides a highly enriched visual experience for detailed and instructive messages, public relations practitioners try to garner as many as YouTube subscribers, who follow YouTube channels and want to stay informed of any new content the practitioners post. Like other social media platforms, YouTube allows subscribers to post comments on the videos they watch. The comments lead to the maintenance of a

29   Anna Clarke, "Will Twitter Continue Dying in 2019?," *Social Media Revolver*, December 12, 2018, https://socialmediarevolver.com/will-twitter-continue-dying-in-2019/.

30   Christina Newberry, "LinkedIn for Business: The Ultimate Marketing Guide," *Hootsuite*, August 13, 2018, https://blog.hootsuite.com/linkedin-for-business/.

31   Spisak, "2019 Social Media."

constant interaction in the YouTube community. One powerful attraction of YouTube is that users go to YouTube for seeking solutions to problems from work and school or tutorials for hobbies and health. The users of YouTube, compared with those of other social media platforms, tend to know what they want and pursue it. Searches of "how-to" videos on YouTube are one of the most popular content categories with music and comedy. Over one billion hours of videos are watched on YouTube every day.[32]

Instagram

A major trend in social media is using visual images rather than words. With over 800 million monthly active users and over 500 million daily active users, Instagram takes advantage of new image effects as the number one visual social media platform. Like Facebook, Instagram differentiates personal accounts from business accounts. The business accounts have proven to be a powerful marketing tool because of the visibility of products and services. Founded in 2010 and acquired by Facebook in 2012, Instagram was exclusively created to be an app for smartphones unlike other major social media platforms, which started out as browser-based sites.[33] Hence, Instagram offers a great method of communicating live organizational posts and stories to smartphone savvy consumers. From a public relations perspective, Instagram is the best social media platform to collaborate with opinion leaders or "influencers," online Instagram celebrities who specialize in promoting a brand or product. The collaboration with influencers enables corporate brands to reach their target audiences in a way that feels friendly since influencers strategize to build a loyal relationship with their followers by sharing life stories in visual content. The collaboration focuses on showing the followers and potential consumers that the product has personality, and it is cool and beneficial to purchase it. According to a 2018 survey, 72 percent of Instagram users said they had made fashion, beauty, or style-related purchases after seeing influencers using the products on the app. It proves Instagram's power in the digital marketing landscape of the future with young users: millennials and Generation Z.[34] Social media analytics firm Klear also found in 2019 that influencer marketing activity on Instagram surged while Instagram influencers boosted their adoption of Instagram Stories, incorporate "several images or videos into a single post that disappears after 24 hours."[35] However, Instagram's popularity has been challenged by TikTok, a video-sharing social networking service, more used by younger people known as the OK Boomer generation in 2020.

Organizations use social media platforms to connect with online users and share their information with consumers. Sharing organizational photos and videos with the target audience or the public on social media is likely to receive more feedback, which leads to a positive two-way communication relationship.

32   Clifford Chi, "51 YouTube Stats Every Video Marketer Should Know in 2019," Hubspot, last modified February 18, 2020, https://blog.hubspot.com/marketing/youtube-stats.

33   Business.com https://www.business.com/articles/10-reasons-to-use-instagram-for-business/

34   Zach Benson, "10 Reasons to Use Instagram for Your Business," Retail Dive, May 10, 2018, https://www.retail-dive.com/news/study-instagram-influences-almost-75-of-user-purchase-decisions/503336/.

35   "2019 State of Influencer Marketing Report," Klear, n.d., https://klear.com/state-of-influencer-marketing.

Social Media is a Public Relations Trend

Organizations strive to communicate with the target audience. They want to know what the audience thinks and needs. In two-way communication, the sender and receiver of information can listen to each other and are willing to negotiate to find a mutual benefit. The Internet and social media serve as the main engine for accelerating two-way communication. Although organizations are able to send information to massive audiences through traditional media channels, they usually receive limited feedback from the audience. The less efficient feedback channels are telephone conversations, comment boxes, letters to editors and face-to-face contact. Therefore, the interaction between organizations and the audience is bound to be limited. In contrast, the Internet introduces the evolution of communication systems, including email, online newsletters, forums, websites, video conferences, and social media. There is no doubt that social media has paved the way for active two-way communication, giving the audience, especially consumers, the power to share information, knowledge, and thoughts. Social media represents a two-way conversational channel that helps organizations build a mutual relationship with the audience in the form of online interaction.

The practice of public relations in the digital age focuses on producing messages and stories with photos, videos, and graphics in which the audience is interested. Customized messages can be embedded into online content. Press releases disseminated through online channels include photos and videos. Journalists visit web and social media sites of organizations to look for their news sources. Public rela-

tions campaigns are customized for Internet users, and social media serves as an amplifier to spread messages about the campaigns. In essence, public relations practitioners rely on the Internet and social media to keep abreast of rapidly changing social trends, aiming to maximize communication effectiveness for their organizations and clients. In addition, the practitioners strive to create social media content tailored for smartphone apps since younger generations consume more media content on mobile than traditional media devices, such as television sets and personal computers.

FIGURE CREDITS

Img. 16.1: Copyright © 2014 Depositphotos/Multirealism.
Fig. 16.2: Copyright © 2014 Depositphotos/Mactrunk.
Fig. 16.3: Copyright © 2019 by Procter & Gamble.
Img. 16.3: Copyright © 2020 by Facebook, Inc.
Img. 16.4: Copyright © 2020 by Twitter, Inc.
Img. 16.5: Copyright © 2020 by LinkedIn Corporation.
Img. 16.5: Copyright © 2020 by YouTube LLC.
Img. 16.6: Copyright © 2016 by Instagram, LLC.
Img. 16.7: Copyright © 2014 Depositphotos/Rawpixel.
Img. 16.8: Copyright © 2020 by Haymarket Media Group Ltd.

CHAPTER SUMMARY AND REVIEW

1. Recognize the timetable of Internet evolution.
2. Identify basic characteristics of online communication.
3. Study how public relations is entangled with the use of the Internet.
4. Explain social media and its developmental stages.
5. Argue why social media is becoming a dominant media channel.

PUBLIC RELATIONS IN PRACTICE

FURTHER READING

PR Week's Awards For **Best PR Social Media**

Winner: Tinder and M Booth
Campaign Name: #RepresentLove

Tinder hoped to highlight its diversity and inclusion efforts and attract new and lapsed users. The campaign had a three-pronged strategy. First, use the emoji launch via earned and owned channels to demonstrate Tinder's commitment to diversity and inclusion. Second, use data to talk about Tinder's diverse users and their openness to interracial relationships. And, finally, create shareable content for users and other targets. The campaign was a hit, generating 200 unique stories. There were also 5.2 million YouTube video views and more than 50,000 signatures on the emoji petition.

Read more at
https://www.prweek.com/article/1579436/prweek-us-awards-2019-winners

17

Celebrities in Public Relations

More than ever before, mostly with the aid of social media, people around the world like to share their personal information and thoughts with others. It is easy for them to express themselves online. One reason they share photos and videos of their lives is to be seen and heard. On social media platforms, parents post their cute baby photos, college students update their party videos, businesspeople upload their meeting photos from conferences, and public figures share all kinds of online content for social causes or self-interest. Such social media activities are considered part of public relations on a personal level. In general, social media allows people to exchange personal information with their friends or followers, highlighting their happy or unfortunate experiences. In return, they expect positive and supportive responses from those who view their online content and messages. Responses such as "your baby is so cute," "I wish I were there," "you look amazing," "I feel your pain," and "I want to buy it too" represent the feedback people hope to gain through social media communication. Now that social media offers such convenient tools to communicate personal information to others, users of social media are able to inform, influence, and promote their personal interests and causes. In other words, public relations is no longer exclusively for organizations or groups of powerful people; public relations is embraced by an individual who wants to build relationships with other people and aims to impress his or her employer with good personal images. Everybody is a public relations practitioner in this regard.

One of the most popular components of public relations is the management function, which creates and maintains mutually beneficial relationships between an organization and its target audience. Public relations practitioners are expected to achieve goals of organizations or clients. They help CEOs look good in media coverage, organize public relations events to build public trust, engage employees to become loyal to their organizations, and strategize public relations campaigns to enhance profits or public support. In fact, public relations in both theory and practice has been advanced and implemented with the focus on organizational accomplishments. In a similar vein, there is another sector of public relations that is receiving rapidly growing attention: entertainment public relations. Individual entertainers facilitate the practice of public relations with professional help from public relations firms. Public figures, such as Hollywood stars, politicians, athletes, and media professionals, are the main clients of entertainment public relations practitioners.

Public Relations for Self-Actualization

Like organizations, celebrities interact with the public to achieve their personal goals. Psychologically speaking, they tend to have a strong desire for success consciousness (a state of mind of expecting success) about what the public thinks about their reputation and image. Their desire for success consciousness can be analyzed based on Maslow's hierarchy of needs, which is a theoretical model that explains what motivates human behavior to achieve individual goals. Abraham Maslow, the creator of the model, was interested in investigating "what makes people happy and the things that they do to achieve that aim"; Maslow believed that people have a natural desire to be self-actualized and to be all they can be.[1] In order for people to achieve their personal goals, people have a number of basic needs. The needs are divided into five levels, which are visualized in the shape of a pyramid. Each level of needs includes unique physical, psychological, and social requirements. The lowest level of the pyramid consists of the most basic physical needs for human survival, whereas the more complex psychological and social needs are placed at the top of the pyramid (Figure 17.1).

Physiological Needs. These include the most basic needs that are vital to survival, such as water, air, food, and sleep. In addition, clothing and shelter are needed to maintain the proper functions of the human body. Sexual instinct for reproduction is also a basic physiological need.

Security and Safety Needs. Individuals, after their physical needs are met, look for security and safety, wanting control and order in their lives. To fulfill security and safety needs, individuals pursue steady employment, financial security, insurance policies, and health care. Adults focus on building a safety net against accidents or illness, while children seek a place to feel safe. When individuals are satisfied with their security and safety, the needs for human survival are met.

Social Needs. Individuals need to feel a sense of love, acceptance, and belonging. Such a sense can be grounded in friendships, families, social groups, romantic relationships, and organizations. At this level, human behavior is affected by the need for psychological relationships because individuals want to be loved and accepted by other people. They want to stay away from a sense of depression and loneliness.

Esteem Needs. After the first three needs have been satisfied, individuals begin to have a need to feel respected. Esteem needs include such things as self-esteem and personal worth. To feel respected, individuals engage in social activities, including going to college, playing a sport, and participating in humanitarian work. Getting an individual's achievement or contribution recognized by other people fulfills esteem needs. In contrast, individuals who fail to get the respect of others are likely to develop feelings of inferiority.

---

1 Kendra Cherry, "The 5 Levels of Maslow's Hierarchy of Needs," Verywell Mind, December 3, 2019, https://www.verywellmind.com/what-is-maslows-hierarchy-of-needs-4136760.

Self-actualizing Needs. At the very peak of Maslow's hierarchy, self-actualizing individuals are concerned with personal growth and fulfilling their potential. "What a man can be, he must be," Maslow explained. Self-actualizers are people "who have developed or are developing to the full stature of which they capable." They are creatively and psychologically satisfied.

Maslow developed this model by studying the biographies of famous historical individuals whom he believed were good examples of self-actualized people. These figures included Albert Einstein, Eleanor Roosevelt, Abraham Lincoln, and Frederick Douglass.[2] Based on the model,

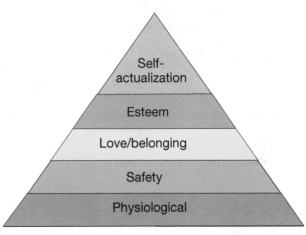

Figure 17.1 Maslow's Hierarchy of Needs.

celebrities probably at least have fulfilled their security and safety needs because of their high-paying professions. Most of them also might have fulfilled their social needs with fans, friends, and even paparazzi. For celebrities, esteem needs can be most important since the level focuses on self-esteem and personal worth, which can be obtained with social contribution and respect. Celebrities seek love, attention, and respect more than anybody. They can be easily loved but hardly respected. To get to the level of self-actualization, celebrities strive to fulfill their esteem needs with positive public images. They hire public relations firms or consult with public relations practitioners to cultivate fame and public respect.

Individual Brands in Public Relations

The practice of public relations to meet organizational goals focuses on creating positive relationships with the target audience or public. For-profit organizations expect public relations practitioners to establish good images of their products or services, including positive attitudes toward corporate brands. In a similar vein, celebrities, as individuals instead of organizations, seek help from the public relations industry to manage their public images. Celebrities in today's mass and social media environment acknowledge that they need better strategies to deal with a wide range of media outlets to establish positive public images and sell personal brands. Social media mentions and news reports about movie stars, the British royal family, TV talk show hosts, politicians, singers, and athletes dominate the 24/7 news cycle ahead of economic and political issues. In reality, the media are obsessed with celebrity news since it drives higher viewership.

Viewers, listeners, and readers are exposed to heavy news stories of celebrity gossip, rumors, and promotion. Celebrity stories appear entertaining, tempting, glorious, and dramatic to media audiences. A staple of American media culture is associated with celebrities. The photos or videos posted on celebrities' social media platforms become news sources for mainstream media. Some media outlets thrive by specializing in celebrity and entertainment:

Magazines. People, US Weekly, Vanity Fair, and Entertainment Weekly
Websites. TMZ, Perez Hilton, E! Online, The Hollywood Reporter, and Just Jared
Television Programs. Extra, E! News, The Insider, Access Hollywood, and Entertainment Tonight

---

2   Cherry, "The 5 Levels."

TABLE 17.1   Five Strategies to Create a Powerful Celebrity Brand

MASTER YOUR CRAFT FIRST	A celebrity should master his or her basic specialty in the entertainment industry. For example, supermodel Gisele Bündchen wore super-high heels on a slippery runway to become the highest-paid model, and actor Dwayne Johnson, known as "The Rock," is a professional wrestler who produces action movies.
BE KNOWN FOR SOMETHING	A celebrity needs to have another skill or character to be branded. For example, TV star Neil Patrick Harris, as an amateur magician, won the Tannen's Magic Louis Award in 2006, and actress Natalie Portman graduated from Harvard University, majoring in psychology.
LEVERAGE WHAT YOU HAVE	A celebrity has the power of being the face of a particular product or service because his or her face is familiar to consumers. For example, actress Jennifer Anniston serves as the brand ambassador for the Aveeno skin care brand, leveraging her beautiful, friendly image with consumers. Further, Aniston, known for her trendy hairstyles on *Friends*, co-owns a hair care company, Living Proof. It is an authentic fit for her, taking advantage of her image as a beauty trend setter.
TRANSFORM THE PERSONAL INTO THE BUSINESS	Celebrities from reality television shows capitalize on this strategy. For example, Martha Stewart, known as the queen of lifestyle, has a variety of home collection products, such as dinnerware, bed sheets, food storage containers, robes, furniture, cookware, and so on. The queen of lifestyle associates her personal ability with the product lines, relating to what homemakers need. More recently, the Kardashian sisters maximized the strategy of using their fame and images for a big business opportunity, launching a clothing collection and cosmetic line.
USE SOCIAL NETWORKS TO KEEP YOUR BUSINESS BRAND PERSONAL	A celebrity builds friendly relationships with fans through social media sites, hoping that his or her personal brand keeps positively growing through online interaction. For example, singer Taylor Swift makes her fans feel listened to and appreciated, as she often offers two-way conversations with her fans through social media.

These media outlets need celebrities for their daily or weekly editions, and celebrities expect the outlets to create and enhance their fame and glory. Between them, public relations practitioners are hired to fulfill both sides' expectations and demands.

Public relations practitioners represent celebrity clients to communicate the "brand of celebrity" to the media and public. The brand of celebrity refers to a comprehensive reputation composed of the celebrity's character, image, and personality. Branding a celebrity is practitioners' top priority in the field of entertainment public relations. A celebrity's familiar face is the known brand to the public. Every celebrity carries his or her own personal brand, and the practitioners focus on strengthening and glorifying the personal celebrity brand. The practitioners strategize to build a powerful brand to please their celebrity clients. A powerful brand for a celebrity does not grow overnight. It takes effort and resources to manufacture. Cheryl Isaac, a business strategist, cited five strategies (Table 17.1) to create a celebrity brand.[3]

For a celebrity client to build a powerful brand, public relations practitioners first work on promoting public awareness about the celebrity and then constructing good public images. When the public begins to recognize the celebrity's name and face, the practitioner promotes the celebrity's talent as an entertainer in his or her special field, such as music, film, or sports. After the celebrity gains public recognition, the practitioner finds a way of enhancing the celebrity's public image, which directly leads to the production of a personal brand.

---

3   Cheryl Isaac and World With a View, "6 Personal Branding Lessons Learned From Forbes Celebrity 100 Women," *Forbes*, May 18, 2012, http://www.forbes.com/sites/worldviews/2012/05/18/5-personal-branding-lessons-learned-from-forbes-celebrity-100-women/.

A powerful celebrity brand generates fame and money, and it is associated with plenty of business opportunities. However, it is a long journey to secure a certain type of a celebrity brand in a favorable light since most celebrities are not as successful as the Kardashian sisters or the Jonas brothers. This is why public relations plays an important role in branding celebrities with media relations, community relations, and corporate relations. More celebrities rely on public relations to build relationships with their fans, corporations, and the public in pursuit of fame, glory, and fortune. They eventually hope to build their own kingdoms and play powerful roles in the entertainment industry.

FIGURE 17.2 Oprah Built Her Celebrity Status through Her Talk Show.

The media revolve around celebrities. The entertainment industry loves it. Celebrities have essential relationships with the US media and entertainment (M&E) industry. The M&E industry is based on businesses that "produce and distribute motion pictures, television programs, and commercials, along with music and audio recordings, radio, games, and publishing."[4] Celebrities are the lifeblood of the M&E industry, which raked in more than $712 billion in revenue in 2018 and is expected to reach $825 billion by 2023.[5]

The film industry pioneered the practice of celebrity public relations before the industry of television was born. Since motion picture studios promoted their stars with glamorous and heroic images, Hollywood became the mecca of the entertainment industry. After the television industry emerged, viewers grew closer to television stars as their idols and heroes. Television created the impression that celebrities were right there in the living room to become everyone's friends. As a result, comedians and actors in soap operas and sitcoms gained popularity and fame while television was becoming the most popular medium in the American family's living room. In addition, television journalists and talk show hosts (see Figure 17.2) built their status as celebrities. Viewers idolized stars on television. In response, television constantly delivers a host of heroes to the living room. The tradition of television shows continues and never ends.

Practitioners in Celebrity Public Relations

Different job titles are used for public relations practitioners who represent celebrities in the entertainment industry. Publicist, representative (or rep), manager, spokesperson, and agent are commonly used titles for celebrity clients. Regardless of job title, their first duty is to deal with the media on behalf of their clients. As a publicist, the practitioner arranges interviews with journalists, manages social media content, organizes television and public appearances, and coaches the client about how to behave in front of the media and public. The practitioner issues press releases, escorts the client to media events, and pitches story ideas about the client to magazines, radio, newspapers, television, and online news outlets. In reality, the practitioner explores any possible opportunity for the celebrity client to gain publicity.

---

4 "MEDIA AND ENTERTAINMENT SPOTLIGHT," Select USA, https://www.selectusa.gov/media-entertainment-industry-united-states

5 Nate Nead, "Media and Entertainment Industry," Investment Bank, n.d., https://investmentbank.com/media-and-entertainment-industry-overview/.

As a manager, the practitioner fosters strategies to develop the client's talents and commercial brand. The practitioner manages the public image of the client, advising the celebrity what to do and where to go. The practitioner also makes tactical recommendations on which products or social movements the client should or should not endorse. If the client is in trouble with negative publicity, the practitioner executes damage control operations. As a spokesperson, the practitioner responds to media requests and questions about the client. The practitioner releases a statement, if necessary, to promote or defend the client. The statement can be either written or spoken. As an agent, the practitioner helps the client choose optimal roles or songs that promote publicity and positive images.

All such activities of the practitioner for the celebrity client can be summarized as the process of communicating with the media and public. The practitioner acknowledges that the public likes to be entertained by reading celebrity magazines, watching celebrities being interviewed on television, and going to the movies or concerts. In a similar vein, the entertainment industry strategizes to fulfill the human desire to feel excited, satisfied, touched, and relaxed in the daily routine of life.

Public relations practitioners are responsible for maintaining positive working relationships with journalists and employees of the entertainment industry while having strong skills in networking to promote the interest of the client. Having a celebrity as a client sounds too good to be true. Things like meeting Hollywood's "A-list" actors, being invited to parties with rich and famous people, having dinner with talk show hosts, and going to clubs with singers can happen to public relations practitioners in entertainment public relations. They can even be paid more than those who work for corporate public relations. Everything sounds just perfect and glamorous. However, not every practitioner is able to have such privileges, especially entry-level public relations practitioners in celebrity public relations. In reality, there are long hours of exhausting work that could include challenging assignments. The following is a list of hard assignments for new public relations practitioners, according to *Ragan's PR Daily*:[6]

- Staring at a computer screen monitoring news stories about his or her clients or cutting, pasting, and photocopying clips
- Making hundreds of follow-up calls to event invitees or journalists
- Booking and confirming car service and hotel reservations
- Conducting dozens of site inspections of venues to meet detailed event specifications
- Taking red-eye flights and heading directly to the office for work
- Standing in the rain, snow, and cold to check on guests
- Stuffing hundreds (even thousands) of gift bags in a windowless closet
- Deflecting nasty come-ons from smarmy clients—politely
- Earning a barely livable salary and being expected to work crazy hours, including weekends

The reality might be a bit disappointing for entry-level practitioners, but they could experience "a huge media turnout, a meeting with a favorite celebrity, or access to a trendy night club" as perks of the reality.[7] More importantly, such rudimentary experiences offer a ladder to the higher professional level: glamorous representation for celebrities.

---

6 Lorra M. Brown, "Glamour? Ha! The Realities of Entertainment and Fashion PR," *PR Daily*, February 1, 2012, http://www.prdaily.com/Main/Articles/Glamour_Ha_The_realities_of_entertainment_and_fash_10701.aspx.
7 Brown, "Glamour?"

Promotional Strategies for Celebrities

There is no standard as to who should be recognized as a celebrity, but once an individual in the entertainment industry receives media coverage, and the media place the term *star* in front of the individual's name, the individual's status as a celebrity is born. A celebrity in today's capitalist market system normally goes through the process of commercialization, which introduces the celebrity to the practice of marketing promotion. Celebrity public relations practitioners specialize in the process of thorough promotional strategies. To promote a celebrity client, the practitioner needs to find opportunities for the client to have media exposure and public engagement. Such exposure includes interviews with journalists, appearances on television and radio talk shows, humanized articles in magazines, personal stories on documentary or reality programs, book promotion, public speeches, and participation in social activism.

Interviews with Journalists

Setting up a media interview for a celebrity client is considered a fundamental task for the practitioner. Although any kinds of interviews with newspapers, television/radio stations, magazines, or Internet podcasts are valued, the practitioner aims to arrange interviews with influential media outlets with a larger audience on behalf of the client.

When the interview is arranged, the specific time, place, and method are discussed between the practitioner and the media outlet to achieve the objectives of the interview. For example, Carsie Blanton was introduced as one of the "10 New Country and Americana Artists You Need to Know in 2019" by *Rolling Stone* magazine. In the interview with *Rolling Stone*, Blanton expressed her dream as an unconventional musician who was unschooled at home on a Virginia farm and spent time in Oregon dumpster-diving at 16. She said her new album, *Buck Up*, "is about two different kinds of edginess: a sexual one and political edginess. It's an expression of the fact that I don't give as much of a damn about making people comfortable as I used to."[8] The interview focused on describing the singer's background, how she became a singer, and how she created a new music genre. Blanton's public relations practitioner deserves kudos for the interview arrangement.

In a different way, interviews are also arranged for already-famous celebrities to send their messages. For example, in September 2014, an unidentified hacker's invasion of a hundred celebrity iCloud accounts occurred, in which mostly self-taken nude photos of female celebrities were leaked to the public. The incident was dubbed "the celebrity nude photo hacking scandal." A-list stars such as Oscar-winning actor Jennifer Lawrence, singer Victoria Justice, *Big Bang Theory* actress Kaley Cuoco, and model Kate Upton were victims of the scandal. After the scandal broke, the media pursued an interview with Jennifer Lawrence (Figure 17.3), who was viewed as the most famous celebrity in the scandal. Lawrence allowed no interview at the time; instead, her spokesman issued a statement: "This is a flagrant violation of privacy. The authorities have been contacted and will prosecute anyone who posts the stolen photos of Jennifer Lawrence."[9] About a

---

8   Jonathan Bernstein, Robert Crawford, Jon Freeman, Joseph Hudak, & Marissa R. Moss, "10 New Country and American Artists You Need to Know: Winter 2019," *Rolling Stone*, February 13, 2019, https://www.rollingstone.com/music/music-country-lists/10-new-country-and-americana-artists-you-need-to-know-winter-2019-793958/carsie-blanton-793999/.

9   Paul Farrell, "Nude Photos of Jennifer Lawrence and Others Posted Online by Alleged Hacker," *The Guardian*, August 31, 2014, http://www.theguardian.com/world/2014/sep/01/

FIGURE 17.3 Jennifer Lawrence on Vanity Fair after the iPhone Nude Scandal.

month after the scandal, Lawrence had an interview with *Vanity Fair* magazine, saying of the hacking, "It is a sexual violation. It's disgusting. The law needs to be changed, and we need to change."[10] The actress used the interview as an opportunity to spread her message against the act of privacy violation, adding that "it is not a scandal. It is a sex crime." Lawrence also explained why she did not respond to the media's interview requests immediately: "I was just so afraid. I didn't know how this would affect my career."[11] Her interview with the magazine was quoted and mentioned numerous times by the media and on other celebrities' social media platforms. Her interview was received with great applause, and her message—"It is a sex crime"—was disseminated all around the world. The interview defended her Hollywood career and reaffirmed her heroic image as the heroine in *The Hunger Games*.

Appearances on Talk Shows

Pursuing radio or television appearances for a celebrity client is a big task for the practitioner. If the client asks for a national television show, the practitioner reaches out to all different ranges of people, such as the station's reporters, producers, editors, writers, and show hosts and staff. Singers and movie stars prefer national television talk shows to promote their new albums and movies since talk shows on television allow them to promote their artistic products.

Talk show hosts create a welcoming and cozy environment to let their celebrity guests feel excited about being on the show. With actor guests, they talk and watch video clips from the guest's new movie while including information about when and where the movie will be released. For singers, talk shows provide the stage to introduce new songs. Morning and afternoon talk shows provide marketing platforms for celebrities to promote themselves or their entertainment products: popular shows are *The Talk, Today, The View, Good Morning America, The Ellen DeGeneres Show*, and *Live! With Kelly and Ryan*. Celebrity appearances on talk shows are win-win situations for show hosts who are pressured to increase the ratings and for celebrities who are obligated to promote their upcoming movies, books, or albums. Higher ratings attract more advertisers who are willing to invest a huge amount of money in popular programs. The advertisers prefer programs that can be exposed to 18 to 49-year-old viewers, categorized as the major consumers of products and services. It is hard to deny that talk shows prioritize celebrity guests with their influence on the target demographic.

Entertainment companies producing movies and albums expect their celebrities to make promotional appearances in the media to generate publicity. More publicity leads to more moviegoers or song downloaders. For example, *Avengers: Endgame*, a 2019 American superhero movie, was produced by Marvel

nude-photos-of-jennifer-lawrence-and-others-posted-online-by-alleged-hacker.

10   "Cover Exclusive: Jennifer Lawrence Calls Photo Hacking a "Sex Crime," *Vanity Fair*, October 7, 2014, http://www.vanityfair.com/hollywood/2014/10/jennifer-lawrence-cover.

11   *Vanity Fair*, "Cover Exclusive."

FIGURE 17.4 Avengers: Endgame Actors on *Jimmy Kimmel Live*.

Studios and distributed by Walt Disney Studios Motion Pictures. Before the release, the movie's actors, including Robert Downey Jr., Chris Evans, Mark Ruffalo, Brie Larson, and Scarlett Johansson, appeared on dozens of television and radio talk shows and had interviews with nearly every entertainment media outlet. Movie critics applauded Downey Jr.'s talents, claiming that "Robert Downey Jr. deserves an Oscar for 'Avengers: Endgame.'"[12] Downey Jr. and his co-actors promoted the movie by appearing on popular television talk shows, such as *Jimmy Kimmel Live* (see Figure 17.4) and *The Ellen DeGeneres Show*, and many other online talk shows. In addition, their promotional interviews with newspapers, magazines, and television celebrity news shows were published a week before the release date. Before its release, the movie generated massive publicity, which led to new records: the highest opening weekend gross and the fastest cumulative grosses worldwide through $2.5 billion.[13]

Personal/Humanized Stories for Publicity

The public likes to read and watch stories similar to their normal lives. Emotionally touching human stories are one of the media's favorite sources to cover. Love, hope, poverty, abuse, friendship, death, parental sacrifice, trauma, depression, and sickness are heart-touching topics in which the media are interested. Human stories focus on these topics, manufactured as an overcoming act of spirit. If a homeless high school student who lost his parents to a drug overdose got into Harvard, the media would report his inspirational story. The coverage would focus on his overcoming all the hardship he went through. Indeed, such a news story is heartwarming and inspirational.

12   Michael Cavna, "Why Robert Downey Jr. deserves an Oscar for 'Avengers: Endgame,' according to its directors," May 2, 2019, *The Washington Post*, https://www.washingtonpost.com/arts-entertainment/2019/05/02/why-robert-downey-jr-deserves-an-oscar-avengers-endgame-according-its-directors/?noredirect=on&utm_term=.bb4acdd6d7aa.

13   "Opening Weekends," Box Office, n.d., https://www.boxofficemojo.com/alltime/weekends/.

FIGURE 17.5 Lindsay Lohan.

Many celebrities had difficult childhoods or still wrestle with chronic problems. Their troubled lifestyles attract media attention; their experience in overcoming illness catches media attention; their tragic loss of family members invites media coverage. On the other side, celebrities who get into trouble with the law seek an opportunity to rebuild their images through the media; celebrities who beat cancer want to be interviewed to give inspirational messages to other patients; celebrities who bounce back from personal tragedy look for media exposure to regain fame and glory.

The public sends their best regards to celebrities who share their troubled stories and make an effort to overcome their problems. When the public hears and watches a celebrity struggle with a personal issue, they begin to see the celebrity as their sister or brother, even if the celebrity had a history of criminal conduct. They tend to forgive the celebrity's troubled past, offering their support instead. The personally troubled life can create sympathetic feelings and gain public support for the celebrity. For example, Lindsay Lohan (see Figure 17.5) has become the icon of a celebrity who made the transition from child star to broken adult. At the age of 12, she played her first movie role as identical twins in *The Parent Trap*, which brought her national fame. Her popularity soared after the success of *Freaky Friday* and *Mean Girls*.

Lohan's image as American's redheaded cutie took a hit in 2006, when she became addicted to partying and drugs. Her disastrous time behind bars and in and out of rehab facilities began with charges for driving under the influence, possession of cocaine, probation violations, and grand theft. The public and media showed no sympathy for her and criticized her hopeless and helpless behavior. After all the arrests, court appearances, trips to jail, and stays in rehab, Lohan had the opportunity to turn her life around with Oprah Winfrey's help. Winfrey's OWN network produced a documentary series about Lohan's attempt to bounce back from her miserable life. Lohan referred to herself as an "addict" while being interviewed by Winfrey.[14] Lohan confessed that she was stressed out from dealing with the paparazzi and her parents, so she did cocaine 10 to 15 times. She admitted that alcohol was a bigger problem for her than cocaine. Being known as "an adjective and verb for bad behavior and child star gone wrong," Lohan told Winfrey that she became a spiritual person after rehab treatments.[15] She vowed to work hard and stay focused to regain the trust of people in her career, calling acting "the thing that has made me happiest my whole life."[16] After the documentary series was aired in 2014, Lohan received a great deal of empathy and support. The social media community posted a host of sympathetic mentions for her, and a journalist wrote, "She's a human. She's a very fragile, volatile, slightly selfish human. But she's one who's working really hard to find peace in the eye of the very large, very tumultuous storm."[17] In a 2019 interview with *Variety* magazine, Lohan said, "There's always going to be something new that I want to do. I just want to make people happy, and I want to stay happy."[18]

14   Lisa Resperns France, "7 Things We Learned from Lindsay Lohan's Sit Down with Oprah Winfrey," CNN, last modified August 19, 2013, http://www.cnn.com/2013/08/19/showbiz/tv/lindsay-lohan-oprah-interview/.

15   France, "7 Things."

16   France, "7 Things."

17   Breanna Hare, "Lindsay Lohan's Reality Show: What's the Verdict?," CNN, last modified March 10, 2014, http://www.cnn.com/2014/03/10/showbiz/tv/lindsay-lohan-own-reality-show/.

18   Elizabeth Wagmeister, "Lindsay Lohan Wants You to Forget Her Past," *Variety*, n.d., https://variety.com/2019/tv/features/lindsay-lohan-beach-house-mtv-mean-girls-sequel-1203101682/.

Reality Television Shows

Not all celebrities belong to the A-list. *Insider* magazine named Kylie Jenner, Ariana Grande, Bradley Cooper, Lady Gaga, Idris Elba, BTS, Meghan Markle, Michael B. Jordan, Carrie Underwood, and Cardi B as 2019's remarkable A-list celebrities.[19] Some celebrities are forgotten by the public while attempting to get their old fame and glory back, and others try to find a way to become more famous so that they can be recognized as A-listers. Either way, they ask their public relations practitioners to help them receive more publicity. Public relations practitioners use reality television shows as a solution for enhancing public awareness and support for less famous or uninfluential celebrities. Although such programs are generally unconventional and unscripted, they have become an important type of television show format. Rather than using professional, famous actors, the programs cast a wide range of people in the entertainment industry, including sports players, fashion models, musicians, socialites, businesspeople, politicians, media people, and even family members of celebrities. Appearing on a reality TV show is a way to achieve fame.

A reality show follows people or the cast to document their lives. The show gives a fair amount of time to each celebrity, who can become a part of the story with little structure. Because of unscripted real-life situations, the show is likely to have longer shooting schedules. Story editors are responsible for sifting through long footage to find entertaining moments. *Survivor* and *Big Brother* led to the explosion of reality show popularity in the early 2000s, but they did not produce A-list celebrities like *The Simple Life*, which aired from December 2003 to August 2007, did.

The Simple Life documented two wealthy spoiled socialites, Paris Hilton and Nicole Richie, who found themselves struggling to survive in the rural reality of Arkansas. They were horribly inept at living on a dairy farm while milking cows, cleaning up manure, and helping with farm work. However, they began to adapt to the simple lifestyle of a small-town family and made an effort to assimilate into the community.

The two socialites kept exploring other tasks while traveling across the United States. They worked at a tanning salon, funeral home, fast-food restaurant, gas station, and wildlife agency. The show won the ASCAP Award for Top TV Series, and Hilton emerged as an A-list celebrity. Because of the show's popularity, international versions of *The Simple Life* were produced in 11 foreign countries. While Hilton was enjoying her celebrity tabloid queen status that attracted an army of paparazzi, her best friend since childhood, Kim Kardashian, came along for the ride. Kardashian's exposure to the media increased as she attended social occasions with Hilton. It was a prelude to the emergence of one of the biggest reality shows.

Kim Kardashian's debut in the reality show *Keeping up with the Kardashians* (Figure 17.6) was broadcast in 2007 on the E! cable network, and she took the tabloid queen title away from Hilton. The show focuses on highlighting the personal and professional lives of the Kardashian-Jenner family: sisters Kim, Kourtney, Khloe; their stepfather Bruce Jenner; Kim's half-sisters Kendall and Kylie Jenner; and their mother Kris. The show became an instant hit, capturing the family's "one-of-a-kind dynamics and hilarious antics."[20]

19   Arielle Tschinkel, "21 Celebrities Who Had a Remarkable 2018," *Insider*, December 14, 2018, https://www.insider.com/biggest-celebrities-in-2018-2018-2018-12.

20   Cristina Kinon, "E! Renews 'Keeping Up With the Kardashians,'" *Daily News*, November 13, 2007, http://www.nydailynews.com/entertainment/tv-movies/e-renews-keeping-kardashians-article-1.260586.

FIGURE 17.6 The Kardashians.

Thanks to the huge success of the show, in 2010, the Kardashian family was making headlines in the media. The sisters were on magazine covers nearly every week, and entertainment programs reported what the Kardashians did and said every day. Some fans were obsessed with the family. Based on the massive publicity, the Kardashian sisters built a business dynasty, shooting spin-off reality show series, endorsing a variety of products, and launching clothing, shoe, and cosmetic lines. Since the sisters boast about their social media fan base, they are reportedly paid to tweet about specific products and post photos or videos of sponsored products on Instagram. *Business Insider* reported in 2019 that Kylie Jenner made "an estimated $1.2 million per Instagram post," which makes her the highest paid celebrity influencer on the social media platform.[21] She has more than 140 million Instagram followers. Kim Kardashian was paid $910,000 per sponsored post in 2019.[22] Season 16 of *Keeping up with the Kardashians* was aired in 2019. Although criticized often for emphasizing the "famous for being famous" concept, *Keeping up with the Kardashians* has created a new reality show trend for celebrity families in the entrainment industry.

Activism for a Cause

Celebrities, whether they intend to or not, use their fame for a cause, and they usually gain massive publicity. Some celebrities and their public relations practitioners thoroughly orchestrate a strategy to attend public events to maximize celebrity power and shine their images. When such a public

---

21   Mary Hanbury, "The 35 celebrities and athletes who make the most money per Instagram post, ranked," Business Insider, July 23, 2019, https://www.businessinsider.com/kylie-jenner-ariana-grande-beyonce-instagrams-biggest-earners-2019-2019-7

22   Mary Hanbury, "The 35

event is related to social movements, celebrities seek the opportunity to give a speech to promote the public interest. They also use such events to promote their own public-appropriate images. Although controversial celebrities exploit social movements as a way of rebuilding their ruined images, many devote their time and energy to activism for various issues, including animal rights, climate change, women's rights, medical research, anti-war movements, genocide prevention, and sustainability for people in need.

For example, Angelina Jolie uses her international fame to raise global awareness of the plight of poor children and women in developing nations. Visiting refugee camps in Africa and Southeast Asia, she uses her influential power to persuade the governments to create better policies that help people in need around the world. She has been recognized as the paragon of celebrity activism. Her image is tied to the heartfelt cause of poor people. Early in her career, however, she did not have such a good image. She was seen as a naughty, wicked person with personal struggles: she had multiple tattoos; she wore a tiny vial of blood on a chain around her neck; she kissed her brother on the lips; and she was accused of prompting Brad Pitt to leave his wife, Jennifer Aniston. She was a bad girl, and no Hollywood star could have had a worse image than her. "I have all that gossip in my life that has gotten so out of control," Jolie told *Forbes* magazine. "In my early 20s I was fighting with myself. There's a lot of bad things written about me and my behavior."[23] The United Nations reports on global poverty and refugees, however, changed her life and her image. Since reading the UN reports in 2000, Jolie has devoted her life to activism with a cause. She says, "Now I take that punk in me to Washington, and I fight for something important."[24]

Book Promotion

Fame and glory for celebrities can be bound to wax and wane. Few celebrities are able to maintain their powerful and influential status for good. Public relations practitioners agree that writing a book is another way to gain publicity and promote professional images for celebrities, regardless of their popularity or writing ability. *The New York Times* reported that, like a branded fragrance or clothing line, a "novel—once quaintly considered an artistic endeavor sprung from a single creative voice" became "another piece of merchandise stamped with the name of celebrities."[25] Nicole Richie, Hilary Duff, Lauren Conrad ,and the Kardashian sisters (Kourtney, Kim, and Khloe) wrote books, and so did Nicole Polizzi, better known as Snooki of the MTV show *Jersey Shore*, who had read only two books in her entire life before she published her first novel.[26]

Public relations practitioners coach celebrities on how to promote their books to stay in the limelight. The issue of who really wrote the book is not important for celebrities, their practitioners, and publishers because books to them can be seen as a business opportunity. There is certainly a "wink-nod" agreement in the entertainment industry, meaning that ghostwriters are behind many novels by celebrities, even though few celebrities would admit that they had ghostwriters. When asked by *Today* show host Matt Lauer if she really wrote her book, Snooki answered, "I did. Because if you read it, you'll know from the

23   Matthew Swibel, "Bad Girl Interrupted," *Forbes*, July 3, 2006, http://www.forbes.com/free_forbes/2006/0703/118.html.

24   Swibel, "Bad Girl."

25   Julie Bosman, "In Their Own Words? Maybe, *New York Times*, January 1, 2011, http://www.nytimes.com/2011/06/02/fashion/noticed-celebrity-books-and-ghostwriters.html?_r=0.

26   Bosman, "In Their Own Words?"

first page that I wrote it. Cause, like, it's all my language."[27] Snooki eventually caved with more pressure from Lauer, admitting that there was a ghostwriter. In the same vein, *The Simple Life* star Nicole Richie told *USA Today*, "I write all my own stories," while promoting her novel, but her publisher confessed that "a ghostwriter did most of the writing" of Richie's book.[28] The motivation to capitalize on fame leads such celebrities and publishers to be involved with ghostwritten books. Not only do their book promotion events offer massive publicity, but the events also produce multiple business opportunities. Robert Gottlieb, chairman of the Trident Media Group, explained, "They hire a writer, come up with an idea, and do a novel that can be turned into a film or a television show. It's a way to extend the footprint of the celebrity."[29] In a nutshell, book promotion is an effective way to trigger publicity.

Promotional strategies can be more comprehensive. Celebrities and their public relations practitioners are inclined to adopt more than one strategy to maximize the effectiveness of public relations–organized promotion. Some celebrities hire an entire public relations firm to launch their promotional events from the beginning. Bruce-Caitlyn Jenner is a good example (Box 17.1).

BOX 17.1   A HISTORIC ORCHESTRATION OF CELEBRITY PUBLIC RELATIONS: BRUCE/CAITLYN JENNER

Born in 1949, Bruce Jenner was a high school athlete, participating in football, basketball, water skiing, and track. After struggling with an injury in college as a football player, Jenner switched to track and field to train for the Olympic decathlon.

Jenner crossed the finish line during the 1976 Summer Olympic Games in Montreal, Quebec, Canada, setting a world record for the decathlon. He won a gold medal, becoming an iconic Olympian who was loved by all Americans. However, it was not the gold medal that made him one of the most beloved sports stars of the 1970s but the American flag he grabbed for a victory lap after crossing the finish line. It was seen as a noble gesture to inspire American pride in people at the height of the Cold War. He was America's greatest athlete.

Soon after the Olympic Games, Jenner appeared on the front of the Wheaties cereal box, featured as a spokesperson for the brand. His career skyrocketed when he pursued appearances on television and film in the 1980s. Jenner's third marriage to Kris Kardashian occurred in 1991, and they starred in the E! reality series *Keeping Up with the Kardashians*.

As the show became a multimillion-dollar empire with spin-offs, tie-ins, endorsement deals, and books, the family shared seemingly every bit of their lives, and nothing was off limits. According to the *Washington Post*, entertaining story lines included Kim's 72-day marriage to professional basketball player Kris Humphries, Khloe's marriage to Los Angeles Lakers star Lamar Odom and their subsequent divorce, Kourtney's refusal to marry the father of her three kids, Kim's butt X-rays, and Jenner and Kris's separation in 2014.

(Continued)

---

27   Bosman, "In Their Own Words?"
28   Bosman, "In Their Own Words?"
29   Bosman, "In Their Own Words?"

The separation was caused by Jenner's gender dysphoria, which he'd recognized since his youth. In December 2014, he insinuated to TMZ that he would transition into a woman. The media were frantic to capture his every move, and Jenner hired Rogers & Cowan, a public relations firm. The firm's vice president, Alan Nierob, strategized his client's celebrity public relations campaign. As Jenner became a celebrity tabloid king, Nierob guided Jenner through a storm of media attention, aiming to make his gender transformation smooth in the eyes of the public.

Jenner's transitioning process was thoroughly staged and exposed as Nierob planned from December 2014 to March 2015. Jenner was spotted leaving a plastic surgeon's office after having his Adam's apple removed, getting a manicure, putting his hair in a ponytail, wearing a pair of diamond earrings, and sporting fuller lips. The media were revolving around him and relayed countless opinions and rumors from the public until Nierob reached out to Diane Sawyer, asking her to interview Jenner for a publicity stunt, according to *Variety* magazine.

Jenner sat down with Diane Sawyer for the two-hour *20/20* interview special in April 2015. During the exclusive interview, he declared, "For all intents and purposes, I'm a woman." He added, "My brain is much more female than it is male." He also promoted his upcoming reality show. The interview attracted 17 million viewers.

If the interview was Jenner's public announcement of his debut as transgender, the *Vanity Fair* magazine cover in June 2015 was the final goodbye to "Bruce." On the cover, he posed in a corset, and the headline read, "Call Me Caitlyn." The cover officially declared that Bruce was replaced by Caitlyn. The media have used Jenner's new name since. She—not he—racked up more than one million followers in a few hours (a new Twitter record) after the cover was published.

"I'm so happy after such a long struggle to be living my true self," she tweeted. "Welcome to the world Caitlyn. Can't wait for you to get to know her/me."

Caitlyn Jenner and her public relations team planned and performed the successful practice of celebrity public relations. Jenner and Nierob allowed paparazzi, entertainment television shows, online celebrity news sites, and magazines to expose her step-by-step transformation to make a smooth transition with the public, and then Jenner had an interview with the reputable journalist Diane Sawyer on ABC to confirm her gender identity. Finally, Jenner showed off her female look on a *Vanity Fair* cover. In short, Nierob and his public relations firm fulfilled their celebrity client's needs and wants.

Sources: *The Washington Post*, http://www.washingtonpost.com/lifestyle/style/the-forgotten-history-of-bruce-jenner-how-the-1970s-all-american-hero-ended-up-here/2015/02/04/3c594ae0-abdf-11e4-ad71-7b9eba0f87d6_story.html.

Variety Magazine, http://variety.com/2015/tv/news/bruce-jenner-caitlyn-jenner-transition-new-york-times-story-1201513335/.

Damage Control

Not all celebrities are set to be in trouble, but their fame and lifestyles often tend to drive them into drug abuse, domestic violence, alcoholism, and promiscuity. Because the elements of conflict, prominence, impact and novelty make a story newsworthy, no one can satisfy all the newsworthy elements except for celebrities. When a celebrity is arrested, the media rush to the police station. When a celebrity walks into a rehab facility, the media roam around the facility. Where there is a troubled celebrity, there are cameras and journalists. Bad news travels fast, and a celebrity's bad news travels faster. Hence, celebrities in trouble turn to public relations practitioners to seek professional help in dealing with the media.

A celebrity public relation practitioner is responsible for protecting the celebrity client from bad publicity after the client committed a crime, cheated on his or her spouse, or made a provocative statement in public. Although what's done is done, the practitioner's duty is to find a way to minimize the harm already done to the client's public image, which is reported by the media and established by the public. This duty is called damage control.

The process of damage control for a celebrity client is simple in theory. When hit by negative publicity, the celebrity wants his or her public relations practitioner to perform image rehabilitation that can put the celebrity right back on top. The practitioner should move quickly to respond to media inquiries and calm down the public. More importantly, the practitioner needs to find strategies to generate positive media coverage of the client that offsets the bad publicity. In the process of damage control, the practitioner first asks the client to refrain from saying or writing things in public because the practitioner is going to come up with the appropriate responses.

Issuing a statement is one of the most common tactics practitioners use with the aim of protecting the misbehaved client from criticism. For example, as soon as the *Desperate Housewives* star Felicity Huffman was indicted and arrested for paying $15,000 to have someone take the SAT test for her oldest daughter amid the 2019 college admissions bribery scandal, she hired the crisis public relations firm, the TASC Group, to handle the media circus. Although Huffman had her regular public relations team, the special case led her to retain the crisis-specialized firm. The firm issued a press release right after Huffman pled guilty to charges, including using bribery and other forms of fraud: "I am in full acceptance of my guilt, and with deep regret and shame over what I have done, I accept full responsibility for my actions and will accept the consequences that stem from those actions."[30] The firm, painting her in the best light possible, handled all media inquiries and press requests in the middle of her public relations nightmare.

Howard Bragman, a founder of Fifteen Minutes public relations firm, advised that, when faced with public relations nightmares, celebrities have three options to address their crises regarding image management:[31]

- Don't talk. Let the practitioner handle it.
- Go on record and deny it.
- Admit it. Say, "Yes, I did it, and I'm going to get help for it.

Drug abuse, alcoholism, and divorce are not uncommon for celebrities to experience while they are in the entertainment business. When celebrities deal with one of these problems, their practitioners issue a statement to apologize for the drug issue, or to promise to fix the alcohol problem, or to ask for privacy to protect the children of troubled celebrities. Drugs, alcohol, and divorce are considered to do minor career damage, and public relations practitioners are able to handle such issues with ease. However, allegations that wind up in court are a different story.

30 Alyssa Bailey, "Felicity Huffman Makes First Statement After Pleading Guilty in College Admissions Cheating Case," *ELLE*, April 8, 2019, https://www.elle.com/culture/celebrities/a27077619/felicity-huffman-college-admissions-scandal-guilty-plea-statement/.
31 Aly Weisman, "PR Guru's Advice to Bill Cosby: 'Shut Up and Disappear,'" *Business Insider*, November 25, 2014, http://www.businessinsider.com/bill-cosby-response-2014-11.

FIGURE 17.7 Bill Cosby and His Public Relations Team.

America's favorite dad, Bill Cosby, was accused of sexual assault by more than 40 women since November 2014. The media highlighted the trail of the iconic comedian's sexual behavior, asking for a comment from him, but he avoided the media. Amid the wave of accusations, Cosby appeared on National Public Radio's *Weekend Edition Saturday* and declined to publicly discuss the matter. His appearance turned into a public relations nightmare for Cosby because "when he did the NPR interview and literally said 'no' to making a comment, it's interpreted as stonewalling, and guilt is associated with that tactic," said Michael Bilello , CEO of Centurion Strategies.[32] Cosby sent a signal to the public that he was hiding something. Bilello saw it as the worst public relations strategy any troubled celebrity could choose. Although Cosby's legal and public relations teams (Figure 17.7) issued a statement denying the allegations, his legacy was crashing down. Public relations practitioners admit that Cosby's crisis was the worst public relations nightmare and hard to fix. One possible way for Cosby to free himself from the court of harsh public opinion is to find another celebrity who "does something really stupid that attracts even more attention and claims the spotlight," said Bragman.[33] Cosby lost in both courts of law and public opinion. Cosby was sentenced to three to ten years at State Correctional Institute Phoenix in Pennsylvania for aggravated indecent assault in 2018 and entered the general population in 2019 where he has been treated just the same as any other inmate.[34]

32   Itay Hod, "Hollywood Crisis Experts to Bill Cosby: 'Shut the F-ck Up!" Yahoo News, November 17, 2014, https://www.yahoo.com/news/hollywood-crisis-experts-bill-cosby-shut-f-ck-031000351.html

33   Itay Hod, "Hollywood Crisis Experts to Bill Cosby

34   Evan Simko-Bednarski and Eric Levenson, "Bill Cosby Has Been Moved to a General Population Cell at a Pennsylvania Prison," CNN, February 8, 2019, https://www.cnn.com/2019/02/07/us/bill-cosby-general-population-prison/index.html.

Public Relations for Celebrity Products

Celebrities and the media need each other. The entertainment industry produces stars and promotes their fame. Higher public awareness of celebrities brings more money and power. Public relations practitioners play an important role in connecting celebrities' needs and nurturing their benefits. Practitioners are hired to orchestrate a campaign for celebrities who are directly or indirectly tied to the entertainment industry. Such a campaign for celebrities focuses on building positive public images and increasing their commercial value.

The practitioners commonly conduct the campaign by following a standard drip-drip-drip technique. The technique takes two steps: (1) a steady output of information about the celebrity's entertainment product and (2) a barrage of promotion for the product. For example, if a celebrity starred in a television show, the celebrity's practitioner would disseminate information to the media about the show a few weeks before it aired. In addition, the practitioner would arrange interviews with newspapers and magazines for the celebrity to promote the show. The celebrity would appear on television talk shows as the practitioner posted interview articles and television appearances on social media to increase potential viewers' interest in the upcoming show. Shortly before the show is first aired, media promotion is conducted by using any possible media outlets.

Public relations practitioners who represent celebrities or anybody in the entertainment industry specialize in publicity, damage control, and promotion. They seek a way of thrusting their star clients into the limelight by organizing media events. If the client is already famous, the practitioner focuses on managing the client's public image, including the client's online persona. The practitioner manages several social media platforms, posting the client's event schedule on Facebook, photos on Instagram, and breaking news on Twitter. As both traditional and social media offer multiple outlets for the practitioner to diversify promotional strategies, the practitioner has heavier duties to deal with, including a wide variety of media outlets. In conclusion, celebrity public relations is a glamorous profession, looking after celebrity clients, but it requires high expectations and responsibilities, especially when the client gets involved in any controversial behavior. Most public relations practitioners with celebrity clients are on call 24 hours a day, 7 days a week.

CHAPTER SUMMARY AND REVIEW

1. Identify the reason why an individual hires public relations practitioners.

2. Understand the basic processes of celebrity promotion.

3. Study major tactics that boost celebrity publicity.

4. Explain how troubled celebrities are helped to regain fame.

5. Describe what celebrities should do to handle personal trouble.

PUBLIC RELATIONS IN PRACTICE

FURTHER READING

PR Week's Awards For **Best PR Crisis**

Winner: Discover Puerto Rico and Ketchum
Campaign Name: #CoverTheProgress

Hurricane Maria was a devastating event for tourist-dependent Puerto Rico, leaving the island with no electricity, a broken infrastructure, and a mounting death toll. In the aftermath of the disaster, Ketchum helped Puerto Rico engineer one of the fastest recoveries in tourism history that became a comeback story for the ages. As the island rebuilt, the agency strategically targeted socially conscious travelers with a meaningful message and enlisted travel influencers to show followers firsthand that Puerto Rico was back in business.

Read more at
https://www.prweek.com/article/1579436/prweek-us-awards-2019-winners

18

Global Public Relations

ccording to the United Nations, there are the 193 sovereign states with about seven billion people in the world. Regardless of time and space, they are able to communicate globally due to modern communication technology tools. Relating to the trend of communication, public relations has evolved into a process of global communication. When people from different cultures, socioeconomic systems, political situations and languages recognize their differences, they try to interact with one another by sharing their knowledge, ideas and thoughts for a better world. Each nation and its people may know what public relations is, although notions of public relations vary in each nation because of the cultural and social differences.

Whether the term and concept of *public relations* are diverse globally, public relations is practiced all around the world. One good example is government executing the practice of public information toward publics even in Syria and North Korea. In a similar way, many types of organizations are in the practice of communicating with their domestic and foreign audiences to build a good relationship. Some of these organizations plan to build mutually beneficial relationships with foreign audiences or have already built a dynamic set of relationships with foreign governments. The process of building a mutual relationship with foreign audiences and governments can be conceptualized as an act of global public relations since the core practice of public relations is connected to interactive communication for human relations.

Global Public Relations

It is hard to define global public relations, also known as international public relations, because the scope of the term is too broad and diverse. However, public relations from a global perspective can be understood as international strategic communication used by different types of organizations. Such organizations aim to establish and maintain mutually beneficial relationships with relevant audiences who live in foreign nations of different social and political systems. Organizations that engage in global public relations include governments, NGOs and corporations. They strategically communicate with foreign governments and audiences to conduct their business and influence policies of foreign governments.

Any organization can practice global public relations virtually in any nation. For example, if a Brazilian cosmetic company attempts to penetrate the bikini wax market in Russia with advertising, media events, and community relations, the company is involved in global marketing and public relations. A similar example can be found with a government. If the Mexican government launches a public relations campaign in Sweden, highlighting Mexico's beautiful beaches, golf courses, and luxury resort facilities, the government is engaging in the practice of global public relations in hopes of improving the country's tourism industry.

The Rise of Public Relations around the World

There is no standardized formula or law for how to practice global public relations, but pioneer examples of the development of public relations practices in the United States are copied and followed in many foreign nations. American practitioners initiated and formalized the practice of public relations since the early 1900s, while global public relations was blossoming in foreign nations with the system of global capitalism in the mid-1900s. Foreign organizations since the late twentieth century have emulated the system of public relations in the United States where it has a great influence on the global community with its dominant financial, cultural, and economic power.

After World War II, the United States and the global community moved toward new global systems of trade, investment, political coalitions, information flow, and communication networking. The US government-led movement for new global systems resulted in opening the twenty-first century with global economic phenomena of free trade agreements, foreign direct investments, and international monetary monitoring systems. Moreover, the US political system of democracy emerged as an idealistic political model for nations suffering from long-term autocracy or oppression. Another global phenomenon of the US government-led movement is the rapid development of communication technology. Television in the 1960s became the most influential and popular communication technology tool, and many Americans thought there would be no better revolutionary communication device until the next century.

The late twentieth century witnessed the expansion of the Internet, and the millennium generation presented an entangled communication web of online communication that connects most global citizens at the speed of light. No doubt, the majority of people in the world are beneficiaries of the new Internet technology. It is evolving quickly and globally. In parallel with the phenomenon, the practice of global public relations facilitates the use of new communication technology and the adaptation to global economy and political systems. However, this does not mean that global public relations is synonymous with American public relations.

Public relations practitioners representing organizations and doing business in diverse cultures and different social systems accumulate the knowledge of new global trends. They aim to achieve their organizational goals in foreign nations. To maximize their ability to practice global public relations, they first need to understand the de facto power that has generated today's integrated but still separated global community. The power is globalization.

Globalization and Public Relations

People have traveled long distances for thousands of years to buy and sell products in foreign lands. The Silk Road, a symbol of early globalization, was a 4,000-mile-long network of trade and cultural transmission routes formally established during the Han Dynasty of China. The routes were explored to trade with Eastern Europe. The Silk Road arguably gave birth to globalization because it provided tradesmen with the routes for Chinese silk, teas, salt, sugar, porcelain, and spices in exchange for European and Indian goods, such as cotton, wool, ivory, and gold. More importantly, the Silk Road served as the major global impetus that allowed "ideas, culture, inventions and unique products to spread across much of the settled world," while generating trade and commerce between different kingdoms and empires.[1]

While the volume of trading goods increased with camels as the main transporting vehicle, the social status for merchants and tradesmen rose in parallel with their amassing wealth. The merchants and tradesmen communicated with sellers and buyers by learning the languages and customs of the countries they traded through. As a result, languages, religions, and cultures were shared and exchanged on the road. Two historical and technical advances that were spread on the Silk Road were the technique of making paper and the development of printing press technology.[2] The Silk Road paved the way for today's global communication.

---

1   "Ancient China: The Silk Road," Dusters History, n.d., http://www.ducksters.com/history/china/silk_road.php.

2   "About the Silk Roads," UNESCO, n.d., https://en.unesco.org/silkroad/about-silk-road.

Globalization is the worldwide movement toward interaction and integration among the people, organizations, and governments of different nations. It drives free transmissions of capital, culture, trade, information, and products from domestic markets to international markets. Globalization has effects "on the environment, on culture, on political systems, on economic development and prosperity, and on human physical well-being in societies around the world."[3]

The current wave of globalization has opened economies internationally and developed technology, especially since World War II. Many governments have accepted the free flow of global capital by agreeing to free trade agreements aimed at stimulating faster and cheaper trade in products and services. Governments have supported the wave of globalization with open market policies; corporations have acted as the moving force to expedite the process of globalization with business strategies that take advantage of new global opportunities in foreign markets. Corporations created the concept of globalization as "an international, industrial and financial business structure."[4] They demonstrate their versatility in forming greater flexibility to operate across borders and abroad.

Technology has been another stimulus for the pervasiveness of globalization. Because of advanced communication technology, an increased amount of free-flowing mass communication travels around the globe. People in Greenland have the same access to information about Hollywood as Americans do; people in both countries learn about new fashion and beauty trends by following Hollywood stars at the same time. Consumers in Dubai can use search engines to find the newest information about new BMW vehicles in Germany. As a result, new communication technology enables people to seek swiftly changing economic and cultural trends around the globe and to streamline their knowledge of making wise decisions in consuming global products and services. The technology, in fact, empowers consumers with the ability to study and analyze global trends in economy, culture, and politics.

Globalization is changing the world and the way people live. Although some say globalization has produced positive effects, others say it has not been good for all people. Globalization as an ongoing process bears both pros and cons. Mike Collins, the author of *Saving American Manufacturing*, cited five pros and cons of the current wave of globalization:[5]

Pros

- There is cultural intermingling, and each country is learning more about other cultures.

- Most people see speedy travel, mass communications, and quick dissemination of information through the Internet as benefits of globalization.

- Labor can move from country to country to market their skills.

- Sharing technology with developing nations will help them progress.

- Transnational companies investing in installing plants in other countries provide employment for the people in those countries, often lifting them out of poverty.

3   "What Is Globalization?," Levin Institute, n.d., http://www.globalization101.org/what-is-globalization/.
4   Levin Institute, "What Is Globalization?"
5   Mike Collins, "The Pros and Cons of Globalization," *Forbes*, May 6, 2015, http://www.forbes.com/sites/mikecollins/2015/05/06/the-pros-and-cons-of-globalization/.

Cons

- Globalization has made the rich (such as corporations and financial organizations) richer while making the nonrich (such as working people) poorer.

- The biggest problem for developed countries is that jobs are lost and transferred to lower-cost countries.

- Large multinational corporations can exploit tax havens in other countries to avoid paying taxes.

- Building products overseas in countries like China puts US technologies at risk of being copied or stolen.

- Because of globalization, multinational corporations are gaining the power to influence political decisions.

Collins concluded, "Globalization is an economic tsunami that is sweeping the planet," which nobody can stop.[6] The list of pros and cons reveals that the main influence on globalization is derived from multinational or transnational corporations. Corporations armed with abundant finances and know-how about global operations have risen as the dominant players in global markets.

Multinational or transnational corporations can be characterized as global corporations. In the 1950s, banks in advanced nations, including the United States and Europe, started to invest vast sums of money in industrial stocks, which led to corporate mergers and capital concentration. Big corporations were formed, and major technological advances in shipping, transport (especially by air), digitalization, and communication accelerated the speed of globalization. Big corporations spearheaded global investment and trade while launching media campaigns to expand foreign market share.[7] They run business in foreign countries, strategizing to penetrate other countries' commercial markets, especially when their domestic growth has come to a dead end. A new foreign market can provide an opportunity to keep the corporation going.

Another reason for global corporations to operate foreign facilities is that they find ways to escape tariffs that prevent imported goods from being sold at competitive prices in the foreign market. For example, if the Bulgarian government set a tariff on imported cars that would increase sticker prices by 20 percent, the US carmaker Ford would build manufacturing facilities in Bulgaria to avoid the tariff. Some global corporations, regardless of the tariff issue, manufacture products in foreign nations where they can hire cheap foreign labor to reduce production costs. Not surprisingly, most global corporations are headquartered in the United States, Europe, and Japan, each of which plays a dominant role in the global economy. According to the *Economist* magazine, General Electric (GE) holds more assets abroad than any other nonfinancial corporation in the world—more than $500 billion worth, with more than half of GE's 300,000 employees based outside the United States.[8]

Global corporations employ public relations practitioners who understand the foreign nation's politics, culture, society, economy, and media systems with foreign language skills. Some practitioners are hired

---

6   Collins, "The Pros and Cons."

7   Jed Greer and Kavaljit Singh, "A Brief History of Transnational Corporations," Global Policy Forum, n.d., https://www.globalpolicy.org/empire/47068-a-brief-history-of-transnational-corporations.html.

8   "Biggest Transnational Companies," *The Economist*, July 10, 2012, http://www.economist.com/blogs/graphicdetail/2012/07/focus-1.

locally, but many of the practitioners are deployed to foreign nations from their corporate headquarters. Either way, the practitioners are expected to succeed in implementing the practice of public relations—mainly guided by American-style public relations tools and techniques—to build a relationship with foreign consumers while remembering the old saying, "When in Rome, do as the Romans do." The practice of global public relations emphasizes that corporations and their practitioners embrace the universally accepted business codes of conduct (globalization) and the cultural and social lifestyles of local consumers (localization).

Global Business Code of Conduct

The reputations of many global corporations has been scorched by wrongdoings and operational mistakes in foreign nations, especially developing ones. The lack of credibility of global corporations stems from foreign business practices that violate labor and environmental standards. Such violations bring obstacles to gaining local community support. Sweatshops, environmental pollution, bribery, deforestation, and overtime work without pay are chronic issues created by global corporations; they damage their images in foreign nations. Such problems are due in part to the distorted objectives of foreign governments and corporations. Governments generally welcome global corporations in their countries as the corporate operations create local jobs and boost the local economy. Thus the foreign government is likely to deregulate the corporation's operation, which is seemingly tempting to the corporation in pursuit of maximizing profits while ignoring health and safety risks for employees, local residents, and the environment. When these dangers erupt into a crisis with either protests by local community members or investigative coverage by the media, it is too late for the corporation to fix. The damage is done, especially to the corporation's reputation.

To address the problems of global corporations' harmful operations, the United Nations introduced the UN Global Compact, which encourages corporations worldwide to adopt sustainable and socially responsible practices with a set of core values in human rights, labor standards, the environment, and anticorruption. The compact asks corporations to (1) fight human rights abuses, (2) abolish child labor, (3) eliminate all forms of forced and compulsory labor, (4) promote greater environmental responsibility, (5) develop ecofriendly technologies, and (6) work against corruption in all its forms.[9]

More than 10,000 global corporations have pledged to conduct their business activities guided by the compact. They belong to the group of global corporate citizens. If global corporations run their businesses by following all the UN requirements, there will be no more struggles with the long-term damaged image of bad corporations in the global community. The UN Global Compact offers a milestone for universal business activities; global corporations view it as the global public relations partnership with the largest international organization.

Cultural and Social Differences

Public relations practitioners who work in foreign nations to represent their corporations confront three major challenges: (1) language, (2) culture, and (3) society. While coping with the challenges, the practitioners try to understand the people's general characteristics and adapt to local customs. Simply put, they attempt to assimilate themselves into the local culture and society, making plans and strategies to achieve

---

9 "Communication on progress 2007," The United Nations Global Compact, https://www.unglobalcompact.org/participation/report/cop/create-and-submit/detail/2521

the goals of their corporations. To see the big picture of cultural and social differences in a particular nation, the practitioners get familiar with Hofstede's cultural dimensions. Geert Hofstede, working at IBM from 1967 to 1973, traveled across Europe and the Middle East, conducting interviews and surveys to collect data from more than a hundred thousand individuals of 40 countries. The data were about how people behave in large organizations. Hofstede, who defined culture as "the collective programming of the mind distinguishing the members of one group or category of people from others," established a framework for cross-cultural communication in his research.[10] The framework is called Hofstede's cultural dimensions, which are considered insightful in understanding the intercultural differences within regions and between counties. Hofstede suggested six dimensions of various national cultures:

1. *Power Distance Index.* Power distance is defined as the extent to which the less powerful members of institutions and organizations within a country expect and accept that power is distributed unequally. The less powerful admit individuals are all unequal. This dimension explains that people living in society with a large degree of power distance accept a hierarchical order, whereas people living in society with low power distance strive to equalize the distribution of power and demand equal distribution of power.

2. *Individualism versus Collectivism.* Individualism prefers a loosely knit social framework, in which individuals are expected to take care of only themselves and their immediate families. In contrast, collectivism favors a tightly knit framework in society where individuals can expect their relatives or members of a particular in-group to look after them in exchange for unquestioning loyalty. People living in an individual society advocate "I," as opposed to "we," which the collective society advocates.

3. *Masculinity versus Femininity.* A masculine society is in favor of achievement, heroism, asser- tiveness and material rewards for success because competition is regarded as a natural thing. A feminine society, in contrast, fosters cooperation, modesty, caring for the weak, and quality of life. The fundamental issue here is whether tough action is adored or soft action is admired. Low masculine societies do value gender equality more.

4. *Uncertainty Avoidance Index.* This dimension describes how the members of a society feel uncom- fortable with uncertainty and ambiguity. Uncertainty and ambiguity can bring anxiety, and different cultures learn to deal with this anxiety in different ways. Members of a culture who feel threatened by ambiguous or unknown situations exhibit strong uncertainty avoidance, whereas members with a more relaxed attitude (in which practice counts more than principles) are associ- ated with weak uncertainty avoidance. The main question in this dimension is, "Should we try to control the future or just let it happen?"

5. *Long-Term Orientation versus Short-Term Normative Orientation.* This dimension describes how every society has to maintain some links with its own past while dealing with the challenges of the present and future. People who value long-term orientation attach more importance to the future, fostering pragmatic values like modern education as a way to prepare for the future. In contrast, people who value short-term orientation believe that change can occur more rapidly, and the present time is important.

---

10   Marianna Pogosyan, "Geert Hofstede: A Conversation About Culture The Hofstede Centre," Psy- chology Today, February 21, 2017 https://www.psychologytoday.com/us/blog/between-cultures/201702/ geert-hofstede-conversation-about-culture

FIGURE 18.1A–B Culture of High Power versus Culture of Low Power Distance.

6. *Indulgence.* This dimension is defined as the extent to which people try to control their desires and impulses, based on the way they were raised. A tendency toward relatively weak control over their impulses is called "indulgence," whereas relatively strong control over their urges is called "restraint." Indulgent societies have a tendency to believe that free gratification of basic and natural human desires is permitted for their members to enjoy life.

According to the dimensions, the United States is a culture of low power distance, high individualism, high masculinity, low uncertainty avoidance, low long-term orientation, and high indulgence.[11] In the same dimensions, China is a culture of high power distance, low individualism, high masculinity, low uncertainty avoidance, high long-term orientation, and low indulgence.[12]

Localization of Global Corporation in Public Relations

Now that more corporations operate their businesses across borders, globalization has provided more complex responsibilities to public relations practitioners. There is no question that the United States and European global corporations opened foreign markets with their advanced human and financial resources (Case Study 18.1). In the mid-1900s, they applied their management formulas to their foreign businesses, pushing foreign labor and consumers to comply with their westernized or advanced systems.

However, such one-way enforcement backfired in many nations since foreign workers and consumers recognized the unfair and arrogant business operations. For example, Walmart was expanding outside the United States in the 1990s. Given Walmart's formidable record at home, the giant corporation was confident that it would maximize its profits with more stores in foreign nations. It imposed its management styles around the world as the world's largest retailer with 11,000 retail units in 28 countries.[13] However, the corporation experienced global operation failures in 2006 after pulling out of Germany and South Korea. Instead of paying attention to South Koreans' local preferences for buying small packages at a variety of local stores, Walmart stacked goods in boxes, "forcing shoppers to use ladders or stretch

11 "NATIONAL CULTURE," The Hofstede Centre, https://hi.hofstede-insights.com/national-culture

12 "NATIONAL CULTURE," The Hofstede Centre

13 "Location Facts," Walmart, n.d., http://corporate.walmart.com/our-story/our-business/locations/.

for items on high shelves."[14] In Germany, Walmart initially installed American executives who had little knowledge about what German consumers wanted. The American executives tried to sell "packaged meat when Germans liked to buy meat from the butcher."[15] Walmart also imposed its corporate culture on German salesclerks, who were instructed to smile at customers. In German culture, male shoppers interpreted the smiles as flirting. These two foreign operations provided a lesson to Walmart: a uniquely powerful American enterprise trying to impose its values around the world has vulnerability. In the same vein, imposing a global corporation's culture and values on foreign employees and consumers can be doomed to failure, unless the corporation takes a localized approach to the foreign market.

If globalization opened global markets for corporations, localization gave an assignment to corporations in terms of understanding and adapting to foreign cultures, languages, and regions. Global corporations undertake special efforts to localize their values and policies to sell products or services. McDonald's, for example, is one of the most successful global restaurant chains with more than 30,000 restaurants worldwide. It facilitates effective management and global expansion strategies to penetrate new foreign markets. While focusing on opening new restaurants in emerging markets, McDonald's has succeeded in dealing with cultural differences and consumer sensitivities through franchising. McDonald's entered the Indian market in 1996, taking aim at changing the local perception of the new product being "American" and removing the fear of the unknown. Indians were afraid that McDonald's restaurants would threaten the local economy and Indian food culture, in which having a meal is a family affair at home. To soothe such negative perceptions, the corporation launched public relations campaigns to create a new image in the mind of Indian consumers: McDonald's as a stimulator and an advocate for Indian family and cultural values.[16]

In India where Hindus hold cows sacred and Muslims view pigs as filthy, McDonald's used no beef or pork on the menu. It was the main strategy of localization; instead, it developed new menus with chicken. The Big Mac beef burger was replaced with the Chicken Maharajah Mac. Next, McDonald's introduced a version of a cheap street burger to change the eating habits of Indian consumers: "One hundred meals that people ate in a month, only three were eaten out."[17] In 2014, eating out went up to nine to ten times per hundred meals, and McDonald's in India had more than 320 million customers a year.[18] The corporation promoted a family dining experience with affordable prices.

McDonald's also partnered up with local suppliers to grow their businesses together. As a result, McDonald's India won awards as "the most trusted family restaurant brand" and "the Company with the best corporate conscience."

Like McDonald's, global corporations attempt to localize. Public relations campaigns play an important role in winning the hearts and minds of the people whom global corporations target in foreign nations. If a US corporation is going to penetrate the Chinese market, for example, a public relations practitioner for the corporation commonly goes through the following five communication steps to raise awareness of the corporation.

14   Mark Landler and Michael Barbaro, "Wal-Mart Finds That Its formula Doesn't Fit Every Culture," *New York Times*, August 2, 2006, http://www.nytimes.com/2006/08/02/business/worldbusiness/02walmart.html?pagewanted=all.
15   Landler and Barbaro, "Wal-Mart Finds."
16   "McDonalds Entry Strategies in India," Assignment Point, n.d., http://www.assignmentpoint.com/business/mcdonalds-entry-strategies-in-india.html.
17   Shilpa Kannan, "How McDonald's Conquered India," BBC, November 19, 2014, http://www.bbc.com/news/business-30115555.
18   Kannan, "How McDonald's Conquered."

1. **Website.** Create the corporation's website, which features Chinese-friendly items in Mandarin. The corporation's address and phone number are listed, including the map and directory listings.

2. **Press Release.** Send a press release to Chinese media to build a relationship with Chinese journalists. The release should be written in Mandarin. The release includes information about the corporation's products or services that will benefit the Chinese people, confirming that a spokesperson who speaks Mandarin will be available for questions and interviews.

3. **Messages.** Develop a localized message to launch a public relations campaign. The message should be more than enough to impress the target audience in China, demonstrating that the corporation wants to be part of the Chinese culture and society with its good quality products or services.

4. **Cross-National Team.** Organize a special team in the corporation that consists of employees specializing in Chinese culture, language, and sociopolitical systems. They can exchange new information and knowledge about the Chinese government and consumers. The public relations practitioner develops communication strategies and campaigns based on the comprehensive information.

5. **Events.** Organize events to communicate with journalists. Inviting journalists to a corporation party or tour is a natural way to promote corporate reputation. Hosting a community event, such as a sponsorship agreement with a local high school soccer team, attracts local media attention. More public relations events produce a higher opportunity to stimulate the interest of Chinese journalists. Practicing CSR for local residents will be highly appreciated by the local media.

Case Study 18.1   Coca-Cola's Localization in the Philippines

The Philippines has had a special meaning to Coca-Cola since 1912 when American businessman M.A. Clarke decided to distribute Coca-Cola in the Philippines—the company's first venture in Asia. Over one hundred years, Coca-Cola has run its business in the nation, fulfilling the four pillars that best signify the company's philosophies to practice global business for the local people: education, entrepreneurship, environment and nutrition.

In 1997, when the Department of Education and the Philippine Business for Social Progress called on corporations doing business in the country to help improve the poor public education system in rural areas, Coca-Cola launched the Little Red Schoolhouse project, taking aim at the country's classroom shortage. The corporation focused on improving elementary education for children in the country's remote and underserved areas.

"We choose (far-flung) areas where there is the most need for classrooms," says Gilda Maquilan, Coca-Cola's corporate communication manager. By 2016, a total of 122 schools nationwide had electricity, running water, furniture and basic necessities thanks to the project.

The corporation invigorated its effort to be a part of rural communities. It provided nutritious drinks to thirty-five thousand schoolkids who suffered from iron-deficiency anemia. With the Agos Ram Pump Water Project, Coca-Cola installed one hundred water-pump systems to pump one hundred thousand liters of water per day to communities where clean water was scarce. In 2013, one hundred thousand Filipino women who owned small stores were invited to Coca-Cola-hosted seminars and workshops on business management, operational training, and financial planning.

"We do all of these to thank the Filipino people for trusting the brand and accepting Coca-Cola in their homes," said, Adel Tamano, Vice President for Public Affairs & Communications for Coca-Cola Philippines. In late 2013, when Typhoon Haiyan claimed more than five thousand Filipino lives and displaced at least four million people from their homes, Coca-Cola suspended advertising money and reallocated the budget to disaster-relief programs.

Coca-Cola projects in the Philippines show how a global corporation can assimilate itself into a foreign nation, building good relationships and a strong reputation for its business through localization practices. The Philippines is one of Coke's ten biggest markets worldwide in terms of volume sales.

Sources: Inquirer, http://business.inquirer.net/67125/coca-cola-marks-100th-year-in-philippines-with-activities-projects.

US-ASEAN Business Council, https://www.usasean.org/csr/member-projects/little-red-schoolhouse

Public Relations Firms for Foreign Clients

In the era of globalization, governments engage in the practice of global public relations. When a government seeks to influence a foreign nation's public opinion, a public relations firm in the foreign nation is often hired to create a positive public atmosphere for the government client. In a similar way, when a government attempts to influence a foreign nation's policies and actions, a public relations firm in the foreign nation is hired to persuade the foreign government to take action in favor of the government client. It is not uncommon for foreign governments to hire US public relations firms to influence American public opinion and US government policies and actions.

Foreign governments hire US public relations firms for five reasons:

1. The foreign government needs the help of the US government to solve domestic issues.

2. The foreign government aims to increase its national image and brand among US citizens and corporations, so it can invite more US investment and tourists into the country.

3. The foreign government wants to turn international criticism into international favoritism.

4. The foreign government makes an effort to change the negative international and US media narrative about the country.

5. The foreign government expects the US government to be on its side when international conflict occurs with another foreign government.

The global public relations industry grew by 5 percent every year, and the size of the global public relations firm industry is over $11 billion, according to the 2019 Holmes Report.[19] Such numbers certainly suggest that global public relations continues to grow faster than the overall global economy.[20] Big US public relations firms are known for their competent abilities to represent foreign government clients

19   Arun Sudhaman, "Global PR Industry Growth Slows to 5% as Networks Struggle," *The Holmes Report*, April 26, 2018, https://www.holmesreport.com/long-reads/article/global-pr-industry-growth-slows-to-5-as-networks-struggle
20   Sudhaman, "Global PR Industry."

to the US government and public. Hill & Knowlton, Edelman, Levick, McGuireWoods Consulting, Fleishman-Hillard, APCO, BGR, and Ketchum are several public relations firms that foreign governments hire to achieve their national goals through the practice of global public relations. The following three cases are well known for the cooperative relationships between US public relations firms and foreign governments.

Case Study 18.2 The Russian Government and Ketchum

In 2006, executives from the public relations firm Ketchum flew to Moscow after the Russian government hired the firm to provide advice on "the Group of 8 meeting" hosted by the government in St. Petersburg. The main reason for the government to hire the US firm was that Russian President Vladimir V. Putin at the time "cared a great deal about what other leaders, especially presidents, thought about him," according to Michael A. McFaul, a former United States ambassador to Russia.[21] *PR Watch* revealed that Ketchum was paid $845,000 for two months of work around the G8 Summit, visited by US Secretary of State Condoleezza Rice and Defense Secretary Robert Gates.[22] The firm not only held dozens of media briefings in Moscow, New York, and Washington, DC, by monitoring media coverage of Russia, but also tracked sentiment on Capitol Hill that might affect Russia.

Ketchum continued to work for Russia, and it boasted its public relations expertise when Putin appeared on the cover of *Time* magazine in 2007. Ketchum successfully lobbied *Time* magazine to name Putin its "Person of the Year" after having meetings with *Time* staffers.[23] The magazine wrote of Putin, "He expanded his outsize—if not always benign—influence on global affairs."[24] In addition, Ketchum lobbied both the US State Department and journalists to soften their assessments of Russia's human rights record that year.

While boosting Putin's global leadership image, Ketchum attempted to build the nation's general image in US media outlets, encouraging journalists to positively write about Russian-hosted international events, including the 2014 Winter Olympics in Sochi. The public relations firm aimed to cordially build "the relationship between representatives of the Russian Federation and the Western media."[25]

In 2013, Ketchum scored another public relations accomplishment for President Putin, who placed an op-ed article in the *New York Times*. In the article, Putin painted himself as a peacemaker, explaining that "decisions affecting war and peace should happen only by consensus," so an American-led strike against the Syrian regime "could throw the entire system of international

---

21   Ravi Somaiya, "P.R. Firm for Putin's Russia Now Walking a Fine Line" *New York Times*, August 31, 2014 https://www.nytimes.com/2014/09/01/business/media/pr-firm-for-putins-russia-now-walking-a-fine-line.html

22   Diane Farsetta, "Ketchum Caught 'Man of the Year' Title for Putin, *PR Watch*, February 20, 2008, http://www.prwatch.org/spin/2008/02/7021/ketchum-caught-man-year-title-putin.

23   Andy Sullivan, "U.S. Public-Relations Firms Helps Putin Make His Case to America," Reuters, September 12, 2013, http://www.reuters.com/article/2013/09/13/us-syria-crisis-usa-ketchum-idUSBRE98C00S20130913.

24   Sullivan, "U.S. Public-Relations."

25   Sullivan, "U.S. Public-Relations."

law and order out of balance."[26] In fact, the process of getting the op-ed article published in the *Times* was orchestrated by Ketchum. "The opinion piece was written by President Putin and submitted to the *New York Times* on his behalf by Ketchum for their consideration," admitted Jackie Burton, Ketchum's senior vice president of external relations.[27] In response to the article, the US government accused Putin of taking advantage of press freedoms unavailable in Russia. US House Speaker John Boehner said he was "insulted," and Sen. Bob Menendez (D-NJ), the chair of the Senate Foreign Relations Committee, said it made him "want to vomit." Critics believe that the article was written and submitted by Ketchum to glorify Putin's global power and influence. From 2006 to 2013, the Russian government paid Ketchum $25 million in fees and expenses.

26   Vladimir V. Putin, "A Plea for Caution From Russia," *New York Times*, September 11, 2013, http://www.nytimes.com/2013/09/12/opinion/putin-plea-for-caution-from-russia-on-syria.html.

27   Brett LoGiurato, "Meet the PR Firm That Helped Vladimir Putin Troll the Entire Country," *Business Insider*, September 12, 2013, http://www.businessinsider.com/vladimir-putin-nyt-op-ed-ketchum-pr-2013-9.

Case Study 18.3 The Kuwait Government and Hill & Knowlton

In August 1990, Iraqi troops, led by dictator Saddam Hussein, invaded the oil-producing nation of Kuwait. The invasion of Kuwait changed the George H.W. Bush administration's attitude toward Hussein, who was regarded as a valuable ally during the US confrontation with Iran. Hussein crossed the line that President Bush could not tolerate. The United Nations Security Council called for Iraq to withdraw from Kuwait the next day and imposed a worldwide ban on trade with Iraq. However, the US government was reluctant to militarily punish Iraq because Kuwait and Iraq were geographically too far away from the United States, and they were oil producers and that could affect global oil prices. Moreover, the US public would not be convinced about sending US soldiers to the Middle East for helping Kuwait, which hardly looked like the sort of country that deserved defending because of the ruling family, accused of suppressing the people in Kuwait.[28] It was a difficult task for the Bush administration to sell the war against Iraq to the American public, who would not understand why billions of their tax dollars needed to be spent on oil-rich sheiks. President Bush collaborated with the United Nations to resolve the conflict. The UN Security Council gave the withdrawal deadline to Iraq: by January 15, 1995.

To wage war against Iraq, the Bush administration found a way to justify US involvement. Iraq's history of human rights abuses under Hussein and the US alliance with Saudi Aribia served as public justifications to enter the war against Iraq. However, such justifications did not receive strong public support until public relations campaigns were launched by the public relations firm Hill & Knowlton, hired by the organization Citizens for a Free Kuwait, established in the United States shortly after Iraq's invasion of Kuwait. The organization paid Hill & Knowlton

28   "How PR Sold the War in the Persian Gulf," *PR Watch*, n. d., http://www.prwatch.org/books/tsigfy10.html.

(Continued)

around $11 million, funded by Kuwait's government in desperate pursuit of selling the war to the American public.

The firm began to devise a campaign to win American support for the war. It organized the campaign of "Kuwait Information Day" on 20 college campuses and a national day of prayer for Kuwait while distributing thousands of "Free Kuwait" bumper stickers. The firm also produced dozens of video news releases depicting Kuwait as a striving young democracy and loyal ally of the United States. The campaigns were slowly gaining US public support, which was still lukewarm at the time.

Hill & Knowlton orchestrated a stronger public relations tactic with an irresistible impact in October 1990. The firm arranged to have a 15-year-old girl named Nayirah appear in front of the Congressional Human Rights Caucus, chaired by California Democrat Tom Lantos and Illinois Republican John Porter. Nayirah's full name was kept confidential to prevent Iraqi reprisals against her family in occupied Kuwait.[29] She told the committee, "I saw the Iraqi soldiers come into the hospital with guns and go into the room where 15 babies were in incubators. They took the babies out of the incubators, took the incubators, and left the babies on the cold floor to die."[30] Her testimony being recorded by the firm's camera crew shocked the committee. Hill & Knowlton disseminated details of her speech to media outlets, and the incubator story dominated national headlines. Sentimental feelings for the people in Kuwait were formed among the American public, and Congress authorized the use of US military intervention. The Gulf War began with extensive aerial bombing on January 17, 1991.

About one year after the inception of the Gulf War, Nayirah's real identity was revealed. She was the daughter of Kuwait's ambassador to the United States, and she had never been in the hospital where Iraqi soldiers allegedly committed the atrocities. More surprisingly, Congressman Lantos knew the girl's real identity but concealed it from the public and his co-chairman, Porter. It turned out that Nayirah's father sat listening in the hearing room during her testimony, and Lauri Fitz-Pegado, vice president of Hill & Knowlton, had coached Nayirah.[31] It is interesting that no journalist bothered to find out the identity of the young woman after the testimony.

---

29   *PR Watch*, "How PR Sold."

30   Tom Regan, "When Contemporary War, Beware of Babies in Incubators," *Christian Science Monitor*, September 6, 2002, http://www.csmonitor.com/2002/0906/p25s02-cogn.html.

31   *PR Watch*, "How PR Sold."

Case Study 18.4 The Nigerian Government and Levick

On the night of April 14, 2014, in the town of Chibok in northeastern Nigeria, the Islamist extremist group Boko Haram kidnapped 276 schoolgirls aged between 16 and 18 years old. Boko Haram militants stormed the all-girl secondary school, arriving in a convoy of trucks and buses and killing school security guards. They forced the girls out of their dormitories and packed them onto trucks, disappearing into a remote area along the border with Cameroon. Boko Haram leader Abubakar

Shekau released a video, saying that the Islamist organization would sell the girls: "I abducted your girls. Allah has instructed me to sell them. They are his property and I will carry out his instructions."[32] The US government vowed to help track down the girls, and the world was appalled. On Twitter, the hashtag #BringBackOurGirls began trending and spread around the world.

The kidnappings were hugely embarrassing for the Nigerian government and threatened to overshadow its first hosting of the World Economic Forum for Africa, starting in a few days. "The abducted girls put Nigeria on the world media stage more than any other event in its history," said Executive Vice President Lanny Davis of Levick.[33] "It's a page one story around the world. It doesn't happen to Nigeria very often." Upset and embarrassed by the tragedy, the government declared war against the kidnappers, but no progress was made in the next two months. Parents and relatives of the girls organized protests, criticizing the lack of action and the failure of Nigerian authorities to rescue them. The Nigerian public supported the parents, arguing that the government was doing nothing. They were losing their faith in government, and it was bad news to President Goodluck Jonathan, who was up for reelection in February 2015. The international and local media also highlighted the inaction of the government in its efforts aimed at securing the release of the girls.

In response, the president had to counter the public anger and frustration. In June 2014, his administration signed a contract worth more than $1.2 million with the Washington public relations firm Levick. The Levick public relations team, led by Davis, arrived in Nigeria and advised the Nigerian president to go on the offensive after months of silence about the criticism. The president defended himself, placing an op-ed article in the *Washington Post*. He wrote, "My silence has been necessary to avoid compromising the details of our investigation."[34] He added, "Nothing is more important to me than finding and rescuing our girls."[35] In August, President Jonathan had an off-the-record breakfast meeting with key American reporters in a hotel room and "disclosed for the first time that he was reaching out to Boko Haram through third parties in an effort to secure the girls' safe release."[36] Levick team leader Davis was in the hotel room as well. In the end, the team altered "false perceptions of those in the media while providing Nigeria with advice to communicate to the international community their leadership in combating terrorism, respecting global human rights norms and promoting government transparency."[37]

32 Martin Cuddihy, "Nigerian Schoolgirl Abduction: Boko Haram Claims Responsibility for Kidnapping 276 Students," ABC News, May 6, 2014, http://www.abc.net.au/news/2014-05-05/boko-haram-claims-responsibility-for-abducting-schoolgirls/5432068.

33 Jeffrey Scott Shapiro, "U.S. Public Relations, Consulting Firms Find Political Gold in Nigeria," *The Washington Times*, August 13, 2014, http://www.washingtontimes.com/news/2014/aug/13/us-public-relations-consulting-firms-find-politica/?page=all.

34 Goodluck Jonathan, "Goodluck Jonathan: Nothing Is More Important Than Bringing Home Nigeria's Missing Girls," *The Washington Post*, June 26, 2014, http://www.washingtonpost.com/opinions/goodluck-jonathan-nothing-is-more-important-than-bringing-home-nigerias-missing-girls/2014/06/26/7739275e-fd4b-11e3-b1f4-8e77c632c07b_story.html.

35 Jonathan, "Goodluck Jonathan."

36 Shapiro, "U.S. Public Relations."

37 Shapiro, "U.S. Public Relations."

Global Public Relations and Global Community

The global community communicates and shares information. Global citizens are informed of what is happening on the other side of the world in the era of globalization, which has popularized democracy, new communication technology, free trade, and corporate global operations. Globalization accelerates the new practice of global public relations by focusing on localization with four suggestions:

1. Obey the local regulations and laws.

2. Enhance the activity of corporate social responsibility for local communities.

3. Focus on ethical relationship building with local journalists.

4. Harmonize western-style public relations with localized public relations.

Different cultures, languages, and sociopolitical systems are obstacles for public relations practitioners in foreign nations. However, the practice of public relations in foreign nations also embraces the basic functions of public relations, such as media relations, employee relations, consumer relations, community relations, and government relations. Global public relations adds one more practice: localization. Global corporations find a way to strike a balance between globalization and localization to penetrate foreign markets for better business opportunities. Public relations practitioners with in-depth knowledge of localization serve on the front lines to help global corporations manage good relationships with their foreign target audiences.

FIGURE CREDITS

Img. 18.1: Copyright © 2013 Depositphotos/Mazirama.
Img. 18.2: Copyright © 2015 Depositphotos/Rawpixel.
Fig. 18.1a: Copyright © 2013 Depositphotos/realinemedia.
Fig. 18.1b: Copyright © 2011 Depositphotos/AndreyPopov.
Img. 18.3: Copyright © 2020 by Haymarket Media Group Ltd.

CHAPTER SUMMARY AND REVIEW

1. Explain what globalization is and how it evolves.
2. Identify fundamental items for localization.
3. Study Hofstede's six dimensions.
4. Explain why some corporations fail to penetrate foreign markets.
5. Discuss US public relations firms' strategies when representing foreign clients.

PUBLIC RELATIONS IN PRACTICE

FURTHER READING

PR Week's Awards For **Best PR Influencer Impact**

Winner: Tourism Australia, Droga5, and Kovert Creative
Campaign Name: Dundee: The Son of a Legend Returns Home

The team created a trailer for *Dundee: The Son of a Legend Returns Home*, a star-studded sequel to the iconic 1986 film—featuring Danny McBride, Chris Hemsworth, Hugh Jackman, Margot Robbie, and Russell Crowe—that cleverly switched into a showcase for Australian tourism. In a carefully orchestrated public relations and social campaign, the team dropped four teaser films in press and celebrity social channels and created a website, social handles, an IMDb page, and behind-the-scenes set imagery.

Read more at
https://www.prweek.com/article/1579436/prweek-us-awards-2019-winners

Printed in the USA
CPSIA information can be obtained
at www.ICGtesting.com
LVHW022356140823
755211LV00012B/1072